Pathways Out of the Polycrisis

Reproducible Research Repository

https://reproducibility.worldbank.org

A reproducibility package is available for this
book in the Reproducible Research Repository at
https://reproducibility.worldbank.org/index.php/catalog/189

Scan the QR code to see all titles in this series.

Pathways Out of the Polycrisis

WORLD BANK GROUP

ISBN (paper): 978-1-4648-2123-3
ISBN (electronic): 978-1-4648-2126-4
DOI: 10.1596/978-1-4648-2123-3

Cover image: Carlos Reyes
Cover design: Bill Pragluski, Critical Stages, LLC

Library of Congress Control Number: 2024947151

Contents

BOXES

FIGURES

CONTENTS

MAPS

TABLES

Foreword

For a quarter of a century, economies across the world whittled down poverty at an extraordinary clip. Beginning in 1990, rapid economic growth—especially in China and India—liberated more than 1 billion people from the scourge of extreme poverty. Over the next 25 years, as the incomes of the poorest nations began to converge with those of the wealthiest, the world came closer than ever to extinguishing extreme poverty altogether.

Then, after 2020, starting with the COVID-19 pandemic, a major reversal began. Poverty reduction slowed to a crawl. Poorer countries did worse than the wealthier economies in responding to the pandemic. Conflict in Europe and the Middle East then disrupted the supplies of foodgrains and fuel. Two years ago, the World Bank's *Poverty and Shared Prosperity 2022* report took stock and came to a dismal conclusion: poverty had risen for the first time in decades. The global goal of cutting the extreme-poverty rate to 3 percent by 2030 had slipped out of reach. At the current pace, it will not be met for three decades.

The delay would be longer still for people living on less than $6.85 a day—the poverty threshold for middle-income countries. It would take more than a century to eliminate poverty at this higher level, which now affects half of humanity. The 2020s, in short, are shaping up to be a lost decade—not just for a small set of countries but for the world as a whole.

That threatens reversals on two other fronts: the fight against climate change and the struggle to expand the middle class everywhere. Poverty, prosperity, and planet are the three corners of the iron triangle of economic development: to achieve durable progress on one, it is imperative to make substantial gains on the other two. In an era of economic populism, rising debt, and aging populations, that will not happen easily. In fact, without the right policy framework, it is far more likely that progress on one front will come at the expense of another.

This report aims to provide exactly that framework—one that can manage the trade-offs and deliver the best possible outcomes on all three fronts. For the first time, it gives governments a comprehensive way to monitor progress, identify new pathways to success, and choose the right policy priorities. The *Poverty, Prosperity, and Planet Report 2024* constitutes the World Bank Group's first integrated progress report on the three goals since the COVID-19 pandemic—and it serves as a central tool in our institution's efforts to realize its updated vision: to create a world free of poverty on a livable planet.

The analysis yields several sobering conclusions—as well as clear evidence that progress is possible even under daunting conditions. The good news is that progress on extreme poverty reduction has finally resumed at the global level: in 2024, the extreme poverty rate was 8.5 percent, marking the first time it has dipped below the 8.8 percent rate that prevailed on the eve of the COVID-19 pandemic. The bad news is that the recovery is bypassing the places that need it most: extreme poverty in the poorest economies is still 1 percentage point higher than it was in 2019.

Across the world, governments have also made notable progress in combating inequality within national borders. In 2024, the number of economies with high inequality stood at a 24-year low, reflecting a one-third reduction since the turn of the century. Yet 1.7 billion people—20 percent of the global population—still live in high-inequality economies, which are concentrated in Sub-Saharan Africa and Latin America and the Caribbean. Poverty and inequality are conjoined. Speeding up the reduction of within-country inequality accelerates progress on poverty reduction. It also builds a stronger foundation for peace and stability.

Another finding of this report is that well-off countries have been making considerable progress in adapting to climate change—but poor countries remain far behind. Since 2010, the number of people exposed to extreme-weather events has grown not only in the poorest economies eligible to borrow from the World Bank's International Development Association (IDA) but also in non-IDA countries. These countries have managed to shield nearly all their populations from extreme-weather events—a function of their wealth and access to finance, which enables greater investment in climate adaptation. IDA countries, by contrast, have been able to protect barely one out of every two people from the risk of actual harm from an extreme-weather event.

That disparity underscores the need for a differentiated approach to managing the trade-offs in play at the intersection of poverty, prosperity, and planet. The poorest economies must be allowed to prioritize climate resilience. Sub-Saharan Africa, for example, has the largest share of people at high risk from extreme-weather events—more than a third. And half its people lack electricity or sanitation.

The policy priorities in the poorest economies *must* be different from those in wealthier parts of the world: to roll back extreme poverty, low-income economies must prioritize long-term growth and better health and education. They must be careful, however, to avoid getting locked into carbon-intensive technologies and growth strategies that will become progressively more costly and less efficient in the future. At higher levels of income, however, the policy predicament intensifies. Ending poverty for the 3 billion people who struggle on less than $6.85 a day would come at a high cost to the environment. By the middle of this century, it would boost global emissions by nearly 50 percent over 2019 levels.

The implications are clear: in the poorest economies, the focus should be on economic growth and investing in human, financial, and physical capital. For lower-middle-income countries, the focus should shift to growth and shared prosperity—and measures to increase the efficiency of policies that increase incomes, improve resilience to shocks, and lower emissions. Just by reducing air pollution, for example, they can reap large rewards on multiple fronts, including better health outcomes. For upper-middle- and high-income countries, which account for four-fifths of global carbon emissions, the emphasis must be on slashing emissions while finding ways to alleviate the job losses and other short-term pains that will result from these cuts.

None of this will be easy, but it can and must be done. The world today enjoys a historic opportunity to change course—to overcome the rising dangers of climate change, systemic inequality, social instability, and conflict. With closer international cooperation, it's possible to build the type of progress that ensures a broad and lasting rise in prosperity. It's an opportunity that must not be passed up.

Indermit S. Gill
Chief Economist and Senior Vice President for Development Economics

Axel van Trotsenburg
Senior Managing Director for Development Policy and Partnerships

Acknowledgments

The preparation of this report was co-led by Maria Eugenia Genoni and Christoph Lakner. The chapter co-leads included Henry Stemmler, Samuel Kofi Tetteh-Baah, and Nishant Yonzan. The core team included Maria Gabriela Farfan Betran, Niklas Buehren, Benoit Decerf, Carolyn Fischer, David Groves, Federico Haslop, Ruth Hill, Daniel Gerszon Mahler, Regina Pleninger, Sutirtha Sinha Roy, Sharad Tandon, and Nele Warrinnier. The extended team included Miki Khanh Doan, Roshen Fernando, Bilal Malaeb, and Christian Schoder. Specific inputs were received by Patrick Behrer, Thijs Benschop, Juliana Bedoya Carmona, Alan Fuchs, Nagaraja Rao Harshadeep, Alexandra Christina Horst, Macha Petronella Kemperman, Yeon Soo Kim, Samuel Jovan Okullo, Marko Olavi Rissanen, and Forhad Shilpi. Ben Brunckhorst, Andres Castaneda, Cameron Nadim Haddad, Rose Mungai, Minh Cong Nguyen, Zander Prinsloo, Mariano Ernesto Sosa, Martha Viveros, and Haoyu Wu, as well as the Global Economic Prospects team, contributed to the production and update of the data used for the report. Jessica Adler, Kimberly Blair Bolch, Michelle Chester, Karem Edwards, and Jaya Karki provided general support to the team.

The authors are especially appreciative of the Global Poverty and Inequality Data team, the Data for Goals (D4G) team, and the World Bank's regional statistical teams for their work to ensure consistency and accuracy in global poverty monitoring and projections.

This work was conducted under the general direction of Deon Filmer, Haishan Fu, and Luis Felipe Lopez-Calva, with additional input from Benu Bidani and Umar Serajuddin. The team is also grateful for the overall guidance received from Indermit S. Gill, Pablo Saavedra, and Axel van Trotsenburg.

The report would not have been possible without the communications, editorial, and publishing teams. Chisako Fukuda led the communications strategy and engagement with support from Paul Clare, Paul Gallagher, Nicholas Nam, Joe Rebello, and Leslie J. Yun. The report was edited by Katherine Theresa Elizabeth Ward and designed by Carlos Reyes. Deborah Appel-Barker, Mary Fisk, and Patricia Katayama from the Publishing Program managed the editing, design, typesetting, translation, and printing of the report.

The team gratefully acknowledges the advice from peer reviewers and advisers. Peer reviewers for this report included François Bourguignon, Jed Friedman, Stephane Hallegatte, Santiago Levy, and Maria Ana Lugo. Advisers included Dean Jolliffe and Aart Kraay.

The team also benefited from many helpful discussions with teams across the World Bank Group, including sector and regional Chief Economist Offices and Directors of Strategy and Operations, and the Poverty and Equity Extended Management Team. The team is also grateful for helpful feedback from the Poverty and Equity External Advisory Committee. In particular, the team is grateful for comments from Kimberly Blair Bolch, Andrew Dabalen, Richard Damania, Samuel Freije, Roberta Gatti, Gabriela Inchauste, Somik Lall, Ambar Narayan, Carlos Rodriguez-Castelan, Carolina Sanchez-Paramo, Norbert Schady, and Stephane Straub.

The report is a joint project of the Development Data and Development Research Groups in the Development Economics Vice Presidency, and the Poverty and Equity Global Practice in the Prosperity Vice Presidency of the World Bank. Financing from the government of the United Kingdom helped support analytical work through the Data and Evidence for Tackling Extreme Poverty Research Programme.

About the Team

Co-leads of the report

Maria Eugenia Genoni is a Senior Economist in the Poverty and Equity Global Practice of the World Bank. She has led analytical work and operations on statistics, poverty and inequality, and household risk management in the Latin America and the Caribbean, Middle East and North Africa, and South Asia regions. Maria's areas of expertise include poverty measurement and survey design, statistical capacity building, migration and forced displacement, and analytics related to poverty and economic mobility. Prior to joining the World Bank, Maria worked in the Economics department at Duke University, the Research department at the Inter-American Development Bank, and the Ministry of Finance of Argentina. She holds a PhD in economics from Duke University.

Christoph Lakner is the Program Manager for Global Poverty and Inequality Data in the Development Data Group at the World Bank. His research interests include global poverty and inequality, inequality of opportunity, intergenerational mobility, and top incomes. He is also involved in the World Bank's global poverty monitoring. He leads the Global Poverty and Inequality Data team in the Development Data Group, which co-produces the Poverty and Inequality Platform, the home of the World Bank's global poverty numbers. He holds a DPhil, an MPhil, and a BA in economics from the University of Oxford.

Chapter co-leads

Henry Stemmler is a Consultant in the Poverty and Equity Global Practice at the World Bank. His research interests include poverty and labor markets in developing countries and how these are affected by global trade and climate change. Prior to joining the World Bank, he was a Postdoctoral Researcher at the Food Systems Economics and Policy Group at ETH Zürich and has worked as an Economist at the International Labor Organization and as a Consultant for the World Bank and Oxfam. He holds a PhD in economics from the University of Göttingen.

Samuel Kofi Tetteh-Baah is an Economist in the Development Data Group (Indicators and Data team) at the World Bank. He is involved in research to improve the quality of global poverty estimates by incorporating new data (for example, on purchasing power parities) and new methods of poverty measurement (for example, accounting for household economies of scale). He is part of the Global Poverty and Inequality Data team in the Development Data Group, which is jointly responsible for updating the World Bank's global poverty estimates twice a year. He prepares the poverty data used for monitoring Sustainable Development Goal 1. Samuel holds a PhD in development economics from ETH Zürich.

Nishant Yonzan is an Economist in the Development Data Group (Indicators and Data team) at the World Bank. His work involves improving the monitoring of global poverty, shared prosperity, and inequality. He is part of the Global Poverty and Inequality Data team in the Development Data Group that co-manages the Poverty and Inequality Platform, the home of the World Bank's global poverty and shared prosperity numbers. He is interested in measuring inequality and poverty as well as exploring the social implications of changes in these variables. Nishant holds a PhD in economics from the Graduate Center of the City University of New York.

Core team

Maria Gabriela Farfan Betran is a Senior Economist in the Poverty and Equity Global Practice. She joined the practice in 2015, following a one-year tenure with the Living Standards Measurement Study in the Development Research Group. During the past 10 years, she has led policy dialogue, analytical work, lending operations, and primary data collection efforts in various countries across lower- and middle-income settings in Latin America and the Caribbean, Sub-Saharan Africa, and Southeast Asia. She holds a bachelor's degree in economics from the Universidad Nacional de Cuyo and a PhD in economics from Duke University.

Niklas Buehren is a Senior Economist in the World Bank's Africa Gender Innovation Lab. He coordinates a portfolio of impact evaluations across various sectors. His work and research interests primarily focus on technology adoption in agriculture, land tenure, entrepreneurship, microfinance, and adolescent development. Prior to joining the World Bank, Niklas worked in the research unit of a nongovernmental organization in Uganda, Tanzania, and Southern Sudan. He received a master's degree in economics from the London School of Economics and Political Science and a PhD in economics from the University College London.

Benoit Decerf is a Senior Economist in the Development Research Group at the World Bank. He is an applied micro-theorist whose research interests include poverty measurement, welfare economics, and mechanism design. His current research on poverty measurement focuses on the design of poverty indicators aggregating different dimensions of deprivation, for example, combining subsistence and social participation, or combining poverty and mortality. Benoit holds an MS from KU Leuven and a PhD from the Université Catholique de Louvain.

Carolyn Fischer is Research Manager of the Sustainability and Infrastructure Team in the Development Research Group at the World Bank. Her research addresses issues of technical change, trade, and emissions leakage in environmental policy instrument design. She was previously appointed professor of environmental economics at Vrije Universiteit Amsterdam, held the Canada 150 Research Chair in Climate Economics, Innovation and Policy at University of Ottawa, and was the Marks Visiting Professor at Gothenburg University. She enjoys research fellow affiliations with Resources for the Future and the CESifo Research Network. She has served on the boards of both the American and European Association of Environmental and Resource Economists, as well as expert advisory councils for research institutes in Europe and North America, and is co-editor of *Environmental and Resource Economics*. She earned her PhD in economics from the University of Michigan, Ann Arbor.

David Groves is a Lead Economist in the Climate Finance and Economics Unit with the Climate Change Group at the World Bank. He co-leads the World Bank's global program on long-term, low-emissions development strategies and supports the compilation of the World Bank's Country Climate and Development Reports. Prior to joining the World Bank in 2021, he was a Senior Policy Researcher at the RAND Corporation, where he co-directed its Climate Resilience Center and Center on Decision Making Under Uncertainty. David has a PhD in policy analysis from the Pardee RAND Graduate School, an MS in atmospheric sciences from the University of Washington, and an MS in earth systems from Stanford University.

Federico Haslop is a Consultant in the Poverty and Equity Global Practice at the World Bank. He is interested on how health and environmental challenges affect the developing world and its cities. He has carried out research on the effect of aridification of lakes, the consequences of epidemics on fertility, and the impact of heat on labor productivity. Federico holds a master's in economics from the Universidad de San Andrés and is currently a PhD candidate in economics at The George Washington University.

Ruth Hill is a Lead Economist in the Poverty and Equity Global Practice at the World Bank. Ruth has been at the World Bank for 10 years and has led work on the distributional impacts of climate change, fiscal policy, markets, and institutions. She co-led the *Poverty and Shared Prosperity Report 2022* and the development of the Rural Income Diagnostics, and she conducted poverty assessments and systematic country diagnostics in East Africa and South Asia. From 2019 to 2021, she was on external service as the Chief Economist at the UK government's Centre for Disaster Protection. Prior to joining the World Bank in 2013, she was a Senior Research Fellow at the International Food Policy Research Institute, conducting impact evaluations on insurance and market interventions. Ruth has published in the *Journal of Development Economics*, *World Bank Economic Review*, *Economic Development and Cultural Change*, *Experimental Economics*, the *American Journal of Agricultural Economics*, and *World Development*. She has a PhD in economics from the University of Oxford.

Daniel Gerszon Mahler is an Economist in the Development Data Group at the World Bank. He conducts research related to the measurement of poverty, inequality, justice, and climate change. Prior to joining the World Bank, he was a Visiting Fellow at Harvard University's Department of Government and worked for the Danish Ministry of Foreign Affairs. He holds a PhD in economics from the University of Copenhagen.

Regina Pleninger is an Economist in the Prosperity Chief Economist Office. Her research interests include topics on inequality, poverty, growth, and jobs. She has worked on the distributional effects of financial development, globalization, and natural disasters. Since she joined the World Bank in 2022, she has worked on the *Africa Poverty and Inequality Report 2024* and contributed to the "Central African Republic Poverty Assessment 2023." She holds a PhD in economics from ETH Zürich.

Sutirtha Sinha Roy is an Economist with the Poverty and Equity Global Practice in the East Asia and Pacific Region of the World Bank. His current work includes examining vulnerability in conflict settings, addressing disparities in learning outcomes, and evaluating interventions to combat child malnutrition. Previously, he conducted research on poverty in India, analyzed the welfare impacts of portable social protection policies, and led technical assistance programs for India's survey and census organizations. Prior to joining the World Bank in 2017, he worked in the office of the Chief Economic Adviser at India's Ministry of Finance. He holds a degree from the Johns Hopkins University School of Advanced International Studies.

Sharad Tandon is a Senior Economist in the Poverty and Equity Global Practice. He joined the World Bank in 2017 and has been working on poverty-related issues in East Asia and Pacific, the Middle East and North Africa, and West Africa. His current research interests include the measurement and analysis of food insecurity and its determinants, building the evidence base to alleviate poverty in conflict and fragile settings, and the measurement and analysis of gender inequities and their determinants. Sharad holds an AB in economics from Cornell University and an MA and PhD in economics from the University of California at Berkeley.

Nele Warrinnier is an Economist in the Global Unit of the Poverty and Equity Global Practice at the World Bank. Her research interests lie at the intersection of development and labor economics, focusing on inequality in labor markets and human capital formation in developing countries. As an applied microeconomist, she has worked on a wide range of topics, including early childhood education, female labor force participation, inequality, informality, and technology adoption. Prior to joining the World Bank, she was awarded a Marie Curie postdoctoral fellowship at the School of Economics and Finance at Queen Mary University of London. Nele holds an MSc from the London School of Economics and Political Science and a PhD in economics from KU Leuven.

Main Messages

The World Bank has set a clear mission: ending extreme poverty and boosting shared prosperity on a livable planet. This report offers the first postpandemic assessment of global progress on this agenda. This report explores different potential pathways out of the polycrisis—an environment where multiple and interconnected challenges are affecting the world simultaneously—taking seriously the trade-offs and complementarities across objectives that are embedded in different policy approaches. The main messages are presented around **Progress** in terms of the goals, **Pathways** to move forward, and **Priorities** depending on where countries stand on the interlinked goals.

Progress: Global poverty reduction and improvements in shared prosperity have stalled

Global poverty reduction has slowed to a near standstill, with 2020–30 set to be a lost decade. Today, 8.5 percent of the world lives in extreme poverty (those living on less than $2.15 per person per day) (figure 1, panel a). At a poverty standard more relevant for upper-middle-income countries ($6.85 per person per day), 44 percent of the world's population lives in poverty. The number of people living under this higher standard has barely changed since 1990 due to population growth (figure 1, panel b). At the current pace of progress, it would take decades to eradicate extreme poverty and more than a century to lift people above $6.85 per day.

Progress has stalled amid multiple shocks and growth patterns that have not enabled the poorest to catch up. The COVID-19 pandemic had scarring impacts, and extreme poverty in the poorest countries today is still above prepandemic rates. Poverty continues to concentrate in settings with historically low economic growth and fragility. Gains in reducing the Global Prosperity Gap, the World Bank's new measure of shared prosperity, have also stopped since the pandemic due to a reduction in economic growth and a divergence in mean incomes across countries (figure 2, panel a). Today, incomes around the world, on average, would have to increase fivefold to reach a prosperity standard of $25 per person per day, which in many places remains completely aspirational.

FIGURE 1

Global extreme poverty reduction has slowed to a near standstill, with 2020–30 set to be a lost decade

a. Progress in reducing extreme poverty has come to a halt

b. Number of people living on less than $6.85 per day has remained unchanged since 1990

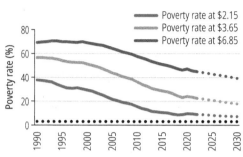
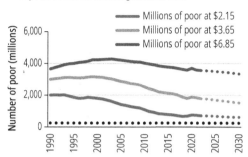

Sources: Original figures for this publication based on World Bank calculations.

Note: All $ values are expressed in per person per day in 2017 purchasing power parity dollars. 2022–30 are projections and are shown in dots at the ends of lines. In panel a, the black horizontal dotted line is drawn at 3 percent and indicates the World Bank's target of ending extreme poverty by 2030. In panel b, it is drawn at 256 million, which represents 3 percent of the global population projected for 2030.

FIGURE 2

Progress on boosting shared prosperity around the world has slowed down

a. Recent progress on the Global Prosperity Gap was hindered by increasing inequality between countries due to divergent growth

b. Latin America and the Caribbean and Sub-Saharan Africa have a large share of high-inequality economies

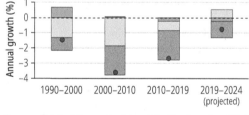
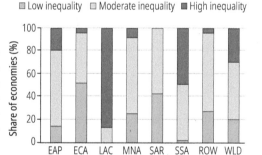

Sources: Original figures for this publication based on World Bank calculations.

Note: EAP = East Asia and Pacific; ECA = Europe and Central Asia; LAC = Latin America and the Caribbean; MNA = Middle East and North Africa; SAR = South Asia; SSA = Sub-Saharan Africa; ROW = rest of the world; WLD = world.

Panel a. Change in the Global Prosperity Gap decomposed into (negative of) the growth in mean incomes, between-country inequality, and within-country inequality. The Global Prosperity Gap for 2024 is projected.

Panel b. Share of economies in 2022 with Gini less than 30 (low), between 30 and 40 (moderate), and greater than 40 (high). Regional classifications follow the Poverty and Inequality Platform: https://datanalytics.worldbank.org/PIP-Methodology /lineupestimates.html#regionsandcountries.

The number of economies with high inequality has fallen. The number of economies with high income or consumption inequality—defined as a Gini coefficient above 40—has fallen from 61 to 49 in a decade. High-inequality economies are concentrated in Latin America and the Caribbean and Sub-Saharan Africa (figure 2, panel b) and are home to 1.7 billion people in 2022, approximately one-fifth of the world's population, a share that has remained roughly the same over the past decade. Seventy percent of the global population lives in an economy with moderate inequality (Gini between 30 and 40), and only 7 percent live in economies with low inequality (Gini below 30).

Moreover, nearly one in five people are at risk of experiencing welfare losses due to an extreme weather event from which they will struggle to recover. The World Bank has developed a new vision indicator that counts the number of people at high risk from climate-related hazards globally. Being at high risk is defined as being exposed to hazards and also being vulnerable to their impacts (defined as the physical propensity to experience severe losses and the inability to cope with and recover from losses). Sub-Saharan Africa has the largest share of people at high risk from extreme weather events, with almost everyone who is exposed to an extreme weather event also being at high risk (figure 3, panel a). South Asia has the largest total population at high risk from extreme weather events (32 percent of the population).

FIGURE 3

Risks from extreme weather events are high and may increase without action

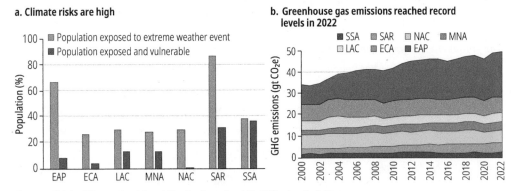

a. Climate risks are high

b. Greenhouse gas emissions reached record levels in 2022

Sources: Original figures for this publication based on World Bank calculations.

Note: GHG = greenhouse gas; gt CO_2e = gigatons carbon dioxide equivalent; EAP = East Asia and Pacific; ECA = Europe and Central Asia; LAC = Latin America and the Caribbean; MNA = Middle East and North Africa; NAC = North America; SAR = South Asia; SSA = Sub-Saharan Africa. Regional classifications follow the World Bank region classifications: https://datahelpdesk.worldbank.org/knowledgebase/articles/906519-world-bank-country-and-lending-groups.

Panel a. Population exposed to extreme weather events, and the population at high risk from extreme weather events (exposed and vulnerable).

Panel b. Total GHG emissions in gt CO_2e.

By contrast, the share of people at risk is the lowest in North America, where less than 1 percent of the population is at high risk. Although exposure in Sub-Saharan Africa is not as high as in other regions, high levels of vulnerability keep people at high risk. The likelihood of experiencing losses has declined with growing income levels globally, but less for the poorest and those in more fragile settings. For example, between 2010 and 2019, despite the number of people exposed increasing, non-International Development Association (IDA) countries were able to reduce the number of people at risk significantly over this period. This pattern is not the case for IDA countries, where the number of people at risk rose almost one to one with the population exposed. In non-IDA countries, the population at risk fell due to the large gains in income and financial access, developments from which people in IDA countries did not benefit as much.

In 2022, greenhouse gas (GHG) emissions reached record levels (figure 3, panel b), trapping nearly 50 percent more heat than in 1990. Climate change will likely lead to more frequent and more intense extreme weather events, which will negatively affect welfare.

Large gaps in human capital, basic infrastructure, and life essentials affect significant populations in the poorest regions. One-half or more of the people in Sub-Saharan Africa and in fragile and conflict-affected situations lack electricity and sanitation. Large education gaps also persist, but investments in education in low-income countries remain very low. Air pollution is a leading environmental risk to people's health, which must be prioritized: it carried a health cost representing 6.1 percent of global GDP in 2019. The prevalence of undernourishment is also on the rise globally and remains particularly high in Sub-Saharan Africa. These large multidimensional gaps have also contributed to the vulnerability to shocks in lower-income countries.

The global environment is facing multiple and interconnected crises or a "polycrisis." The global environment that has become more challenging amid a polycrisis—from slow growth prospects and high levels of debt to increased uncertainty, fragility, and polarization. Economic growth in the poorest countries is projected to remain weaker than in the decade before the pandemic. In addition, debt interest payments in the poorest settings are reaching an all-time high, diverting spending away from critical needs.

Pathways: Eradicating poverty and boosting shared prosperity on a livable planet requires managing trade-offs

Progress on the interlinked goals requires faster and inclusive growth and protecting people from extreme weather events. Enabling the poor to benefit more from economic growth involves better-functioning labor markets, investments in the productive capacity of people, and structural conditions that enable socioeconomic mobility so that everyone can use their productive capacity to their full extent. Protecting people from extreme weather events requires acting on two fronts: (a) lowering vulnerability by enhancing risk management and (b) preventing the escalation of future climate hazards by accelerating transformations to reduce the emissions intensiveness of growth.

With limited budgets, high uncertainty, and conflicting interests, policy makers must prioritize and make difficult choices. To inform their decisions, policy makers must understand the trade-offs between growing incomes and lowering GHG emissions, find ways to scale up synergistic policies that can help advance on multiple fronts or reduce trade-offs (for example, tackling high air pollution), and manage transition costs to specific groups and communities affected by labor market or price shifts.

Actions need to recognize that emissions are primarily generated by richer countries and that poorer countries are the most at risk. Whereas upper-middle- and high-income countries currently account for four-fifths of global GHG emissions, low- and lower-middle-income

FIGURE 4

Priorities to advance on the interlinked goals

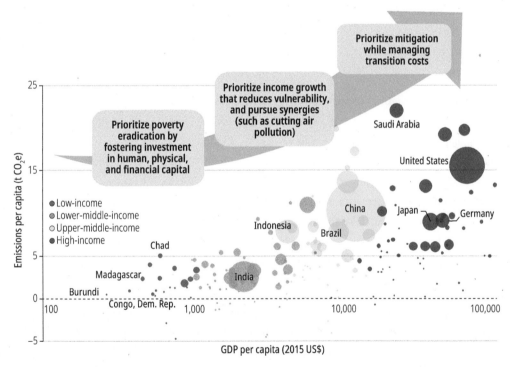

Source: Original figure for this publication based on World Bank calculations.

Note: GDP = gross domestic product; GHG = greenhouse gas; t CO_2e = tons, carbon dioxide equivalent. The size of the bubbles indicates total GHG emissions. Negative emissions occur when ecosystems absorb more carbon than the country emits. A few small countries with very high per capita emissions (Bahrain, Guyana, Iceland, Kuwait, Oman, Palau, Qatar, Trinidad and Tobago, United Arab Emirates) and countries with very low per capita emissions (Central African Republic, Vanuatu) are omitted for visual purposes. The horizontal axis uses a logarithmic scale.

countries contribute a relatively small share of emissions, although they are home to one-half of the world's population. For example, Sub-Saharan Africa accounts for only 5 percent of global emissions. On the other hand, the share of people at risk from weather hazards is significantly higher in poorer settings.

Advancing on the eradication of extreme poverty does not come at a big cost for the planet because the poorest countries contribute so little to emissions. Eradicating extreme poverty would increase emissions by less than 5 percent above 2019 levels. Achieving higher living standards than this bare minimum—that is, by moving more than 3 billion people above $6.85 per day—would lead to a significant increase in emissions assuming historic emission intensities: the increase would be 46 percent above 2019 levels.

Priorities: Doing what matters where it matters

Figure 4 brings these considerations together and illustrates a simplified way to identify priorities. A key guiding element to set priorities is considering where the poor and vulnerable live and where the emissions are and will be generated. Each unique situation requires its own tailored solutions, and the results from this report do not aim to be prescriptive for a specific country. Country-specific studies are recommended to guide prioritization at that level. The following discussion aims to shed light on where attention should be placed from a broader global perspective.

Low-income and fragile countries need to prioritize poverty reduction by fostering investment in human, physical, and financial capital. Two-thirds of the world's extreme poor live in Sub-Saharan Africa, rising to three-quarters when including all fragile and conflict-affected countries. More broadly, IDA countries account for 7 in 10 of the global extreme poor today. In those settings, higher growth is an essential foundation. To have the maximum impact on poverty reduction, that growth must be inclusive by creating employment opportunities while ensuring that the poor can take advantage of opportunities (for example, through quality education). Promoting economic growth, basic investments, and insurance are fundamental to sustainably improve the lives of the poor. Those actions reduce multidimensional poverty and enhance resilience against extreme weather and other shocks.

Middle-income countries must prioritize income growth that reduces vulnerability and pursue synergistic actions. Middle-income countries have successfully exited low-income status and have been able to reduce extreme poverty substantially; however, they are struggling to maintain the momentum needed to reach high-income levels and lift people above the $3.65 and $6.85 poverty lines. As in low-income countries, accelerating economic growth, enhancing the productive capacity of poorer households, and risk management are key. At the same time, emissions of many middle-income countries cannot be neglected. Without action, their emissions will increase over the next decades and surpass those of upper-middle-income countries and higher-income countries in absolute terms. For this purpose, identifying synergistic policies that can contribute to all goals and scaling them up is key. Tackling local environmental hazards such as air pollution is an area with multiple gains.

High-income and upper-middle-income countries with high emissions must accelerate mitigation to advance on the interlinked goals globally while managing transition costs. Upper-middle-income countries and, especially, high-income countries must step up the transition to low-carbon economies. Although emissions in those settings are projected to decline under current policies, the current progress is not nearly fast enough to limit global warming. Potential transition costs associated with climate mitigation, such as higher energy prices or job losses in carbon-intensive sectors, must be managed—particularly for the poor and more vulnerable. Wealthier nations hastening their climate mitigation actions could significantly alter the distribution of future environmental risks worldwide. Upper-middle-income countries also have a significant share of the population facing climate risks, and it is in their own population's interest to accelerate this process to protect them from future hazards.

Advancing on these interlinked global challenges requires a solid foundation of evidence. Across the board, more and better data are needed to address these complex policy issues and monitor impacts. Although data availability has improved in many countries, less than one-half of IDA countries had a household survey available for global poverty monitoring in 2020 or later. More investment is needed to produce reliable, granular, and timely information, and that requires foundational efforts to strengthen national statistical systems and innovative approaches to advance the frontier of data and modeling for welfare analysis. When collected, data should be made public to better monitor policy impact and facilitate further policy design. Because the lived experience of poverty goes well beyond monetary measures, it is important to ensure that data efforts also invest in understanding other dimensions of well-being, such as deprivations in access to services, health, or food security.

Urgent and coordinated global action is essential to meet these interlinked goals. The financing gap for sustainable development is growing, which hinders lower-income countries' ability to invest across multiple objectives. This constrained environment creates an urgent need to focus and prioritize the actions that will have the highest return for development and that can allow the world to make significant progress. It calls for fundamental changes in how countries approach their national development strategies and their contribution to global public goods. The potential policy pathways in each context often differ drastically depending on a country's historical development trajectory, access to technology and financing, and national priorities. However, countries must also consider their global responsibilities and that international actors have a critical coordination role to play. Ending poverty and boosting shared prosperity on a livable planet will require novel ways of organizing economic activity.

Abbreviations

AI	artificial intelligence
ALPM	active labor market program
CBAM	Carbon Border Adjustment Mechanism
CEMS	Continuous Emissions Monitoring Systems
CEQ	Commitment to Equity (Institute)
CO_2	carbon dioxide
EDGAR	Emissions Database for Global Atmospheric Research
EFDVM	Emission Factors and Default Values Methods
EMDEs	emerging market and developing economies
ETS	emission trading systems
EU-SILC	European Union Statistics on Income and Living Conditions
FAM	fuel analysis method
FCS	fragile and conflict-affected situations
FIES	Food Insecurity Experience Scale
FNS	food and nutrition security
GDP	gross domestic product
GHG	greenhouse gas
GHSL	Global Human Settlement Layer with gridded population data (GHS-POP)
GMD	Global Monitoring Database
HCES	Household Consumption and Expenditure Survey
ICP	International Comparison Program
IDA	International Development Association

IIASA	International Institute of Applied Systems Analysis
IHME	Institute for Health Metrics and Evaluation
IPCC	Intergovernmental Panel on Climate Change
LULUCF	land use, land use change, and forestry
MDBs	multilateral development banks
MMRP	Modified Mixed Reference Period
MPI	Multidimensional Poverty Index
MPM	Multidimensional Poverty Measure
NDC	Nationally Determined Contribution
NGFS	Network for Greening the Financial System
NSS	National Sample Survey
ODIN	Open Data Inventory
OECD	Organisation for Economic Co-operation and Development
PIP	Poverty and Inequality Platform
PoU	Prevalence of Undernourishment
PPP	purchasing power parity
PSPR	Poverty and Shared Prosperity report
PV	photovoltaic
RTM	real-time modeling
SDGs	Sustainable Development Goals
SPL	societal poverty line
SSPs	Shared Socioeconomic Pathways
UNFCCC	United Nations Framework Convention on Climate Change
WASH	water, sanitation, and hygiene
WBGT	wet bulb globe temperature
WDI	World Development Indicators
WHO	World Health Organization
WID	World Inequality Database

The term *country*, used interchangeably with *economy*, does not imply political independence but refers to any territory for which authorities report separate social or economic statistics.

Overview

The World Bank has set a clear mission: ending extreme poverty and boosting shared prosperity on a livable planet. This new edition of the biennial series, previously titled *Poverty and Shared Prosperity*, assesses the three components of the mission and emphasizes that reducing poverty and increasing shared prosperity must be achieved without high costs to the environment. The current polycrisis—where the multiple crises of slow economic growth, increased fragility, climate risks, and heightened uncertainty have come together at the same time—makes national development strategies and international cooperation difficult.

This overview summarizes the **progress** toward achieving these goals, outlines promising **pathways** to speed up the progress on multiple fronts, and proposes **priorities** tailored to countries at various levels of poverty, income, and environmental vulnerability. Offering the first post-COVID-19 (Coronavirus) pandemic assessment of global progress on this interlinked agenda, the report finds that global poverty reduction has resumed but at a pace slower than before the COVID-19 crisis. It also provides evidence that the number of countries with high levels of income inequality has declined considerably during the past two decades, but the pace of improvements in shared prosperity has slowed and that inequality remains high in Latin America and the Caribbean and in Sub-Saharan Africa. The report also finds evidence of countries' increasing ability to manage natural hazards where there has been progress in poverty reduction and shared prosperity; but in the poorest settings, the report finds that climate risks are significantly higher.

Progress: Global poverty reduction and improvements in shared prosperity have stalled

Global poverty reduction slowed to a near standstill during the past five years, raising concerns that 2020–30 would be a lost decade

About 8.5 percent of the global population lives in extreme poverty in 2024. This means that 692 million people worldwide live on less than $2.15 per person per day.[1] While the extreme poverty rate fell from 38 percent in 1990 to 8.5 percent in 2024, it has stalled more recently amid lower economic growth and multiple shocks such as the COVID-19 pandemic, high inflation, and increased conflict and fragility. Extreme poverty today is only slightly below the rate observed before the pandemic in 2019 and in many poor settings, poverty rates remain higher than they were five years ago. Using the slightly higher poverty line of $3.65 a day per person (representative of the national poverty lines used in lower-middle-income countries), about 1.7 billion people are living in poverty in 2024 (21.4 percent, or about one-fifth, of the global population). At the still higher standard of $6.85 per person per day that is more typical of upper-middle-income countries, almost one-half of the world's population (43.6 percent) is living in poverty. This means that the living standards of 3.5 billion people are below this higher poverty line in 2024 (figure O.1). While the share of people under $6.85 declined from 70 percent to 43.6 percent since the 1990s, the actual number of people living on less than $6.85 a day has barely changed since 1990 because of population growth.

Even more serious, by the end of this decade, a projected 7.3 percent of the world population will be living in extreme poverty—more than double the World Bank global goal of 3 percent and even further away from the Sustainable Development Goal of ending extreme poverty in all countries by 2030. In fact, between now and 2030, only 69 million people are projected to escape extreme poverty (figure O.1). At the higher poverty line of $6.85, reductions in the poverty rate are projected to continue more noticeably with slightly less than 40 percent of the global population being projected to live on less than $6.85 per person per day in 2030 (more than 3 billion people).

If economic growth continues to be slow and inequality remains unchanged, the 3 percent goal will remain out of reach for decades. If gross domestic product (GDP) per capita growth stays at the average rates observed during 2010–19, extreme poverty rates will remain above 7 percent until 2050 (figure O.2, panel a). If every country grew by 2 percent in per capita terms annually, extreme poverty would not reach 3 percent for another 60 years. Even with 4 percent per capita growth rates, which seem out of reach for many countries, it would take until 2048 to reach 3 percent. Reductions in inequality can help accelerate progress. For example, under the 2 percent per capita growth scenario, if the Gini index in every country were to also decrease by 2 percent annually, it would take 40 years less to eradicate poverty (20 versus 60 years).

Poverty rates at $6.85 a day are projected to fall faster under the current growth forecast scenario than extreme poverty rates (figure O.2, panel b). Still, under the current growth forecast, it would take more than a century to reach a poverty rate of less than 3 percent at $6.85 per person per day.

FIGURE O.1

Progress has stagnated for the poor

a. Progress in reducing extreme poverty rate has resumed but at a slower pace than before 2020

—— Poverty rate at $2.15   —— Poverty rate at $3.65   —— Poverty rate at $6.85

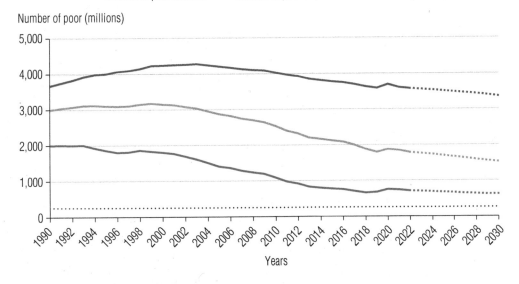

b. The number of people living on less than $6.85 has remained unchanged over the past 30 years

—— Millions of poor at $2.15   —— Millions of poor at $3.65   —— Millions of poor at $6.85

Source: World Bank, Poverty and Inequality Platform (version September 2024), https://pip.worldbank.org/.
Note: Poverty rates are reported for the $2.15, $3.65, and $6.85 per person per day poverty lines (expressed in 2017 purchasing power parity dollars). Between 2022 and 2029 poverty is projected based on per capita gross domestic product growth projections in *Global Economic Prospects, June 2024* (World Bank 2024c) complemented by the *Macro Poverty Outlook, Spring Meetings 2024* (World Bank 2024e) and the *World Economic Outlook* (IMF 2024); for 2030, average annual historic per capita growth rates (2010–19) are used. See annex 1A for more details on the projection methods. In panel a, the black horizontal dotted line is drawn at 3 percent and indicates the World Bank's target of ending extreme poverty by 2030. In panel b, it is drawn at 256 million, which represents 3 percent of the global population projected for 2030.

FIGURE O.2

Projections of poverty until 2050 under different scenarios

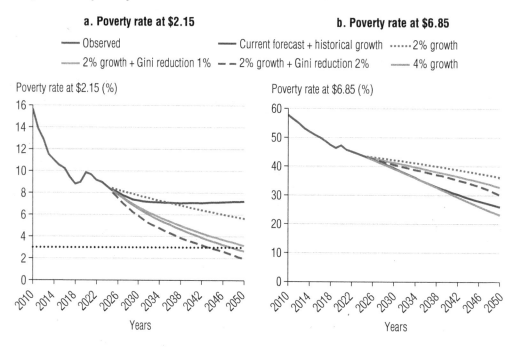

a. Poverty rate at $2.15   b. Poverty rate at $6.85

—— Observed   —— Current forecast + historical growth   ······ 2% growth
—— 2% growth + Gini reduction 1%   – – 2% growth + Gini reduction 2%   —— 4% growth

Sources: World Bank calculations using data from World Bank, Poverty and Inequality Platform (version September 2024), https://pip.worldbank.org/; World Bank 2024c; IMF 2024; and World Bank 2024e.

Note: Poverty rates are reported for the $2.15 and $6.85 per person per day poverty lines (expressed in 2017 purchasing power parity dollars). Poverty rates are projected after 2022 based on country-level growth in gross domestic product per capita. "Current forecast + historical growth" is based on growth projections in the *Global Economic Prospects, June 2024* (World Bank 2024c) complemented by the *Macro Poverty Outlook* (World Bank 2024e) and the *World Economic Outlook* (IMF 2024) until 2029 and average annual per capita historical growth rates (2010–19) thereafter (see annex 1A for details). Inequality reduction scenarios refer to a reduction in the country-level Gini index by 1 percent or 2 percent annually. The horizontal dotted line indicates a poverty rate of 3 percent.

Overlapping crises have slowed or stalled poverty reduction

The slow progress on poverty reduction in the past years reflects global conditions characterized by multiple and overlapping crises or a "polycrisis." *Polycrisis* refers to multiple and interconnected crises occurring simultaneously, where their interactions amplify the overall impact. The scarring effects of the pandemic, slow economic growth, increased conflict and fragility, and insufficient progress on shared prosperity, for instance, are connected and have been behind the slow progress in poverty reduction. The risk of a polycrisis is growing due to heightened uncertainly, fragility, climate change, and other vulnerabilities that tie together diverse sectors and regions.

The poorest countries have still not recovered from the poverty increase caused by the COVID-19 pandemic

The poorest countries still have higher poverty rates than before the pandemic. In low-income countries, the extreme poverty rate rose in 2020 and 2021 and has not fallen much since (figure O.3). In 2024, 43 percent of people in low-income countries are in extreme poverty. Lower-middle-income countries managed to recover from the COVID-19 shock only in 2022. In contrast, upper-middle-income countries continued to make progress in 2021 and 2022 against poverty (as measured against the $6.85 line, which is more relevant in these settings). Low-income countries have shown less resilience, as the compounded effects of the pandemic and rising food and energy prices have led to poverty rates remaining higher than in 2019.[2]

FIGURE O.3

Poverty is still above prepandemic levels in the poorest countries

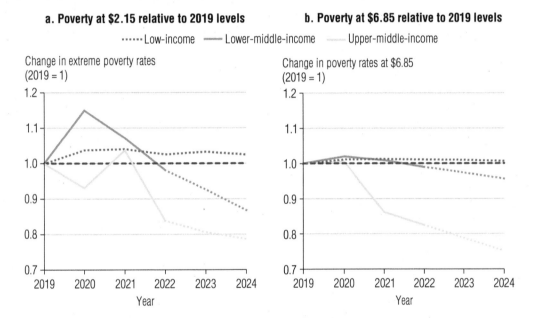

a. Poverty at $2.15 relative to 2019 levels　　**b. Poverty at $6.85 relative to 2019 levels**

······ Low-income ── Lower-middle-income ── Upper-middle-income

Source: World Bank, Poverty and Inequality Platform (version September 2024), https://pip.worldbank.org/.
Note: Poverty rates are shown relative to 2019 levels for the $2.15 and $6.85 per person per day poverty lines (expressed in 2017 purchasing power parity dollars). The line for low-income countries is dotted because the surveys covered less than 50 percent of the group's population between 2019 and 2022. Poverty rates for 2022–24 are projected based on per capita gross domestic product growth projections in *Global Economic Prospects, June 2024* (World Bank 2024c). High-income countries are omitted because poverty rates at both lines are small. Poverty rates at the $6.85 poverty line did not increase in high-income countries between 2019 and 2024, and changes at the $2.15 poverty line were less than 0.05 percentage points. Income group is kept fixed using the fiscal year 2024 classifications.

In addition to a slower recovery in terms of income, poor people experienced setbacks in human capital and employment, further compromising their resilience and capacity to generate higher incomes in the future. The pandemic had a devastating effect on global health, causing a significant number of excess deaths and reducing the global life expectancy at birth by over 1.5 years.[3] Countries with higher inequalities in income and access to quality care had higher excess mortality during the pandemic (Sepulveda and Brooker 2021). The health and food systems disruptions caused by the pandemic also reversed progress on child nutrition, with an estimated additional 9.3 million children suffering from acute malnutrition and 2.6 million more children stunted by 2022 (Osendarp et al. 2020). In addition, school closures led to learning losses in language, literacy, and mathematics of around 30 percent in multiple countries. In 2021, in several countries a quarter of all young people were not in education, employment, or training (Schady et al. 2023). Poorer households were also less likely to use remote work and schooling (Narayan et al. 2022). Schooling disruptions affected poorer households more than richer ones. It is estimated that students in low-income and lower-middle-income countries could face future earning losses of up to 10 percent because of the pandemic, suggesting a permanent scarring effect (Schady et al. 2023). This generation of students now risks losing $21 trillion in potential lifetime earnings in present value, or the equivalent of 17 percent of today's global GDP (World Bank et al. 2022). The loss in schooling is likely to have a larger effect on poverty in the future than the immediate effect of the pandemic has had (Decerf et al. 2024).

Extreme poverty has been increasingly concentrated in countries with slow economic growth

A large factor in the slowing of global poverty reduction over the last decade is the changing regional composition of poverty. In 1990, East Asia and Pacific had a higher poverty rate than Sub-Saharan Africa, and South Asia had rates similar to Sub-Saharan Africa. This picture changed markedly over the years. Fueled by rapid growth, East Asia and Pacific experienced unprecedented progress that also drove poverty reduction at the global level. Until 2013, global extreme poverty reduction was led by China's rapid economic growth, which lifted more than 800 million people out of extreme poverty over three decades. Between 1990 and 2024, the rest of East Asia and Pacific also made remarkable progress, with 210 million people exiting extreme poverty during this period. Extreme poverty also fell significantly in South Asia, despite recent stagnation (see chapter 1).

Since the early 2010s, progress in reducing global extreme poverty has depended on the reduction of poverty in Sub-Saharan Africa much more than it did before. Although the extreme poverty rate in Sub-Saharan Africa has fallen over the past three decades, it did so at much slower rates than in other regions, and the number of people living in extreme poverty in the region has come fairly close to doubling—rising from 282 million in 1990 to 464 million in 2024. Similarly, in the Middle East and North Africa, the number of people living in extreme poverty doubled from 15 million in 1990 to 30 million in 2024. Extreme poverty in that region has surged since 2014, driven by fragility, conflict, and inflation (Gatti et al. 2023).

In 2000, only one-quarter of the extreme poor were living in a country in Sub-Saharan Africa or in a country in fragile and conflict-affected situations (FCS). By 2014, every second person in extreme poverty lived in either Sub-Saharan Africa or in FCS. The share of extreme poor in FCS in Sub-Saharan Africa then grew starkly in the late 2010s, driven by countries with large poor populations becoming fragile (for example, Niger or Nigeria). By 2024, the share of the extreme poor in Sub-Saharan Africa or FCS had increased to three-quarters, and 42 percent of the global extreme poor were in FCS in Sub-Saharan Africa.[4] More broadly, countries eligible for support through the International Development Association (IDA) account for 7 in 10 of the global extreme poor.[5]

IDA countries, particularly those in Sub-Saharan Africa, have not been able to achieve the high rates of income growth seen in East Asia and Pacific and South Asia. While IDA countries are different in many respects, they share common challenges, including low per capita incomes, widespread extreme poverty, and heightened fragility (World Bank 2024d). In Sub-Saharan Africa, which is home to about half of the IDA countries, economic growth has neither been large enough nor inclusive enough to reduce poverty significantly, especially since 2015 (Wu et al. 2024). Between 1990 and 2022, GDP per capita in Sub-Saharan Africa only grew by 0.7 percent annually (compared with 1.6 percent for the world). GDP growth in IDA countries is forecast to strengthen in 2024–25 but remain weaker than in the decade before the pandemic (World Bank 2024d).

Progress in improving shared prosperity has stalled since the pandemic

How growth benefits the least well-off is an important dimension to consider for improvements in societal well-being. Average income growth alone is not a good marker of development. Therefore, it is important to track a measure of the inclusiveness of growth or shared prosperity. The Global Prosperity Gap is the World Bank's new measure of shared prosperity (see box O.1). It is the average factor by which incomes need to be multiplied to bring everyone in the world to the prosperity standard of $25 per person per day, which is roughly equal to the average income when countries reach high-income status. The measure gives greater weight to the incomes of the poor, and hence income growth among the poorest households matters significantly more for reducing the Global Prosperity Gap.

Progress in reducing the Prosperity Gap has stalled since the pandemic, highlighting a slowdown in inclusive income growth over this period (figure O.4, panel a). Today, incomes around the world would have to increase fivefold, on average, to reach the prosperity standard of $25 per person per day. In many places, the convergence of incomes to the $25 per person per day level remains purely aspirational. The Prosperity Gap ranges from 1.7 in Europe and Central Asia to over 12 in Sub-Saharan Africa, signaling large disparities in income levels across regions. In Sub-Saharan Africa, incomes on average would need to rise more than twelvefold to reach the $25 standard. Sub-Saharan Africa accounts for 39 percent of the Global Prosperity Gap but 16 percent of the global population (figure O.4, panel b). This disparity highlights the large share of the region's population that is far away from the prosperity threshold.

BOX 0.1

How is the Prosperity Gap calculated?

The Prosperity Gap captures how far a society is from $25 per person per day, which is close to the average per capita household income when countries reach high-income status. The society's shortfall is the average shortfall among all individuals living in that society but giving poorer people a greater weight. The Prosperity Gap is defined as the average income multiple needed to reach that $25 standard for every member of that society (Kraay et al. 2023).

Note that the typical person in Tanzania, the Lao People's Democratic Republic, and Uzbekistan has less than $25 per day so they contribute with a factor greater than 1, and the typical person in Bulgaria has $25 per day so they contribute

FIGURE B0.1.1

The Prosperity Gap captures how far societies are from $25 per person per day

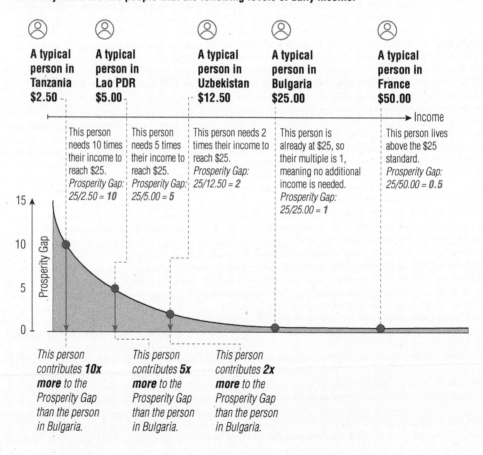

(continued)

BOX 0.1

How is the Prosperity Gap calculated? *(continued)*

with a factor of 1 (figure BO.1.1). The typical person in France lives above the $25 standard and makes only a small contribution to the measure. While income growth experienced by any person in the world will help reduce the Prosperity Gap, the magnitude of that reduction grows exponentially the poorer the individual is. That means that the typical person in Tanzania—the poorest person in this example—will contribute more to the Prosperity Gap, and gains in their income will count more than the others.

To find the Prosperity Gap in this example, these numbers are averaged:

$$\text{Prosperity Gap} = (10 + 5 + 2 + 1 + 0.5)/5 = 18.5/5 = \mathbf{3.7}$$

So, the society's Prosperity Gap is 3.7. This means that, on average, everyone's incomes need to be multiplied by 3.7 to reach the $25 per day standard. If the five people in the example were the only people in the world, the Global Prosperity Gap would be 3.7.

Source: World Bank.
Note: All $ values are in 2017 purchasing power parity dollars.

FIGURE 0.4

Stalled progress in Global Prosperity Gap reduction

a. Progress in reducing the Global Prosperity Gap

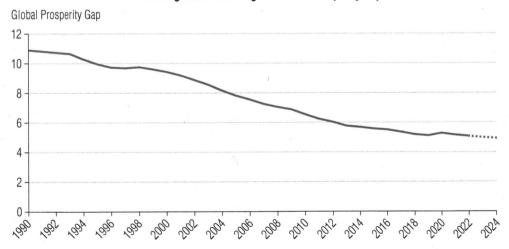

(continued)

FIGURE O.4

Stalled progress in Global Prosperity Gap reduction *(continued)*

b. The poorest regions are furthest behind and contribute more to the Global Prosperity Gap relative to their population in 2024

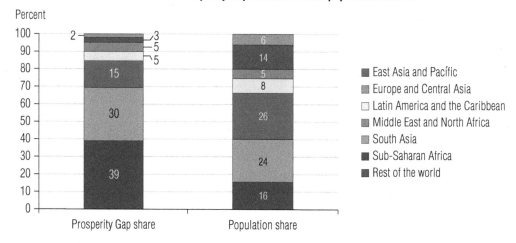

Source: World Bank, Poverty and Inequality Platform (version September 2024), https://pip.worldbank.org/.
Note: The estimates after 2022 are nowcasts (see annex 1A for further details on nowcasts and forecasts). See box O.1 for a calculation of the Global Prosperity Gap. Regional contribution (percent) of the Global Prosperity Gap in 2024 is shown in panel b, compared with the regional population shares (see chapter 2 for further details). The label values may not add to 100 percent due to rounding.

Historically, gains in global prosperity have been driven by both overall economic growth and a decline in inequality between countries. Between 1990 and 2024, the Global Prosperity Gap improved at an annual rate of 2.34 percent, with global mean income increasing at an annual rate of 1.48 percent and global inequality declining by 0.86 percent. The decline in global inequality has been driven by a decline in the inequality between countries, which is measured by the disparities in average living standards across countries (Kraay et al. 2023; Lakner and Milanovic 2016). However, from 2019 to 2024, the gains in prosperity were limited by a slowdown of global growth during the COVID-19 pandemic as well as an increase in global inequality driven by a divergence in average incomes between countries (figure O.5).

FIGURE 0.5

Limited gains in the Global Prosperity Gap due to a slowdown of global growth and an increase of global inequality during the COVID-19 pandemic

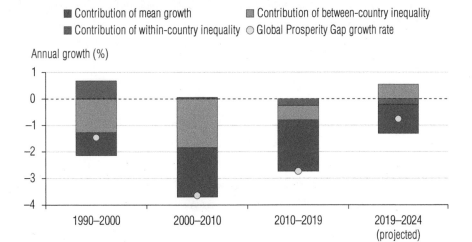

Source: World Bank calculations using data from the Poverty and Inequality Platform (version September 2024), https://pip.worldbank.org/.

Note: A decrease in the Prosperity Gap is an improvement in welfare. Growth is calculated as the log difference. Change in the Prosperity Gap is the sum of the (negative) growth in the mean income and the decline in total inequality. Positive growth in the mean decreases (improves) the Prosperity Gap; thus, in the figure, the contribution of the mean growth is shown as the negative of mean growth. That is, for all the periods in the graph, there was positive growth in the global mean, which is displayed as a negative contribution. Inequality is measured using the inequality measure related to the Prosperity Gap. Change in total inequality is the sum of changes in between-country and within-country inequality. See annex 2B for further details.

The number of economies with high inequality has fallen, and high-inequality economies are now concentrated in Latin America and the Caribbean and in Sub-Saharan Africa

High inequality reflects a lack of opportunities for socioeconomic mobility, which can further hinder prospects for poverty reduction and shared prosperity over time. In countries where levels of income or consumption inequality are higher, an increase in growth results in a smaller reduction in poverty (Bourguignon 2003). Simulations have shown that declines in inequality can have a significant effect on reducing poverty (Bergstrom 2022; Lakner et al. 2022). However, this double dividend has been missed in some cases. Poverty reduction in Sub-Saharan Africa has been slow, largely because of slow growth. But a lack of improvement in equality has also been a missed opportunity for poverty reduction (Sinha, Inchauste, and Narayan 2024) in a region where many countries have abnormally high levels of inequality.

There is a broad consensus that when inequality in a country is high it is harmful. High levels of inequality within a country can be symptomatic of the inability of some population groups to rise along the economic and social ladder for reasons that are outside of their control, such as their gender, race, parental background, or place of birth. This is not only unjust but also inefficient, because it means that some population groups cannot participate in economic activity using their full potential. Furthermore, the inequality of outcomes and opportunities in the present directly affects the opportunities for the next generation (Atkinson 2015; van der Weide et al. 2024; World Bank 2017). For instance, unequal societies tend to exhibit greater inequalities among schools or neighborhoods, so inequalities today have a strong effect on children's opportunities (Alesina et al. 2021; Asher, Novosad, and Rafkin 2024; Chetty, Hendren, and Katz 2016). This is also important as societal frictions have been linked to actual or perceived high inequality levels—for example, the social discontent seen during the Arab Spring (World Bank 2016). Concurrently, lower inequality is correlated with higher levels of political and social stability as well as social cohesion (World Bank 2016). Evidence suggests that high inequality has been disproportionately reducing political participation among low-income voters relative to high-income voters (Erikson 2015) and at the same time increasing the share of political contributions of high-income households (Cagé 2023).

Inequality is a broad concept, and it should be studied with a broad range of measures to capture its multiple dimensions (see box O.2). This report focuses on a specific measure of inequality—the Gini index—and a specific threshold to differentiate high-inequality economies—a Gini index above 40. The Gini index is based on income (or consumption) using household surveys, which are the only ones available to monitor inequality globally. Chapters 2 and 4 in the report discuss the indicator in more detail as well as implications for measurement and interpretation.

Using the latest survey available for each economy, 49 out of 166 economies had a Gini index above 40 (map O.1).[6] About 1.7 billion people lived in high-inequality economies in 2022. The number of economies with high inequality has fallen, from 66 a decade earlier to 49 in the most recent year. At the same time, the percentage of people living in economies with high inequality has remained roughly the same in the past decade (about 22 percent of the world population).

At present, high-inequality economies are concentrated in Sub-Saharan Africa and Latin America and the Caribbean. Over 80 percent of the economies in Latin America and the Caribbean had a Gini index above 40 in their most recent household survey. Within Sub-Saharan Africa, inequality is highest in Southern and Central Africa.[7] High income or consumption inequality is more prevalent in low- and middle-income economies as well as economies affected by FCS (figure O.6, panel b). Around one-third of low-income economies and two-fifths of middle-income economies exhibit high levels of inequality.[8] For FCS economies with data, two-fifths of them have high levels of inequality. Of the 68 IDA countries with data on inequality, less than 15 percent were in the low-inequality group and 37 percent were in the high-inequality group.

BOX 0.2

Concepts of welfare and differences in measured inequality

The level of inequality depends on the underlying concept of welfare that is captured. Economic inequality is generally captured in three different welfare spaces—income, consumption, or wealth—each reflecting different aspects of welfare and different observed levels of inequality. Whereas *income* signals an individual's or family's potential buying power, *consumption* expenditure is the realization of that buying power. Households generally do not consume all their income. What is left over, that is, savings, tends to be greater for the richer households compared with poorer households. This implies that the distribution of consumption tends to be more equal than the distribution of income (see annex 2D and chapter 4 for further detail). Whereas income and consumption both represent the flow of resources—that is, how much one earns or spends in a given time frame, typically a year—*wealth* represents a stock of resource such as accumulated assets, including property, corporate stock holdings, or savings, as well as other investments that can be inherited or acquired. For example, a house (or stock) is wealth, and the rent (or dividends) is the income generated from this asset. The distribution of wealth tends to be much more unequal than either income or consumption.[a]

These concepts are interlinked. For instance, recent increases in income inequality have been attributed to the higher rate of return of wealth among the richest (Piketty 2014). Nevertheless, these concepts of welfare are distinct in several crucial ways. Unlike income, which can fluctuate annually, wealth tends to accumulate over time and is more resistant to short-term economic changes. This likely makes wealth a better indicator of long-term resilience and a better signal for economic opportunity or mobility. However, among the three concepts outlined here, wealth remains the most difficult to capture. This is in part due to measurement challenges that also plague income measurement in developing countries, as well as the potential to "hide" wealth offshore, which is a concern even for the countries with the most comprehensive data (Zucman 2015). Given these challenges, this report uses income or consumption depending on the type of survey available.

a. For example, see the studies by Saez and Zucman (2020) for the United States and by Alvaredo, Atkinson, and Morelli (2018) for the United Kingdom.

This report also notes that more analytical work is needed to better capture top incomes in household surveys and adjust for methodological differences between countries—such as differences between income and consumption—to improve inequality monitoring (see chapter 4).

MAP 0.1

Income and consumption inequality among economies

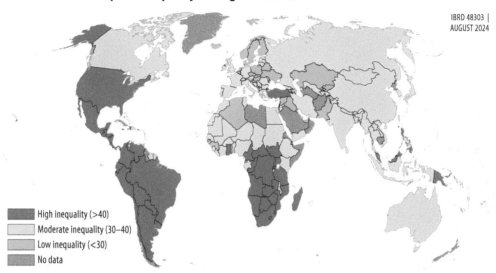

IBRD 48303 |
AUGUST 2024

High inequality (>40)
Moderate inequality (30–40)
Low inequality (<30)
No data

Sources: World Bank, Poverty and Inequality Platform (version September 2024), https://pip.worldbank.org/; Haddad et al. 2024.
Note: The map presents Gini indexes for the latest available survey (after 2000), which measures the inequality of income or consumption, depending on the economy. High-inequality economies have a Gini index above 40, moderate-inequality economies are those with a Gini index between 30 and 40, and low-inequality economies are those with a Gini index below 30. See annex table 2F.1 for the economy classifications, Gini indexes, year of survey, and the type of welfare—income, or consumption—used.

FIGURE 0.6

Poorer and conflict-affected economies tend to be more unequal

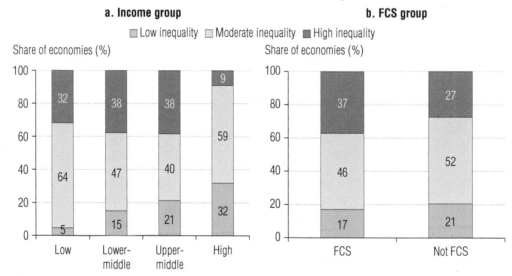

a. Income group

b. FCS group

Low inequality Moderate inequality High inequality

Source: World Bank, Poverty and Inequality Platform (version September 2024), https://pip.worldbank.org/.
Note: FCS = fragile and conflict-affected situations. High-inequality economies have a Gini index above 40, moderate-inequality economies are those with a Gini index between 30 and 40, and low-inequality economies are those with a Gini index below 30. The data cover 166 economies with at least one household survey in the Poverty and Inequality Platform between 2000 and 2022. Gini is calculated from the latest survey year. Income group and FCS status are based on World Bank fiscal year 2024 lists. The label values may not add to 100 percent due to rounding.

Risks of gain reversals remain high for the poorest countries

Although the global distribution of income has improved since 1990, a sizable portion of the population continues to live close to the poverty lines discussed in this report (figure O.7). This means that even moderate shocks can rapidly push people back into extreme poverty. Recent shocks highlight this risk. For example, in the Middle East and North Africa, the extreme poverty rate was below 3 percent between 2000 and 2014. Today, almost 7 percent of people in the region live in extreme poverty due to increased fragility and conflict. Another example is the COVID-19 pandemic, which pushed about 73 million people worldwide into extreme poverty in a single year, predominantly in lower-income countries. The pandemic has shown how shocks can have a long-lasting effect on welfare. Shocks are expected to increase with more frequent and severe extreme weather events.

Nearly one in five people is likely to experience a severe weather shock that they are going to struggle to recover from

Climate change will likely lead to an increasing occurrence and severity of extreme weather events (IPCC 2023). Since the 1970s, floods, storms, droughts, and heatwaves are occurring more often. Every year, millions of households are pushed into or trapped in poverty by natural disasters (Baquie and Fuje 2020; Hallegatte and Walsh 2021; Hill and Porter 2017; Kochhar and Knippenberg 2023; Pape and Wollburg 2019). In addition, droughts and heatwaves have been occurring at a higher frequency in countries where poverty rates are already high.

The World Bank has developed an indicator that tracks the number of people at high risk from climate-related hazards across the world (World Bank, n.d.). Nearly one in five people (17.9 percent) is at high risk from climate-related hazards globally, meaning they are likely to experience a severe climate shock in their lifetime that they will struggle to recover from. People are considered at risk from climate-related hazards if they are exposed to a hazard (specifically floods, heat, drought, cyclones) *and* are vulnerable to experiencing severe welfare effects from these events when they occur. Vulnerability, which is a person's propensity or predisposition to be adversely affected, is what moves people from being exposed to being at risk. Box O.3 summarizes how the indicator was constructed.

Countries can have similar shares of their population exposed, but different shares of their population at risk (map O.2). South Asia is the region with the largest share of its population exposed to shocks (88.1 percent), followed by East Asia and Pacific (67.9 percent). But Sub-Saharan Africa has the largest share of people who are at high risk from extreme weather events, even though the share of people exposed is smaller than Asia. In Sub-Saharan Africa, nearly the same proportion of people exposed to an extreme weather event is also at high risk (39.2 percent and 37.3 percent, respectively, of the total population). In comparison, even though two-thirds of the population in East Asia and Pacific is exposed, less than one-tenth is at risk. Vulnerability is lowest in North America, with less than 1 percent of the population at high risk, despite 31 percent of the population being exposed to a weather shock. In absolute terms, South Asia has the largest number of people at high risk from extreme weather events (594 million people, or 32 percent of its population).

FIGURE O.7

Income levels in the world have grown between 1990 and 2024, but many people remain vulnerable to falling back into poverty

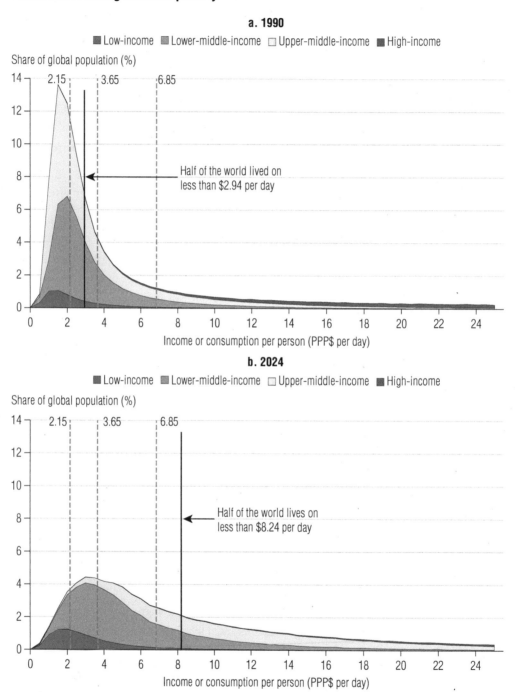

Source: World Bank, Poverty and Inequality Platform (version September 2024), https://pip.worldbank.org/.
Note: PPP$ = purchasing power parity dollars. This figure shows the distribution of the population over income and consumption levels in 1990 and in 2024, cut off at $25 per person per day and expressed in 2017 purchasing power parity dollars (PPP$). More than 86 percent of the global population lived below the $25 per person per day threshold in 1990 and about 80 percent live under the threshold in 2024.

MAP 0.2

Large populations are exposed to extreme weather events in South Asia and East Asia and Pacific, and vulnerability is high in Sub-Saharan Africa

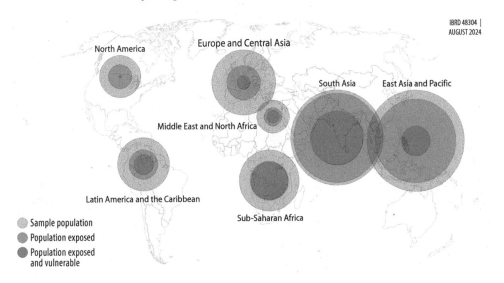

Source: World Bank calculations using data from the World Bank Group Scorecard indicator: the percentage of people at high risk of climate-related hazards globally, https://scorecard.worldbank.org/en/scorecard/home.
Note: Gray circles depict the overall population in the region, blue circles depict the population exposed to any type of hazard, and red circles depict the population exposed to any type of climate-related hazard and vulnerable along at least one dimension. There is a blue circle in Sub-Saharan Africa, but it is barely visible in the figure because almost everyone in Sub-Saharan Africa who is exposed is also vulnerable. The circles represent regions; their placement on the map does not have any meaning. See annex 3B for more details.

BOX 0.3

How is the number of people at risk from extreme weather hazards calculated?

The percentage of people at high risk from climate-related hazards globally is defined as the number of people globally who are both exposed to a set of key climate-related hazards (floods, droughts, cyclones, and heatwaves) and are also highly vulnerable (that is, have a propensity to be adversely affected or unable to cope with the effects), as a share of global population. People are counted as being at high risk from climate-related hazards if they are exposed to at least one hazard and are identified as highly vulnerable on at least one dimension of vulnerability.

(continued)

BOX 0.3

How is the number of people at risk from extreme weather hazards calculated? *(continued)*

This indicator follows the traditional risk framework in which risk is the combination of hazard, exposure, and vulnerability. The hazard is the potential occurrence of an extreme event, exposure indicates the people affected in the hazard's location, and vulnerability is the propensity or predisposition of these people to be adversely affected. Here, vulnerability is proxied by a set of indicators measuring (a) the physical propensity to experience severe losses (proxied by the lack of mobility and access to basic infrastructure services, such as water and electricity) and (b) the inability to cope with and recover from losses (proxied by low income, not having education, not having access to financial services, and not having access to social protection). Figure BO.3.1 summarizes the measure.

The indicator is based on a sample of 103 countries with data on all vulnerability dimensions and covers 86 percent of the world population. The latest available data within three years, before or after 2021, are used. The indicator currently considers a subset of climate hazards using historical data, a subset of vulnerability dimensions, and an aggregation methodology similar to approaches used for multidimensional poverty measures. Chapter 3 provides more details on how the indicator is constructed, and chapter 4 discusses measurement challenges with respect to the indicator in more detail, as well as some areas in which the indicator will be updated in future rounds.

FIGURE BO.3.1

Measuring the vulnerability of people at high risk from climate-related hazards

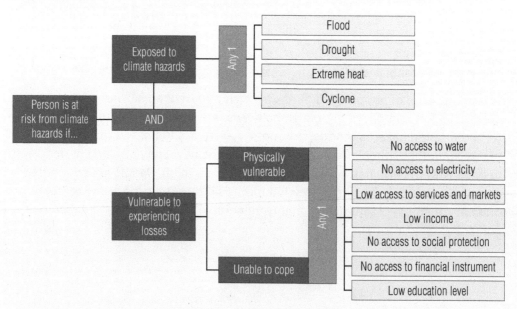

Source: World Bank Group Scorecard indicator: the percentage of people at high risk of climate-related hazards globally, https://scorecard.worldbank.org/en/scorecard/home.

Without more rapid action, climate-related hazards will likely intensify. In 2022, the three main anthropogenic greenhouse gases—carbon dioxide (CO_2), methane, and nitrous oxide—reached record levels, trapping nearly 50 percent more heat than in 1990.[9,10] Greenhouse gas emissions, which lead to global warming, are linked to the occurrence and severity of extreme weather events (IPCC 2023). If GHG emissions are not reduced, climate risks will worsen. While economic growth has become less carbon intensive, progress in reducing GHG emissions per unit of growth has slowed down recently (chapter 3 discusses in more detail the trends and patterns in GHG emissions). That progress needs to be speeded up.

To summarize, comparisons between exposure and risk show that risks can be mitigated by reducing vulnerability. While exposure in Sub-Saharan Africa is not as high as in other regions, high levels of vulnerability keep people at high risk. The availability in the region of factors that are important for resilience, such as access to basic infrastructure services (for example, water and electricity), income, education, and financial services, is limited. For instance, only 50 percent of the population in Sub-Saharan Africa has access to electricity, and 65 percent has access to basic drinking water.[11] These deprivations make people more vulnerable to adverse shocks.

Pathways: Eradicating poverty and boosting shared prosperity on a livable planet requires managing trade-offs

Ending extreme poverty and boosting shared prosperity on a livable planet requires actions in two areas: delivering faster and inclusive growth (that is, growing labor incomes by delivering more and better jobs and investing in the productive capacity of the poor) and protecting people from climate shocks (that is, enhancing risk management and accelerating climate change mitigation).

Progress requires more economic growth and climate actions

Delivering faster and more inclusive growth

The 1990 World Development Report highlighted that the most effective way to improve the lives of the poor is through (a) promoting economic growth that uses labor, the poor's most abundant asset; (b) investing in human capital, particularly primary education, and health care; and (c) promoting well-targeted social safety nets. These priorities are still appropriate more than 30 years later and are even more urgent given the losses in human capital due to COVID-19 and increasing environmental shocks.

Enabling the poor to benefit more from economic growth will require better-functioning labor markets, as labor is the main source of income for the poor (World Bank 2013a). It is therefore crucial to ensure that the conditions are in place for strong private sector–led growth—the main creator of jobs. Governments can support job creation by ensuring that the fundamental elements of macroeconomic stability, a business-friendly environment, and the rule of law are in place. Developing effective job strategies leading to sustained labor productivity enhancements (which are essential for fostering economic growth), reducing poverty, and ensuring inclusive outcomes in the long term depend heavily on essential job transformations across sectors, occupations, and space (see box 1.5 in chapter 1). For example, the transition from agriculture to nonagricultural sectors is vital for economic growth, and it is marked by substantial productivity gains. The move from rural to urban areas is associated with higher wages and productivity if urban labor markets work well. Completing these job transitions is essential to closing massive income gaps and combatting poverty. Evidence suggests that progress in these transitions can significantly reduce poverty rates by shifting people into more productive activities.[12]

Growth that is most effective in poverty reduction creates opportunities for those at the bottom of the income distribution. If poorer households possess lower productive capacity, the potential for income growth and overall economic growth is more limited (López-Calva and Rodríguez-Castelán 2016).[13] Moreover, growth that reduces poverty requires structural conditions that enable socioeconomic mobility, thereby ensuring that everyone can use their full productive capacity.

Enabling the poor to benefit more from economic growth will require substantive investments in human capital, basic infrastructure, improved opportunities and access to markets, and progressive fiscal policies that reduce inequality and raise domestic revenue (Lakner et al. 2022; World Bank 2022e; Wu et al. 2024).

Protecting people from climate shocks by enhancing risk management

A large body of evidence highlights the importance of risk management for increasing resilience to negative shocks (World Bank 2013b). Risk management must integrate the ability to prepare for risks with the capacity to respond effectively afterward. Building on the foundational work of Ehrlich and Becker (1972), preparation should encompass three proactive measures: self-insurance, market insurance, and self-protection. In addition to these three measures, a comprehensive risk management strategy includes support for sensible coping measures. Better knowledge can lead to more informed decisions about allocating resources between insurance and protection (World Bank 2013b). Similarly, improved insurance and protection can make coping with risks less challenging and less costly. Effective ways to promote resilience to climate risks are discussed in more detail in box 3.4 in chapter 3.

Investments in education and infrastructure are fundamental for risk management

Development strategies that bolster households' productivity and income-generating capacities often concurrently enhance their ability to manage climate risks by enhancing prevention and coping (Doan et al. 2023; Hallegatte and Rozenberg 2017; IPCC 2022a) and should be prioritized in poorer and more vulnerable countries.

Investing in education is fundamental to increasing incomes, but it also allows households to better prepare and cope with shocks. One important aspect of risk management is knowledge, and an increase in education leads to an increase in knowledge. Furthermore, evidence suggests that households with higher levels of education have a better understanding of and ability to process risk information such as weather forecasts and early warnings (Hoffmann and Muttarak 2017; Muttarak and Lutz 2014; Muttarak and Pothisiri 2013). In addition, households with more education are less likely to engage in negative coping strategies (Dimitrova 2021; Hill and Mejia-Mantilla 2017; Le and Nguyen 2023).

Improving infrastructure increases access to markets and productivity and also supports risk management and resilience. For example, better infrastructure can improve access to energy, water, and communication, which can allow households to better cope with shocks when they occur. Infrastructure improvements are beneficial for both economic development and resilience, but unlocking synergies depends on how infrastructure is built. Infrastructure investments need to account for future risks, such as an increased frequency and intensity of flooding (Hallegatte et al. 2016; Hallegatte, Rentschler, and Rozenberg 2019). It is important to consider that constructing infrastructure in a resilient manner improves its cost-effectiveness in the long run, and higher up-front investment costs can reduce damages and repair costs in the future (Hallegatte, Rentschler, and Rozenberg 2019).[14]

Expanding insurance is also crucial

Beyond these foundational investments in human capital and infrastructure, it is important to strengthen insurance mechanisms that protect individuals from severe poverty and prevent deeper hardship during crises (Gill, Revenga, and Zeballos 2016).

Financial development is important to enable access to credit, formal insurance, and other financial products that can help households and businesses manage climate risk. One of the primary objectives of financial inclusion is to enhance households' capacity to manage common but unpredictable events that entail financial expenses. Mobile money is an example: when a weather crisis strikes, mobile money can allow households to quickly receive transfers or remittances from relatives or migrant family members who live elsewhere (Batista and Vicente 2023; Jack and Suri 2014). For instance, Sub-Saharan Africa has shown significant growth in financial inclusion driven by mobile money account adoption. Yet many adults still conduct transactions in cash, which suggests opportunities to increase financial inclusion through continued payment digitalization (Demirgüç-Kunt et al. 2022). Many people exposed to severe climate hazards are not financially included (figure O.8). These issues are particularly prevalent in Sub-Saharan Africa and the Middle East and North Africa regions, where about one in three people exposed to extreme weather events does not have a financial account (including mobile money).

Developing insurance markets and increasing the demand for insurance is central. Household demand for insurance is constrained by several factors. In 2023, the estimated global economic losses due to natural disasters was $380 billion,[15] of which only about one-third were covered by insurance. In low-income countries, less than 10 percent of losses were covered by insurance, forcing governments to redirect limited development funds toward disaster recovery. Despite its importance for risk management, access to insurance remains insufficient, leaving billions unprotected. One important challenge is affordability, as the demand for insurance is price sensitive (Cai, de Janvry, and Sadoulet 2020; Cole et al. 2013; Hill et al. 2019; Karlan et al. 2014; McIntosh, Sarris, and Papadopoulos 2013). Interventions to reduce prices (for example, reducing reinsurance costs or reducing taxes on insurance products) can increase demand. Moreover, insurance is a more complex financial product than savings or credit products, and financial literacy training also increases demand for insurance (Cai and Song 2017; Vasilaky et al. 2020). Liquidity constraints also limit the use of insurance, but moving payment of the insurance premium to the end of the coverage period can increase demand (Casaburi and Willis 2018; Liu, Chen, and Hill 2020).

Noncontributory social assistance programs, or social safety nets, aimed at those who are chronically or extremely poor also serve as last-resort insurance. The use of adaptive social protection can help vulnerable people manage risks from climate-related hazards by timely transferring resources to disaster victims (World Bank Group 2023). Post-disaster transfers have a benefit-cost ratio above 1.3 (Hallegatte et al. 2016). For example, the Philippines supported recipients of its flagship social safety net program, the Pantawid Pamilyang Pilipino Program, when they were hit by Typhoon Yolanda in 2013 (World Bank 2022c). In Kenya, the Hunger Safety Net Programme provided aid to over 100,000 additional households in response to droughts during 2015 and issued a special transfer to 200,000 households in anticipation of expected droughts (Hallegatte et al. 2016). Anticipatory cash transfers before the traditional humanitarian response would normally arrive can have a significant additional welfare effect (Pople et al. 2021). Yet, in Sub-Saharan Africa, 71.2 percent of the people exposed to severe cyclones, floods, droughts, and heatwaves are neither covered nor contributing to social protection and are unlikely to receive public support when one of these severe events occurs (figure O.8). Additionally, not all of those covered will have their climate risk fully covered by public safety nets.

FIGURE O.8

A large share of the population in Sub-Saharan Africa does not have access to social protection or a financial account

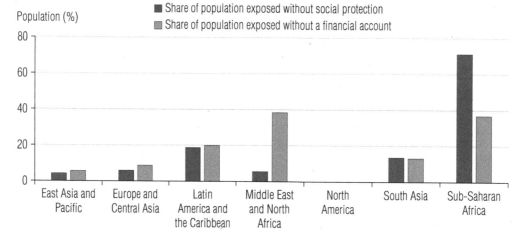

Source: World Bank calculations using data from the World Bank Group Scorecard indicator: the percentage of people at high risk of climate-related hazards globally, https://scorecard.worldbank.org/en/scorecard/home.
Note: The figure shows the share of population exposed to any hazard that neither receives social protection benefits nor contributes to social insurance, and the share of population exposed to any hazard that does not have a financial account (including mobile money). For North America, the share of population exposed to any climate-related hazard and without social protection or access to a financial account is zero. See annex 3B in chapter 3 for more details.

22

While safety nets serve as last-resort insurance, they need to be complemented by social insurance programs designed to protect a broader segment of the population from falling back into poverty because of individual or systemic shocks. Additionally, global insurance mechanisms are essential to help countries manage the effects of large-scale natural disasters affecting multiple nations or pandemics.

Basic systems to deliver timely information on climate risk are fundamental

Climate risk management can be enhanced through expanded early warning systems, hazard maps, and climate knowledge. In Bangladesh, Cyclone Bhola caused 300,000 deaths in 1970, and Cyclone April killed 138,000 people in 1991. Since then, investments in resilient infrastructure, road networks, and early warning systems have significantly reduced fatalities. Cyclone Sidr in 2007 resulted in 3,363 deaths, Cyclone Fani in 2019 caused five, and in 2020, Bangladesh evacuated 2.4 million people for Cyclone Amphan, with 20 fatalities. Yet, one-fifth of the world's population is not covered by an early warning system, even though these systems save lives and greatly reduce climate-related disaster losses in developing countries.[16]

Faster economic transformations to reduce the emissions intensiveness of growth

Faster transformations of the global economy are necessary to limit global warming and reduce climate risks.[17] Since 2015, when the Paris Agreement was adopted, GHG emissions were expected to rise by 16 percent until 2030 based on existing policies. At present, the expected increase is 3 percent, showing that transformations have already occurred over the past years. However, figure O.9 shows that with current policies, temperatures are projected to increase close to 2°C. Even if currently pledged Nationally Determined Contributions (NDCs)[18] were to be enacted, emissions would not fall enough to limit global warming to below 1.5°C (IPCC 2022b). Only a Net Zero 2050 scenario, which is shaped by stringent climate policies and innovation, would have the chance to limit warming to around 1.5°C.[19] A net-zero path would require emissions to decline by 80 percent in advanced economies and 60 percent in emerging market and developing economies by 2035 compared with the 2022 level (IEA 2023b).

Both expanded use of renewable energy and improved energy efficiency are necessary. The energy sector produces three-quarters of global emissions. Despite progress, in 2022 renewable sources added up to just 7 percent of total global energy, up from 4 percent in 1990 (see chapter 3 of the full report). Petroleum (with other liquid fuels) and coal remain the largest sources of energy (32 percent each). To reduce GHG emissions, the reliance on coal and oil will need to be brought down substantially. Doubling the pace of progress in energy efficiency could cut energy bills by one-third and constitute 50 percent of CO_2 reductions by 2030 (IEA, IRENA, et al. 2023). Further advancements and adoption of technology have the potential to speed up the necessary transformations for cutting GHG emissions. Without the growth of key clean energy technologies since 2019 (for example, solar photovoltaic [PV], wind power, heat pumps, electric cars), the increase in emissions would have been three times larger (IEA 2023a).

Carbon pricing policies are key to internalize the externalities of greenhouse gas emissions, incentivize efficiency gains, reduce the reliance on fossil fuels, and spur innovation in less emission-intense technologies (World Bank 2024f). The coverage of carbon taxes and emission trading systems (ETS) has increased from 0.15 percent of global emissions in 1990 to 24 percent in 2024. Despite the progress, three-quarters of global emissions remain unaccounted for, and many emissions have negative effective prices due to pervasive fossil fuel subsidies. Thus, while coverage is increasing, the global total carbon price—which takes into account the additional net effect of indirect pricing from fossil fuel taxes and subsidies—has not increased much since 1994 (Agnolucci et al. 2023). Repurposing fossil fuel subsidies is thus important to remove market distortions and to help move resources to sustainable projects (Damania, Balseca, et al. 2023). Investing in research and development and digitalization is crucial to spur innovation and transitions.

FIGURE O.9

Projections of emissions and temperatures to 2050

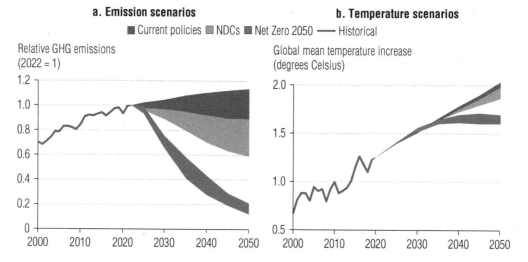

Sources: Panel a: Network for Greening the Financial System (NGFS) 2023, harmonized to historical 2022 emissions estimations from EDGAR data. Panel b: World Bank calculations using projections from NGFS 2023, harmonized to historical 2020 temperature estimations from IPCC 2021.
Note: EDGAR = Emissions Database for Global Atmospheric Research; GHG = greenhouse gas; IPCC = Intergovernmental Panel on Climate Change; NDCs = Nationally Determined Contributions. Ranges for each policy scenario are based on four different projection models: GCAM 6.0, MESSAGEix-GLOBIOM 1.1-M-R12, REMIND-MAgPIE 3.2-4.6 Integrated Physical Damages [95th-high], and REMIND-MAgPIE 3.2-4.6 Integrated Physical Damages (median). In panel b, temperature increases are relative to the average global surface temperature of the period 1850–1900 (pre-industrial) (IPCC 2021). Temperature projections refer to the AR6 Surface Temperature increase (50th percentile) from the MAGICC 7.5.3 model.

Informed decisions require understanding trade-offs and synergies and managing transition costs

To inform decisions, it is important to understand the trade-off between growing incomes and lowering GHG emissions, find ways to scale up synergistic policies that can help advance on multiple fronts or reduce trade-offs, and manage transition costs to specific groups and communities.

The trade-off between growing incomes and lowering emissions

Past economic growth and poverty reduction have been associated with high GHG emissions. This marks an apparent tension between advancing on poverty reduction, growing people's incomes, and reducing emissions. Unsurprisingly, research suggests that additional emissions attributed to moving individuals out of *extreme* poverty does not materially undermine climate goals, as emissions of low-income households are miniscule (Bruckner et al. 2022). Wollburg, Hallegatte, and Mahler (2023) calculate the additional economic growth that would be required to eradicate extreme poverty, and the additional emissions implied using historical emission intensities (2010–19). Eradicating extreme poverty would entail 4.7 percent more emissions than in 2019 (figure O.10). This number becomes larger at higher poverty lines. At $6.85 per person per day, additional emissions would reach 46 percent with historical emission intensities (figure O.10). This trade-off is different across countries, depending on their levels of poverty and the sources of economic growth and emission levels. Yet, it is clear that the foregone reduction in GHG emissions from extreme poverty eradication is minimal.

FIGURE O.10

Additional emissions associated with poverty alleviation increase with the level of ambition

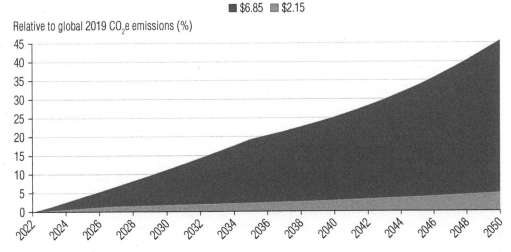

Source: Wollburg, Hallegatte, and Mahler 2023.
Note: CO_2e = carbon dioxide equivalent. The figure shows additional emissions relative to 2019 if poverty were to be alleviated at the $2.15 and $6.85 per person per day poverty lines (expressed in 2017 purchasing power parity dollars) using historical emission intensities.

Synergistic policies can ameliorate the trade-offs

Investment in renewable energy and energy efficiency offers multiple benefits beyond reducing emissions

Studies show that renewable energy investments not only help lower emissions but also meet growing energy demands and improve energy security (World Bank Group 2023). For some countries with low energy access, it can be more cost-effective to develop renewable energy infrastructure than to expand fossil fuel generation (World Bank Group 2023).[20] Solar and wind energy are particularly efficient for connecting sparsely populated areas, and lower-income regions can benefit directly from them. For example, in countries such as Uzbekistan and Côte d'Ivoire, where gas supplies are decreasing and electricity demand is rising, transforming power systems to renewable energy is the most cost-efficient solution (World Bank Group 2023).

These investments are also synergistic in the sense that they can ease the trade-off between economic growth, poverty reduction, and emissions. Simulations indicate that investing in renewable energy and energy efficiency combined would in fact lower the additional emissions that accompany the economic growth needed to reduce poverty by more than half (figure O.11) (Wollburg, Hallegatte, and Mahler 2023).

FIGURE O.11

Lower emissions from poverty alleviation projected with energy efficiency and decarbonization

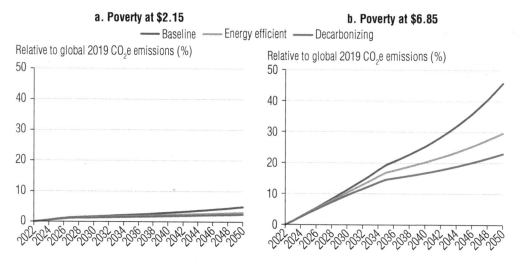

a. Poverty at $2.15   **b. Poverty at $6.85**

—— Baseline   —— Energy efficient   —— Decarbonizing

Source: Wollburg, Hallegatte, and Mahler 2023.
Note: CO_2e = carbon dioxide equivalent. The figure shows additional emissions relative to 2019 if poverty were to be alleviated at the $2.15 and $6.85 per person per day poverty lines (expressed in 2017 purchasing power parity dollars). The baseline scenario uses historical emission intensities. Energy-efficient and decarbonizing scenarios assume that all countries achieve the top 10 percent historical performance in energy efficiency and decarbonization.

Tackling air pollution is a clear win-win strategy that should be prioritized

Air pollution is a leading environmental risk to people's health (World Bank 2022a). Air pollution is estimated to be responsible for a staggering 6.7 million deaths[21] annually worldwide, almost the total number of deaths due to COVID-19 to date[22] or an amount roughly equivalent to one-third of the combined deaths due to communicable, maternal, neonatal, and nutritional diseases in 2021.[23] Air pollution today carries a global health cost representing 6.1 percent of global GDP in 2019 (World Bank 2022a).

For some countries, particularly those in South Asia and Sub-Saharan Africa, annual exposure levels are particularly high, exceeding 10 times the recommended levels. Indeed, South Asia is home to 37 of the 40 most polluted cities in the world (World Bank 2023e). In South Asia, air pollution causes an estimated 2 million premature deaths each year and imposes significant economic costs. World Bank (2023e) shows that cost-effective strategies to lower air pollution in South Asia not only can save lives but also bring important climate benefits. For example, reduction of air pollution concentrations to World Health Organization (WHO) Interim Target 1 by 2030 would reduce CO_2 by 22 percent and methane by 21 percent.[24] Urban development that focusses on mass transit systems can lower both CO_2 emissions and air pollution levels (Mukim and Roberts 2023).

Several other actions can help depending on the context

Another area with sizable synergies is improving agricultural productivity through climate-smart practices, especially for low-income countries (Sutton, Lotsch, and Prasann 2024). In regions where agriculture is an important contributor to emissions, such as Latin America and the Caribbean and Sub-Saharan Africa, such practices will be crucial. For instance, in Colombia, agriculture accounts for 22 percent of the country's GHG emissions, and agricultural expansion over the past two decades has primarily occurred at the expense of forests and natural ecosystems. Climate-smart agriculture increases agricultural productivity, spurring economic growth without deforestation. However, only 15 percent of farms in Colombia use innovative technologies, and most climate-smart agricultural initiatives have remained in the pilot stage. Public policy is needed to promote these practices more widely. This can be achieved by redirecting agricultural support, strengthening innovation systems, facilitating financing services, and improving land information systems and administration (World Bank 2023c). In Cambodia, which could suffer one of the largest losses in rice yields in Southeast Asia because of climate change, analysis indicates that the negative effects of droughts can be entirely mitigated through irrigation or crop-rotation practices (World Bank 2023b).

Repurposing agricultural subsidies to climate-smart and productivity-enhancing practices can reduce overall agricultural emissions by more than 40 percent, the land footprint of agriculture by 2.2 percent, and higher productivity could reduce global extreme poverty by about 1 percent (Laborde et al. 2022). This is not only relevant for lower-income countries, as removing inefficient subsidies alleviates market distortions and also reduces deforestation and biodiversity loss in high-income countries (Damania, Balseca, et al. 2023). Agricultural and energy subsidies constitute around 3 percent of GDP in lower-middle-income and low-income countries, but only 20 percent of spending on subsidies reaches the bottom 40 percent of the populations (World Bank 2022d).

Moreover, sustainable forest management initiatives not only protect biodiversity and reduce emissions but also provide livelihood opportunities for local communities, thereby reducing poverty and enhancing resilience to climate-related disasters (Barbier 2010; Damania, Polasky, et al. 2023; Grosset, Papp, and Taylor 2023). In Peru, transitioning to a zero-carbon forest sector could generate employment opportunities, yield $3.5 billion in benefits from restored ecosystem services, and increase the value added of the sector sevenfold by 2050 (World Bank 2022b). More efficient land use could sequester an additional 85.6 billion metric tons of CO_2 equivalent without adverse economic impacts—an amount equivalent to approximately 1.7 years' worth of global emissions (Damania, Polasky, et al. 2023).[25]

It is important to identify and remove constraints to scale up synergistic policies

While synergistic strategies exist across different geographical contexts and sectors, challenges may still arise in their implementation. For instance, agroforestry may require a fundamental shift in traditional farming techniques, necessitating new skills or knowledge that farmers may not initially possess. Risk aversion can also be a challenge; farmers might be hesitant to adopt new practices because of uncertainty about the outcomes or fear of initial yield reductions. Financial constraints are another common barrier, as up-front costs for resources or training might be prohibitive for lower-income households. Moreover, cultural and social norms can influence the willingness to adopt new methods, as practices deeply ingrained in community identity may not be easily altered. Lastly, the lack of supportive policies or incentives from governments can impede widespread adoption, as can inadequate access to markets or resources necessary to implement these new practices effectively. Addressing these barriers through finance, comprehensive support systems, education, and community engagement is essential for the successful adoption and long-term sustainability of synergistic strategies.

Managing transition costs is important for the poor and vulnerable

Transitioning toward a low-carbon, climate-resilient economy may involve a trade-off between a cost today and benefits in the future, as well as opportunity costs between different priorities. These transitions bring future climate benefits by altering the probability distribution of climate-related hazards, but they can be costly for specific people now.

Transitioning to green industries may lead to or accelerate job displacement in traditional industries that rely heavily on fossil fuels. Reductions in coal production are unlikely to have substantial effects on national employment and output in many economies because of the industry's low labor share. For example, in Indonesia, the world's second-largest coal exporter, the coal industry's share of the GDP is less than 2 percent, and it employs only 0.2 percent of the workforce (World Bank Group 2023). However, effects on local communities can be substantial in some instances (World Bank Group 2023). Challenges arise as displaced workers may face difficulties transitioning to alternative employment because of differences in skills, wages, and geographic locations (World Bank 2023a). For instance, in six South Asian countries (Bangladesh, India, the Maldives, Nepal, Pakistan, and Sri Lanka), workers in pollution-intensive jobs are systematically less educated and are often informally employed; the opposite applies to workers in green jobs. Going beyond education levels to consider foundational skills, analysis in Poland shows that people in green jobs on average have higher numeracy, literacy, and problem-solving skills. There are also major gender differences in green employment across all major occupation groups, with women tending to have browner jobs (World Bank 2022d).

Workers in carbon-intensive sectors can be affected not only by local energy transition policies but also by the global consequences of carbon mitigation policies on trade flows. Changes in goods and labor demands may originate from abroad. Take, for example, the Carbon Border Adjustment Mechanism (CBAM), a carbon tariff that penalizes high-carbon exports to the European Union. If industries in certain countries fail to decarbonize, such systems may redirect demand to producers elsewhere.[26] While CBAM is not likely to have a large effect on countries' GDP or trade balances, it may negatively affect workers in some sectors in lower-income countries (World Bank Group 2022).

Consumers, especially those with lower purchasing power or who allocate a significant portion of their budget to food and energy, may encounter challenges from policies aimed at reducing emissions that affect prices. For example, carbon pricing schemes and the removal of fossil fuel subsidies could lead to short-term increases in poverty in several low- and middle-income countries if policies are not carefully designed (World Bank Group 2022). Indirect subsidies, like those for energy, often constitute a higher share of the market income for poorer households (World Bank Group 2022).

The transition costs and how to manage them will vary depending on each country's context. These challenges will also depend on how policies are implemented and how political and economic institutions align to support these transitions (Lankes et al. 2024; Rizk and Slimane 2018). Transition costs, such as higher energy prices or job losses in carbon-intensive sectors, can be particularly hard for poorer people to manage. Therefore, assessing how the green transition affects poor and vulnerable people and designing policies to reduce negative effects are essential.

Policies that invest in skills and reskilling can play a vital role in facilitating the transition of workers affected by industry changes. Active labor market programs, for instance, not only help workers acquire the skills needed for this transition but also ensure a workforce is ready to meet the demand in green industries. Programs supporting internal migration can be particularly valuable (Rigolini 2021). To support communities most affected by job losses, targeted policies are essential. These include initiatives to promote job creation, especially in areas facing employment challenges, and support for climate-smart agricultural practices, job training, and skills development. Such measures are crucial for facilitating the transition to low-carbon and sustainable livelihoods.

It is also important to implement compensatory measures to not disproportionately affect poor households. Well-designed redistribution measures can mitigate the effects on households, especially those with lower incomes (Blanchard, Gollier, and Tirole 2023). According to the findings of Steckel et al. (2021), redistributing revenues generated from carbon pricing to all individuals, not just the poor, results in a net income gain for poor households. Similarly, redistributing domestic carbon revenues as an equal-per-capita climate dividend more than offsets the negative effects of higher prices, lifting approximately 6 million people out of poverty globally.

To counteract the adverse effects of fuel price hikes on the poor, governments have various policy tools at their disposal beyond cash transfers. For instance, in urban areas, making public transportation more affordable or providing subsidies to assist low-income households in securing housing closer to job opportunities can help mitigate these effects (Liotta, Avner, and Hallegatte 2023). Such incentives also align with emission reduction objectives.

Priorities: Doing what matters, where it matters most

Acting on these multiple fronts requires fundamental changes in how countries approach their national development strategies and their contributions to global public goods. However, there are no simple solutions. The pathways presented above involve difficult trade-offs across objectives and transition costs.

It is important to recognize that low growth and high debt servicing severely constrain the ability of many countries to act. The financing gap for sustainable development is mounting (United Nations and Inter-agency Task Force on Financing for Development 2024; World Bank 2024d). The COVID-19 pandemic, inflation, and the global economic slowdown have exacerbated the already high debt levels in poorer countries (World Bank 2024d). These debt burdens further constrain the already limited fiscal space of lower-income countries (World Bank 2023d, 2024b). Interest payments on their total external debt stock in IDA countries have quadrupled since 2012, reaching an all-time high of $23.6 billion, which diverts spending away from health, education, and other critical needs (World Bank 2023d). Low-income countries are spending about 2 percent of GDP on interest payments to service debt in 2024 (World Bank 2024c), which is more than half of what they spend on education (about 3.6 percent of GDP [Bend et al. 2023]).

In this constrained environment, there is an urgent need to prioritize the actions that will have the highest return for development and that can allow the world to make progress on the interlinked goals of eradicating poverty, boosting shared prosperity, and making the planet more livable. The guiding principle is to focus on where the poor and vulnerable live and where the emissions are highest and where they are likely to increase most. As shown in chapter 1, extreme poverty will be concentrated increasingly in Sub-Saharan Africa and fragile and conflict-affected countries (in Sub-Saharan Africa and elsewhere). The poorest countries are also most at risk from climate hazards.

Yet, emissions are largely generated by high-income and upper-middle-income countries. Priorities in terms of mitigating emissions should also consider how emissions are evolving.

Under current policies, GHG emissions from high-income and upper-middle-income countries are projected to decline, but not nearly fast enough to limit warming to around 1.5°C. To reach this goal, additional CO_2 emissions will need to fall to practically zero in these countries. In addition, lower-middle-income countries do not contribute much to emissions today, but without action, they will have a significant role in total emissions in a few decades.

Figure O.12 brings these considerations together and illustrates a simplified way to identify priorities. Importantly, each unique situation requires its own tailored solutions, and the results from this report do not aim to be prescriptive for a specific country. Country-specific studies are recommended to guide prioritization at that level. The following discussion aims to shed light on where attention should be placed from a broader global perspective.

FIGURE O.12

Priorities to advance on the interlinked goals

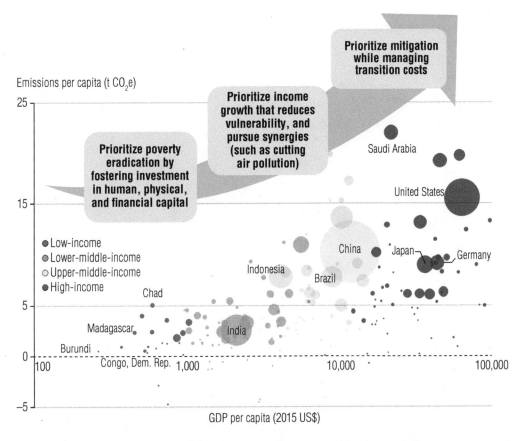

Source: Global Atmospheric Research (EDGAR), Grassi et al. 2023, and World Development Indicators.
Note: GHG = greenhouse gas; t CO_2e = tons, carbon dioxide equivalent. The size of the bubbles indicates total GHG emissions. Negative emissions occur when ecosystems absorb more carbon than the country emits. A few small countries with very high per capita emissions (Bahrain, Guyana, Iceland, Kuwait, Oman, Palau, Qatar, Trinidad and Tobago, United Arab Emirates) and countries with very low per capita emissions (Central African Republic, Vanuatu) are omitted for visual purposes. The horizontal axis uses a logarithmic scale.

Low-income settings: Prioritize poverty reduction by fostering investment in human, physical, and financial capital

Going forward, extreme poverty will be concentrated increasingly in countries in Sub-Saharan Africa and in FCS (figure O.13). By 2030, one-half of the global extreme poor will be in today's FCS within Sub-Saharan Africa, and an additional one-quarter is projected to be in countries in Sub-Saharan Africa that are not in FCS today. Effectively, the relative concentration of extreme poverty in FCS or Sub-Saharan Africa versus in non-FCS and non-Sub-Saharan Africa will have reversed over the course of three decades. The share of poor in FCS and Sub-Saharan Africa will have grown from one-quarter to more than four-fifths. Current IDA countries will comprise 82 percent of the global poor in 2030 with the currently projected growth rates, and 90 percent of the global extreme poor in 2050.

Increased concentration of extreme poverty in Sub-Saharan Africa and FCS

□ Non-FCS in SSA ▨ FCS in SSA ■ FCS outside SSA ■ Rest of the world

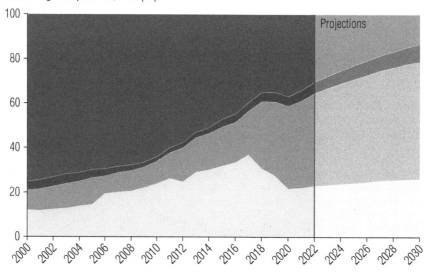

Source: World Bank calculations using data from the Poverty and Inequality Platform (version September 2024), https://pip.worldbank.org/.
Note: FCS = fragile and conflict-affected situations; GDP = gross domestic product; SSA = Sub-Saharan Africa. The extreme poverty rate is calculated at $2.15 per person per day (expressed in 2017 purchasing power parity dollars). Countries in FCS are defined following the World Bank classification of fragility and conflict-affected situations for each year until 2022, and keeping the definition fixed in 2022 for the years after. Between 2022 and 2029, poverty is projected based on per capita GDP projections in *Global Economic Prospects, June 2024* (World Bank 2024c) complemented by the *Macro Poverty Outlook, Spring Meetings 2024* (World Bank 2024e) and the *World Economic Outlook* (IMF 2024), and for 2030, average annual historic growth rates (2010–19) are used. Population coverage is below 50 percent for Sub-Saharan Africa after 2019, and for countries in FCS in 2000 and after 2017.

In these settings, higher economic growth is an essential foundation to support poverty reduction and build resilience. Per capita income growth is expected to remain at a meager 1.5 percent in Sub-Saharan Africa and 2.3 percent in IDA countries in 2025 (World Bank 2024c, 2024d). Various factors have contributed to the slow economic growth in IDA countries. First, many of these countries have not benefited from globalization as much as countries that historically had high poverty rates have, in particular Asian countries (Lakner and Milanovic 2016; Milanovic 2016). IDA countries engage less in international trade than other lower-middle-income countries and rely heavily on food imports, making them vulnerable to food price inflation (Laborde, Lakatos, and Martin 2019; World Bank 2024d). Moreover, compared with other countries, IDA economies have exhibited limited technological change (World Bank 2024a) and are still heavily dependent on agriculture and natural resources. IDA countries are also characterized by weak institutions, inhibiting investment and growth (World Bank 2024d).

Poverty reduction in IDA countries is hindered by big gaps in human capital and basic infrastructure and services. About one-half of the people in Sub-Saharan Africa and FCS countries lack electricity or sanitation (figure O.14, panel a). Large education gaps also persist. In 20 low-income countries with available data, more than 90 percent of children cannot read or understand a basic text by the end of primary school.[27] Yet, investments in education in low-income countries remain very low.[28] In 2021, the average low-income country spent only $54 per student per year, compared with more than $8,500 in the typical high-income country (Bend et al. 2023). In some of the poorest countries in Sub-Saharan Africa, only 20 percent of respondents surpass the education of their parents, compared with 80 percent in East Asia (van der Weide et al. 2024). In addition, in 15 out of 18 countries with available data in Sub-Saharan Africa, more than half of the inequality in consumption is due to factors beyond an individual's control, such as their place of birth or ethnicity (Sinha, Inchauste, and Narayan 2024). The result is that many people are deprived of the opportunity to use their full potential.

These large gaps and more broadly limited progress on multidimensional poverty have also increased vulnerability to shocks in these countries. For example, of the population in IDA countries covered by the data on risks from extreme weather events used for this report, 56 percent are exposed to extreme weather hazards and 47 percent are at risk. This means that 84 percent of those who are exposed are also at risk. In comparison, while a larger share of people is exposed to an extreme weather event in non-IDA countries (59 percent), only 11 percent are at risk. Between 2010 and 2019, the number of people exposed to extreme weather events rose in both IDA and non-IDA countries, but twice as fast in IDA countries (figure O.14, panel b).[29] However, despite the increase in the exposed population, non-IDA countries were able to reduce the population at risk significantly over this period. This is not the case for IDA countries, where the population at risk rose almost one-to-one with the population exposed. In non-IDA countries, the population at risk fell because of the large gains in income and financial access, developments from which people in IDA countries did not benefit as much.

Accelerating economic growth in these settings will not lead to significantly higher GHG emissions. Low-income countries barely contribute to emissions and emissions are not expected to grow significantly under current policies (see chapter 3 of the full report). Still, low-income countries must be careful to avoid getting locked into carbon-intensive technologies and growth paths that will become more costly and less efficient in the future (Hallegatte, Rentschler, and Rozenberg 2019). This is where international financing plays a key role—in enabling these countries to invest in future-oriented technologies now and not lock in on a pathway that will leave them with inefficient and stranded assets in the future (Hallegatte, Rentschler, and Rozenberg 2019).

FIGURE 0.14

Rates of multidimensional poverty and increased risks from extreme weather in IDA countries compared with other countries

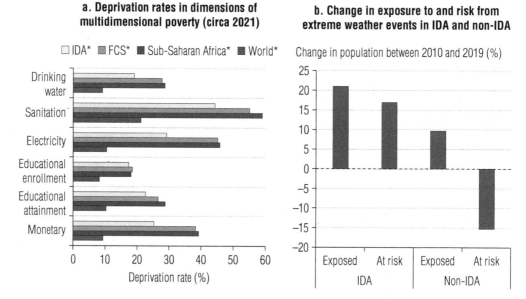

a. Deprivation rates in dimensions of multidimensional poverty (circa 2021)

b. Change in exposure to and risk from extreme weather events in IDA and non-IDA

Sources: Panel a: World Bank calculations using data from the Global Monitoring Database. Panel b: World Bank calculations using data from Doan et al. 2023.

Note: FCS = fragile and conflict-affected situations; IDA = International Development Association. Panel a: The figure presents the share of population deprived in each indicator of the multidimensional poverty measure for selected regions and country groupings circa 2021. For more information on the multidimensional poverty measure and its components, see chapter 1 of the full report. Panel b: The sample consists of 45 countries that have data both for 2010 and 2019. These countries represent 52 percent of the population in IDA and 63 percent of the population in non-IDA countries. The variables used to compute the risk indicator for the years 2010 and 2019 differ slightly from the risk indicator for the year 2021 used in other parts of the report. *The surveys available for 2020 or later cover less than 50 percent of the population.

Middle-income countries: Prioritize income growth that reduces vulnerability and pursue synergies such as cutting air pollution

Growth in middle-income countries needs to continue and accelerate to lift people above poverty lines of $3.65 and $6.85 per person per day, but many countries in this group are stuck in a middle-income trap (World Bank 2024g). As for low-income countries, fast growth that creates jobs and enhances the productive capacity of poorer households is important to serve the dual function of increasing incomes and improving the resilience of these households.

At the same time, the GHG emissions of many middle-income countries cannot be neglected. Even though lower-middle-income countries currently contribute less than higher-income countries to GHG emissions (19 percent versus 29 percent of total emissions in 2022), their emissions will increase over the next decades under current policies and surpass those of high-income countries by 2030 and those of upper-middle-income countries in the 2040s in absolute terms. Therefore, it is essential that lower-middle-income countries start transitioning to a less carbon-intensive pathway soon.

Because growth needs to be less carbon intensive, it is crucial to identify and scale up synergistic policies that can contribute significantly across the intertwined goals. As discussed, tackling air pollution is a clear area with multiple gains, particularly for low- and middle-income countries. In countries where agriculture is important, climate-smart agriculture and repurposing agricultural subsidies could be an important area of action. It is also important to invest early in renewable energy.

High-income and upper-middle-income countries: Accelerate mitigation while managing transition costs

High-income countries and upper-middle-income countries respectively account for 32 percent and 52 percent of global CO_2 emissions, while accounting only for 15 percent and 35 percent of the global population. Ten economies emit two-thirds of global emissions annually (figure O.15, panel a). The next 30 economies, by total emissions, contribute 24 percent of global emissions. The 140 least-emitting economies, which comprise 12 percent of the total population, produce less than 5 percent of GHG emissions.[30]

Upper-middle-income countries are responsible for an increasing share of global GHG emissions, having overtaken high-income countries in 2004 in terms of total emissions. Today, upper-middle-income countries produce as many GHG emissions as all other income groups combined (see chapter 3 for more details). The trend in per capita emissions in upper-middle-income countries is particularly striking, as they are rapidly converging to the levels of high-income countries (figure O.15, panel b). However, it is also important to note that the stock of GHG emissions in the atmosphere is what matters for warming (Eyring et al. 2021; IPCC 2022a). Today's high-income countries started emitting large amounts of CO_2 in the mid-nineteenth century, and upper-middle-income countries have caught up quickly over the past 40 years (figure O.15, panel c). In 2022, high-income countries and upper-middle-income countries were responsible for 90 percent of all historical CO_2 emissions, of which emissions from high-income countries make up roughly two-thirds.

FIGURE O.15

Positive relationship between income levels and GHG emissions

a. Ten economies produce two-thirds of global emissions

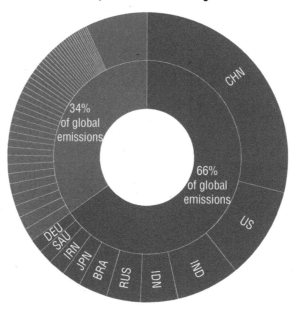

b. Emissions per capita are converging between high- and upper-middle-income countries

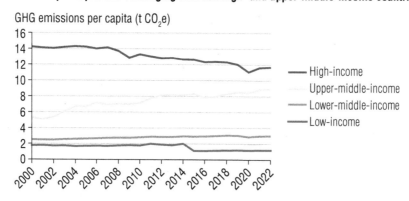

(continued)

FIGURE O.15

Positive relationship between income levels and GHG emissions *(continued)*

c. High-income and upper-middle-income countries are responsible for 90 percent of historical emissions

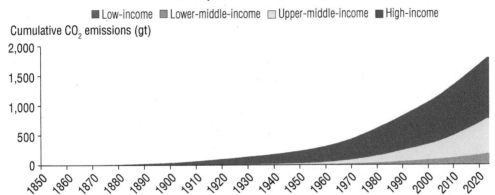

■ Low-income ■ Lower-middle-income □ Upper-middle-income ■ High-income

Sources: Panels a and b: World Bank calculations based on data from EDGAR, Grassi et al. 2023, and WDI data; panel c: PRIMAP-hist data from Gütschow, Pflüger, and Busch 2024.

Note: CO_2e = carbon dioxide equivalent; EDGAR = Emissions Database for Global Atmospheric Research; GHG = greenhouse gas; LULUCF = land use, land use change, and forestry; WDI = World Development Indicators. Panel a: The 10 economies are Brazil (BRA), China (CHN), Germany (DEU), India (IND), Indonesia (IDN), Iran, Islamic Republic of (IRN), Japan (JPN), Russian Federation (RUS), Saudi Arabia (SAU), and the United States (US). Data are from 2022. Panel b: Emissions per capita are in tons of CO_2e. Panel c: CO_2 emissions are cumulative in gigatons (gt) and do not include emissions from LULUCF. Panels b and c: Country income groups are fixed at 2022 definitions. In panel b, the drop in emissions from low-income countries in 2015 comes from the Democratic Republic of Congo, where LULUCF emissions declined substantially after 2014.

The quickest way to reduce future climate risks is for high-income countries and upper-middle-income countries with high emissions to drastically cut their emissions while managing transition costs. Accelerated actions by wealthier nations to reduce current emissions could significantly affect global emissions and alter the distribution of future environmental risks worldwide. Upper-middle-income countries also have significant populations at risk from extreme weather events, so it is in their own population's interest to act on reducing GHG emissions.

High-income and upper-middle-income countries need to prioritize and accelerate the shift away from primary energy generated by fossil fuels, which would have to fall by around 60 percent by 2035 and by 90 percent by 2050 compared with 2020 levels. The use of energy will also need to become more efficient.[31] Recent evidence indicates that countries with significant renewable potential, like Brazil, can fully decarbonize their power systems without higher costs or compromising resilience (World Bank 2023a).

In contrast to lower-income countries, these countries are in a better position to leverage funds and technology to transition to net zero. Research and development is needed to spur technological innovation to accelerate progress in fully decoupling economic growth from GHG emissions. Several countries have already managed to decouple growth from emissions, and more need to follow. Fostering technology infusion and innovation in upper-middle-income countries will be decisive for these countries to raise incomes while lowering emissions and transition to high-income status (see *World Development Report 2024* [World Bank 2024g]). These processes can catalyze a widespread adoption of renewable energy, the deployment of which requires a higher level of technological sophistication. Yet, it will be important to manage transitions costs to protect their more vulnerable populations.

Across the board: Better data and more international cooperation are needed

Achieving the interlinked goals of eradicating poverty and boosting shared prosperity on a livable planet requires decisive actions. This needs to be achieved in a global environment that has already become more challenging amid the polycrisis—from slow growth prospects and high levels of debt to increased uncertainty, fragility, and polarization. Solutions and policies exist to achieve the interlinked objectives, but these issues are complex and there will be trade-offs. Decisions must be made with a clear understanding of both the trade-offs and complementarities across objectives.

Across the board, more and better data are needed to design solutions that can address these complex policy issues and monitor their effects on vulnerable populations. Data provide the infrastructure for policy. This is essential to both designing and targeting interventions as well as monitoring progress. While data availability has improved in many countries, less than half of IDA countries had a household survey available in 2020 or later. Making progress on these interlinked global challenges requires a solid foundation of evidence. More investment is needed to produce reliable, granular, and timely information. This requires foundational efforts to strengthen national statistical systems and innovative approaches to advance the frontier of data and modeling for welfare analysis. Because the lived experience of poverty goes well beyond what can be captured by monetary measures, it is important to ensure that data efforts also invest in understanding other dimensions of well-being, such as deprivations in access to services, health, or food security.

Moreover, international development cooperation needs to play a larger and more effective role. There is a pressing need for more and better alignment of funding, as well as stronger international cooperation to meet the escalating challenges posed by climate change and development goals. International cooperation to achieve the Sustainable Development Goals (SDGs) and climate goals is ongoing but faces significant challenges and requires urgent action and increased investment. The United Nations 2024 World Economic Situation and Prospects report highlights the need for robust global cooperation to tackle economic vulnerabilities, rising interest rates, and climate disasters. The report stresses that without significant investments in sustainable development and climate action, achieving the SDGs will remain elusive (United Nations 2024; United Nations and Inter-agency Task Force on Financing for Development 2024).

The financing gap for sustainable development is growing, with many developing countries lacking access to affordable finance and facing high debt burdens, which hinder their ability to invest in both development and climate resilience (United Nations and Inter-agency Task Force on Financing for Development 2024; World Bank 2024d). Estimates suggest an additional annual investment of $4 trillion is needed to meet the SDGs by 2030 (United Nations and Inter-agency Task Force on Financing for Development 2024). Despite reaching the $100 billion climate finance goal in 2022, significant gaps remain. More financing is needed for adaptation and building resilient infrastructure in the first place. Climate adaptation costs alone for developing countries are expected to be between $160 billion and $340 billion annually by 2030 (UNEP 2022).

In particular, lower-income countries will need substantial and immediate investment in both adaptation and mitigation actions (World Bank 2024d). For instance, there is a significant gap between the required and actual funding for climate adaptation and mitigation in Sub-Saharan Africa. Current international adaptation finance flows are estimated to be 5–10 times below the needed levels. Current adaptation costs in Africa are estimated to be in the range of $7–$15 billion per year, with projections suggesting these could rise to $35 billion annually by the 2040s and up to $200 billion per year by the 2070s if warming exceeds 2°C. If no adaptation measures are implemented, costs could escalate to 7 percent of Africa's GDP by 2100 (UNEP 2022).

It is sometimes argued that climate finance is crowding out other development finance. As this report lays out, most of the policies that support climate resilience generally support development. At the same time, richer countries need to step up their support to low-income countries with financing and technologies so they can accelerate growth in a sustainable way.

The implementation of development and climate policy solutions requires a robust financial framework capable of navigating the fragmented global aid landscape—effectively incorporating domestic resource mobilization with external funding sources, including concessional funding. In particular, it is essential to promote a greater balance and complementarity between leveraged and unleveraged approaches to aid delivery (see box 3.5 in chapter 3 for a discussion on the current challenges in the aid ecosystem). Scaling up both public and private financing for SDGs and climate investments also entails closing policy gaps, enhancing international cooperation, and reforming financial institutions to provide more substantial and sustainable support.

The potential policy pathways can differ drastically depending on a country's historical development trajectory, access to technology and financing, and national priorities. However, countries must also consider their global responsibilities, and international actors have a critical coordination role to play. Ending poverty and boosting shared prosperity on a livable planet will require novel ways of organizing economic activity.

Notes

1. This is expressed in 2017 purchasing power parity dollars.
2. Using the coverage rules in the Poverty and Inequality Platform (Castaneda et al. 2024), data coverage for low-income countries fell somewhat below 50 percent of the population in 2018 and 2019. Comparing poverty rates from 2020 onward to data from 2017 would still show an increase in the headcount at the $2.15 and $6.85 poverty lines.
3. Florina Pirlea and Emi Suzuki, "The Impact of COVID-19 on Public Health," published on Data Blog, World Bank Group (July 26, 2023), https://blogs.worldbank.org/en/opendata/impact-covid-19-global-health; "Chapter 2: Current Context: the COVID-19 Pandemic and Continuing Challenges to Global Health," in *A Healthy Return*, World Health Organization (May 17, 2022), https://www.who.int/about/funding/invest-in-who/investment-case-2.0/challenges#:~:text=The%20global%20toll%20of%20COVID,extent%20of%20cases%20and%20deaths.
4. Not only is the share of poor in FCS increasing, but the poverty rates in FCS have also been rising over the past decade (see annex 1D).
5. IDA, a part of the World Bank Group, provides grants and concessional loans to the world's poorest countries. As of 2024, there are 75 countries eligible for support from IDA, with 75 percent of total commitments concentrated in Sub-Saharan Africa. See the following for more information: https://ida.worldbank.org/en/ida-financing.
6. The data set for inequality is based on surveys starting in 2000. Those economies with surveys older than 2000 are excluded. The data set covers 166 economies out of the 170 economies in the Poverty and Inequality Platform.
7. Note that Sub-Saharan Africa measures inequality based on consumption. Inequality based on income would tend to be higher than the numbers reported here.
8. The economies in the low-income and lower-middle-income categories predominantly have consumption surveys that are known to have lower levels of inequality than the income survey widely used in upper-middle-income and high-income countries. This implies that if inequality was measured with income, the levels of inequality would be even higher in low-income and lower-middle-income settings.
9. For more information, see the World Meteorological Organization's 2022 Greenhouse Gas Bulletin at https://wmo.int/publication-series/greenhouse-gas-bulletin.
10. NOAA Research News, "Greenhouse Gas Pollution Trapped 49 Percent More Heat in 2021 than in 1990, NOAA Finds," NOAA Research, May 23, 2022, https://research.noaa.gov/2022/05/23/greenhouse-gas-pollution-trapped-49-more-heat-in-2021-than-in-1990-noaa-finds/.
11. These figures are based on the definitions used to construct the climate risk indicator described in box O.3 and chapter 3. Therefore, figures are consistent but slightly different from the ones presented in chapter 1 as part of the multidimensional poverty measure.
12. For more information, see https://datatopics.worldbank.org/jobsdiagnostics/.
13. A household's capacity to generate income depends on the assets they own or have access to, the existing returns to these assets, and how intensively they are used. In the short term, the distribution of household assets does not change, and variables such as prices, the composition of economic growth, and fiscal transfers will play a more significant role in driving household incomes and reducing poverty. In the medium and long term, however, the level and distribution of assets, along with the returns on the assets that reflect their productivity, will be the primary drivers of household incomes and poverty reduction.
14. Hallegatte, Rentschler, and Rozenberg (2019) estimate that improving the infrastructure resilience of assets exposed to hazards would cost less than 0.1 percent of the GDP of low- and middle-income countries.
15. Jennifer Rudden, "Natural disaster losses cost worldwide 2000–2023," Statista (February 23, 2024), https://www.statista.com/statistics/612561/natural-disaster-losses-cost-worldwide-by-type-of-loss/#:~:text=In%202023%2C%20there%20was%20a,to%20118%20billion%20U.S.%20dollars.

16. For more information about early warning systems, see the United Nations website at https://www.un .org/en/climatechange/early-warnings-for-all.

17. Warming beyond 1.5°C will increase the magnitude and the share of people exposed to climate hazards substantially (IPCC 2023).

18. Nationally Determined Contributions are climate action plans to cut emissions and adapt to climate change. All parties to the Paris Agreement are required to stablish one and update it every five years (https://www.un.org/en/climatechange/all-about-ndcs#:~:text=Simply%20put%2C%20an%20 NDC%2C%20or,update%20it%20every%20five%20years).

19. Note that some, but not all, Network for Greening the Financial System (NGFS) countries are projected to have no greenhouse gas emissions in 2050 in the Net Zero 2050 scenario. Moreover, the Net Zero 2050 scenario refers to net-zero CO_2 emissions only, while total greenhouse gas emissions are not net zero across all countries. There is also heterogeneity between the models used by NGFS as to when net-zero emissions need to be reached in order to limit warming to 1.5°C.

20. See, for example, World Bank Climate Change and Development Reports for Benin, Brazil, Cameroon, or Tunisia.

21. "Household Air Pollution," World Health Organization (December 15, 2023), https://www.who.int /news-room/fact-sheets/detail/household-air-pollution-and-health.

22. As of May 17, 2024, the data were obtained from https://data.who.int/dashboards/covid19 /deaths?n=o.

23. The data are from IHME, https://vizhub.healthdata.org/gbd-results/.

24. WHO Interim Target 1 refers to a PM2.5 level of 35 micrograms per cubic meter.

25. The mitigation potential estimates indicate total amount mitigated over time (with a 20-year time horizon) through changes in land use and land management.

26. M. Haddad, B. Hansl, and A. Pechevy, "Trading in a New Climate: How Mitigation Policies Are Reshaping Global Trade Dynamics," blog (February 13, 2024), https://blogs.worldbank.org/en /developmenttalk/trading-new-climate-how-mitigation-policies-are-reshaping-global-trade-dynamics.

27. See World Bank SDG Atlas: https://datatopics.worldbank.org/sdgatlas/goal-4-quality-education? lang=en.

28. Though there is a consensus of spending at least 4–6 percent of GDP or 15–20 percent of public expenditure on education, only 1 in 10 countries and territories meets the 20 percent benchmark, and only 4 in 10 meet the 15 percent benchmark (UNICEF 2022).

29. Note that this calculation is based on a smaller sample of countries and that the probability of experiencing a hazard is kept constant over time. Changes are therefore driven by population growth and people settling in more exposed areas (Doan et al. 2023).

30. Twenty-five countries in the world with an aggregate population of 100 million people, out of which 10 countries with 75 million people are in Sub-Saharan Africa, had negative greenhouse gas emissions in 2022, so their ecosystems absorbed more carbon than the country emitted.

31. The availability of technology for carbon capture and storage is also assumed to increase under the Net Zero 2050 scenario of Network for Greening the Financial System (NGFS), though only at a limited scale. See for example the NGFS scenarios portal: https://www.ngfs.net/ngfs-scenarios-portal /explore/.

References

Agnolucci, Paolo, Carolyn Fischer, Dirk Heine, Mariza Montes de Oca Leon, Joseph Pryor, Kathleen Patroni, and Stéphane Hallegatte. 2023. "Measuring Total Carbon Pricing" *The World Bank Research Observer* 39 (2): 227–58. https://doi.org/10.1093/wbro/lkad009.

Alesina, Alberto, Sebastian Hohmann, Stelios Michalopoulos, and Elias Papaioannou. 2021. "Intergenerational Mobility in Africa." *Econometrica* 89 (1): 1–35. https://doi.org/10.3982/ECTA17018.

Alvaredo, Facundo, Anthony B. Atkinson, and Salvatore Morelli. 2018. "Top Wealth Shares in the UK Over More Than a Century." *Journal of Public Economics* 16w: 26–47.

Asher, Sam, Paul Novosad, and Charlie Rafkin. 2024. "Intergenerational Mobility in India: New Measures and Estimates Across Time and Social Groups." *American Economic Journal: Applied Economics* 16 (2): 66–98. https://doi.org/10.1257/app.20210686.

Atkinson, Anthony B. 2015. *Inequality: What Can Be Done?* Cambridge, MA: Harvard University Press.

Baquie, Sandra, and Habtamu Fuje, H. 2020. "Vulnerability to Poverty Following Extreme Weather Events in Malawi." Policy Research Working Paper 9435 [preprint], World Bank, Washington, DC.

Barbier, Edward B. 2010. "Poverty, Development, and Environment." *Environment and Development Economics* 15 (6): 635–60. https://doi.org/10.1017/S1355770X1000032X.

Batista, Cátia, and Pedro C. Vicente. 2023. "Is Mobile Money Changing Rural Africa? Evidence from a Field Experiment." *The Review of Economics and Statistics*: 1–29. https://doi.org/10.1162/rest_a_01333.

Bend, May, Yitong Hu, Yilin Pan, Harry Anthony Patrinos, Thomas Poulson, Angelica Rivera-Olvera, Nobuyuki Tanaka, et al. 2023. *Education Finance Watch 2023*. Washington DC: World Bank Group. https://documents.worldbank.org/en/publication/documents-reports/documentdetail/0991031231637 55271/P17813506cd84f07a0b6be0c6ea576d59f8.

Bergstrom, Katy. 2022. "The Role of Income Inequality for Poverty Reduction." *The World Bank Economic Review* 36 (3): 583–604. https://doi.org/10.1093/wber/lhab026.

Blanchard, Olivier, Christian Gollier, and Jean Tirole. 2023. "The Portfolio of Economic Policies Needed to Fight Climate Change." *Annual Review of Economics* 15 (1): 689–722. https://doi.org/10.1146/annurev-economics-051520-015113.

Bourguignon, François. 2003. "The Growth Elasticity of Poverty Reduction: Explaining Heterogeneity Across Countries and Time Periods." In *Inequality and Growth: Theory and Policy Implications*, edited by Theo S. Eicher and Stephen J. Turnovsky, 3–26. Cambridge, MA: MIT Press. https://doi.org/10.7551/mitpress/3750.003.0004.

Bruckner, Benedikt, Klaus Hubacek, Yuli Shan, Honglin Zhong, and Kuishuang Feng. 2022. "Impacts of Poverty Alleviation on National and Global Carbon Emissions." *Nature Sustainability* 5 (4): 311–20. https://doi.org/10.1038/s41893-021-00842-z.

Cagé, Julia. 2023. "Political Inequality." Working Paper No. 2023/22 [preprint], World Inequality Lab, Paris. https://wid.world/document/political-inequality-wid-world-working-paper-2023-22/.

Cai, Jing, Alain de Janvry, and Elisabeth Sadoulet. 2020. "Subsidy Policies and Insurance Demand." *American Economic Review* 110 (8): 2422–53. https://doi.org/10.1257/aer.20190661.

Cai, Jing, and Changcheng Song. 2017. "Do Disaster Experience and Knowledge Affect Insurance Take-up Decisions?" *Journal of Development Economics* 124: 83–94. https://doi.org/10.1016/j.jdeveco.2016.08.007.

Casaburi, Lorenzo, and Jack Willis. 2018. "Time Versus State in Insurance: Experimental Evidence from Contract Farming in Kenya." *American Economic Review* 108 (12): 3778–813. https://doi.org/10.1257/aer.20171526.

Castaneda, Aguilar, R. Andres, Adriana Castillo, Nancy P. Devpura, Reno Dewina, Carolina Diaz-Bonilla, Ifeanyi Edochie, et al. 2024. *March 2024 Update to the Poverty and Inequality Platform (PIP): What's New*. Washington, DC: World Bank. https://doi.org/10.1596/41341.

Chetty, Raj, Nathaniel Hendren, and Lawrence F. Katz. 2016. "The Effects of Exposure to Better Neighborhoods on Children: New Evidence from the Moving to Opportunity Experiment." *American Economic Review* 106 (4): 855–902. https://doi.org/10.1257/aer.20150572.

Cole, Shawn, Xavier Giné, Jeremy Tobacman, Petia Topalova, Robert Townsend, and James Vickery. 2013. "Barriers to Household Risk Management: Evidence from India." *American Economic Journal: Applied Economics* 5 (1): 104–35. https://doi.org/10.1257/app.5.1.104.

Damania, Richard, Esteban Balseca, Charlotte de Fontaubert, Joshua Gill, Kichan Kim, Jun Rentschler, Jason Russ, et al. 2023. *Detox Development: Repurposing Environmentally Harmful Subsidies*. Washington, DC: World Bank. http://hdl.handle.net/10986/39423.

Damania, Richard, Stephen Polasky, Mary Ruckelshaus, Jason Russ, Markus Amann, Rebecca Chaplin-Kramer, James Gerber, et al. 2023. "Nature's Frontiers: Achieving Sustainability, Efficiency, and Prosperity with Natural Capital." Washington, DC: World Bank Group.

Decerf, Benoit Marie A., Jed Friedman, Arthur Galego Mendes, Michael Pennings, and Nishant Yonzan. 2024. "Lives, Livelihoods, and Learning: A Global Perspective on the Well-Being Impacts of the COVID-19 Pandemic." Policy Research Working Paper WPS10728 [preprint], World Bank, Washington, DC. http://documents.worldbank.org/curated/en/099537503202413127/IDU1f944e1ca18e2814ce0198221694a75dd5654.

Demirgüç-Kunt, Asli, Leora Klapper, Dorothe Singer, and Saniya Ansar. 2022. *The Global Findex Database 2021: Financial Inclusion, Digital Payments, and Resilience in the Age of COVID-19*. Washington, DC: World Bank Group. https://www.worldbank.org/en/publication/globalfindex/Report.

Dimitrova, Anna. 2021. "Seasonal Droughts and the Risk of Childhood Undernutrition in Ethiopia." *World Development* 141: 105417. https://doi.org/10.1016/j.worlddev.2021.105417.

Doan, Miki Khanh, Ruth Hill, Stephane Hallegatte, Paul Corral, Ben Brunckhorst, Minh Nguyen, Samual Freije-Rodriguez, et al. 2023. *Counting People Exposed to, Vulnerable to, or at High Risk From Climate Shocks: A Methodology*. Washington, DC: World Bank. https://doi.org/10.1596/1813-9450-10619.

Ehrlich, Isaac, and Gary S. Becker. 1972. "Market Insurance, Self-Insurance, and Self-Protection." *Journal of Political Economy* 80 (4): 623–48. https://doi.org/10.1086/259916.

Erikson, Robert S. 2015. "Income Inequality and Policy Responsiveness." *Annual Review of Political Science* 18: 11–29. https://doi.org/10.1146/annurev-polisci-020614-094706.

Eyring, Veronika, Nathan P. Gillett, Krishna M. Achuta Rao, Rondrotiana Barimalala, Marcelo Barreiro Parrillo, Nicolas Bellouin, Christophe Cassou, et al. 2021. "Human Influence on the Climate System." In *Climate Change 2021: The Physical Science Basis. Contribution of Working Group I to the Sixth Assessment Report of the Intergovernmental Panel on Climate Change*, edited by V. Masson-Delmotte, P. Zhai, A. Pirani, S.L. Connors, C. Péan, S. Berger, N. Caud, Y. Chen, L. Goldfarb, M.I. Gomis, M. Huang, K. Leitzell, E. Lonnoy, J.B.R. Matthews, T.K. Maycock, T. Waterfield, O. Yelekçi, R. Yu, and B. Zhou, 423–552. Cambridge, UK and New York: Cambridge University Press. https://www.ipcc.ch/report/sixth-assessment-report-working-group-i/.

Gatti, Roberta, Daniel Lederman, Asif M. Islam, Bo Andree, Pieter Johannes, Rana Lotfi, Mennatallah Emam Mousa, et al. 2023. *Altered Destinies: The Long-Term Effects of Rising Prices and Food Insecurity in the Middle East and North Africa*. Middle East and North Africa Economic Update. Washington, DC: World Bank Group. https://doi.org/10.1596/978-1-4648-1974-2.

Gill, Indermit S., Ana Revenga, and Christian Zeballos. 2016. "Grow, Invest, Insure: A Game Plan to End Extreme Poverty by 2030." Policy Research Working Paper 7892, World Bank, Washington, DC. https://papers.ssrn.com/abstract=2870160.

Grassi, Giacomo, Clemens Schwingshackl, Thomas Gasser, Richard A. Houghton, Stephen Sitch, Josep G. Canadell, Alessandro Cescatti, et al. 2023. "Harmonising the Land-Use Flux Estimates of Global Models and National Inventories for 2000–2020." *Earth System Science Data* 15 (3): 1093–1114. https://doi.org/10.5194/essd-15-1093-2023.

Grosset-Touba, Florian, Anna Papp, and Charles Taylor. 2023. "Rain Follows the Forest: Land Use Policy, Climate Change, and Adaptation." https://doi.org/10.2139/ssrn.4333147.

Gütschow, Johannes, Mika Pflüger, and Daniel Busch. 2024. The PRIMAP-Hist National Historical Emissions Time Series (1750–2022) v2.5.1. https://doi.org/doi:10.5281/zenodo.10705513.

Haddad, Cameron Nadim, Daniel Mahler, Carolina Diaz-Bonilla, Ruth Hill, Christoph Lakner, and Gabriel Lara Ibarra. 2024. "The World Bank's New Inequality Indicator: The Number of Countries with High Inequality (English)." Policy Research Working Paper WPS 10796, World Bank, Washington, DC.

Hallegatte, Stephane, Jun Rentschler, and Julie Rozenberg. 2019. *Lifelines: The Resilient Infrastructure Opportunity*. Washington, DC: World Bank Group. http://hdl.handle.net/10986/31805.

Hallegatte, Stephane, and Julie Rozenberg. 2017. "Climate Change Through a Poverty Lens." *Nature Climate Change* 7 (4): 250–56. https://doi.org/10.1038/nclimate3253.

Hallegatte, Stephane, Adrian Camille Vogt-Schilb, Mook Bangalore, and Julie Rozenberg. 2016. *Unbreakable: Building the Resilience of the Poor in the Face of Natural Disasters*. Washington, DC: World Bank Group.

Hallegatte, Stephane, and Brian Walsh. 2021. "Natural Disasters, Poverty and Inequality: New Metrics for Fairer Policies." In *The Routledge Handbook of the Political Economy of the Environment*. Oxfordshire, UK: Routledge.

Hill, Ruth Vargas, Neha Kumar, Nicholas Magnan, Simrin Makhija, Francesca de Nicola, David J. Spielman, and Patrick S. Ward. 2019. "Ex Ante and Ex Post Effects of Hybrid Index Insurance in Bangladesh." *Journal of Development Economics* 136: 1–17. https://doi.org/10.1016/j .jdeveco.2018.09.003.

Hill, Ruth, and Carolina Mejia-Mantilla. 2017. "With a Little Help: Shocks, Agricultural Income, and Welfare in Uganda." Policy Research Working Paper 7935, World Bank, Washington, DC.

Hill, Ruth Vargas, and Catherine Porter. 2017. "Vulnerability to Drought and Food Price Shocks: Evidence from Ethiopia." *World Development* 96: 65–77. https://doi.org/10.1016/j.worlddev.2017.02.025.

Hoffmann, Roman, and Raya Muttarak. 2017. "Learn from the Past, Prepare for the Future: Impacts of Education and Experience on Disaster Preparedness in the Philippines and Thailand." *World Development* 96: 32–51. https://doi.org/10.1016/j.worlddev.2017.02.016.

IEA (International Energy Agency). 2023a. *Energy Efficiency 2023*. Paris: IEA. https://www.iea.org /reports/energy-efficiency-2023.

IEA (International Energy Agency). 2023b. *Net Zero Roadmap: A Global Pathway to Keep the 1.5 °C Goal in Reach*. Paris: IEA. https://www.iea.org/reports/net-zero-roadmap-a-global-pathway-to-keep -the-15-0c-goal-in-reach.

IEA (International Energy Agency), IRENA (International Renewable Energy Agency), United Nations Statistics Division, World Bank, and WHO (World Health Organization). 2023. *Tracking SDG 7: The Energy Progress Report 2023*. Washington, DC: International Bank for Reconstruction and Development/The World Bank.

IMF (International Monetary Fund). 2024. *World Economic Outlook—Steady but Slow: Resilience amid Divergence*. Washington, DC: IMF.

IPCC (Intergovernmental Panel on Climate Change). 2021. *Climate Change 2021: The Physical Science Basis: Working Group I Contribution to the Sixth Assessment Report of the Intergovernmental Panel on Climate Change*. Cambridge, UK and New York: Cambridge University Press. https://doi.org /10.1017/9781009325844.

IPCC (Intergovernmental Panel on Climate Change). 2022a. *Climate Change 2022: Impacts, Adaptation and Vulnerability: Working Group II Contribution to the Sixth Assessment Report of the Intergovernmental Panel on Climate Change*. Cambridge, UK and New York: Cambridge University Press. https://doi.org/10.1017/9781009325844.

IPCC (Intergovernmental Panel on Climate Change). 2022b. *Climate Change 2022: Mitigation of Climate Change: Working Group III Contribution to the Sixth Assessment Report of the Intergovernmental Panel on Climate Change*. Cambridge, UK and New York: Cambridge University Press. https://doi .org/10.1017/9781009157926.

IPCC (Intergovernmental Panel on Climate Change). 2023. *Climate Change 2023: Synthesis Report. Contribution of Working Groups I, II and III to the Sixth Assessment Report of the Intergovernmental Panel on Climate Change*. Geneva, Switzerland: IPCC. [Core Writing Team, H. Lee and J. Romero (eds.)]. https://www.ipcc.ch/report/ar6/syr/downloads/report/IPCC_AR6_SYR_LongerReport.pdf.

Jack, William, and Tavneet Suri. 2014. "Risk Sharing and Transactions Costs: Evidence from Kenya's Mobile Money Revolution." *American Economic Review* 104 (1): 183–223. https://doi.org/10.1257/aer .104.1.183.

Karlan, Dean, Robert Osei, Isaac Osei-Akoto, and Christopher Udry. 2014. "Agricultural Decisions After Relaxing Credit and Risk Constraints." *The Quarterly Journal of Economics* 129 (2): 597–652. https://doi.org/10.1093/qje/qju002.

Kochhar, Nishtha, and Erwin Knippenberg. 2023. "Droughts and Welfare in Afghanistan." Policy Research Working Paper 10272, World Bank, Washington, DC.

Kraay, Aart, Christoph Lakner, Berk Özler, Benoit Decerf, Dean Jolliffe, Olivier Sterck, and Nishant Yonzan. 2023. *A New Distribution Sensitive Index for Measuring Welfare, Poverty, and Inequality.* Policy Research Working Paper 10470, World Bank, Washington, DC. https://doi.org/10.1596/1813-9450-10470.

Laborde, David, Madhur Gautam; Abdullah Mamun, Valeria Pineiro, Will Martin, and Rob Vos. 2022. *Repurposing Agricultural Policies and Support: Options to Transform Agriculture and Food Systems to Better Serve the Health of People, Economies, and the Planet.* Washington, DC: World Bank Group.

Laborde, David, Csilla Lakatos, and Will J. Martin. 2019. "Poverty Impact of Food Price Shocks and Policies." Policy Research Working Paper 8724, World Bank, Washington, DC. https://papers.ssrn.com/abstract=3335091.

Lakner, Christoph, Daniel Gerszon Mahler, Mario Negre, and Espen Beer Prydz. 2022. "How Much Does Reducing Inequality Matter for Global Poverty?" *The Journal of Economic Inequality* 20 (3): 559–85. https://doi.org/10.1007/s10888-021-09510-w.

Lakner, Christoph, and Branko Milanovic. 2016. "Global Income Distribution: From the Fall of the Berlin Wall to the Great Recession." *The World Bank Economic Review* 30 (2): 203–32. https://doi.org/10.1093/wber/lhv039.

Lankes, Hans Peter, Rob Macquarie, Éléonore Soubeyran, and Nicholas Stern. 2024. "The Relationship Between Climate Action and Poverty Reduction." *The World Bank Research Observer* 39 (1): 1–46. https://doi.org/10.1093/wbro/lkad011.

Le, Kien, and My Nguyen. 2023. "Rainfall Shocks, Health and Well-being in Rural Vietnam." *Studies in Microeconomics.* https://doi.org/10.1177/23210222221144873.

Liotta, Charlotte, Paolo Avner, and Stéphane Hallegatte. 2023. "Efficiency and Equity in Urban Flood Management Policies: A Systematic Urban Economics Exploration." Policy Research Working Paper 10292, World Bank, Washington, DC. https://doi.org/10.1596/1813-9450-10292.

Liu, Yanyab, Kevin Chen, and Ruth V. Hill. 2020. "Delayed Premium Payment, Insurance Adoption, and Household Investment in Rural China." *American Journal of Agricultural Economics* 102 (4): 1177–97. https://doi.org/10.1002/ajae.12038.

López-Calva, Luis F., and Carlos Rodríguez-Castelán. 2016. *Pro-Growth Equity: A Policy Framework for the Twin Goals.* Policy Research Working Paper, World Bank, Washington, DC. https://doi.org/10.1596/1813-9450-7897.

McIntosh, Craig, Alexander Sarris, and Fotis Papadopoulos. 2013. "Productivity, Credit, Risk, and the Demand for Weather Index Insurance in Smallholder Agriculture in Ethiopia." *Agricultural Economics* 44 (4–5): 399–417. https://doi.org/10.1111/agec.12024.

Milanovic, Branko. 2016. *Global Inequality: A New Approach for the Age of Globalization.* Cambridge, MA: Harvard University Press. https://doi.org/10.2307/j.ctvjghwk4.

Mukim, Megha, and Mark Roberts (eds.). 2023. *Thriving: Making Cities Green, Resilient, and Inclusive in a Changing Climate.* Washington, DC: World Bank Group. http://hdl.handle.net/10986/38295.

Muttarak, Raya, and Wolfgang Lutz. 2014. "Is Education a Key to Reducing Vulnerability to Natural Disasters and Hence Unavoidable Climate Change?" *Ecology and Society* 19 (1). https://www.jstor.org/stable/26269470.

Muttarak, Raya, and Wiraporn Pothisiri. 2013. "The Role of Education on Disaster Preparedness: Case Study of 2012 Indian Ocean Earthquakes on Thailand's Andaman Coast." *Ecology and Society* 18 (4). https://www.jstor.org/stable/26269420.

Narayan, Ambar, Alexandru Cojocaru, Maria Davalos, Natalia Garcia, Christoph Lakner, Daniel Gerszon Mahler, and Nishant Yonzan. 2022. "COVID-19 and Economic Inequality: Short-Term Impacts with Long-Term Consequences." Policy Research Working Paper 9902, World Bank, Washington, DC. https://doi.org/10.1596/1813-9450-9902.

NGFS (Network for Greening the Financial System). 2023. *NGFS Scenarios Technical Documentation.* Paris: NGFS.

Osendarp, Saskia, Jonathan Akuoku, Robert Black, Derek Headey, Marie Ruel, Nick Scott, Meera Shekar, et al. 2020. "The Potential Impacts of the COVID-19 Crisis on Maternal and Child Undernutrition in Low and Middle Income Countries." [preprint]. Research Square, Durham, NC. https://doi .org/10.21203/rs.3.rs-123716/v1.

Pape, Utz, and Philip Wollburg. 2019. "Impact of Drought on Poverty in Somalia." [Preprint]. Policy Research Working Paper 8698, World Bank, Washington, DC.

Piketty, Thomas. 2014. *Capital in the Twenty-First Century*. Cambridge, MA: Harvard University Press. https://www.jstor.org/stable/j.ctt6wpqbc.

Pople, Ashley, Ruth Hill, Stefan Dercon, and Ben Brunckhorst. 2021. "Anticipatory Cash Transfers in Climate Disaster Response." Working paper 6, Centre for Disaster Protection, London, UK.

Rigolini, Jamele. 2021. "Social Protection and Labor: A Key Enabler for Climate Change Adaptation and Mitigation." Social Protection and Jobs Discussion Paper 2108, World Bank Group, Washington, DC.

Rizk, Reham, and Mehdi Ben Slimane. 2018. "Modelling the Relationship Between Poverty, Environment, and Institutions: A Panel Data Study." *Environmental Science and Pollution Research* 25 (31): 31459–73. https://doi.org/10.1007/s11356-018-3051-6.

Saez, Emmanuel, and Gabriel Zucman. 2020. 'The Rise of Income and Wealth Inequality in America: Evidence from Distributional Macroeconomic Accounts." *Journal of Economic Perspectives* 34 (4): 3–26.

Schady, Norbert, Alaka Holla, Shwetlena Sabarwal, Joana Silva, and Andres Yi Chang. 2023. *Collapse and Recovery: How the COVID-19 Pandemic Eroded Human Capital and What to Do About It*. Washington, DC: World Bank Group.

Sepulveda, Edgardo R., and Ann-Sylvia Brooker. 2021. "Income Inequality and COVID-19 Mortality: Age-Stratified Analysis of 22 OECD Countries." *SSM—Population Health* 16: 100904. https://doi .org/10.1016/j.ssmph.2021.100904.

Sinha, Nistha, Gabriela Inchauste, and Ambar Narayan. 2024. *Leveling the Playing Field: Addressing Structural Inequalities to Accelerate Poverty Reduction in Africa*. Washington, DC: World Bank Group.

Steckel, Jan C., Ira I. Dorband, Lorenzo Montrone, Hauke Ward, Leonard Missbach, Fabian Hafner, Michael Jakob, et al. 2021. "Distributional Impacts of Carbon Pricing in Developing Asia." *Nature Sustainability* 4 (11): 1005–14. https://doi.org/10.1038/s41893-021-00758-8.

Sutton, William R., Alexander Lotsch, and Ashesh Prasann. 2024. *Recipe for a Livable Planet: Achieving Net Zero Emissions in the Agrifood System*. Agriculture and Food Series. Conference Edition. Washington, DC: World Bank. http://hdl.handle.net/10986/41468.

UNEP (United Nations Environment Programme). 2022. *Adaptation Gap Report 2022: Too Little, Too Slow—Climate Adaptation Failure Puts World at Risk*. Nairobi: UNEP. https://www.unep.org /adaptation-gap-report-2022.

UNICEF (United Nations Children's Fund). 2022. *Financing Education Recovery: A Piece of Cake?* Policy brief. New York: United Nations. https://www.unicef.org/reports /financing-education-recovery-piece-cake.

United Nations. 2024. *World Economic Situation and Prospects 2024*. New York: United Nations.

United Nations and Inter-agency Task Force on Financing for Development. 2024. *Financing for Sustainable Development Report 2024: Financing for Development at a Crossroads*. New York: United Nations. https://developmentfinance.un.org/fsdr2021.

van der Weide, Roy, Christoph Lakner, Daniel Gerszon Mahler, Ambar Narayan, and Rakesh Gupta. 2024. "Intergenerational Mobility Around the World: A New Database." *Journal of Development Economics* 166: 103167. https://doi.org/10.1016/j.jdeveco.2023.103167.

Vasilaky, Kathryn, Rahel Diro, Michael Norton, Geoff McCarney, and Daniel Osgood. 2020. "Can Education Unlock Scale? The Demand Impact of Educational Games on a Large-Scale Unsubsidised Index Insurance Programme in Ethiopia." *The Journal of Development Studies* 56 (2): 361–83. https://doi.org/10.1080/00220388.2018.1554207.

Wollburg, Philip, Stephane Hallegatte, and Daniel Gerszon Mahler. 2023. "Ending Extreme Poverty Has a Negligible Impact on Global Greenhouse Gas Emissions." *Nature* 623 (7989): 982–86. https://doi .org/10.1038/s41586-023-06679-0.

World Bank. 2013a. *World Development Report 2013: Jobs*. Washington, DC: World Bank Group.

World Bank. 2013b. *World Development Report 2014: Risk and Opportunity—Managing Risk for Development*. World Development Report. Washington, DC: World Bank Group. https://doi .org/10.1596/978-0-8213-9903-3.

World Bank. 2016. *Poverty and Shared Prosperity 2016: Taking on Inequality*. Washington, DC: World Bank Group. https://doi.org/10.1596/978-1-4648-0958-3.

World Bank. 2017. *Monitoring Global Poverty: Report of the Commission on Global Poverty*. Washington, DC: World Bank Group. doi: 10.1596/978-1-4648-0961-3.

World Bank. 2022a. *The Global Health Cost of PM 2.5 Air Pollution: A Case for Action Beyond 2021*. Washington, DC: World Bank Group. https://doi.org/10.1596/978-1-4648-1816-5.

World Bank. 2022b. *Peru Country Climate and Development Report*. Washington, DC: World Bank Group.

World Bank. 2022c. *Philippines Country Climate and Development Report*. Washington, DC: World Bank Group.

World Bank. 2022d. *Poland Country Economic Memorandum: The Green Transformation in Poland— Opportunities and Challenges for Economic Growth*. Washington, DC: World Bank Group. http://hdl .handle.net/10986/38116.

World Bank. 2022e. *Poverty and Shared Prosperity 2022: Correcting Course*. Washington, DC: World Bank Group. https://www.worldbank.org/en/publication/poverty-and-shared-prosperity.

World Bank. 2023a. *Brazil Country Climate and Development Report*. Washington, DC: World Bank Group.

World Bank. 2023b. *Cambodia Country Climate and Development Report (English)*. Washington, DC: World Bank Group.

World Bank. 2023c. *Colombia Country Climate and Development Report*. Washington, DC: World Bank Group.

World Bank. 2023d. *International Debt Report 2023*. Washington, DC: World Bank. http://hdl.handle .net/10986/40670.

World Bank. 2023e. *Striving for Clean Air: Air Pollution and Public Health in South Asia*. Washington, DC: International Bank for Reconstruction and Development/The World Bank.

World Bank. 2024a. *Digital Progress and Trends Report 2023*. Washington, DC: World Bank Group. http://hdl.handle.net/10986/40970.

World Bank. 2024b. *Global Economic Prospects, January 2024*. Washington, DC: World Bank Group. https://doi.org/10.1596/978-1-4648-2017-5.

World Bank. 2024c. *Global Economic Prospects, June 2024*. Washington, DC: World Bank. https://doi .org/10.1596/978-1-4648-2058-8.

World Bank. 2024d. *The Great Reversal: Prospects, Risks, and Policies in International Development Association (IDA) Countries*. Washington, DC: World Bank Group. https://www.worldbank.org/en /research/publication/prospects-risks-and-policies-in-IDA-countries.

World Bank. 2024e. *Macro Poverty Outlook, Spring Meetings 2024*. Washington, DC: World Bank.

World Bank. 2024f. *State and Trends of Carbon Pricing 2024*. Washington, DC: World Bank. http://hdl .handle.net/10986/41544.

World Bank. 2024g. *World Development Report 2024: The Middle-Income Trap*. Washington, DC: World Bank Group.

World Bank. n.d. "Translating Our Vision." World Bank Group Scorecard, accessed August 22, 2024. https://scorecard.worldbank.org/en/scorecard/home.

World Bank, UNESCO, UNICEF, FCDO, USAID, and the Bill & Melinda Gates Foundation. 2022. *The State of Global Learning Poverty: 2022 Update*. https://thedocs.worldbank.org/en/doc /e52f55322528903b27f1b7e61238e416-0200022022/original/Learning-poverty-report-2022-06-21 -final-V7-0-conferenceEdition.pdf.

World Bank Group. 2022. *Climate and Development: An Agenda for Action—Emerging Insights from World Bank Group 2021–22 Country Climate and Development Reports*. http://hdl.handle.net/10986/38220.

World Bank Group. 2023. *The Development, Climate, and Nature Crisis: Solutions to End Poverty on a Livable Planet—Insights from World Bank Country Climate and Development Reports Covering 42 Economies*. https://doi.org/10.1596/40652.

Wu, Haoyu, Aziz Atamanov, Tom Bundervoet, and Pierella Paci. 2024. "The Growth Elasticity of Poverty: Is Africa Any Different?" Policy Research Working Paper 10690, World Bank Group, Washington, DC.

Zucman, Gabriel. 2015. "The Hidden Wealth of Nations: The Scourge of Tax Havens." in *The Hidden Wealth of Nations*. Chicago: University of Chicago Press. https://www.degruyter.com/document/doi /10.7208/9780226245560/html.

Global Poverty Update and Outlook

1

Summary

- *Today, 692 million people (8.5 percent of the world's population) live in extreme poverty—that is, on less than $2.15 per day. Progress has stalled amid low growth, setbacks due to COVID-19 (Coronavirus), and increased fragility. Poverty in low-income countries is greater than before the pandemic.*

- *About 44 percent of the world population remains poor by a standard that is more relevant for upper-middle-income countries ($6.85 per day), and the number of people living on less than this standard has barely changed since the 1990s because of population growth.*

- *In 2024, Sub-Saharan Africa accounted for 16 percent of the world's population, but 67 percent of the people living in extreme poverty. Two-thirds of the world's extreme poor lives in Sub-Saharan Africa, rising to three-quarters when all fragile and conflict-affected countries are included. About 72 percent of the world's extreme poor lives in countries that are eligible to receive assistance from the International Development Association (IDA).*

- *Based on the current trajectory, 7.3 percent of the global population is projected to live in extreme poverty in 2030. This means that about 69 million people are projected to escape extreme poverty between 2024 and 2030, compared to about 150 million who did so between 2013 and 2019. In addition, nearly 40 percent of the world's population will likely live on less than $6.85 per day.*

- *If growth does not accelerate and become more inclusive, it will take decades to eradicate extreme poverty and more than a century to lift everyone over $6.85 per day.*

- *Improving labor incomes by creating more and better jobs and investing in the productive capacity of the poor by investing in fundamentals such as education, infrastructure, and basic services will be important to enable the poor to benefit more from and contribute to growth, and enhance their resilience amid increasing shocks.*

Ending poverty remains a major global challenge

Global poverty reduction has slowed to a near standstill, with 2020–30 set to mark a lost decade

This report presents the first global poverty numbers for the post-COVID-19 pandemic period that are based primarily on survey data up to 2022, as well as nowcasts up to 2024. In 2024, about 8.5 percent of the global population lives in extreme poverty, just slightly below the rate observed before the pandemic (extreme poverty was 8.8 percent in 2019) (figure 1.1). This means that 692 million people in the world still live on less than $2.15 per day, up from 684 million in 2019.

The extreme poverty line (currently set at $2.15 per person per day) is a very frugal standard, typical of the cost of basic needs in the poorest countries (Jolliffe and Lakner 2023; Ravallion, Datt, and van de Walle 1991). Using a slightly higher poverty line, which is typical of the national poverty lines used in lower-middle-income countries ($3.65 per day), about 1.73 billion people are living in poverty in 2024 (21.4 percent of the global population). Using a more widely applicable standard that is typical of upper-middle-income countries ($6.85 per day), about 43.6 percent of the world's population is living in poverty. The World Bank is now tracking the $6.85 poverty rate, in addition to the extreme poverty rate, as part of its corporate mission to end extreme poverty and boost shared prosperity on a livable planet (see box 1.1 for the rationale behind this shift). The living standards of 3.53 billion people are below this higher poverty line in 2024, compared with 3.59 billion in 2019.

These estimates offer the first postpandemic assessment of global poverty using household surveys for most of the world population (box 1.2). Previous estimates of poverty during and after the COVID-19 pandemic were based largely on nowcasts, rather than actual survey data, because of the adverse impact of the pandemic on face-to-face survey data collection in many countries (Cuesta and Pico 2020; Mahler, Yonzan, and Lakner 2022; Sumner, Hoy, and Ortiz-Juarez 2020; World Bank 2022).[1] The new estimates of extreme poverty during the pandemic generally align with previously reported projections (annex 1B). The broad patterns of an economic recovery after 2020 are confirmed in the current report. Thus, the direction of change in extreme poverty between 2021 and 2022 predicted from gross domestic product (GDP) growth data has been largely consistent with the new survey-based poverty estimates. For example, the 2020 *Poverty and Shared Prosperity* report predicted an increase of 0.7 percentage points for the world in 2020, and the 2022 edition of the report estimated an increase of 0.9 percentage points, which is similar to the 0.85 percentage point reported in the current report (World Bank 2020, 2022). While differences are small globally, they are larger for some regions, mostly explained by new survey data from specific countries (see annex 1B for further details).

Poverty between 1990 and 2030 at $2.15, $3.65, and $6.85 per person per day

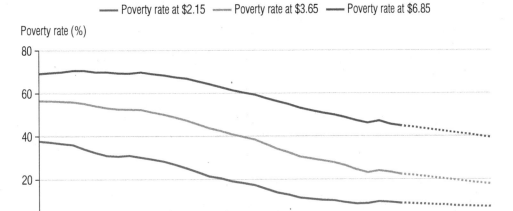

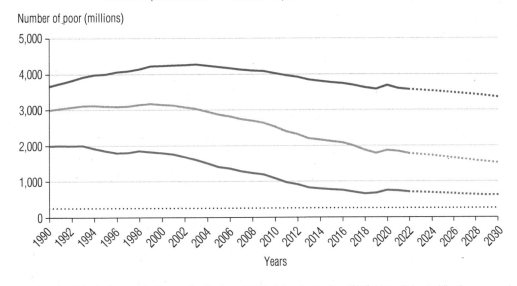

Source: World Bank, Poverty and Inequality Platform (PIP) (version September 2024), https://pip.worldbank.org.
Note: Poverty rates are reported for the $2.15, $3.65, and $6.85 per person per day poverty lines (expressed in 2017 purchasing power parity dollars). Between 2022 and 2029 poverty is projected based on per capita gross domestic product growth projections in *Global Economic Prospects, June 2024* (World Bank 2024d) complemented by the *Macro Poverty Outlook, Spring Meetings 2024* (World Bank 2024e) and the *World Economic Outlook* (IMF 2024); for 2030, average annual historic per capita growth rates (2010–19) are used. See annex 1A for more details on the projection methods. In panel a, the black horizontal dotted line is drawn at 3 percent and indicates the World Bank's target of ending extreme poverty by 2030. In panel b, it is drawn at 256 million, which represents 3 percent of the global population projected for 2030.

BOX 1.1
Revisiting the poverty line for a changing global population

The World Bank applies different thresholds to define poverty globally, relying on national definitions that countries around the world use to describe poverty within their borders. Anyone with an income or consumption below the international poverty line—currently set at $2.15 per person per day (2017 purchasing power parity dollars, or PPP$)—lives in extreme poverty. The international poverty line is the median of the national poverty lines in low-income countries. The second poverty line that this report emphasizes is $6.85 per person per day (2017 PPP$), which is the median national poverty line in upper-middle-income countries. The poverty line typical of lower-middle-income countries is $3.65. This report focuses on the extreme poverty line of $2.15 and the higher line of $6.85; poverty measures for any other poverty line are available on the Poverty and Inequality Platform website.[a] All these amounts are frugal by rich-country standards—the poverty line typical of high-income countries is $24.35.

For several decades, the World Bank has monitored extreme poverty, which has also become enshrined in the Sustainable Development Goals as target 1.1. Poverty was also monitored using higher poverty lines but not as an institutional goal. Starting in 2024, the World Bank will also start tracking poverty at the $6.85 poverty line as part of its vision indicators to reflect evolving conditions (Jolliffe and Lakner 2023; Pritchett 2024; World Bank, n.d.). This shift in focus reflects the facts that the world has become richer and there has been substantial population growth, especially in lower-middle- and upper-middle-income countries. Low-income countries now constitute only 9 percent of the world's population, compared to 58 percent in 1990 when the World Bank started tracking extreme poverty (figure B1.1.1, panel a). Conversely, lower-middle- and upper-middle-income countries now account for three-quarters of the world's population, compared to about one-quarter in 1990. In addition, the distribution of income around the world has evolved. More than half of the global population lives on more than $6.85 per day today, compared to less than one-third in 1990 (figure B1.1.1, panel b).

With growing income levels, the definition of basic needs expands beyond food, clothing, and shelter and now also includes a healthy diet, good sanitation, internet connectivity, access to electricity, and education, among others (Herforth et al. 2020; Jolliffe and Prydz 2016). The $6.85 poverty line captures these patterns and helps present a more relevant picture of poverty in many countries. Another poverty concept, the World Bank's societal poverty line, captures more systematically that the cost of meeting basic needs increases as an economy grows and allows for the poverty line to vary across countries over time (see box 1.4).

(continued)

Revisiting the poverty line for a changing global population *(continued)*

Notwithstanding this expanded vision, eradicating extreme poverty remains at the core of the World Bank's mission. The World Bank is the custodian of Sustainable Development Goals target 1.1., which is to eradicate extreme poverty in the world. Today, more people live in extreme poverty in middle-income countries than in low-income countries (Mahler, Yonzan, and Lakner 2023). Thus, tracking poverty using the international poverty line of $2.15 remains relevant both for low- and middle-income countries.

FIGURE B1.1.1

The composition of the global population has changed since 1990

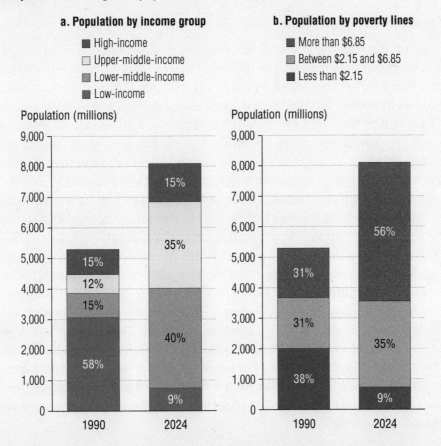

a. Population by income group
- High-income
- Upper-middle-income
- Lower-middle-income
- Low-income

b. Population by poverty lines
- More than $6.85
- Between $2.15 and $6.85
- Less than $2.15

Source: World Bank, Poverty and Inequality Platform (version September 2024), https://pip.worldbank.org.
Note: Panel a uses changing income groups over time. Poverty rates are reported for the $2.15, $3.65, and $6.85 per person per day poverty lines (expressed in 2017 purchasing power parity dollars).

a. For more information, see the Poverty and Inequality Platform at https://pip.worldbank.org.

Although there is sufficient recent data coverage globally, the recent survey data available for populous countries, especially in Sub-Saharan Africa, remain limited (box 1.2). As a result, the 2022 estimates reported for Sub-Saharan Africa, as well as the Middle East and North Africa, are based on less than half of the regional population covered by a recent survey. Also note that in recent months new data sets have been released that could not be analyzed in time for inclusion in this report (see box 1.3 and annex 1C). This includes new survey data for Ethiopia, India, Madagascar, Mozambique, and Nigeria, as well as new purchasing power parities (PPPs) for the 2021 reference year. Estimates using these new sources of data are expected to be published in the Poverty and Inequality Platform in 2025.

BOX 1.2

Improvements in survey coverage

This report presents the first estimates for the postpandemic period based on actual survey data for many countries in the world. The 2022 *Poverty and Shared Prosperity* report relied on prepandemic data for most of the world's population (figure B1.2.1). The survey data available for 2020 or later accounted for 14 percent of the world's population and spanned an even smaller share in low- and lower-middle-income countries. In contrast, this report has survey data collected from 98 countries in 2020 or later, representing more than three-quarters of the world's population and two-thirds of the population in low- and lower-middle-income countries. The entire Poverty and Inequality Platform database of household surveys that is used in this report covers 97 percent of the world's population.[a] However, this progress is notably missing in Sub-Saharan Africa and the Middle East and North Africa, where survey data are lacking for more than half of the population for 2020 or later (figure B1.2.1, panel a). Similarly, there is a lack of data coverage for low-income countries, International Development Association (IDA) countries, and fragile and conflicted countries (figure B1.2.1, panel b). Although there are sufficient recent global data, the lack of available survey data from such populous countries as Ethiopia and Nigeria increases the uncertainty surrounding global poverty estimates reported in this chapter for the most recent years, especially for the poorest regions and countries. See chapter 4 for a discussion on survey data availability and challenges.

(continued)

Improvements in survey coverage *(continued)*

FIGURE B1.2.1

Share of population with survey data in 2020 or later for global poverty monitoring

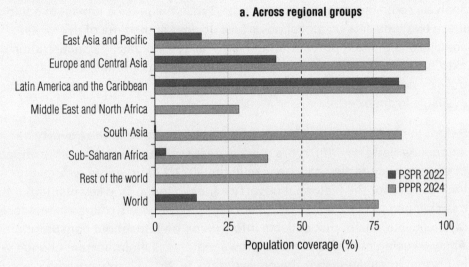

a. Across regional groups

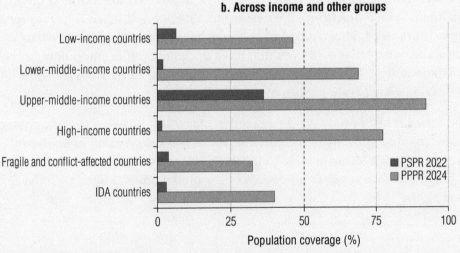

b. Across income and other groups

Source: World Bank, Poverty and Inequality Platform (version September 2024), https://pip.worldbank.org.

Note: IDA = International Development Association; PSPR 2022 = *Poverty and Shared Prosperity* report 2022; PPPR 2024 = *Poverty, Prosperity, and Planet Report 2024.* IDA countries are countries eligible for grants and concessionary loans from the World Bank's IDA, which provides support to the poorest countries in the world (consisting of low-income countries and some countries in other income groups). Data coverage for 2022 is adequate when there are survey data for the year 2020 or later covering at least 50 percent of the population of a region or country group of interest. This condition is consistent with the coverage rules applied in the Poverty and Inequality Platform for reporting regional and global poverty estimates (Castañeda Aguilar et al. 2024).

a. For more information, see the Poverty and Inequality Platform at https://pip.worldbank.org.

BOX 1.3
New data for India and international price levels

In recent months, the 2022/23 Household Consumption and Expenditure Survey (HCES) for India and purchasing power parities (PPPs) for 2021 were released. These new data sets are not reflected in the report, since the necessary analysis could not be completed in time. While the precise impact of adding these two data sets on global poverty is unclear at the time of this writing, key conclusions of the report are robust, such as the increasing concentration of extreme poverty in Sub-Saharan Africa and fragile countries, and that extreme poverty eradication by 2030 is out of reach. Further details on the new data are available in annex 1C.

Before the India 2022/23 HCES survey can be included in the Poverty and Inequality Platform (PIP), more work is necessary to understand the impact of various methodological changes in the 2022/23 survey, as well as the implications for the historical poverty series in India. One key element that has changed in the 2022/23 HCES survey from previous rounds is the design of the questionnaire that collects information on household consumption. Analysis using previous surveys shows that this is an important change with important implications for the poverty rate. In 2011/12, the extreme poverty rate in India changes from 22.9 percent to 13.4 percent when different recall periods are used. These types of changes are not unprecedented when compared with other countries that have updated their methodologies (Castañeda Aguilar et al. 2022). However, they need to be analyzed carefully to provide an accurate picture of poverty.

The new 2021 PPPs data were released in May 2024, allowing for an updated assessment of price levels around the world. Work is ongoing to analyze changes in price levels relative to the 2017 PPP round that is used in this report. This process also requires an update of the global poverty lines with the new prices.

The pandemic had scarring effects, and the poorest countries still have not recovered

The COVID-19 pandemic hit at an unprecedented scale, causing the biggest setback in the fight against global poverty since World War II (World Bank 2022). Global extreme poverty jumped by 0.85 percentage points in 2020, and 73 million people fell into poverty that year. While the pandemic hit globally, low- and lower-middle-income countries experienced much larger increases in poverty than upper-middle-income countries (figure 1.2). The recovery from the increase in poverty during COVID-19 has been uneven across countries (Mahler, Yonzan, and Lakner 2022; World Bank 2024d).

Low-income countries have shown less resilience, as the compounded effects of the pandemic and rising food and energy prices have led to poverty rates remaining higher than in 2019.[2] In low-income countries, extreme poverty is above prepandemic levels (figure 1.2, panel a). The same is true for IDA countries (see annex 1D). Lower-middle-income countries managed to recover from the COVID-19 shock only in 2022: extreme poverty rates fell to 10.5 percent in 2024, after jumping from 12.1 to 13.9 percent between 2019 and 2020. At the $6.85 poverty line, poverty rebounded to prepandemic levels in 2022 in lower-middle-income countries (figure 1.2, panel b). In contrast, upper-middle-income countries continued to see progress against poverty (as measured against the $6.85 line) in 2021 and 2022.

FIGURE 1.2

Extreme poverty is still above prepandemic levels in low-income countries

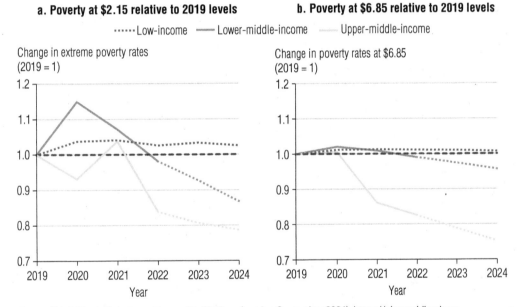

a. Poverty at $2.15 relative to 2019 levels   b. Poverty at $6.85 relative to 2019 levels

······· Low-income   ——— Lower-middle-income   ——— Upper-middle-income

Source: World Bank, Poverty and Inequality Platform (version September 2024), https://pip.worldbank.org.
Note: Poverty rates are shown relative to 2019 levels for the $2.15 and $6.85 per person per day poverty lines (expressed in 2017 purchasing power parity dollars). The line for low-income countries is dotted because the surveys covered less than 50 percent of the group's population between 2019 and 2022. Poverty rates for 2022–24 are projected based on per capita gross domestic product growth projections in *Global Economic Prospects* (World Bank 2024d). High-income countries are omitted because poverty rates at both lines are small. Poverty rates at the $6.85 poverty line did not increase in high-income countries between 2019 and 2024, and changes at the $2.15 poverty line were marginal (less than 0.05 percentage points). Income group is kept fixed using the fiscal year 2024 classification.

The outlook for poverty reduction is grim under the current pace and inclusiveness of economic growth

Progress in poverty reduction is projected to remain slow, and the goal of eradicating poverty is far out of reach. Even before the COVID-19 pandemic, the pace of poverty reduction was not fast enough to reach 3 percent by the end of the decade (World Bank 2018). The pandemic put the goal even further out of reach (Mahler, Yonzan, and Lakner 2022). Poverty rates are projected to continue to decline only gradually until 2030. Only 69 million people are projected to escape extreme poverty between 2024 and 2030 (figure 1.1). At this rate, 7.3 percent of the global population will remain in extreme poverty in 2030, more than double the 3 percent target.

At the higher poverty lines, reductions in the poverty rate are projected to continue more noticeably. By 2030, it is expected that slightly less than 40 percent of the global population (equal to more than 3 billion people) will live on less than $6.85 per day—an 8-percentage-point decline in a decade—and less than 20 percent will have less than $3.65 per day. This means that poverty at the higher lines is projected to decline at rates similar to the ones achieved in the beginning of this century, while progress in reducing extreme poverty is slowing significantly. This projection reflects several factors, including differences in where the poor at the various lines live and the associated countries' projected growth rates over the next half-decade.

If growth continues to be slow and inequality continues to stagnate or even increase, reaching a global extreme poverty rate of 3 percent will be a lengthy endeavor. In 2023, GDP per capita grew only by 1 percent in low-income countries, and it is expected to rise to only 2.5 percent in 2025. One-third of low-income countries is projected to have lower per capita incomes in 2026 than in 2019 (World Bank 2024d). Under the current forecast scenario—currently projected GDP per capita growth rates until 2029 and historical growth rates thereafter—extreme poverty will not change much between 2030 and 2050 (figure 1.3, panel a). This is due largely to high poverty rates and slow projected and historical growth in Sub-Saharan Africa. If per capita growth were to reach 2 percent annually in every country, extreme poverty would still be almost twice as high in 2050 as the 3 percent goal for 2030, and it would not reach the 3 percent goal for another 60 years. Even with a 4 percent growth rate, which seems out of reach for many countries, it would take until 2048 to reach 3 percent—two decades after the goal of 2030.

In the current slow-growth environment, the projections show the importance and potential of reducing inequality to accelerate progress. If the Gini index in every country were to decrease by 2 percent annually in addition to 2 percent growth, the extreme poverty rate would fall to 2 percent in 2050, compared to about 5.7 percent without changes in inequality (see chapter 2 for more information on the Gini index).

Poverty rates at $6.85 are projected to fall faster under the current forecast scenario than extreme poverty rates because of higher historical growth rates in East Asia and Pacific and in South Asia (figure 1.3, panel b). Still, it would take more than a century to reach a poverty rate of less than 3 percent at $6.85 per day. According to the current forecast, 26 percent of the global population would remain below the upper poverty line in 2050, which is not very different from the scenario of 4 percent per year.

FIGURE 1.3

Projections of poverty until 2050 under different scenarios

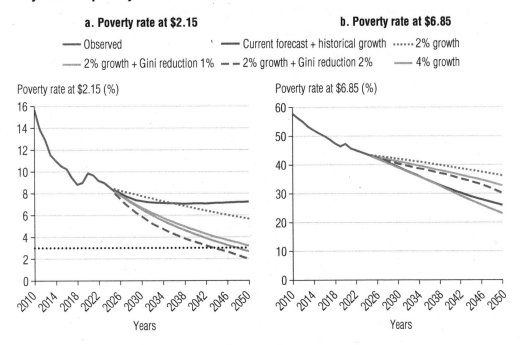

a. Poverty rate at $2.15

b. Poverty rate at $6.85

— Observed   — Current forecast + historical growth   ⋯⋯ 2% growth
— 2% growth + Gini reduction 1%   − − 2% growth + Gini reduction 2%   — 4% growth

Poverty rate at $2.15 (%)

Poverty rate at $6.85 (%)

Years   Years

Sources: World Bank calculations using data from the Poverty and Inequality Platform (version September 2024), https://pip.worldbank.org; World Bank 2024d; World Bank 2024e; IMF 2024.

Note: Poverty rates are reported for the $2.15 and $6.85 per person per day poverty lines (expressed in 2017 purchasing power parity dollars). Poverty rates are projected after 2022 based on country-level growth in gross domestic product per capita. "Current forecast + historical growth" is based on growth projections in the *Global Economic Prospects, June 2024* (World Bank 2024d), complemented by the *Macro Poverty Outlook* (World Bank 2024e) and the *World Economic Outlook* (IMF 2024) until 2029 and average annual per capita historical growth rates (2010–19) thereafter (see annex 1A for more details). Inequality reduction scenarios refer to a reduction in the country-level Gini index by 1 percent or 2 percent annually. The horizontal dotted line indicates a poverty rate of 3 percent.

Poverty has been increasingly concentrated in Sub-Saharan Africa and fragile settings, but it is more widespread at higher poverty lines

Sub-Saharan Africa is home to two-thirds of the global extreme poor and 9 of the 10 countries with the highest extreme poverty rates in the world as of 2024.[3] While Sub-Saharan Africa accounts for 16 percent of the world's population, it is home to 67 percent of the global population living in extreme poverty (see table 1D3 in annex 1D). The regional distribution of poverty changes depending on the standard, but overall, most poor people are concentrated in Sub-Saharan Africa and South Asia (figure 1.4). South Asia accounts for one-fifth of the global extreme poor, roughly in line with its global population share (one-quarter).

FIGURE 1.4

The regional distribution of poverty changes depending on the standard, but overall, most poor people are concentrated in Sub-Saharan Africa and South Asia

a. Extreme poverty ($2.15 per person per day) is concentrated in Sub-Saharan Africa

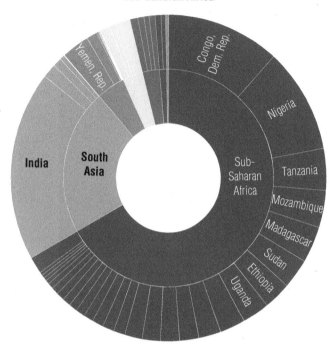

b. Poverty at the $3.65 line is concentrated in Sub-Saharan Africa and South Asia

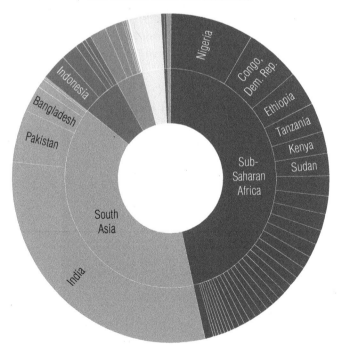

(continued)

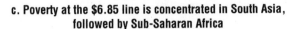

FIGURE 1.4

The regional distribution of poverty changes depending on the standard, but overall, most poor people are concentrated in Sub-Saharan Africa and South Asia *(continued)*

c. Poverty at the $6.85 line is concentrated in South Asia, followed by Sub-Saharan Africa

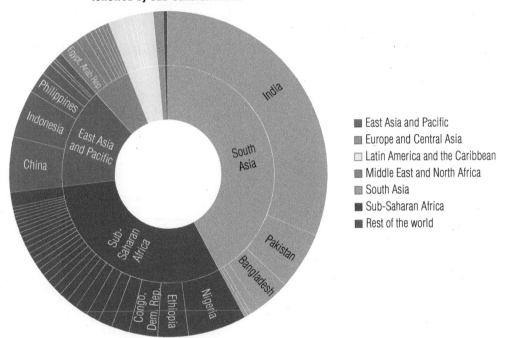

Legend:
- East Asia and Pacific
- Europe and Central Asia
- Latin America and the Caribbean
- Middle East and North Africa
- South Asia
- Sub-Saharan Africa
- Rest of the world

Source: World Bank, Poverty and Inequality Platform (version September 2024), https://pip.worldbank.org.

Note: Figures show the composition of poverty at the $2.15, $3.65, and $6.85 per person per day poverty lines (expressed in 2017 purchasing power parity dollars). In all figures, the inner ring shows the share of the total number of poor living in a particular region, and the outer ring refers to the shares by country. The 10 countries with the most poor people are labeled.

Extreme poverty has been concentrated not only in Sub-Saharan Africa but also in fragile and conflict-affected situations (FCS). In 2000, only one-quarter of the extreme poor was living in a country in Sub-Saharan Africa or one that was fragile (see figure 1.6, panel a). However, by 2014, every second person in extreme poverty was in either Sub-Saharan Africa or FCS. The share of extreme poor in FCS in Sub-Saharan Africa then grew starkly in the late 2010s, driven by countries with large poor populations becoming fragile, such as Niger and Nigeria. By 2024, the share of the extreme poor in Sub-Saharan Africa or FCS had increased to three-quarters, and 42 percent of the global extreme poor was in FCS in Sub-Saharan Africa.[4]

At higher poverty lines, poverty becomes less concentrated. South Asia accounts for the largest share of the poor at the $6.85 poverty line (figure 1.4, panel b). Of the global population with less than $6.85 per day, 42 percent live in South Asia, 32 percent in Sub-Saharan Africa, and 15 percent in East Asia and Pacific. About one-quarter of the populations in Latin America and the Caribbean and in East Asia and Pacific is living on less than $6.85 per day in 2024 (figure 1.5, panel b). Around three-quarters of the population in South Asia and almost the entire regional population in Sub-Saharan Africa (87 percent) live below this higher poverty line. At the higher poverty standard of $6.85, the share of Sub-Saharan Africa and FCS has also increased, but it is still less than 50 percent (figure 1.6, panel b).

FIGURE 1.5

Poverty forecasts through 2030 by region

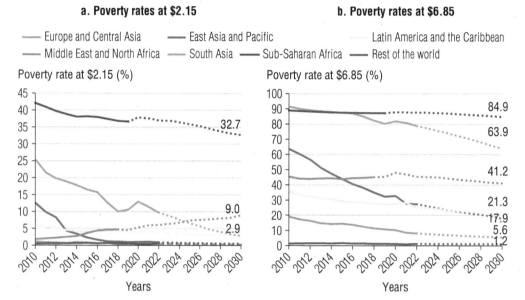

a. Poverty rates at $2.15

b. Poverty rates at $6.85

— Europe and Central Asia   — East Asia and Pacific   ⋯ Latin America and the Caribbean
— Middle East and North Africa   — South Asia   — Sub-Saharan Africa   — Rest of the world

Source: World Bank, Poverty and Inequality Platform (version September 2024), https://pip.worldbank.org.
Note: Poverty rates are reported for the $2.15 and $6.85 per person per day poverty lines (expressed in 2017 purchasing power parity dollars). Between 2022 and 2029 poverty is projected based on per capita gross domestic product growth projections in *Global Economic Prospects, June 2024* (World Bank 2024d), complemented by the *Macro Poverty Outlook* (World Bank 2024e) and the *World Economic Outlook* (IMF 2024); for 2030, average annual historic per capita growth rates (2010–19) are used. In Sub-Saharan Africa and in the Middle East and North Africa, surveys cover less than 50 percent of the population after 2019 and 2018, respectively. See annex 1A for more details on the projections.

The Middle East and North Africa and Sub-Saharan Africa are the two regions where extreme poverty is not projected to be eradicated by 2030

While poverty is projected to fall in Sub-Saharan Africa, progress will not be nearly fast enough to eradicate extreme poverty by 2030. About one in three people in Sub-Saharan Africa in 2030 is projected to still be living with less than $2.15 (figure 1.5, panel a). The Middle East and North Africa is the only region that has seen a reversal in poverty eradication. In 2014, the Middle East and North Africa had almost eradicated poverty, with an extreme poverty rate of less than 3 percent. Post-2014, slow economic growth, limited job creation, increased fragility and conflict, inflation, and other shocks such as the pandemic led to a reversal in that progress (Gatti et al. 2023; World Bank 2024d). Extreme poverty in the Middle East and North Africa is projected to continue to rise to 2030 (figure 1.5, panel a).

FIGURE 1.6

Increased concentration of extreme poverty in Sub-Saharan Africa and fragile and conflict-affected situations

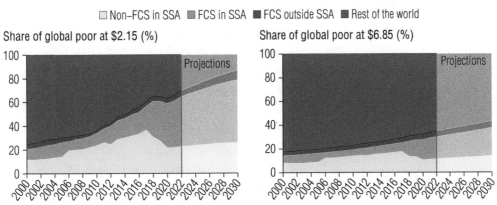

a. Share of poor at $2.15
b. Share of poor at $6.85

□ Non–FCS in SSA ■ FCS in SSA ■ FCS outside SSA ■ Rest of the world

Source: World Bank, Poverty and Inequality Platform (version September 2024), https://pip.worldbank.org.
Note: FCS = fragile and conflict-affected situations; SSA = Sub-Saharan Africa. Poverty rates are reported for the $2.15 and $6.85 per person per day poverty lines (expressed in 2017 purchasing power parity dollars). Countries in FCS are defined following the World Bank classification of fragile and conflict-affected situations for each year until 2022, and keeping the definition fixed in 2022 for the years after. Between 2022 and 2029 poverty is projected based on per capita gross domestic product growth projections in *Global Economic Prospects, June 2024* (World Bank 2024d), complemented by the *Macro Poverty Outlook, Spring Meetings 2024* (World Bank 2024e) and *World Economic Outlook* (IMF 2024); for 2030, average annual historic per capita growth rates are used. See annex 1A for more details on the projections. Surveys cover less than 50 percent of the population for Sub-Saharan Africa after 2019, and for countries in FCS in 2000 and after 2017.

Regional trajectories of poverty using the higher poverty line of $6.85 per day are also expected to diverge (figure 1.5, panel b). Globally, 39 percent of the population is projected to live below that line in 2030. In Sub-Saharan Africa, only 15 percent of the population will have levels of daily consumption greater than $6.85. In South Asia, poverty rates will continue to fall faster, widening the gap with Sub-Saharan Africa, but 64 percent of the population is still projected to be poor by this standard in 2030. The forecasts show that East Asia and Pacific as well as Europe and Central Asia will continue to make progress, while in Latin America and the Caribbean and the Middle East and North Africa reductions in poverty will be small.

The concentration of extreme poverty in fragile countries and Sub-Saharan Africa will continue

The concentration of poverty in Sub-Saharan Africa and FCS is forecasted to intensify (figure 1.6). By 2030, one-half of the global extreme poor will be in today's FCS within Sub-Saharan Africa, and another one-quarter is projected to be in countries in Sub-Saharan Africa that are not in FCS today. Effectively, the relative concentrations of extreme poverty in FCS or Sub-Saharan Africa versus in non-FCS and non-Sub-Saharan Africa will have reversed over the course of three decades. The share of poor in FCS and/or Sub-Saharan Africa will have grown from one-quarter to more than four-fifths.

To eradicate extreme poverty, global support for FCS and Sub-Saharan Africa will be key. People in FCS face numerous challenges that could potentially perpetuate their experience of poverty, including violence, displacement, limited access to basic services, food insecurity, limited opportunities for income generation, and adverse institutional and macroeconomic environments (Evans 2009; FAO-WFP 2019; Keho 2009; Lukunka and Grundy 2020; Mueller and Tobias 2016). Conflict not only has immediate detrimental impacts on human lives, infrastructure and business activity, it also hinders long-term progress by adversely affecting human capital and productivity (Corral et al. 2020; World Bank 2024h).

The changing regional composition of poverty partly explains the role of economic growth behind past gains and current stagnation in poverty reduction

A longer-term view shows that extreme poverty fell significantly between 1990 and 2013, but progress has slowed dramatically since then. From 1990 to 2013, the rate dropped from 37.9 to 11.5 percent (figure 1.1, panel a; figure 1.7, panel a) and 1.2 billion people exited extreme poverty (figure 1.7, panel c). Thereafter, the pace of reduction slowed—even before the COVID-19 pandemic hit (World Bank 2020). From 2013 to 2018, the extreme poverty rate decreased by only 2.8 percentage points. From 2018 on, the trend even reversed.

A large factor that explains the slowing of global poverty reduction over the last decade is the changing regional composition of poverty (see figure 1.7, panels a and c). In 1990, East Asia and Pacific had a higher poverty rate than Sub-Saharan Africa, and South Asia had rates not very different from those of Sub-Saharan Africa. This picture changed markedly over the years. Fueled by rapid growth, East Asia and Pacific experienced historic progress on poverty that also drove the reduction at the global level. Until 2013, global extreme poverty reduction was led by China's rapid economic growth, which lifted more than 800 million people out of extreme poverty over three decades (figure 1.7, panel c). The rest of East Asia also made remarkable progress, with 210 million people exiting extreme poverty between 1990 and 2024. Moreover, in South Asia (excluding India) the number of extreme poor fell significantly, from 141 to 20 million, over the same period, despite recent stagnation. In India alone, the number of extremely poor people fell from 431 million to 129 million over this period.

Since the early 2010s, progress in reducing global extreme poverty has depended to a much greater extent on Sub-Saharan Africa than it did before. Although the extreme poverty rate in Sub-Saharan Africa has fallen over the past three decades, it did so at much lower rates than in other regions, and not fast enough relative to population growth. Hence, the number of people living in extreme poverty in the region has increased by almost 200 million, rising from 282 million in 1990 to 464 million in 2024. Similarly, in the Middle East and North Africa, the number of people living in extreme poverty doubled, from 15 million in 1990 to 30 million in 2024. Extreme poverty in that region has surged since 2014, driven by fragility, conflict, and inflation (Gatti et al. 2023).

At the higher poverty standard of $6.85, the 1990s were a period of stagnation. Thereafter, however, the poverty rate at this level also declined sharply, falling from 69.0 to 43.6 percent between 2000 and 2024. This staggered picture is explained largely by China's progress in moving people out of extreme poverty before they could later cross the $6.85 poverty line (figure 1.7, panel d). In East Asia and Pacific as a whole, the poverty rate in 2024 was one-fourth of the level in 1990 (figure 1.7, panel b). Latin America and the Caribbean and South Asia have also experienced declines, although progress has stalled more recently. Despite this progress in the percentage of people below the $6.85 line, due to high population growth, the number of people living on less than that has barely changed, declining by about 130 million between 1990 and 2024 (figure 1.1, panel b). In India, there are more people living on less than $6.85 in 2024 than in 1990, driven by population growth. The same is true for South Asia as a whole and also for Sub-Saharan Africa and the Middle East and North Africa. While many people in East Asia and Pacific have moved from below $6.85 to above it, shifts in South Asia were concentrated from below $2.15 to between $2.15 and $6.85 (figure 1.7, panel d). See annex 1C for regional poverty estimates for selected years in the period 1990–2024.

FIGURE 1.7

Regional disparities in poverty reduction

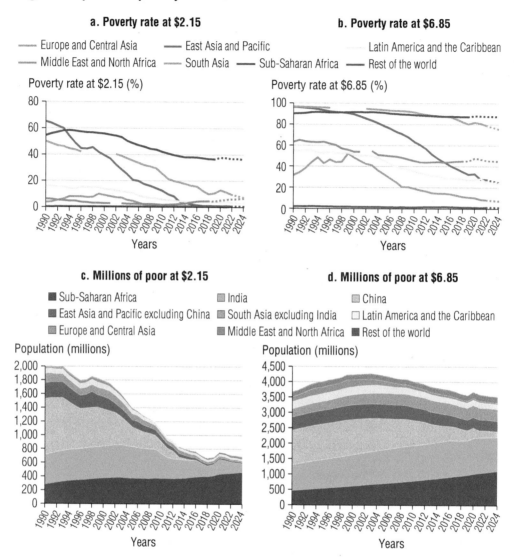

a. Poverty rate at $2.15

— Europe and Central Asia — East Asia and Pacific
— Middle East and North Africa — South Asia — Sub-Saharan Africa

b. Poverty rate at $6.85

Latin America and the Caribbean
— Rest of the world

Poverty rate at $2.15 (%)

Poverty rate at $6.85 (%)

Years

Years

c. Millions of poor at $2.15

d. Millions of poor at $6.85

■ Sub-Saharan Africa ■ India ▫ China
■ East Asia and Pacific excluding China ■ South Asia excluding India ▫ Latin America and the Caribbean
▫ Europe and Central Asia ■ Middle East and North Africa ■ Rest of the world

Population (millions)

Population (millions)

Years

Years

Source: World Bank, Poverty and Inequality Platform (version September 2024), https://pip.worldbank.org.
Note: Poverty rates are reported for the $2.15 and $6.85 per person per day poverty lines (expressed in 2017 purchasing power parity dollars). In panels c and d, millions of poor from South Asia and East Asia and Pacific do not include numbers from India and China, respectively, which are shown separately. Poverty rates for 2022–24 are projected based on per capita gross domestic product growth projections in *Global Economic Prospects* (IMF 2024). See annex 1A for more details on the projections. Discontinuity in the series in panels a and b indicates years with insufficient data coverage (that is, survey data do not cover at least 50 percent of the population). More recent estimates for Sub-Saharan Africa and the Middle East and North Africa are projections shown with dotted lines, as survey data do not cover at least 50 percent of the population after 2019 and 2018, respectively. To obtain the global count of millions of poor, panels c and d include all regional estimates of the millions of poor, whether or not there is data coverage.

Reigniting economic growth and making it more inclusive are key to eradicating poverty

Economic growth has been a key factor behind poverty reduction and the differential progress across regions (Bergstrom 2022; Kraay 2006; Lakner et al. 2022). Figure 1.8 shows that high economic growth is strongly linked to rapid reduction in extreme poverty in 39 countries with poverty data that were designated low-income countries in 1990.[5] Notably, China has recorded the highest annual growth rate (exceeding 9 percent) and has virtually eradicated extreme poverty. In general, countries in East Asia and Pacific and South Asia have shown higher rates of economic growth and poverty reduction than those in Sub-Saharan Africa.

FIGURE 1.8

Economic growth has been an important driver of extreme poverty reduction

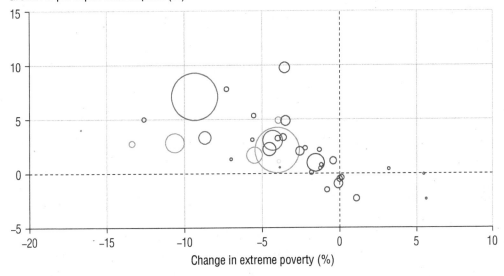

Sources: World Bank, Poverty and Inequality Platform (PIP) (version September 2024), https://pip.worldbank.org; World Development Indicators database.

Note: This chart plots the annualized growth rate in per capita consumption (or income) against the annualized change in extreme poverty (living on less than $2.15 per person per day expressed in 2017 purchasing power parity dollars) using the longest comparable spell for each country in the PIP. The first and last survey years in the longest comparable spell vary by country. The countries represented here were designated as low-income countries in 1990 (and have survey data in PIP). The Arab Republic of Egypt and Myanmar are outliers and are not included for presentational purposes. The size of the marker is proportional to population size in the second survey year. For details on survey comparability, see https://datanalytics.worldbank.org/PIP-Methodology/welfareaggregate.html#comparability.

The same level of economic growth need not translate into the same level of poverty reduction (Kakwani and Pernia 2000; Lakner et al. 2022; Ravallion 2004). Countries differ in their ability to translate economic growth into poverty reduction. A fundamental nexus between growth and poverty reduction is the labor market and labor incomes. In many settings where poverty is stagnating, the labor market has not been able to deliver more and better jobs.[6]

An important factor to enhance the impact of economic growth on poverty reduction is the level of inequality. Chapter 2 of this report discusses in greater detail the role of inequality in efforts to boost shared prosperity around the world. Relative measures of poverty, such as the World Bank's societal poverty measure, are another way to capture these distributional concerns. As explained in more detail in box 1.4, poverty is assessed largely against absolute lines that are held fixed across countries and over time. In contrast, a relative poverty line increases in tandem with average income. To reduce relative poverty, growth needs to reduce inequality.

BOX 1.4

Progress in societal poverty has stagnated since 2020

The poverty lines of \$2.15, \$3.65, and \$6.85 per person per day (expressed in 2017 purchasing power parity dollars) used in this report are absolute measures, which are fixed in real terms for all countries over time. As highlighted in box 1.1, the definition of what it means to be poor evolves as countries get richer, which motivated the introduction of the \$6.85 line in the World Bank's vision alongside the extreme poverty line (World Bank, n.d.). Applying the same idea more broadly suggests that poverty lines should vary across countries, as well as over time for a particular country. Since 2018, the World Bank has been monitoring the societal poverty line, which is a weakly relative poverty line that increases with a country's income once countries move beyond an income level where extreme poverty is the primary concern (Jolliffe and Prydz 2021; World Bank 2018).[a] A decline in relative poverty requires that the poorest parts of the population within a country grow faster than average income, leading to a reduction in inequality.

Progress in societal poverty has been slower than the changes at the absolute lines (see figure B1.4.1, panel a). This is as expected, because the societal poverty line is a stricter assessment of poverty in growing economies than the absolute poverty lines. The societal poverty line is more relevant for assessing poverty in higher-income countries and regions. Figure B1.4.1, panel b, shows quite different distributions of poverty across regions, depending on the poverty line used. In particular, the distribution of global poverty is more even across regional groups when the societal poverty line is used.

(continued)

BOX 1.4

Progress in societal poverty has stagnated since 2020 *(continued)*

FIGURE B1.4.1

Societal poverty line

a. Global poverty trends

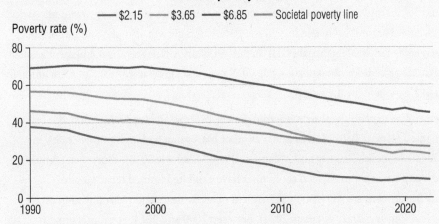

b. Share of global poor by region, 2022

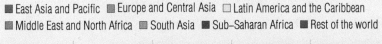

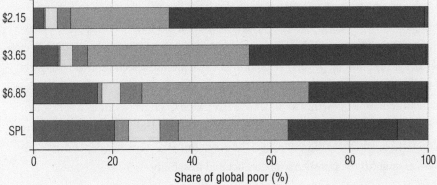

Source: World Bank, Poverty and Inequality Platform (PIP, version September 2024), https://pip.worldbank.org.
Note: SPL = societal poverty line. The poverty lines of $2.15, $3.65, $6.85, and the SPL are per person per day (expressed in 2017 purchasing power parity dollars).

a. The measure was introduced following the recommendation of the Atkinson Commission on Global Poverty to "introduce a societal headcount ratio measure of global consumption poverty" (World Bank 2017, 144). The societal poverty line is defined as $1.15 plus half the median level of consumption or income, with the international poverty line of $2.15 as a floor (Jolliffe et al. 2022). By construction, $2.15 is the societal poverty line as long as the median level of consumption or income is less than $2 per person per day, which applies only to the poorest countries. For example, considering two low-income countries, Burundi had a median consumption of $1.80 (2020–21), compared with $3.10 (2021–22) for Burkina Faso. The relative component of the societal poverty line applies to countries with levels of consumption exceeding $2.

To eradicate extreme poverty, Sub-Saharan Africa will need to accelerate economic growth and make it more pro-poor

In Sub-Saharan Africa, economic growth has been historically slower than in other regions, and the outlook is not promising. While progress in poverty reduction is highly varied across countries in Sub-Saharan Africa (see figure 1.8), the region is a systemically low-growth environment, especially since 2015 (Wu et al. 2024). Much of the progress in poverty reduction in East Asia and Pacific and South Asia has been driven by high rates of income growth, rates which Sub-Saharan Africa has not been able to achieve. Population growth also plays an important role: between 1990 and 2022, aggregate GDP in Sub-Saharan Africa grew by 3.4 percent annually (compared to 2.9 percent for the world), while GDP per capita grew only by 0.7 percent annually (compared to 1.6 percent for the world).

Various factors may explain the slow economic growth in Sub-Saharan Africa. First, the region has not benefited from globalization as much as other places that had high poverty rates, in particular Asian countries (Lakner and Milanovic 2016; Milanovic 2016). Moreover, compared to other regions, Sub-Saharan African economies have exhibited limited technological change (World Bank 2024b) and are still heavily dependent on agriculture and natural resources (Thorbecke and Ouyang 2022; Wu et al. 2024). Between 2000 and 2014, economic growth on the continent was driven by the use of natural capital rather than rising levels of productivity (World Bank 2024a). Per capita income growth in Sub-Saharan Africa is expected to remain at a meager 1.5 percent in 2025, further dampening prospects of poverty reduction (World Bank 2024d).

In addition to being slower, economic growth has also been less pro-poor in Sub-Saharan Africa. The impact of economic growth on poverty reduction has been limited, particularly because of high levels of inequality (Bourguignon 2003; Klasen and Misselhorn 2008; Wu et al. 2024). Wu et al. (2024) find that poverty reduction in the region has been limited because of factors that constrain the productive capacity of the poor and their ability to generate income and contribute to economic growth. Examples of such factors include (a) limited access to education, which hinders the accumulation of human capital; (b) lack of basic infrastructure (electricity, sanitation, and drinking water); (c) the economic structure and dependence on natural resources; and (d) the prevalence of conflict and instability.

Reducing poverty requires focusing on job creation and investing in the productive capacity of people

The 1990 *World Development Report* highlighted that the most effective ways to improve the lives of the poor are by (a) promoting growth that uses labor, the poor's most abundant asset, and (b) ensuring widespread access to basic social services, particularly primary education and health care (World Bank 1990). These priorities are still appropriate more than 30 years later and are even more urgent given the losses in human capital due to COVID-19. Enabling the poor to benefit more from economic growth will require better-functioning labor markets (see box 1.5) and substantial investments in the productive capacity of people. Key areas include more education, basic infrastructure, and economic diversification, as well as a progressive income and property taxation that reduces inequality and raises domestic revenue (Lakner et al. 2022; Wu et al. 2024).

BOX 1.5
Better labor markets for poverty reduction

The private sector creates jobs.[a] The roles of government are to ensure that the conditions are in place for strong private sector–led growth, to analyze job market conditions and outcomes, and to remove or mitigate the constraints that prevent the creation of more and better jobs. Government can fulfill these roles by ensuring that the fundamental aspects of macroeconomic stability, the business environment, and rule of law are in place.

In addition, governments can help set priorities to increase the ability of the labor market to create jobs. As economies evolve and new challenges emerge, so too must the policies aimed at fostering employment, ensuring that they remain relevant and effective over time. This dynamic nature of policy design allows for the anticipation of future labor market trends and to preemptively address potential obstacles to job creation and improvements in job quality. Effective job strategies, leading to sustained labor productivity enhancements that are essential for fostering economic growth, reducing poverty, and ensuring inclusive outcomes in the long term, depend heavily on the following job transitions:

- *Sectoral Transition.* The transition from agriculture to nonagricultural sectors is vital for economic growth, accompanied by substantial productivity gaps. In low-income countries, the share of employment in nonagricultural sectors remains minor compared to that in high-income countries, highlighting the growth potential through sectoral transitions. **Removing structural barriers, such as improving access to credit and resolving land-tenure issues, can facilitate this transition.**

- *Spatial Transition.* The move from rural to urban areas is associated with higher wages and greater productivity, yet the share of urban workers in low-income countries is much lower than in high-income countries. **Addressing skill mismatches and improving rural education quality can enhance urban employment opportunities and thus support spatial transitions.**

- *Occupational Transition.* The high skill premium and the smaller share of skilled workers in low-income countries than in high-income countries suggest significant growth opportunities through occupational transitions. **Investing in education and training to increase the skilled labor supply is essential for meeting the demand in more productive sectors.**

(continued)

BOX 1.5

Better labor markets for poverty reduction *(continued)*

- *Organizational Transition.* Exporting activities, indicative of organizational transitions, are significantly more productive than nonexporting activities but involve only a small fraction of the workforce in lower-income countries. **Reducing the cost of formal employment and encouraging technology adoption can facilitate this transition, highlighting the productivity potential through organizational transition.**

Completing these job transitions is key to closing massive income gaps and combating poverty. Evidence suggests that poverty rates among workers are significantly lower on the advanced side of each transition, indicating that progress in these transitions can significantly reduce poverty rates by shifting people to more productive activities.[b]

a. See World Bank (2012) and references therein.
b. For more information, see https://datatopics.worldbank.org/jobsdiagnostics/.

These elements are important not only to raise incomes but also to reduce the risk of people falling back into poverty. Even though the distribution of incomes has changed significantly since 1990, a significant share of the population continues to live close to the poverty lines discussed in this chapter (figure 1.9, panels a and b). With 50 percent of the global population living below or close to the two poverty lines, even small shocks can push many people back into poverty. For example, in 2014, the Middle East and North Africa had almost eradicated extreme poverty, but in 2030 almost 1 in 10 people in the region is projected to live in extreme poverty. Globally, the COVID-19 pandemic pushed about 73 million people into extreme poverty in a single year. While the pandemic was a global shock, the impacts and the ability to recover were not the same for people with different household characteristics such as their location, demographics, employment, and levels of incomes, among other factors.

FIGURE 1.9

Income levels in the world have grown between 1990 and 2024, but many people remain vulnerable to falling back into poverty

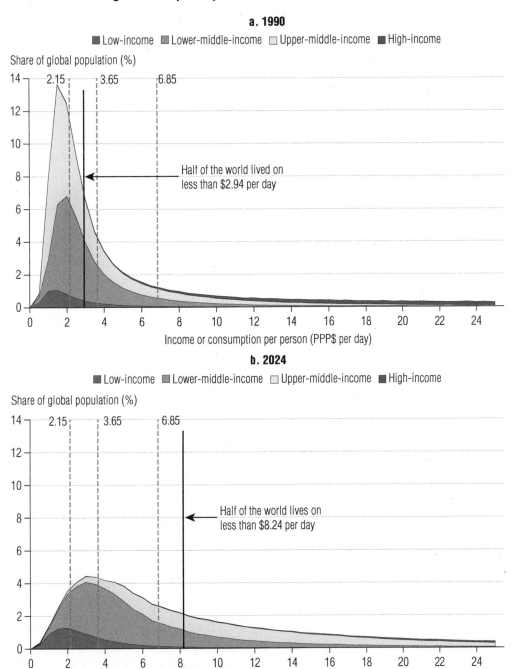

a. 1990

■ Low-income   ■ Lower-middle-income   □ Upper-middle-income   ■ High-income

Share of global population (%)

Half of the world lived on less than $2.94 per day

Income or consumption per person (PPP$ per day)

b. 2024

■ Low-income   ■ Lower-middle-income   □ Upper-middle-income   ■ High-income

Share of global population (%)

Half of the world lives on less than $8.24 per day

Income or consumption per person (PPP$ per day)

Source: World Bank, Poverty and Inequality Platform (version September 2024), https://pip.worldbank.org.
Note: This figure shows the distribution of the population over income or consumption levels in 1990 and 2024, cut off at $25 per person per day and expressed in 2017 purchasing power parity dollars (PPP$). More than 86 percent of the global population lived below the $25 per person per day threshold in 1990, and about 80 percent live under the threshold in 2024.

Profile of the global poor: People living in poverty typically live in rural areas and are younger and less educated

To inform policies that target the poor with the aim of raising incomes and enhancing resilience, it is key to understand the spatial and demographic profile of the population living in poverty at different levels and the extent of multidimensional poverty. The remainder of this chapter presents this evidence, using harmonized data to provide a global perspective.

This section profiles the global poor in terms of where they live, as well as their age and educational attainment. The analysis spans up to 152 countries with microdata from or around 2022, the latest year with sufficient data coverage. The data represent 87 percent of the world's population.[7] The spatial and demographic profiles of the poor at both the $2.15 poverty line (extreme poverty line) and the $6.85 poverty line are presented.

Global poverty estimates, and hence the profiling of the global poor, assume an equal allocation of resources within households, regardless of the age and gender composition of these households. That is, a household's poverty status is defined if per capita household income or consumption falls below the poverty line and all individuals living in a poor (nonpoor) household are counted as individually poor (nonpoor) as well. However, the costs of basic needs differ for children and adults, and within-household inequality can be traced back to individuals' age and gender (Bargain, Lacroix, and Tiberti 2022; World Bank 2018). Given that the within-household inequality, particularly between men and women, is not observable with the data at hand, the breakdowns by gender are not reported here.[8] In addition, poverty estimates ignore potential economies of scale benefits at the household level. Larger households typically enjoy economies of scale in consumption because goods such as housing or consumer durables can be shared within the household, leading to an overestimation of poverty for children and rural areas (Jolliffe and Tetteh-Baah 2024; Salmeron-Gomez et al. 2023).

Extreme poverty in rural areas remains high, but a large share of the poor lives in urban areas

More than three-quarters of the global extreme poor lived in rural areas in 2022, and half of the global extreme poor lived in rural Sub-Saharan Africa alone (figure 1.10, panel a).[9] In nearly all regions, the rate of extreme poverty is higher in rural areas than urban areas, with rural poverty at 16 percent and urban poverty at 5 percent for the world as a whole (see figure 1.10, panel c). The difference between rural and urban poverty is most pronounced in Sub-Saharan Africa, where the rural poverty rate is 46 percent and the urban poverty rate is 20 percent.

Comparison of rural and urban poverty rates, 2022

a. Share of global poor at $2.15

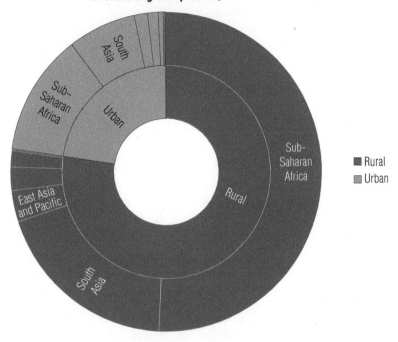

b. Share of global poor at $6.85

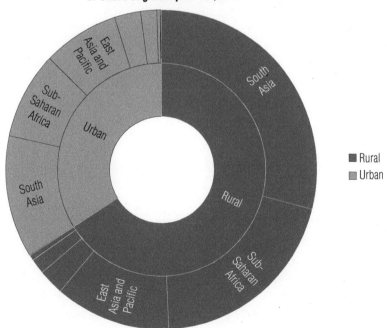

(continued)

FIGURE 1.10

Comparison of rural and urban poverty rates, 2022 *(continued)*

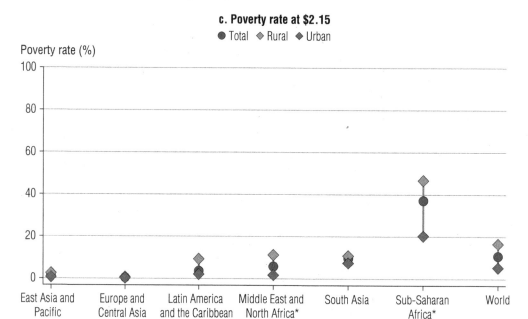

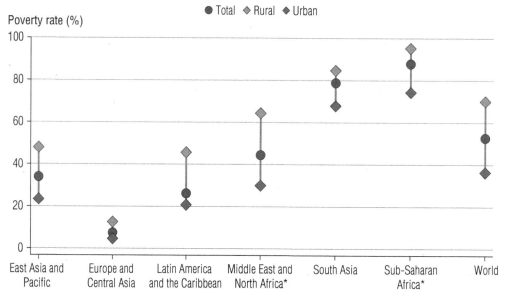

Source: World Bank, Global Monitoring Database (GMD) (version September 2024).

Note: Poverty rates are reported for the $2.15 and $6.85 per person per day poverty lines (expressed in 2017 purchasing power parity dollars). In panels a and b, selected regions are labeled. In panels c and d, estimates are not reported for the rest of the world, where poverty rates are low and there may be only a few observations for population subgroups.

*For the Middle East and North Africa and Sub-Saharan Africa, the recent survey data do not cover at least 50 percent of the population.

At the $6.85 poverty line, both rural and urban poverty rates are higher, as expected; however, importantly, rural-urban poverty gaps are larger in nearly all regions (figure 1.10, panel d). The absolute difference in rural and urban poverty rates is most pronounced in East Asia and Pacific and in Latin America and the Caribbean (around 25 percentage points each), especially compared with South Asia (17 percentage points). Globally, the difference in the rural and urban poverty rates is 35 percentage points at the $6.85 poverty line, compared to 11 percentage points at the $2.15 extreme poverty line. Poverty is still largely a rural phenomenon at the higher poverty line, but from a global point of view it is less concentrated in rural areas than extreme poverty. This is explained largely by the large share of the extreme poor in Sub-Saharan Africa who live in rural areas. At the $6.85 poverty line, 66 percent of the global poor lived in rural areas in 2022 (figure 1.10, panel b).

Against this background, rural populations need to be in the focus of poverty reduction efforts, especially in Sub-Saharan Africa and South Asia, particularly when extreme poverty is addressed. Yet urban areas cannot be ignored since that is where around a third of the global poor lives (according to the $6.85 line).

Poverty rates vary greatly across subnational areas

The Global Subnational Atlas of Poverty uses detailed survey data to capture regional differences in poverty within a country. Figure 1.11 shows the distribution of these subnational poverty rates, grouping countries by their income group. There is large variation among the subnational areas. While the median subnational area among lower-middle-income countries has a poverty rate of less than 10 percent, the poorest 5 percent of subnational areas have poverty rates exceeding 60 percent, well above the median among the low-income countries.

Similarly, there are also very poor subnational areas in upper-middle-income countries. For example, in some parts of Namibia, an upper-middle-income country, over 30 percent of the population lives on less than $2.15. The poorest areas in the country are sparsely populated and not well connected to the rest of the country. In South Africa, also an upper-middle-income country, the province Eastern Cape has a poverty rate of 36 percent, which is five times higher than the poverty rate in Western Cape and Gauteng and more similar to poverty rates in regions in Guinea-Bissau or Lesotho. In the capital region of Chad, only 3 percent of the population lives on less than $2.15, while the poverty rate of the whole country is 31 percent. Similar patterns are seen with the poverty line of $6.85, where some subnational areas in Latin America and the Caribbean or East Asia and Pacific show rates comparable to countries in Sub-Saharan Africa.

FIGURE 1.11

Distribution of subnational extreme poverty rates by income group, 2021

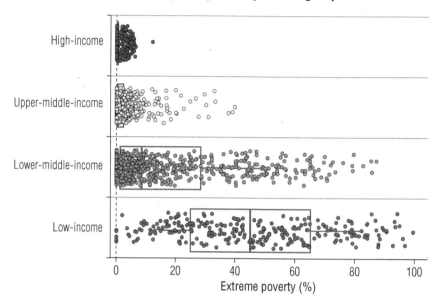

Sources: World Bank, Poverty and Inequality Platform (version September 2024), https://pip.worldbank.org; Global Subnational Atlas of Poverty (database).

Note: The extreme poverty rate reported for the $2.15 per person per day poverty line (expressed in 2017 purchasing power parity dollars). Each dot refers to one subnational area, which is assigned to income groups based on the country it is in. The boxes depict the interquartile range and the vertical line in each box depicts the respective median values. The lower whisker represents the 10th percentile, while the upper whisker represents the 90th percentile.

The poor still have large educational gaps, and COVID-19 increased the gaps for children

The 2022 data confirm the negative correlation between educational attainment and poverty. In nearly all regions of the world, the rate of extreme poverty declines with education (figure 1.12, panel a).[10] Among the population age 15 or above globally, one-fifth of those without any formal education lives in extreme poverty, while 3 percent of those with tertiary education lives in extreme poverty. These patterns are compounded by regional effects. Adults age 15 or above without formal education who live in Sub-Saharan Africa show the highest rate of extreme poverty at 39 percent, while only 0.6 percent of the same demographic group residing in Europe or Central Asia lives in extreme poverty. Tertiary education in Sub-Saharan Africa is associated with lower levels of extreme poverty, but it is still 9 percent—a rate comparable to that of secondary school graduates in South Asia or that of people having no formal education in Latin America and the Caribbean.

At the poverty line of $6.85, the gradient between educational attainment and poverty becomes even more pronounced across all regions. Around three-quarters of the population age 15 or above without any formal education lives on less than $6.85 a day (figure 1.12, panel b). Obtaining even primary education reduces the likelihood of living in poverty to 65 percent, and a secondary education further reduces it to 44 percent. About one-third of the population age 15 or above with tertiary education lives in poverty.

Focusing on closing education gaps is also a policy priority, given the significant educational losses due to the pandemic, particularly for the poor. School closures led to learning losses in language, literacy, and mathematics of around 30 percent in multiple countries. In 2021, in several countries a quarter of all young people were not in education, employment, or training (Schady et al. 2023). Poorer households were also less likely to use remote work and schooling (Narayan et al. 2022). Schooling disruptions affected poorer households more than richer ones. It is estimated that students in low- and lower-middle-income countries could face future earning losses of up to 10 percent due to the pandemic, suggesting a permanent scarring effect (Schady et al. 2023). This generation of students now risks losing $21 trillion in potential lifetime earnings in present value—the equivalent of 17 percent of today's global GDP (World Bank et al. 2022). The loss in schooling is likely to have a larger impact on poverty in the future than the immediate effect of the pandemic on poverty (Decerf et al. 2024).

Children and young adults are more likely to be living in poor households

Globally, 6 of 10 extremely poor people (living on less than $2.15 per day) are children or young adults.[11] In nearly all regions of the world, the share of children who live in extreme poverty is higher than the equivalent share for youth or adults (figure 1.13). More precisely, the extreme poverty rate for children is 17 percent, compared with about 12 percent for youth and 7 percent for adults (figure 1.13, panel a). In Sub-Saharan Africa, the region that drives the global estimates of extreme poverty, poverty rates for children and adults are 42 and 31 percent, respectively. At the poverty line of $6.85, while poverty rates are significantly higher across several regions, the poverty rate is still higher for children and youth than for adults. Sub-Saharan Africa and South Asia have similarly high poverty rates for the different age groups. Europe and Central Asia has the lowest poverty rates.

FIGURE 1.12

Percent of population living in poverty by educational attainment, 2022

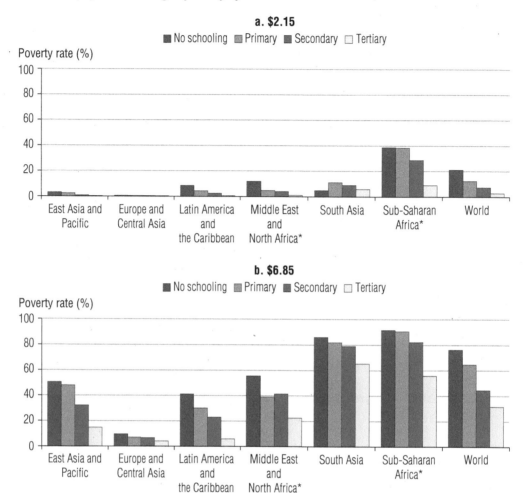

a. $2.15

■ No schooling ▨ Primary ■ Secondary □ Tertiary

Poverty rate (%)

b. $6.85

■ No schooling ▨ Primary ■ Secondary □ Tertiary

Poverty rate (%)

Source: World Bank, Global Monitoring Database (GMD) (version September 2024).

Note: Poverty rates are reported for the $2.15 and $6.85 per person per day poverty lines (expressed in 2017 purchasing power parity dollars). Estimates are based on population age 15 or above. Estimates are not reported for the rest of the world, where poverty rates are low and there might be few observations for some population subgroups. The extreme poverty rate in South Asia is driven by India, where less than 1 percent of the population age 15 or above have no formal education.

*For the Middle East and North Africa and Sub-Saharan Africa, the recent survey data do not cover at least 50 percent of the population.

FIGURE 1.13

Age profile of the poor, 2022

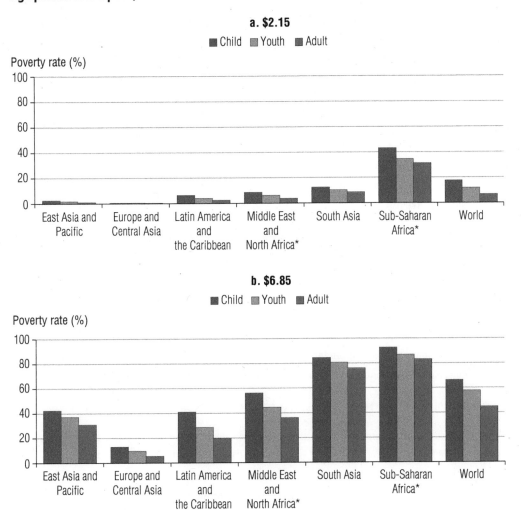

a. $2.15

■ Child ■ Youth ■ Adult

b. $6.85

■ Child ■ Youth ■ Adult

Source: World Bank, Global Monitoring Database (GMD) (version September 2024).
Note: Poverty rates are reported for the $2.15 and $6.85 per person per day poverty lines (expressed in 2017 purchasing power parity dollars). Estimates are not reported for the rest of the world, where poverty rates are low. Age cutoffs are defined as follows: child (<18), youth (15–24), adult (25+). Note that older children (ages 15–17) are included in both the child and youth categories.
*For the Middle East and North Africa and Sub-Saharan Africa, the recent survey data do not cover at least 50 percent of the population.

Poverty reduction policies should prioritize the well-being of children and young adults to give everyone a fair start in life, irrespective of parental resources. Poor households tend to have more children yet have limited financial resources to provide adequate nutrition and education for these children and give them a chance to have a better life in the future (Beegle, Dehejia, and Gatti 2003; Salmeron-Gomez et al. 2023). Young adults fare worse in the labor market, especially if they are women (Kabeer 2021; Mayer, Moorti, and McCallum 2019). Children and women are disproportionately affected by economic and climatic shocks and recover more slowly from such shocks (Escalante and Maisonnave 2023; World Bank 2023b). Beyond their intrinsic value to individual well-being, equal opportunities for young adults and women have instrumental benefits for the whole society (Mayer, Moorti, and McCallum 2019; Mitra, Bang, and Biswas 2015).

Multidimensional poverty broadens the understanding of poverty to guide actions

The World Bank's Multidimensional Poverty Measure (MPM), which was first published in 2018, seeks to provide a broader view of poverty by assessing deprivations across multiple dimensions of well-being to understand poverty beyond monetary deprivation (World Bank 2018). Deprivations in nonmonetary and nonmarket dimensions, such as access to schooling and basic infrastructure, compound poverty and perpetuate cycles of inequality.

A person is considered multidimensionally poor if their consumption is below the extreme poverty line of $2.15 per day or if they live in a household with too many deprivations in education and basic infrastructure. More precisely, the household is considered deprived in education if there is at least one school-age child who is not enrolled in school or if no adult in the household has completed primary education. For basic infrastructure, a household is considered deprived if it lacks access to drinking water, sanitation, or electricity.[12] Therefore, a country's MPM is at least as high as its monetary poverty, but it may be considerably higher, reflecting the additional role of nonmonetary dimensions to impoverishing households.

About 1 in 10 people globally is multidimensionally poor

While it is difficult to compare multidimensional poverty over time, the multidimensional poverty rate has decreased from 14.7 percent in 2019 (World Bank 2022) to 13.4 percent in 2021, the most recent year reported here.[13] The slight reduction in multidimensional poverty, which is driven by the nonmonetary indicators, should be interpreted with caution, as the most recent estimate of 13.4 percent is based on limited recent data (table 1.1 indicates that only about one-third of the world's population had survey data in 2020 or later for estimating multidimensional poverty). Table 1.1 summarizes the different dimensions and indicators that make up the multidimensional poverty rate by region.[14] Estimating multidimensional poverty places greater demands on the data since several dimensions need to be observed for the same set of households. Therefore, the recently available data for several regions, as well as for the whole world, do not represent at least half of the population and are thus shaded gray.[15] This lack of data highlights the importance of improving the availability of multitopic household survey data, as discussed in more detail in chapter 4.

The regional differences in multidimensional poverty mirror those found for the extreme poverty line of $2.15, which is not surprising given that monetary deprivation is an important component in the construction of the MPM. The highest multidimensional poverty rate is found in Sub-Saharan Africa, where 52.6 percent of people face deprivation. In South Asia, multidimensional poverty is also significantly greater than monetary poverty, which is driven by low rates of educational enrollment and attainment, next to low access to sanitation.[16]

TABLE 1.1

Deprivations in educational attainment and access to basic infrastructure lift multidimensional poverty above the extreme poverty rate, 2021

Region	Deprivation rate (%)						Multidimensional poverty rate	Number of economies	Coverage (%)
	Educational attainment		Basic infrastructure						
	Monetary	Educational attainment	Educational enrollment	Electricity	Sanitation	Drinking water			
East Asia and Pacific	2	5	2	1	9	4	2.7	12	26
Europe and Central Asia	0	1	1	2	8	4	2.1	24	78
Latin America and the Caribbean	3	8	2	1	17	3	3.6	18	86
Middle East and North Africa	1	7	2	0	2	1	1.5	3	24
South Asia	4	15	18	6	23	5	11.2	6	11
Sub-Saharan Africa	39	29	18	46	59	29	52.6	24	31
Rest of the world	0	1	2	0	0	0	1.0	23	69
World	9	10	8	10	21	9	13.4	110	37
IDA countries	25	23	17	29	44	19	35.6	38	34
Countries in FCS	38	27	18	45	55	28	50.4	13	27

Source: World Bank, Global Monitoring Database (GMD) (version September 2024).

Note: FCS = fragile and conflict-affected situations; IDA = International Development Association. The table presents the multidimensional poverty rate and share of population deprived in each indicator by region and rest of the world for circa 2021. "Multidimensional poverty rate" is the share of the population in each region defined as multidimensionally poor. "Number of economies" is the number of economies in each region for which information is available in the window between 2018 and 2024, three years within the circa 2021 reporting year. The monetary poverty rate is based on the international poverty line of $2.15 per person per day (in 2017 purchasing power parity dollars). Regional and total estimates are population-weighted averages of survey year estimates for 110 economies and are not comparable with those presented in the previous section because of differences in country coverage. "Coverage" refers to the share of the population that is covered by a recent survey (in 2020 or later). Groupings with less than 50 percent coverage are shaded. The coverage rule applied to the estimates is identical to that used in the rest of the chapter. The absence of data for China and India reduces coverage for the East Asia and Pacific and South Asia regions, as well as the world.

Individuals in countries in FCS, Sub-Saharan Africa, and countries that are eligible for support from the IDA of World Bank are significantly more deprived along all dimensions of the MPM indicator than the average global citizen (figure 1.14). In all three groups, multidimensional poverty is significantly higher than monetary poverty alone (compare table 1.1). In Sub-Saharan Africa and countries in FCS, 40 percent or more of the population is deprived of access to electricity and sanitation. While differences from other countries in educational attainment and enrollment are smaller than in other dimensions, substantial gaps remain, particularly in attainment.

FIGURE 1.14

The poorest countries lag behind in many dimensions of multidimensional poverty in 2021

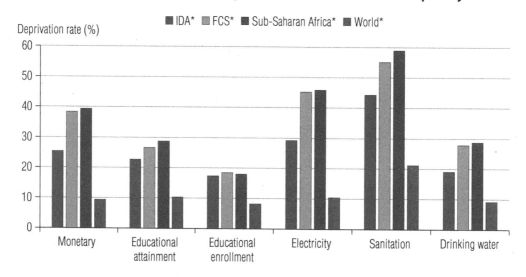

Source: World Bank, Global Monitoring Database (GMD) (version September 2024).
Note: FCS = fragile and conflict-affected situations; IDA = International Development Association. The figure presents the multidimensional poverty rate and share of population deprived for selected groupings and the world circa 2021, using the same data as in table 1.1. See table 1.1 and notes to table 1.1 for more details.
* Less than 50 percent of the population is covered with a recent survey (conducted in 2020 or later).

Especially in Sub-Saharan Africa countries, multidimensional poverty is considerably higher than monetary poverty alone

There can be significant differences in the poverty rate, depending on whether monetary deprivation alone or other dimensions are considered. In fact, figure 1.15 highlights that in some countries, multidimensional poverty is more than twice as high as monetary poverty at the $2.15 line. Most of these countries are in Sub-Saharan Africa, which is because the MPM, like the extreme poverty line, focuses on the most basic achievements. In other countries in Sub-Saharan Africa, such as Zambia and Zimbabwe, there is almost perfect overlap of the two measures, which is the case for those countries in figure 1.15 that lie on or near the 45-degree line.

In fact, there is considerable heterogeneity across countries in Sub-Saharan Africa when levels of monetary and multidimensional poverty are compared. With the same extreme poverty rate of 31 percent, Angola and Chad vary significantly in the MPM (47 and 81 percent, respectively).

When poverty is assessed across multiple dimensions, the poverty status of Chad is similar to that of countries such as Burundi and Malawi, where extreme poverty levels are above 60 percent. Angola, Benin, Guinea, and Mauritania also have similar levels of multidimensional poverty, with extreme poverty levels ranging from 5 to 31 percent.

Deprivation is multifaceted, and measuring poverty based solely on consumption may fall short of giving a comprehensive perspective on people's well-being. It may also fall short of connecting poverty alleviation to policy options that improve people's welfare even if they do not immediately raise consumption levels.

FIGURE 1.15

Higher rates of multidimensional poverty than monetary poverty, especially in Sub-Saharan Africa

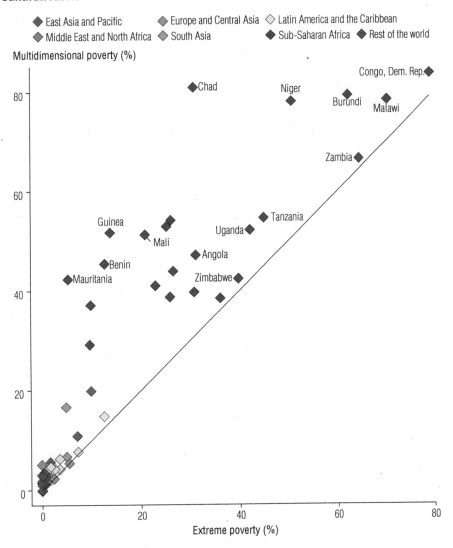

Source: World Bank, Global Monitoring Database (GMD) (version September 2024).
Note: Each marker represents a country in circa 2021. Extreme poverty is reported using the $2.15 per person per day poverty line (expressed in 2017 purchasing power parity dollars). See table 1.1 and notes to table 1.1. for more details on multidimensional poverty. The solid line is a 45-degree line.

Annex 1A. Methodology

Poverty and Inequality Platform data and methodology for the measurement of global poverty

Regional and global poverty rates are computed by estimating poverty in each country and aggregating across regions and for the world. Data for measuring poverty come from the World Bank's Poverty and Inequality Platform (PIP), which aggregates welfare data from country-level household surveys. The platform includes over 2,300 household surveys from 170 countries representing 97 percent of the world's population. Most of these surveys come from the Global Monitoring Database (GMD), which is described in more detail below. For this report, 297 more surveys have been added to the number used for the 2022 *Poverty and Shared Prosperity* report (World Bank 2022). This improvement in survey data coverage has made it possible to report global poverty up to 2022, a two-year lag from the publication year of this report. The 2022 *Poverty and Shared Prosperity* report had a three-year lag.

Welfare is computed using either consumption or income data. In PIP, three-fifths of countries rely on consumption data, while income measures are used mostly by countries in Latin America and the Caribbean and high-income countries. In general, consumption is a smoother measure of welfare than income, which can exhibit large fluctuations, for instance after loss of employment or because of seasonal factors (see annex 2D in chapter 2, chapter 4, and World Bank 2016 for a more in-depth discussion on both concepts). Survey data are converted to internationally comparable welfare measures using the 2017 round of purchasing power parity (PPP). Welfare values of less than $0.25 (2017 purchasing power parity dollars, or PPP$) more likely reflect measurement errors rather than extremely low consumption. Thus, a minimum consumption or income level of $0.25 (2017 PPP$) is assumed for all individuals (see more details on the bottom censoring of welfare distributions in chapter 2, annex 2C).

For countries that do not have survey data for a particular year, poverty rates are estimated on the basis of the most recent available survey data. If a survey is available only prior to the reference year, the most recent welfare distribution is extrapolated forward using growth rates from national accounts, either real GDP per capita or real household final consumption expenditure per capita. Not all economic growth feeds into growth in household income. Therefore, a pass-through rate between national accounts data and household welfare is assumed, which is based on estimations from Mahler, Castañeda Aguilar, and Newhouse (2022). The pass-through rate is 0.7 when the last household survey of the country uses a consumption aggregate and is 1 when the last household survey of the country uses an income aggregate (Mahler and Newhouse 2024). The extrapolation is distribution neutral—that is, no changes in inequality are assumed. For years between two survey years, poverty is interpolated on the basis of the two surveys, again based on data from national accounts while assuming the same pass-through rates. More technical details on the extrapolation and interpolation methods can be found in the *Poverty and Inequality Platform Methodology Handbook* (World Bank 2024f).

Even though PIP contains a large number of surveys, there are countries (less than 3 percent of the global population) for which poverty cannot be estimated for several reasons, such as unavailable survey or national accounts data or unreliable price data. These countries are assigned the average regional poverty rate using countries with data in those regions as defined by PIP regional definitions (World Bank 2024f). This allows the computation of regional and global poverty rates. Regional poverty estimates are reported for a reference year if there is survey data for at least 50 percent of the region's population. Global poverty estimates are reported for a reference year if there is survey data covering at least 50 percent of the world's population and at least 50 percent of the population in low- and lower-middle-income countries. A country is considered covered if a nationally representative survey is conducted in the country within three years on either side of a reference year. As an exception, surveys conducted prior to COVID-19 do not count for coverage in 2020 or later, and vice versa.

The societal poverty line is defined as max($2.15, $1.15 + 0.5*Median), meaning it is the larger of either $2.15 per person per day (international poverty line) or $1.15 plus half of the median consumption or income of the country. For countries with median consumption or income greater than $2.00 per person per day, this is a relative poverty measure, reflecting the fact that national poverty lines increase as economies grow. The societal poverty line corresponds approximately to how national poverty lines vary with average income around the world (Jolliffe and Prydz 2021).

All technical details on how the World Bank estimates and reports monetary poverty can be found in the *Poverty and Inequality Platform Methodology Handbook* (World Bank 2024f).

Projection methods

Projections are used to generate up-to-date and future poverty numbers. In this report, nowcasting refers to the years 2023 and 2024, for which survey data are not yet available to meet the global population coverage. Forecasting refers to the years thereafter, the future at the time of writing. Poverty nowcasting and forecasting are done using growth rates of GDP per capita, like the methods used in earlier years when a country does not have a survey in a particular year. Mahler, Castañeda Aguilar, and Newhouse (2022) find that projections based on per capita GDP growth work nearly as well as using 1,000 development variables combined. There are two key assumptions in projecting poverty on the basis of GDP per capita growth rates. First, it is assumed that all households in a country benefit equally from economic growth. This is called distribution neutrality, as each household's income in a country is scaled by the same fraction of GDP per capita growth and there is no change in inequality. Second, as explained for the imputation of poverty rates in the previous section, pass-through rates are applied to the GDP per capita growth rate. These are 0.7 if the most recent survey uses consumption and 1 if it is an income survey. The methodology used to nowcast and forecast is consistently applied across all countries. This is necessary to ensure comparability. Alternative country and regional nowcasts using a range of methods with assumptions specific to each group are available in the World Bank's *Macro Poverty Outlook*. The differences in estimates from various methodologies are reported on the Poverty and Inequality Platform Nowcast web page.

GDP per capita growth rates up to 2029 are taken from the *Global Economic Prospects, June 2024* report (World Bank 2024d), which are supplemented with the April 2024 *Macro Poverty Outlook* (World Bank 2024e) or the April 2024 *World Economic Outlook* (IMF 2024) when

Global Economic Prospects is not available. When GDP data are missing, average annual historical GDP per capita growth rates (over the period 2010 to 2019) from the World Development Indicators are used to extend the series up to 2030.

Figure 1.3 in the main text includes scenarios that allow for distributional changes, for example, a reduction in the Gini index by 1 or 2 percent. These changes in the Gini index are modeled by assuming a linear growth incidence curve following the methodology introduced by Lakner et al. (2022).

Global Monitoring Database and Global Subnational Atlas of Poverty

The Global Monitoring Database (GMD) is a World Bank repository of nationally representative household surveys. These surveys are conducted by national statistical offices, sometimes in collaboration with the World Bank. These survey data sets have information on household income and consumption (sometimes disaggregated into food and nonfood consumption) as well as harmonized demographic variables, such as household size, age, gender, and rural or urban location of households, among others. The GMD is the main source of data for the World Bank's poverty and inequality estimates published in the Poverty and Inequality Platform (World Bank 2024g).

Beyond monetary indicators of well-being, the GMD has harmonized data on a range of other topics, including school enrollment, educational attainment, and access to basic infrastructure services (for example, electricity and improved sanitation) which are used in estimating the MPM. Since survey instruments differ across countries, harmonization of data is done as best as possible. Researchers can access these harmonized survey data from the Poverty and Inequality Platform (World Bank 2024g). Both the GMD and the Poverty and Inequality Platform are updated periodically; this report uses the latest versions of data available, dated September 2024.

The Global Subnational Atlas of Poverty (World Bank 2023a) combines several sources of data, including household survey data from the GMD, as well as administrative boundaries, among others, to visualize global poverty at subnational levels. The Global Subnational Atlas of Poverty has custom shapefiles that can be linked to the subnational geographic units in the GMD. The custom shapefiles follow a harmonized spatial hierarchy across countries, consisting of four administrative levels, from country to district and finer units.

Annex 1B. Survey-based estimates of the COVID-19 impact confirm previous nowcasts

Because of the lack of timely survey data during the pandemic, previous poverty estimates were based on projections using information on GDP.[17] Throughout the pandemic, the economic growth impacts and poverty projections were revised, sometimes heavily, as new data regarding the spread of COVID-19, how it disrupted economic activities, and how countries responded differently became available.

Estimates based on the latest survey data indicate that 73 million people fell into extreme poverty in 2020.[18] This figure is in between the range 60–86 million estimated in the 2020 *Poverty and Shared Prosperity* report (PSPR) and close to the 71 million presented in the 2022 PSPR. Globally, the 2020 PSPR predicted an increase in extreme poverty between 0.7 and 1 percentage points, the 2022 PSPR estimated an increase of 0.9 percentage points, and this report estimates a 0.85 percentage point rise. Figure 1B1 shows that poverty estimates are generally aligned, at least for the world in 2020. Poverty estimates for some regions have been revised more noticeably, as new surveys became available. Some regions show large changes in poverty estimates, which can be explained mostly by new survey data becoming available.[19] New survey data from Uzbekistan resulted in a downward revision in the extreme poverty series for Europe and Central Asia by about 2 percentage points (Castaneda et al. 2024). The previous reports extrapolated poverty for Uzbekistan from a relatively old survey conducted in 2003. New surveys also reflect the impact of social protection programs in Latin America (mainly Brazil) and the group of advanced countries (classified as the "rest of the world"), which are not captured well by distribution-neutral extrapolations based on national accounts aggregates.

FIGURE 1B.1

Changes in poverty rates during the COVID-19 pandemic

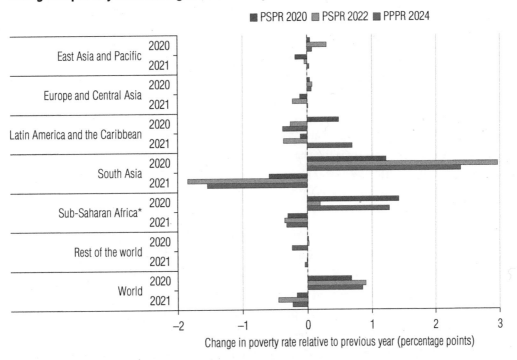

Sources: World Bank 2020, 2022; World Bank, Poverty and Inequality Platform (PIP, version September 2024), https://pip.worldbank.org.

Note: PPPR = *Poverty, Prosperity, and Planet Report;* PSPR = *Poverty and Shared Prosperity* report. Poverty is reported using the $2.15 per person per day poverty line (expressed in 2017 purchasing power parity dollars). Estimates for the Middle East and North Africa are not shown because population coverage is insufficient and was not reported in the earlier publications. Different editions of PIP and growth data have been used for each of the three reports. The latest available growth data used for nowcasting poverty at the time of writing the 2020 PSPR was the June 2020 version of the Global Economic Prospects (GEP) database. The 2022 PSPR used the June 2022 version of GEP and accounted for some distributional impacts of COVID-19 on households. See box 1.3 of the 2022 PSPR for more details (World Bank 2022).

*Less than 50 percent of the population is covered with a recent survey (conducted in 2020 or later).

Annex 1C. New data for India and international price levels have recently become available

After completing the analysis for this report, two important data sets that have implications for global poverty monitoring became available. First, new official household expenditure data for India were published, the first microdata released since 2011–12. Second, new PPPs for 2021 have been released by the International Comparison Program (ICP). Following the World Bank's process to update PIP, when new data become available, extensive analysis and validations are done before the global poverty estimates are updated. This process could not be completed in time for the release of the report. This annex discusses the potential implications of the new data.

New microdata for India available for 2022–23

India is an important country for global poverty measurement because of its population size. In recent months, new Household Consumption and Expenditure Survey (HCES) microdata for 2022–23 were released.[20] As this is the first time that budget survey microdata for India have been released since 2011–12, incorporating these data into the international poverty estimates requires significant background work.[21] Therefore, this report does not incorporate the 2022–23 HCES estimates.

One key element that needs to be analyzed with the new data and that has implications for the estimation of poverty is the change in the recall periods used to capture various consumption items. The World Bank's poverty estimates for India historically have been based on consumption data collected using the Uniform Reference Period (URP), in which all consumption items are collected by asking survey respondents for their consumption in the previous 30-day period. The current series in the PIP, going back to 1977–78 for India, is based on the URP survey instrument. With the 2011–12 round of the National Sample Survey (NSS), the Modified Mixed Reference Period (MMRP) was introduced (in addition to the URP instrument in that round), with the recall period set at 7 days for perishable items, 365 days for the five low-frequency items, and 30 days for the remaining items (Government of India Planning Commission 2014).[22] To maintain comparability with historical data, the World Bank's poverty count for India has thus far been based on consumption measures derived by using the URP instrument. However, with future rounds of the surveys adopting the MMRP instrument, the World Bank has noted the need to switch to using the MMRP-based consumption aggregate for poverty monitoring for India (World Bank 2018).

The implications of different recall periods were discussed in the 2018 version of the PSPR (World Bank 2018). The 2011–12 survey has both the URP and the MMRP aggregates and allows for a comparison of poverty based on the two approaches. In this survey, the extreme poverty rate roughly halves from 22.9 percent when the URP was used to 13.4 percent when the MMRP instrument was used. This is a big change in the poverty rate estimated for India, but it is not unprecedented. Many countries around the world have improved their measurement of consumption, leading to higher measured levels of consumption, similar to India's case. Some recent examples include the Harmonized Surveys on Household Living Conditions program conducted in 10 West African Economic and Monetary Union countries, which, similarly to the change in India, harmonized reference periods across all countries and led to sizeable changes in poverty rates (Castañeda Aguilar et al. 2022).[23] Research has found that changes in survey design can lead to substantial shifts in poverty estimates (De Weerdt, Gibson, and Beegle 2020; Gibson et al. 2015). These changes are particularly large with a poverty line that is fixed in real terms, that is, updated only over time for changes in inflation. At national poverty lines, these revisions are often smaller, since the national poverty lines are updated to consider the change in the consumption measure (see discussion below and Mahler, Foster, and Tetteh-Baah [2024]).

Ongoing work is analyzing the implications of the various recall periods for the poverty estimates in India. In addition, other comparability and methodological issues need to be assessed before the 2022–23 survey can be included in PIP. The 2011–12 and 2022–23 surveys also differ in other ways, such as the mode of survey collection, the number of visits, and the sampling design.

Robustness of the report's findings to different India poverty rates

While more analysis is needed to estimate international poverty for India using new data, robustness checks suggest that key findings of the report would not be affected in a meaningful way. One key conclusion of the report is that extreme poverty currently is concentrated in Sub-Saharan Africa and fragile countries. A reduction in India's poverty rate today, as suggested by the comparison between MMRP and URP in 2011–12, further intensifies this concentration. Figure 1C.1 shows how a reduction in the poverty rate for India from the baseline estimate affects the concentration of extreme poverty in 2022.[24] The vertical line is drawn at the India estimate that is included in the baseline results in the main text (see figure 1.6, panel a, in the main text of this chapter), suggesting that around two-thirds of the extreme poor are in Sub-Saharan Africa and fragile countries. If the India poverty rate is halved, Sub-Saharan Africa and fragile countries would account for three-quarters of the global poor.

Further analysis is needed to update the India trend in recent years with the new data. If the India estimate is revised down also for the recent past, extreme poverty will be further concentrated in Sub-Saharan Africa. As the report has argued, the shift toward Sub-Saharan Africa, a region with slow progress against poverty, has contributed to a slowdown in global poverty reduction. Therefore, such an increasing concentration toward Sub-Saharan Africa by itself strengthens the finding of a slowdown in recent years.

Another conclusion of this report is that extreme poverty eradication will take longer than the original target date of 2030. In the baseline results in the main text, extreme poverty in India was already projected to fall below 3 percent by the end of this decade, so India's contribution to global extreme poverty is projected to decline significantly over the next decade. These estimates are based on projections of growth in GDP per capita over the next decade, as well as historic growth rates (see annex 1A). Even setting the extreme poverty rate in India in 2030 to zero, the global extreme poverty rate in 2030 would only fall from 7.31 to 6.72 percent, still well above the 3 percent target.

Finally, using the 2011–12 data for India, the impact of the new welfare aggregate is smaller for higher poverty lines. Using the $6.85 poverty line, the national poverty rate declines from 90.3 to 87.4 percent, which is considerably smaller than the impact for extreme poverty reported above. This suggests that the impacts of the India revision on global poverty measured at this line will be smaller.

FIGURE 1C.1

Concentration of extreme poverty in Sub-Saharan Africa and fragile and conflict-affected situations under various poverty rates for India in 2022

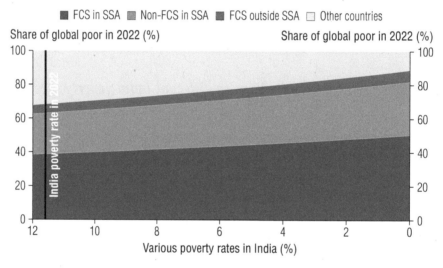

Source: World Bank, Poverty and Inequality Platform (version September 2024), https://pip.worldbank.org.
Note: FCS = fragile and conflict-affected situations; SSA = Sub-Saharan Africa. Figure shows the share of the global extreme poor in 2022 under various scenarios for extreme poverty in India. Extreme poverty is reported using the $2.15 per person per day poverty line (expressed in 2017 purchasing power parity dollars). Moving along the horizontal axis to the right *decreases* extreme poverty in India. Vertical line is drawn at the India estimate included in the baseline results (figure 1.6, panel a, in the main text).

2021 PPPs

New PPPs for the 2021 reference year were released by the ICP in May 2024. Each time the ICP releases new PPPs, it takes some time for the World Bank to analyze and adopt them for global poverty monitoring. For example, the 2017 PPPs currently used for global poverty monitoring were published in May 2020 and adopted in September 2022. Preliminary results of the 2021 PPPs suggest considerable stability with the 2017 PPPs, at least at the aggregate level, so it seems plausible that the 2021 PPPs will be adopted sooner.[25]

PPPs are price indices used to adjust for relative differences in living costs across countries. PPPs are used to convert (a) income or consumption data and (b) national poverty lines, both expressed in local currency units, into a common, comparable currency (typically the US dollar PPP). Poorer countries tend to have lower price levels, especially for nontradables such as labor costs, so they become richer when PPPs instead of standard market exchange rates are used for assessing well-being. The World Bank's global poverty lines have always been based on national poverty lines, expressed in US PPP dollars. For example, the current international poverty line of $2.15 (2017 PPP$) is the median value of the national poverty lines of low-income countries around 2017.

With the 2021 PPPs, an updated list of national poverty lines around 2021 will be used to update the World Bank's poverty lines. Over the next months, World Bank researchers will re-examine national poverty lines and investigate whether there have been updates to these national poverty lines. As national statistical systems around the world build more capacity, improvements in the quality of recent survey data have been observed. As the above example of India highlights, these quality improvements lead to an increase in the amount of measured consumption. When this happens to the aggregates, countries in turn revise upward their national poverty lines, which in the poorest countries are typically based on an estimated minimum cost of basic needs. Mahler, Foster, and Tetteh-Baah (2024) identify 12 countries, mostly low-income countries in West Africa, in which mean consumption has increased by an average of 46 percent, when old and new survey data are compared. Indeed, national poverty lines have also increased by an average of 50 percent in 10 of these 12 countries. This means that if the 2021 PPPs are eventually adopted, the international poverty line could be revised upward by more than what pure price movements would suggest. This will reflect how national poverty lines, as well as the welfare aggregates that underlie the global poverty measure, increase when more consumption is collected in higher-quality surveys.[26]

Net impact of all changes (new India data and PPPs)

At the time of writing, the net impact of these various changes on global poverty is unclear. While the new data in India are expected to bring down India's estimate of extreme poverty, it is possible that there will be an upward revision of the international poverty line when the new PPPs are adopted. While methodological revisions can lead to uncertainty, it is important that the most accurate and up-to-date data are reflected through periodic updates. The improvements that countries have made in their measurement of consumption and poverty, as well as the up-to-date information on international price levels, are welcomed, and they are likely to be adopted once the World Bank's researchers and the broader scholarly community have had an opportunity to assess them.

Annex 1D. Regional and global poverty estimates, 1990–2024

Percentage of population living in poverty by region

Region and poverty line	1990	1995	2000	2005	2010	2015	2019	2020	2021	2022	2023	2024
$2.15 per day												
East Asia and Pacific	65.2	49.0	39.7	20.7	12.6	2.3	1.0	1.1	1.1	1.0	0.9	0.8
Europe and Central Asia	3.6	8.1	9.2	4.7	1.2	0.8	0.5	0.5	0.5	0.5	0.5	0.5
Latin America and the Caribbean	16.3	14.0	13.8	10.7	5.9	4.1	4.2	3.8	4.5	3.5	3.4	3.3
Middle East and North Africa	6.4	4.7	3.0	2.7	1.9	3.7	4.6	5.3	5.9	6.1	6.4	6.7
South Asia	50.0	43.8	--	35.5	25.4	16.6	10.6	13.0	11.4	9.7	8.7	7.6
Sub-Saharan Africa	54.6	58.0	56.0	48.7	42.1	38.2	36.7	37.9	37.6	37.0	36.9	36.5
Eastern and Southern Africa	--	57.5	56.3	50.2	44.2	41.7	43.1	44.5	44.2	43.6	43.7	43.2
Western and Central Africa	55.2	58.8	--	46.5	39.1	33.0	27.3	28.3	27.9	27.3	27.0	26.5
Rest of the world	0.4	0.5	0.5	0.5	0.5	0.7	0.6	0.4	0.3	0.6	0.6	0.6
World	**37.9**	**32.5**	**29.3**	**21.5**	**15.7**	**10.5**	**8.8**	**9.7**	**9.5**	**9.0**	**8.8**	**8.5**
FCS	--	49.9	--	38.1	31.7	29.5	29.2	30.7	30.9	30.8	31.1	30.9
IDA	54.4	50.5	48.3	39.1	31.0	27.5	25.7	26.7	26.5	26.0	26.1	25.8
$3.65 per day												
East Asia and Pacific	87.3	77.3	67.8	49.1	34.2	15.1	7.2	6.4	5.8	5.4	5.1	4.8
Europe and Central Asia	11.7	19.6	21.4	12.3	4.8	3.2	2.0	2.1	1.9	1.7	1.6	1.6
Latin America and the Caribbean	31.3	28.7	27.1	22.5	14.7	10.8	10.2	9.9	10.5	8.9	8.8	8.6
Middle East and North Africa	26.4	25.5	18.7	16.7	12.7	13.1	14.6	16.0	16.7	16.2	16.3	16.4
South Asia	83.5	80.0	--	73.7	65.8	56.9	42.1	44.9	42.2	38.8	36.7	34.3
Sub-Saharan Africa	75.1	77.6	77.6	73.7	69.0	65.7	63.9	65.1	64.8	64.2	64.1	63.5
Eastern and Southern Africa	--	76.4	76.8	73.9	69.6	67.8	68.2	69.2	69.0	68.4	68.4	68.0
Western and Central Africa	76.9	79.5	--	73.3	68.1	62.6	57.6	59.0	58.5	58.0	57.7	57.0
Rest of the world	0.7	0.8	0.8	0.8	0.7	0.9	0.8	0.6	0.5	0.8	0.8	0.8
World	**56.6**	**54.2**	**51.2**	**43.9**	**36.4**	**28.7**	**23.2**	**24.0**	**23.4**	**22.4**	**22.0**	**21.4**
FCS	--	68.2	--	61.4	56.6	54.8	53.4	55.2	55.9	55.8	56.0	55.7
IDA	78.7	77.0	75.9	69.8	62.2	56.8	53.0	53.9	53.5	52.5	52.5	52.0
$6.85 per day												
East Asia and Pacific	96.3	93.4	89.5	78.5	63.7	44.0	32.4	32.9	27.8	27.4	26.1	24.7
Europe and Central Asia	31.7	43.1	48.7	32.6	19.1	14.5	10.8	10.3	8.6	8.2	7.7	7.4
Latin America and the Caribbean	55.3	53.1	50.8	45.7	35.6	29.2	27.2	27.6	28.4	25.2	24.7	24.3
Middle East and North Africa	63.3	63.4	54.1	50.6	45.5	43.8	45.4	48.0	47.0	45.5	45.2	44.9

(continued)

TABLE 1D.1

Percentage of population living in poverty by region *(continued)*

Region and poverty line	1990	1995	2000	2005	2010	2015	2019	2020	2021	2022	2023	2024
South Asia	96.7	95.9	--	93.6	91.5	87.5	80.4	81.9	80.9	78.8	77.3	75.6
Sub-Saharan Africa	90.1	91.4	91.6	91.0	88.9	87.5	87.3	88.0	87.8	87.7	87.6	87.3
Eastern and Southern Africa	--	90.0	90.4	90.1	88.1	87.4	88.2	88.9	88.7	88.5	88.5	88.3
Western and Central Africa	92.7	93.5	--	92.2	90.2	87.7	85.8	86.7	86.5	86.4	86.2	85.9
Rest of the world	2.1	2.0	1.6	1.5	1.4	1.7	1.3	1.2	1.0	1.3	1.3	1.2
World	**69.2**	**69.9**	**69.0**	**64.2**	**57.8**	**51.0**	**46.3**	**47.2**	**45.7**	**44.9**	**44.3**	**43.6**
FCS	--	85.8	--	81.9	79.0	78.6	78.0	79.7	80.2	80.6	80.5	80.4
IDA	93.3	93.1	92.5	90.9	88.0	85.0	82.8	83.5	83.1	82.5	82.3	81.9

Source: World Bank, Poverty and Inequality Platform (version September 2024), https://pip.worldbank.org.

Note: FCS = fragile and conflict-affected settings; IDA = International Development Association. Poverty rates are reported for the poverty lines of $2.15, $3.65, and $6.85 per person per day (expressed in 2017 purchasing power parity dollars). The definition of IDA and FCS is kept fixed using the World Bank fiscal year 2024 classification. Poverty estimates are not reported for years with insufficient data coverage (that is, less than 50 percent of the regional population). These missing observations are marked (--). However, poverty estimates are presented for the recent years (2019–22) using nowcasting methods, even if there is insufficient data coverage, and are thus grayed out (for example, Middle East and North Africa, Sub-Saharan Africa, and FCS). Estimates presented for all regions and country groups for 2023 and 2024 are based on poverty nowcasts and are also grayed out. See chapter 1, annex 1A, for details about coverage rules and the methodology for projecting or nowcasting poverty.

TABLE 1D.2

Millions of people living in poverty by region

Region and poverty line	1990	1995	2000	2005	2010	2015	2019	2020	2021	2022	2023	2024
$2.15 per day												
East Asia and Pacific	1045	840	721	393	248	48	21	22	23	20	19	18
Europe and Central Asia	17	38	43	22	6	4	2	3	3	2	2	2
Latin America and the Caribbean	71	67	71	59	35	25	27	25	29	23	22	22
Middle East and North Africa	15	12	8	8	6	14	19	22	25	26	28	30
South Asia	571	557	--	547	422	294	197	245	218	186	168	149
Sub-Saharan Africa	282	342	376	374	371	385	411	437	444	448	458	464
Eastern and Southern Africa	--	203	226	229	231	250	287	305	311	314	323	327
Western and Central Africa	114	139	--	144	139	135	124	132	134	134	136	137
Rest of the world	4	5	5	5	5	8	7	4	4	7	7	7
World	**2005**	**1862**	**1800**	**1409**	**1093**	**778**	**684**	**757**	**746**	**713**	**705**	**692**
FCS	--	274	--	263	247	259	280	301	310	314	325	332
IDA	470	497	538	492	438	433	443	470	477	479	491	496

(continued)

TABLE 1D.2

Millions of people living in poverty by region (continued)

Region and poverty line	1990	1995	2000	2005	2010	2015	2019	2020	2021	2022	2023	2024
$3.65 per day												
East Asia and Pacific	1397	1326	1232	932	674	310	152	136	124	115	109	103
Europe and Central Asia	54	92	101	58	23	16	10	11	9	9	8	8
Latin America and the Caribbean	137	137	140	124	86	66	66	64	68	58	58	57
Middle East and North Africa	61	66	54	53	44	50	60	67	71	69	71	73
South Asia	953	1018	--	1136	1093	1010	784	844	802	745	712	673
Sub-Saharan Africa	388	457	521	565	607	662	717	749	765	777	796	809
Eastern and Southern Africa	--	270	308	338	364	407	455	474	485	493	506	515
Western and Central Africa	159	187	--	227	243	256	262	275	280	285	290	294
Rest of the world	7	8	8	8	8	10	9	6	6	9	9	9
World	**2996**	**3105**	**3147**	**2876**	**2534**	**2124**	**1797**	**1878**	**1845**	**1783**	**1763**	**1732**
FCS	--	374	--	424	440	481	511	541	560	569	585	597
IDA	681	758	845	877	879	895	912	949	962	967	988	1000
$6.85 per day												
East Asia and Pacific	1542	1603	1626	1490	1255	902	683	696	590	584	557	530
Europe and Central Asia	147	203	229	153	91	70	53	51	43	40	38	36
Latin America and the Caribbean	242	254	263	252	208	180	175	179	185	165	163	162
Middle East and North Africa	146	164	155	159	157	168	186	200	199	195	197	199
South Asia	1103	1221	--	1443	1519	1554	1496	1541	1538	1513	1499	1481
Sub-Saharan Africa	466	539	615	698	782	883	979	1013	1038	1062	1087	1112
Eastern and Southern Africa	--	318	363	412	461	524	589	609	624	638	654	669
Western and Central Africa	192	221	--	286	321	359	390	404	414	424	433	443
Rest of the world	19	19	16	15	15	18	15	13	11	14	14	14
World	**3665**	**4003**	**4239**	**4210**	**4027**	**3775**	**3586**	**3692**	**3602**	**3574**	**3555**	**3534**
FCS	--	471	--	565	615	688	747	781	804	822	841	861
IDA	807	916	1030	1143	1243	1340	1425	1471	1496	1518	1548	1574

Source: World Bank, Poverty and Inequality Platform (version September 2024), https://pip.worldbank.org.

Note: FCS = fragile and conflict-affected settings; IDA = International Development Association. Millions of people living in poverty are reported for the poverty lines of $2.15, $3.65, and $6.85 per person per day (expressed in 2017 purchasing power parity dollars). The definition of IDA and FCS is kept fixed using the World Bank fiscal year 2024 classification. Poverty estimates are not reported for years with insufficient data coverage (that is, less than 50 percent of the regional population). These missing observations are marked (--). However, poverty estimates are presented for the recent years (2019–22) using nowcasting methods, even if there is insufficient data coverage, and are thus grayed out (for example, Middle East and North Africa, Sub-Saharan Africa, and FCS). Estimates presented for all regions and country groups for 2023 and 2024 are based on poverty nowcasts and are also grayed out. See chapter 1, annex 1A, for details about coverage rules and the methodology for projecting or nowcasting poverty.

TABLE 1D.3

Share of global poor (percent)

Region and poverty line	1990	1995	2000	2005	2010	2015	2019	2020	2021	2022	2023	2024
$2.15 per day												
East Asia and Pacific	52.1	45.1	40.1	27.9	22.7	6.2	3.0	2.9	3.1	2.8	2.7	2.6
Europe and Central Asia	0.8	2.1	2.4	1.6	0.5	0.5	0.3	0.3	0.4	0.3	0.3	0.3
Latin America and the Caribbean	3.6	3.6	4.0	4.2	3.2	3.2	3.9	3.3	4.0	3.2	3.1	3.2
Middle East and North Africa	0.7	0.7	0.5	0.6	0.6	1.8	2.7	2.9	3.3	3.7	3.9	4.3
South Asia	28.5	29.9	--	38.9	38.6	37.8	28.9	32.3	29.2	26.1	23.8	21.5
Sub-Saharan Africa	14.1	18.4	20.9	26.5	33.9	49.5	60.1	57.7	59.6	62.9	65.0	67.1
Eastern and Southern Africa	--	10.9	12.6	16.3	21.2	32.2	42.0	40.3	41.7	44.1	45.8	47.3
Western and Central Africa	5.7	7.5	--	10.2	12.7	17.3	18.1	17.4	17.9	18.8	19.3	19.8
Rest of the world	0.2	0.3	0.3	0.4	0.5	1.0	1.0	0.5	0.5	1.0	1.0	1.0
FCS	--	14.7	--	18.6	22.6	33.2	41.0	39.7	41.6	44.0	46.0	47.9
IDA	23.5	26.7	29.9	34.9	40.1	55.6	64.8	62.1	64.0	67.2	69.6	71.7
$3.65 per day												
East Asia and Pacific	46.6	42.7	39.1	32.4	26.6	14.6	8.5	7.3	6.7	6.5	6.2	6.0
Europe and Central Asia	1.8	3.0	3.2	2.0	0.9	0.7	0.6	0.6	0.5	0.5	0.5	0.4
Latin America and the Caribbean	4.6	4.4	4.4	4.3	3.4	3.1	3.6	3.4	3.7	3.3	3.3	3.3
Middle East and North Africa	2.0	2.1	1.7	1.8	1.7	2.4	3.3	3.6	3.8	3.9	4.0	4.2
South Asia	31.8	32.8	--	39.5	43.1	47.5	43.6	45.0	43.5	41.8	40.4	38.9
Sub-Saharan Africa	12.9	14.7	16.5	19.6	24.0	31.2	39.9	39.9	41.5	43.6	45.2	46.7
Eastern and Southern Africa	--	8.7	9.8	11.8	14.4	19.1	25.3	25.3	26.3	27.6	28.7	29.8
Western and Central Africa	5.3	6.0	--	7.9	9.6	12.0	14.6	14.6	15.2	16.0	16.4	17.0
Rest of the world	0.2	0.2	0.2	0.3	0.3	0.5	0.5	0.3	0.3	0.5	0.5	0.5
FCS	--	12.1	--	14.7	17.4	22.6	28.4	28.8	30.3	31.9	33.2	34.5
IDA	22.7	24.4	26.8	30.5	34.7	42.1	50.7	50.6	52.2	54.2	56.1	57.7
$6.85 per day												
East Asia and Pacific	42.1	40.1	38.3	35.4	31.2	23.9	19.0	18.9	16.4	16.3	15.7	15.0
Europe and Central Asia	4.0	5.1	5.4	3.6	2.3	1.9	1.5	1.4	1.2	1.1	1.1	1.0
Latin America and the Caribbean	6.6	6.3	6.2	6.0	5.2	4.8	4.9	4.8	5.1	4.6	4.6	4.6
Middle East and North Africa	4.0	4.1	3.7	3.8	3.9	4.4	5.2	5.4	5.5	5.5	5.5	5.6
South Asia	30.1	30.5	--	34.3	37.7	41.2	41.7	41.7	42.7	42.3	42.2	41.9
Sub-Saharan Africa	12.7	13.5	14.5	16.6	19.4	23.4	27.3	27.4	28.8	29.7	30.6	31.5
Eastern and Southern Africa	--	8.0	8.6	9.8	11.5	13.9	16.4	16.5	17.3	17.9	18.4	18.9
Western and Central Africa	5.2	5.5	--	6.8	8.0	9.5	10.9	10.9	11.5	11.9	12.2	12.5

(continued)

TABLE 1D.3

Share of global poor (percent) *(continued)*

Region and poverty line	1990	1995	2000	2005	2010	2015	2019	2020	2021	2022	2023	2024
Rest of the world	0.5	0.5	0.4	0.4	0.4	0.5	0.4	0.3	0.3	0.4	0.4	0.4
FCS	--	11.8	--	13.4	15.3	18.2	20.8	21.1	22.3	23.0	23.7	24.4
IDA	22.0	22.9	24.3	27.2	30.9	35.5	39.7	39.8	41.5	42.5	43.6	44.6

Source: World Bank, Poverty and Inequality Platform (version September 2024), https://pip.worldbank.org.

Note: FCS = fragile and conflict-affected settings; IDA = International Development Association. The shares of the global poor for regions and other groupings are reported for the poverty lines of $2.15, $3.65, and $6.85 per person per day (expressed in 2017 purchasing power parity dollars). The definition of IDA and FCS is kept fixed using the World Bank fiscal year 2024 classification. Poverty estimates are not reported for years with insufficient data coverage (that is, less than 50 percent of the regional population). These missing observations are marked (--). However, poverty estimates are presented for the recent years (2019–22) using nowcasting methods, even if there is insufficient data coverage, and are thus grayed out (for example, Middle East and North Africa, Sub-Saharan Africa, and FCS). Estimates presented for all regions and country groups for 2023 and 2024 are based on poverty nowcasts and are also grayed out. See chapter 1, annex 1A, for details about coverage rules and the methodology for projecting or nowcasting poverty.

Notes

1. See annex 1A for more details on the methods used for nowcasts and projections.
2. Using the coverage rules in the Poverty and Inequality Platform (Castaneda et al. 2024), data coverage for low-income countries fell somewhat below 50 percent of the population in 2018 and 2019. Comparing poverty rates from 2020 onward to data from 2017 would still show an increase in the headcount at the $2.15 and $6.85 poverty lines.
3. These countries are Madagascar, the Democratic Republic of Congo, Mozambique, South Sudan, Malawi, the Central African Republic, Zambia, Burundi, the Republic of Yemen, and Niger (in descending order of poverty rates).
4. Not only is the share of poor in FCS increasing, but the poverty rate in FCS has also been rising over the past decade (see annex 1D).
5. Tetteh-Baah, Lakner, and Serajuddin (2024) show that the GDP per capita of the 22 countries that have been unable to escape low-income status has grown by only 0.26 percent annually since 1987.
6. For more information, see the World Bank Jobs Group's diagnostics and data site at https://datatopics .worldbank.org/jobsdiagnostics/.
7. The main source of these data is the Global Monitoring Database, a World Bank repository of nationally representative household surveys (see annex 1A for more details). In a few cases, the underlying data and methodology for measuring poverty when profiling the global poor slightly differ from the data and methodology in the Poverty and Inequality Platform (PIP). For example, grouped data are used for China in the Poverty and Inequality Platform (PIP), while micro-level data are used for profiling the poor. Also, the global database for profiling the poor has one survey data set for each country that is closest to the reference year, whereas PIP uses all available surveys and interpolates when necessary.
8. The 2022 edition of the *Poverty and Shared Prosperity* report estimated 101 poor women for every 100 poor men. The assumed equal allocation likely underestimates poverty for women.
9. The Poverty and Inequality Platform includes a spatial price adjustment between urban and rural areas for many countries in the database. The methods are country specific.

10. The only exception is South Asia, where the extreme poverty rate for the population age 15 or above without formal education is relatively low. This may be explained by measurement error, as less than 1 percent of the population age 15 or above in India has no formal education, so the estimation sample is small.

11. Age cutoffs for children, youth, and adults differ across countries and international organizations. This report adopts the United Nations International Children's Emergency Fund definition for children (less than 18 years) and the International Labour Organization definition for youth (or young adults) (15 to 24 years). This means that older children between the ages of 15 and 17 are included in both children and youth. Adults are defined in this report as persons age 25 or above.

12. Each of three dimensions is equally weighted (one-third), and within each of the dimensions, each indicator is equally weighted (one-third for consumption, one-sixth for each education indicator, and one-ninth for each infrastructure indicator).

13. The MPM uses survey data within a three-year window either side of the reporting year, which for multidimensional poverty is 2021 in this report. Within this window, survey estimates are held constant. Therefore, the sample of countries changes across reporting years, and for some countries the same survey estimate is used across several reporting years, giving the impression that there has been no progress. Some of the components of multidimensional poverty, such as adult education, do not change dramatically over a six-year period.

14. Within this window, survey estimates are held constant, which differs from the monetary poverty estimates reported previously in this chapter. In the latter, surveys are interpolated and extrapolated to a common year using growth rates in national accounts (see annex 1A for details). While these methods are well established for monetary poverty, doing so for nonmonetary dimensions, as well as their overlap, is currently not possible.

15. As explained previously in this chapter, a country is covered if it has a survey that is within three years of 2021, as long as that survey was conducted in 2020 or later. However, the MPM, like the monetary poverty estimates, still uses the pre-2020 data in its estimation. In the case of the MPM, a three-year window around 2021 is applied; that is, it uses data from between 2018 and 2024. The number of countries that are used in the MPM estimates is indicated in table 1.1. These surveys cover 49.2 percent for the world population, 66.2 percent for Sub-Saharan Africa, 70 percent for IDA countries, and 49.7 percent for countries in FCS. These figures differ from the coverage rates reported in the table, since the latter do not count pre-2000 data for data coverage in 2021.

16. The estimate for South Asia is based on data from Bangladesh, Bhutan, Maldives, Nepal, Pakistan, and Sri Lanka. However, only the surveys from Bangladesh, Bhutan, and Nepal were conducted after 2019, so they are the only countries that are included in the population coverage reported in table 1.1.

17. More technical details on the methodology for nowcasting or forecasting poverty can be found in the work of Mahler, Castañeda Aguilar, and Newhouse (2022) and Mahler, Yonzan, and Lakner (2022).

18. The estimated number of people falling into poverty reported here includes only the change in the number of poor from 2019 to 2020 and does not account for a counterfactual change in poverty that would have been observed in the absence of COVID-19. See Mahler, Yonzan, and Lakner (2022) for estimates that account for the additional counterfactual impact.

19. Xie et al. (2024) provide a more detailed evaluation of poverty nowcasts for 2020 and 2021.

20. Earlier in 2024, the National Sample Survey Office of the government of India published a fact sheet with key summary statistics based on these data.

21. Two rounds of NSSs have been conducted since 2011–12: 2014–15 and 2017–18. The 2014–15 NSS has the same socioeconomic and demographic information as the 2011–12 round and provides data on household expenditures on services and durables. However, only a subset of the 2014–15 round was released by the government. The 2017–18 NSS round was not released due to concerns over data quality.

22. Since 1999–2000, India has been experimenting with various recall periods to improve the accuracy of consumption data collection. In the 2011–12 survey, India utilized three recall periods: the URP, Mixed Reference Period (MRP), and MMRP. In 2011–12, MRP was adopted for official poverty rate calculations, and it was indicated that future data collection would transition to using MMRP. For the 2022–23 survey, India used exclusively the MMRP recall period for collecting consumption data.

23. For example, in Senegal, the poverty rate was estimated to be 28.8 percent in 2018 using an extrapolation of the older survey compared to 7 percent using the updated harmonized survey. Unlike for India, the two aggregates were not collected in the same survey, which complicates these comparisons. For example, errors in the extrapolation model are also important.
24. For simplicity, the figure shows reductions from the estimate that are included in the main text. Scenarios with greater poverty than currently estimated are omitted.
25. In previous updates of purchasing power parity (PPP) data, large changes in the level of global poverty were observed. For example, the number of poor people in the world increased by 400 million when the 2005 PPPs were adopted (Chen and Ravallion 2010). This outcome led to debates among researchers and the recommendation by the Atkinson Commission that the World Bank should not revise global poverty estimates with new PPP data, which reflected not only real changes in relative prices across countries but also ICP methodological changes (World Bank 2017). Unlike in the past, the ICP methodology has substantially stabilized in the recent 2011 and 2017 rounds (Deaton and Schreyer 2022).
26. An important question that World Bank researchers will investigate is whether this upward revision in national poverty lines reflects (a) an increase in the definition of what it means to be poor or (b) simply a change in the scale on which consumption and the associated poverty lines are measured. As countries get richer, national definitions of poverty increase, which is captured by the World Bank's Societal Poverty Line, which is discussed in box 1.4 in the main text of this chapter. Regardless of the driver, the World Bank's extreme poverty line will remain anchored to how the poorest countries in the world define poverty.

References

Bargain, Olivier, Guy Lacroix, and Luca Tiberti. 2022. "Intrahousehold Resource Allocation and Individual Poverty: Assessing Collective Model Predictions against Direct Evidence on Sharing." *Economic Journal* 132 (643): 865–905.

Beegle, Kathleen, Rajeev H. Dehejia, and Roberta Gatti. 2003. "Child Labor, Income Shocks, and Access to Credit." Policy Research Working Paper 3075, World Bank, Washington, DC. https://papers.ssrn.com/abstract=636437.

Bergstrom, Katy. 2022. "The Role of Income Inequality for Poverty Reduction." *The World Bank Economic Review* 36 (3): 583–604. https://doi.org/10.1093/wber/lhab026.

Bourguignon, Francois. 2003. "The Growth Elasticity of Poverty Reduction: Explaining Heterogeneity across Countries and Time Periods." In *Inequality and Growth: Theory and Policy Implications*, edited by T. S. Eicher and S. J. Turnovsky, 3–26. Cambridge: MIT Press. https://doi.org/10.7551/mitpress/3750.003.0004.

Castañeda Aguilar, R. Andrés, Reno Dewina, Carolina Diaz-Bonilla, Ifeanyi N. Edochie, Tony H. M. J. Fujs, Dean Jolliffe, et al. 2022. *April 2022 Update to the Poverty and Inequality Platform (PIP): What's New (English)*. Washington, DC: World Bank. https://documents.worldbank.org/en/publication/documents-reports/documentdetail/099422404082231105/idu02070690808ee7044720a1e6010de398e6a75.

Castañeda Aguilar, R. Andrés, Adriana Castillo, Nancy P. Devpura, Reno Dewina, Carolina Diaz-Bonilla, Ifeanyi Edochie, et al. 2024. *March 2024 Update to the Poverty and Inequality Platform (PIP): What's New*. Global Poverty Monitoring Technical Note 36. Washington, DC: World Bank. https://doi.org/10.1596/41341.

Chen, Shaohua, and Martin Ravallion. 2010. "The Developing World Is Poorer than We Thought, But No Less Successful in the Fight against Poverty." *The Quarterly Journal of Economics* 125 (4): 1577–1625.

Corral, Paul, Alexander Irwin, Nandini Krishnan, Daniel Gerszon Mahler, and Tara Vishwanath. 2020. *Fragility and Conflict: On the Front Lines of the Fight against Poverty*. Washington, DC: World Bank.

Cuesta, Jose, and Julieth Pico. 2020. "The Gendered Poverty Effects of the COVID-19 Pandemic in Colombia." *The European Journal of Development Research* 32 (5): 1558–91. https://doi.org/10.1057/s41287-020-00328-2.

Deaton, Angus, and Paul Schreyer. 2022. "GDP, Wellbeing, and Health: Thoughts on the 2017 Round of the International Comparison Program." *Review of Income and Wealth* 68 (1): 1–15. https://doi.org/10.1111/roiw.12520.

Decerf, Benoit Marie A., Jed Friedman, Arthur Galego Mendes, Steven Michael Pennings, and Nishant Yonzan. 2024. "Lives, Livelihoods, and Learning: A Global Perspective on the Well-Being Impacts of the COVID-19 Pandemic" (English). Policy Research Working Paper WPS 10728 [preprint], World Bank, Washington, DC. http://documents.worldbank.org/curated/en/099537503202413127/IDU1f944e1ca18e2814ce0198221694a75dd5654.

De Weerdt, Joachim, John Gibson, and Kathleen Beegle. 2020. "What Can We Learn from Experimenting with Survey Methods?" *Annual Review of Resource Economics* 12 (2020): 431–47. https://doi.org/10.1146/annurev-resource-103019-105958.

Escalante, Luis Enrique, and Helene Maisonnave. 2023. "Assessing the Impacts of Climate Change on Women's Poverty: A Bolivian Case Study." *Journal of International Development* 35 (5): 884–96. https://doi.org/10.1002/jid.3711.

Evans, Gareth. 2009. "Conflict and Poverty." Keynote address presented at the DFID Conference on Future of International Development, London, March 10, 2009. https://www.crisisgroup.org/global/conflict-and-poverty.

FAO-WFP (Food and Agriculture Organization–World Food Programme). 2019. *Monitoring Food Security in Countries with Conflict Situations*, issue 5. Food and Agriculture Organization (FAO) and World Food Programme (WFP). https://openknowledge.fao.org/server/api/core/bitstreams/45d68136-6dba-4bb6-bccd-8283840d3885/content.

Gatti, Roberta, Daniel Lederman, Asif M. Islam, Federico R. Bennett, Bo Pieter Johannes Andree, Hoda Assem, Rana Lotfi, and Mennatallah Emam Mousa. 2023. *Altered Destinies: The Long-Term Effects of Rising Prices and Food Insecurity in the Middle East and North Africa*. Middle East and North Africa Economic Update. Washington, DC: World Bank. https://doi.org/10.1596/978-1-4648-1974-2.

Gibson, John, Kathleen Beegle, Joachim De Weerdt, and Jed Friedman. 2015. "What Does Variation in Survey Design Reveal about the Nature of Measurement Errors in Household Consumption?" *Oxford Bulletin of Economics and Statistics* 77 (3): 466–474. https://doi.org/10.1111/obes.12066.

Government of India, Planning Commission. 2014. *Report of the Expert Group to Review the Methodology for Measurement of Poverty*. New Delhi: Government of India. http://planningcommission.nic.in/reports/genrep/pov_rep0707.pdf.

Herforth, Anna, Yan Bai, Aishwarya Venkat, Kristi Mahrt, Alissa Ebel, and William A. Masters. 2020. *Cost and Affordability of Healthy Diets across and within Countries. Background Paper for the State of Food Security and Nutrition in the World 2020*. FAO Agricultural Development Economics Technical Study no. 9. Rome: Food and Agriculture Organization. https://books.google.com/books?hl=en&lr=&id=tmQQEAAAQBAJ&oi=fnd&pg=PR7&dq=info:c_N73DdP97YJ:scholar.google.com&ots=g54a40yw5L&sig=J93I7GT7ceVJ8KrKQB--5CCYkuI.

IMF (International Monetary Fund). 2024. *World Economic Outlook, Steady but Slow: Resilience amid Divergence*. Washington, DC: IMF.

Jolliffe, Dean, and Christoph Lakner. 2023. "Measuring Global Poverty in a Changing World." In *Handbook of Labor, Human Resources and Population Economics*, edited by Klaus Zimmermann. 1–25. Berlin, Germany: Springer Nature. https://link.springer.com/referencework/10.1007/978-3-319-57365-6.

Jolliffe, Dean Mitchell, Daniel Gerszon Mahler, Christoph Lakner, Aziz Atamanov, Samuel Kofi Tetteh-Baah. 2022. "Assessing the Impact of the 2017 PPPs on the International Poverty Line and Global Poverty (English)." Policy Research Working Paper Series 9941, World Bank, Washington, DC. http://documents.worldbank.org/curated/en/353811645450974574/Assessing -the-Impact-of-the-2017-PPPs-on-the-International-Poverty-Line-and-Global-Poverty.

Jolliffe, Dean, and Espen Beer Prydz. 2016. "Estimating International Poverty Lines from Comparable National Thresholds." Policy Research Working Paper 7606, World Bank, Washington, DC.

Jolliffe, Dean, and Espen Beer Prydz. 2021. "Societal Poverty: A Relative and Relevant Measure." *The World Bank Economic Review* 35 (1): 180–206. https://doi.org/10.1093/wber/lhz018.

Jolliffe, Dean Mitchell, and Samuel Kofi Tetteh-Baah. 2024. "Identifying the Poor—Accounting for Household Economies of Scale in Global Poverty Estimates (English)." *World Development* 179 (C): 106593. https://doi.org/10.1016/j.worlddev.2024.106593.

Kabeer, Naila. 2021. "Gender Equality, Inclusive Growth, and Labour Markets." In *Women's Economic Empowerment*, edited by Kate Grantham, Gillian Dowie, and Arjan de Haan, 13–48. Milton Park, UK: Routledge.

Kakwani, Nanak, and Ernesto M. Pernia. 2000. "What Is Pro-Poor Growth?" *Asian Development Review* 18 (01): 1–16. https://doi.org/10.1142/S0116110500000014.

Keho, Yaya. 2009. "Social Capital in Situations of Conflict: A Case Study from Côte d'Ivoire." *African Research Review* 3 (3): 158–180. https://www.ajol.info/index.php/afrrev/article/view/47522/33899.

Klasen, Stephan, and Mark Misselhorn. 2008. "Determinants of the Growth Semi-elasticity of Poverty Reduction." Working Paper. IAI Discussion Paper 176. Georg-August-Universität Göttingen, Ibero-America Institute for Economic Research (IAI), Göttingen, Germany. https://www.econstor.eu /handle/10419/57314.

Kraay, Aart. 2006. "When Is Growth Pro-Poor? Evidence from a Panel of Countries." *Journal of Development Economics* 80 (1): 198–227. https://doi.org/10.1016/j.jdeveco.2005.02.004.

Lakner, Christoph, Daniel Gerszon Mahler, Mario Negre, and Espen Beer Prydz. 2022. "How Much Does Reducing Inequality Matter for Global Poverty?" *The Journal of Economic Inequality* 20 (3): 559–85. https://doi.org/10.1007/s10888-021-09510-w.

Lakner, Christoph, and Branko Milanovic. 2016. "Global Income Distribution: From the Fall of the Berlin Wall to the Great Recession." *The World Bank Economic Review* 30 (2): 203–32. https://doi.org/10.1093 /wber/lhv039.

Lukunka, Barbara, and Sam Grundy. 2020. "Peacebuilding and Human Mobility: IOM's Role in Sustaining Peace." International Organization of Migration (IOM). https://www.un.org/peacebuilding/sites/www .un.org.peacebuilding/files/iom_peacebuilding_thematic_paper_march_2020_0.pdf.

Mahler, Daniel Gerszon, R. Andrés Castañeda Aguilar, and David Newhouse. 2022. "Nowcasting Global Poverty." *The World Bank Economic Review* 36 (4): 835–56. https://doi.org/10.1093/wber /lhac017.

Mahler, Daniel Gerszon, E. Foster, and Samuel Kofi Tetteh-Baah. 2024. "How Improved Household Surveys Influence National and International Poverty Rates." Global Poverty Monitoring Technical Note Series 40 [preprint], Washington, DC: World Bank.

Mahler, Daniel Gerszon, Nishant Yonzan, and Christoph Lakner. 2022. "The Impact of COVID-19 on Global Inequality and Poverty." Policy Research Working Paper WPS 10198, World Bank, Washington, DC. https://doi.org/10.1596/1813-9450-10198.

Mahler, Daniel Gerszon, and David Newhouse. 2024. "Changes to the Extrapolation Method for Global Poverty Estimation." Global Poverty Monitoring Technical Note Series 35, World Bank, Washington, DC. https://ideas.repec.org//p/wbk/wbgpmt/35.html.

Mahler, Daniel Gerszon, Nishant Yonzan, and Christoph Lakner. 2023. "Most of the World's Extreme Poor Live in Middle Income Countries—But not for Long." *World Bank Data Blog.* March 21, 2023. https:// blogs.worldbank.org/opendata/most-worlds-extreme-poor-live-middle-income-countries-not-long.

Mayer, Tamar, Sujata Moorti, and Jamie K. McCallum, ed. 2019. *The Crises of Global Youth Unemployment.* London: Routledge Taylor & Francis Group.

Milanovic, Branko. 2016. *Global Inequality: A New Approach for the Age of Globalization.* Cambridge, MA: Harvard University Press. https://doi.org/10.2307/j.ctvjghwk4.

Mitra, Aniruddha, James T. Bang, and Arnab Biswas. 2015. "Gender Equality and Economic Growth: Is It Equality of Opportunity or Equality of Outcomes?" *Feminist Economics* 21 (1): 110–35. https://doi.org/10.1080/13545701.2014.930163.

Mueller, Hannes, and Julia Tobias. 2016. "The Cost of Violence: Estimating the Economic Impact of Conflict." Growth Brief, International Growth Centre. https://www.theigc.org/sites/default/files/2016/12/IGCJ5023_Economic_Cost_of_Conflict_Brief_2211_v7_WEB.pdf.

Narayan, Ambar, Alexandru Cojocaru, Maria Davalos, Natalia Garcia, Christoph Lakner, Daniel Gerszon Mahler, and Nishant Yonzan. 2022. "COVID-19 and Economic Inequality: Short-Term Impacts with Long-Term Consequences." Policy Research Working Paper 9902, World Bank, Washington, DC. https://doi.org/10.1596/1813-9450-9902.

Pritchett, Lant. 2024. "'Dollar a Day' Poverty Was a Development Mileage Marker, not the Destination." https://lantpritchett.org.

Ravallion, Martin. 2004. "Pro-Poor Growth: A Primer." Policy Research Working Paper 3242, World Bank, Washington, DC. https://papers.ssrn.com/abstract=610283.

Ravallion, Martin, Gaurav Datt, and Dominique van de Walle. 1991. "Quantifying Absolute Poverty in the Developing World." *Review of Income and Wealth* 37 (4): 345–61. https://doi.org/10.1111/j.1475-4991.1991.tb00378.x.

Salmeron-Gomez, Daylan, Solrun Engilbertsdottir, Jose Antonio Cuesta Leiva, David Newhouse, and David Stewart. 2023. "Global Trends in Child Monetary Poverty According to International Poverty Lines." Policy Research Working Paper 10525, World Bank, Washington, DC. https://doi.org/10.1596/1813-9450-10525.

Schady, Norbert, Alaka Holla, Shwetlena Sabarwal, Joana Silva, and Andres Yi Chang. 2023. "Collapse and Recovery: How the COVID-19 Pandemic Eroded Human Capital and What to Do about It." Executive Summary Booklet, World Bank, Washington, DC.

Sumner, Andy, Christopher Hoy, and Eduardo Ortiz-Juarez. 2020. "Estimates of the Impact of COVID-19 on Global Poverty." Working Paper 2020/43, UNU-WIDER, Helsinki, Finland. https://doi.org/10.35188/UNU-WIDER/2020/800-9.

Tetteh-Baah, Samuel Kofi, Christoph Lakner, and Umar Serajuddin. 2024. "Are the Poorest Countries Being Left Behind?" *Data Blog*, March 14, 2024. https://blogs.worldbank.org/en/opendata/are-poorest-countries-being-left-behind.

Thorbecke, Erik, and Yusi Ouyang. 2022. "Towards a Virtuous Spiral between Poverty Reduction and Growth: Comparing Sub Saharan Africa with the Developing World." *World Development* 152: 105776. https://doi.org/10.1016/j.worlddev.2021.105776.

World Bank. 1990. *World Development Report 1990: Poverty.* New York: Oxford University Press. http://hdl.handle.net/10986/5973.

World Bank. 2012. *World Development Report 2013: Jobs.* Washington, DC: World Bank.

World Bank. 2016. *Poverty and Shared Prosperity 2016: Taking on Inequality.* Washington, DC: World Bank. https://www.worldbank.org/en/publication/poverty-and-shared-prosperity-2016.

World Bank. 2017. *Monitoring Global Poverty: Report of the Commission on Global Poverty (English).* Washington, DC: World Bank.

World Bank. 2018. *Poverty and Shared Prosperity 2018: Piecing Together the Poverty Puzzle.* Washington, DC: World Bank. https://www.worldbank.org/en/publication/poverty-and-shared-prosperity-2018.

World Bank. 2020. *Poverty and Shared Prosperity 2020: Reversals of Fortune.* Washington, DC: World Bank. https://www.worldbank.org/en/publication/poverty-and-shared-prosperity-2020.

World Bank. 2022. *Poverty and Shared Prosperity 2022: Correcting Course.* Washington, DC: World Bank. https://www.worldbank.org/en/publication/poverty-and-shared-prosperity.

World Bank. 2023a. Global Subnational Poverty Atlas (GSAP) (database), accessed May 31, 2024, https://datacatalog.worldbank.org/int/search/dataset/0042041/global_subnational_poverty_atlas_gsap.

World Bank. 2023b. *World Bank Gender Strategy 2024–2030: Accelerate Gender Equality for a Sustainable, Resilient, and Inclusive Future—Consultation Draft.* Washington, DC: World Bank. https://documents.worldbank.org/en/publication/documents-reports/documentdetail/099013107142345483/SECBOS04cf7b650208a5e08b784c0db6a4.

World Bank. 2024a. *Africa's Pulse, no. 29, April 2024: Tackling Inequality to Revitalize Growth and Reduce Poverty in Africa*. Washington, DC: World Bank. https://doi.org/10.1596/978-1-4648-2109-7.

World Bank. 2024b. *Digital Progress and Trends Report 2023*. Washington, DC: World Bank. http://hdl.handle.net/10986/40970.

World Bank. 2024c. *Global Economic Prospects, January 2024*. Washington, DC: World Bank. https://doi.org/10.1596/978-1-4648-2017-5.

World Bank. 2024d. *Global Economic Prospects, June 2024*. Washington, DC: World Bank. https://hdl.handle.net/10986/41536.

World Bank. 2024e. *Macro Poverty Outlook (Spring Meeting 2024)*. Washington, DC: World Bank.

World Bank. 2024f. *Poverty and Inequality Platform Methodology Handbook*. Edition 2024-03. https://datanalytics.worldbank.org/PIP-Methodology/.

World Bank. 2024g. Poverty and Inequality Platform (PIP) (data set). World Bank, Washington, DC. https://pip.worldbank.org/home.

World Bank. 2024h. "Impacts of the Conflict in the Middle East on the Palestinian Economy." World Bank Economic Monitoring Report, World Bank, Washington, DC. https://thedocs.worldbank.org/en/doc/ce9fed0d3bb295f0363d690224d1cd39-0280012024/original/Palestinian-Econ-Upd-May2024-FINAL-ENGLISH-Only.pdf.

World Bank. n.d. "Translating Our Vision." 2024 World Bank Group Scorecard online resource. https://scorecard.worldbank.org/en/scorecard/home.

World Bank, UNESCO (United Nations Educational, Scientific, and Cultural Organization), UNICEF (UN Children's Fund), FCDO (Foreign, Commonwealth, and Development Office), USAID (U.S. Agency for International Development), and Bill & Melinda Gates Foundation. 2022. *The State of Global Learning Poverty: 2022 Update*. https://thedocs.worldbank.org/en/doc/e52f55322528903b27f1b7e61238e416-0200022022/original/Learning-poverty-report-2022-06-21-final-V7-0-conferenceEdition.pdf.

Wu, Haoyu, Aziz Atamanov, Tom Bundervoet, and Pierella Paci. 2024. "The Growth Elasticity of Poverty: Is Africa any different?" Policy Research Working Paper WPS 10690, World Bank Group, Washington, DC.

Xie, Jing, Daniel Gerszon Mahler, Nishant Yonzan, Samuel Kofi Tetteh-Baah, and Christoph Lakner. 2024. "Off Target? Assessing Poverty Nowcasting amidst the COVID-19 Crisis." *Data Blog*, June 21, 2024. https://blogs.worldbank.org/en/opendata/off-target--assessing-poverty-nowcasting-amidst-the-covid-19-cri.

Shared Prosperity

2

Summary

- *Growth in average income alone is not a sufficient marker of development, and that is why it is important to track a measure of the inclusiveness of growth or shared prosperity. The Global Prosperity Gap, a new indicator of shared prosperity, tracks how far the world is, on average, from a threshold of $25 per person per day, with a specific emphasis on the incomes of the poorest.*

- *Progress in reducing the Prosperity Gap has stalled since the COVID-19 (Coronavirus) pandemic, highlighting a slowdown in inclusive income growth over this period.*

- *A high level of inequality can reflect a lack of opportunities for socioeconomic mobility, which can further hinder prospects for inclusive growth and poverty reduction over time. A longer-term view shows that within-country inequality has declined for the average country. The number of economies with high inequality, defined as having a Gini index above 40, has also continuously declined since the 2000s.*

- *Despite a reduction in the number of economies with high inequality, the percentage of people living in economies with high inequality has stayed roughly the same in the last decade, from over 23 percent of the global population in 2013 to 22 percent (1.7 billion) in 2022. Another 70 percent (5.6 billion) lives in an economy with moderate inequality, and just 7 percent (612 million) lives in economies with low inequality according to this measure. The number of economies with high inequality could be higher if income surveys were available for all economies.*

- *Today, high levels of income or consumption inequality are concentrated among countries in Sub-Saharan Africa and in Latin America and the Caribbean.*

- *Faster and more inclusive growth is needed to accelerate progress in achieving shared prosperity. At current growth rates, a typical upper-middle-income country will need 100 years to close the Prosperity Gap. The number of years needed can be reduced if income growth is substantially faster or more inclusive. Countries can achieve the same level of prosperity with less growth and a decrease in the level of inequality.*

- *Inclusive growth efforts need to be focused on creating opportunities for everyone to proactively contribute to the economy. Moreover, this requires structural conditions that enable socioeconomic mobility, so that everyone can use their productive capacity to its full extent. Addressing inequality for low- and lower-middle-income countries requires tackling all phases of inequality; fiscal redistribution alone is not the solution.*

Introduction: A new take on shared prosperity

Two new measures of shared prosperity: The Global Prosperity Gap and the number of economies with high inequality

Since 2013, the World Bank has been tracking a measure of shared prosperity, recognizing that growth in average income alone is not a sufficient indicator of development. How growth benefits the least well-off is an important dimension to consider for improvements in societal welfare. Starting with this report, the World Bank has adopted two new measures of shared prosperity: the *Global Prosperity Gap* and the *number of economies with high inequality* to better capture the notion of shared prosperity, combining concerns for economic progress and equity. Box 2.1 discusses the change in the measures, and annex 2A includes some comparisons between the old and new measures.

BOX 2.1

Why the new shared prosperity measures?

The concern for shared prosperity is not new to the World Bank, but the precise measures have changed. The two new indicators are replacing the growth in income or consumption of the poorest 40 percent of the population in a country (the bottom 40)—the measure used since 2013. Growth in the bottom 40 effectively moved attention away from growth in the average toward growth among the poorer segments of the distribution, thereby influencing country-level policy design and policy discussions to address their impact on the most disadvantaged.

However, 10 years of implementing the bottom 40 growth indicator has exposed some limitations. First, growth in the bottom 40 was defined as a country-level measure and could not be aggregated to a global estimate. Similarly, a country's growth in the bottom 40 cannot be broken down among regions or demographic groups, making it difficult to understand drivers of aggregate changes.[a] Second,

(continued)

106

BOX 2.1

Why the new shared prosperity measures? *(continued)*

the bottom 40 tracks most closely the growth in incomes of those who live close to the 40th percentile of the country and largely ignores the growth of the poorest people in the country. Third, data demands have resulted in a selective assessment of global progress. While the Global Prosperity Gap, like global poverty estimates, can be assessed using a single round of data, growth in the bottom 40 requires two comparable rounds of data over a particular time window. Meeting this condition has been challenging due to infrequent surveys and frequent breaks to survey comparability, particularly among the poorest countries. As a result, in its latest edition, growth in the bottom 40 was available for only 26 of 80 low- and lower-middle-income countries (Global Database of Shared Prosperity, 13th edition, circa 2016–21),[b] while the data underpinning the global measures of poverty and the Prosperity Gap provide more complete coverage. Last, while the bottom 40 captures inequality when explicitly compared with the growth in the mean, it leaves the link to inequality open to interpretation.[c]

Together, the new indicators address the shortcomings of the bottom 40 measure: they will track the degree to which global growth is pro-poor, allow for identification of the countries driving the changes, and will retain a focus on country-level inequality irrespective of the prosperity achieved.

a. The adoption of the Prosperity Gap adds the focus on *global* shared prosperity in addition to *country-level* shared prosperity, which was the only focus of the previous shared prosperity measure. The new measure is thus similar to the reporting on global poverty in chapter 1, which gives equal weight to all citizens of the world. Moreover, like the poverty measure, the Prosperity Gap can also be reported for each country. The high-inequality indicator, on the other hand, gives equal weight to every economy.
b. For the latest update of the Global Database of Shared Prosperity, see https://www.worldbank.org/en/topic/poverty/brief/global-database-of-shared-prosperity.
c. Contrary to the Sustainable Development Goal target, which measures explicitly whether the growth of the bottom 40 is higher than the growth in the national average.

The Global Prosperity Gap brings together the notions of *progress* (measured by growth in average income) and improvements in *equity* (measured by the reduction in inequality in society) into one indicator of inclusive growth. The Global Prosperity Gap captures how far people's incomes are from a global prosperity standard, which is set at $25 per person per day. This benchmark represents the average income when countries transition from upper-middle-income to high-income status. This measure gives a greater weight to the incomes of the poor: poorer households contribute significantly more to the gap than their better-off counterparts.[1] Consequently, income growth among the poorest households also matters significantly more for reducing the Global Prosperity Gap than growth among the better-off.

Three main reasons why tracking within-country inequality is important

In addition to the Global Prosperity Gap, which focuses on the income differences of everyone around the world, the World Bank is now tracking an indicator that emphasizes within-country inequality directly. That indicator is the number of economies with high inequality as measured by the Gini index, based on income or consumption. While complete equality is neither feasible nor necessarily desirable—for instance, a part of inequality of wages reflects differences in efforts—there is a broad consensus that when inequality in a country is too high, it is harmful.

Tracking inequality is important for various reasons. First, high inequality within countries slows the pace of poverty reduction. How economic growth translates into raising the income of the poor strongly depends on the existing levels of inequality. In countries where levels of income or consumption inequality are higher, a given increase in growth delivers a smaller reduction in poverty (Bourguignon 2003). Simulations have shown that declines in inequality can have a significant impact on reducing poverty (Bergstrom 2022; Lakner et al. 2022). This means that policies to reduce inequality can have a double dividend over time. However, the double dividend has been missed in some cases. As chapter 1 has shown, poverty reduction in Sub-Saharan Africa has been slow, driven largely by slow growth. However, a lack of improvement in inequality has also been a missed opportunity for poverty reduction (Sinha, Inchauste, and Narayan 2024) in a region where a large share of countries have high inequality (see discussion on within-country inequality below). As discussed later in this chapter, achieving shared prosperity, like reducing poverty, is affected negatively by the level of inequality. There is a separate question whether inequality impedes the level of growth, but the evidence on this is ambiguous, both conceptually and empirically (Banerjee and Duflo 2003; Baselgia and Foellmi 2022; Brueckner and Lederman 2018; Forbes 2000; Gründler and Scheuermeyer 2018; Li and Zou 1998).[2]

Second, high inequality often reflects a lack of opportunities for socioeconomic mobility. Inequality of outcomes today is closely related to inequalities in opportunities and thus a sign of more deep-rooted problems (Brunori, Ferreira, and Peragine 2013; Chetty et al. 2017; Corak 2013). High levels of inequality within a country can therefore be symptomatic of the inability of some population groups to rise along the economic and social ladder for reasons that are outside of their control, such as their gender, race, parental background, or place of birth. This is not only unjust, but also inefficient, because it means that some groups cannot participate in economic activity using their full potential.[3] Furthermore, inequality of outcomes and opportunities today directly affects the opportunities for the next generation (Atkinson 2015; van der Weide et al. 2024; World Bank 2017b). For instance, very unequal societies tend to exhibit greater inequalities among schools or neighborhoods, so inequalities today have a strong impact on children's opportunities tomorrow.

Third, monitoring inequality is important since perceptions of inequality matter for policy and have broad social implications. Societal frictions have been linked to actual or perceived high inequality levels—for example, the social discontent seen during the Arab Spring (World Bank 2016). Concurrently, lower inequality is correlated with higher levels of political and social stability as well as social cohesion (World Bank 2016). Evidence also suggests that high inequality has been disproportionately reducing political participation among low-income voters relative to high-income voters (Erikson 2015) and at the same time increasing the share of political contributions of high-net-worth households (Cagé 2023). How individuals perceive inequality is correlated with their perceived position in income distribution as well as with the shocks they face. Perceptions do change, however, as the nature of shocks changes and as people are informed about their actual positions in the income distribution (Cruces, Perez-Truglia, and Tetaz 2013; Hvidberg, Kreiner, and Stantcheva 2023). Studies on advanced economies emphasize that people are most sensitive to income comparison with those they view as peers (Amendola, Dell'Anno, and Parisi 2019; Card et al. 2012; Hvidberg, Kreiner, and Stantcheva 2023); however, those studies also highlight that people tend to underestimate inequality most within these groups (Hvidberg, Kreiner, and Stantcheva 2023). Given the implications of the perception of inequality, the gaps between actual and perceived inequalities, and individuals' willingness to adjust their perceptions monitoring inequality with objective measures can potentially add to a more informed public discourse.

The next section of this chapter introduces the Global Prosperity Gap as one of two new measures of the World Bank to monitor shared prosperity and presents historical trends and projections. It also discusses the roles of growth in average incomes and changes in inequality in explaining these trends. The third section discusses the trends in country-level inequality. The final section summarizes policy actions that support inclusive growth.

Progress in shared prosperity has stalled since the COVID-19 pandemic

Today, the Global Prosperity Gap is about five: On average, incomes around the world have to increase fivefold to reach the prosperity standard of $25 per person per day

In 2024, the typical person in Tanzania lives on $2.50 per day. In the Lao People's Democratic Republic, a typical person lives on almost $5 per day, while in Uzbekistan the corresponding figure is around $12.50. In contrast, in a country like Bulgaria, which recently entered high-income status, the typical person earns close to $25 per day.[4] What would it take to bring the typical person in Tanzania or in Lao PDR or in Uzbekistan to the level of prosperity enjoyed by people in countries as they enter high-income status? Their incomes would have to increase by factors of 10, 5, and 2 for people in Tanzania, Lao PDR, and Uzbekistan, respectively. These factors highlight the massive shortfalls from a global standard of prosperity that are a harsh reality for most people in most developing countries.

In this report, the World Bank is introducing a new measure of shared prosperity that combines these shortfalls into a single number for the world. The Global Prosperity Gap is the average factor by which every person in the world would need to increase their income to reach a prosperity standard of $25 per day (see box 2.2).

In 2024, the Prosperity Gap is 4.9—meaning that incomes on average would have to increase almost fivefold to reach the prosperity standard of $25 per person per day (figure 2.1, panel a). Reductions in the Global Prosperity Gap correspond to increases in shared prosperity, as the average shortfall from the global prosperity standard is reduced. The global prosperity standard is set at $25 per person per day—roughly equal to the average per capita household income at the point where countries transition from upper-middle-income to high-income status, according to the World Bank's income classification (Kraay et al. 2023).[5] The Prosperity Gap includes income of every person in the world, which is characteristic of a shared prosperity measure; however, it places much more weight on the income shortfalls of the poor than of the rich.[6] The typical person in Tanzania who lives on just $2.50 per day contributes 10 times more to the Global Prosperity Gap than a person who enjoys $25 per day.[7] See box 2.2 for an intuitive explanation and annex 2B for a more technical presentation.

BOX 2.2

How is the Prosperity Gap calculated?

The Prosperity Gap captures how far a society is from $25 per person per day, which is close to the average per capita household income when countries reach high-income status. The society's shortfall is the average shortfall among all individuals living in that society but giving poorer people a greater weight. The Prosperity Gap is defined as the average income multiple needed to reach that $25 standard for every member of that society (Kraay et al. 2023).

Note that the typical person in Tanzania, the Lao People's Democratic Republic, and Uzbekistan has less than $25 per day so they contribute with a factor greater than 1, and the typical person in Bulgaria has $25 per day so they contribute with a factor of 1 (figure B2.2.1). The typical person in France lives above the $25 standard and makes only a small contribution to the measure. While income growth experienced by any person in the world will help reduce the Prosperity Gap, the magnitude of that reduction grows exponentially the poorer the individual is. That means that the typical person in Tanzania—the poorest person in this example—will contribute more to the Prosperity Gap, and gains in their income will count more than the others.

(continued)

How is the Prosperity Gap calculated? *(continued)*

FIGURE B2.2.1

The Prosperity Gap captures how far societies are from $25 per person per day

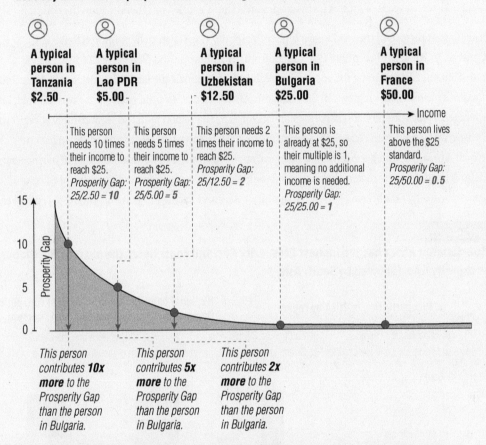

Let's say there are five people with the following levels of daily income:

| A typical person in Tanzania $2.50 | A typical person in Lao PDR $5.00 | A typical person in Uzbekistan $12.50 | A typical person in Bulgaria $25.00 | A typical person in France $50.00 |

→ Income

This person needs 10 times their income to reach $25.
Prosperity Gap: 25/2.50 = **10**

This person needs 5 times their income to reach $25.
Prosperity Gap: 25/5.00 = **5**

This person needs 2 times their income to reach $25.
Prosperity Gap: 25/12.50 = **2**

This person is already at $25, so their multiple is 1, meaning no additional income is needed.
Prosperity Gap: 25/25.00 = **1**

This person lives above the $25 standard.
Prosperity Gap: 25/50.00 = **0.5**

*This person contributes **10x** more to the Prosperity Gap than the person in Bulgaria.*

*This person contributes **5x** more to the Prosperity Gap than the person in Bulgaria.*

*This person contributes **2x** more to the Prosperity Gap than the person in Bulgaria.*

To find the Prosperity Gap in this example, these numbers are averaged:

Prosperity Gap = *(10 + 5 + 2 + 1 + 0.5)*/5 = 18.5/5 = **3.7**

So, the society's Prosperity Gap is 3.7. This means that, on average, everyone's incomes need to be multiplied by 3.7 to reach the $25 per day standard. If the five people in the example were the only people in the world, the Global Prosperity Gap would be 3.7.

Source: World Bank.

Note: All $ values are in 2017 purchasing power parity dollars.

An advantage of this new measure is that it can be easily decomposed, allowing for a better understanding of the main drivers of shared prosperity. The Prosperity Gap for a person is just the factor by which their income must increase to achieve $25 per day. The Prosperity Gap for a country is the average of these gaps for all people in the country. The Prosperity Gap for a region, such as Sub-Saharan Africa, is the population-weighted average of the Prosperity Gaps for all countries in the region. Finally, the Prosperity Gap for the world is a population-weighted average of the Prosperity Gaps for all regions in the world. Country Prosperity Gaps can thus be expressed as population-weighted average gaps of groups (provincial, state, ethnic, gender, or others) within the country.

The poorest regions of the world have higher Prosperity Gaps than richer regions (figure 2.1, panel a). In 2024, the Prosperity Gap ranges from 1.7 in Europe and Central Asia to 12.2 in Sub-Saharan Africa among the geographic regions.[8] This signals the large disparities in income and inequality levels across regions. In Sub-Saharan Africa, incomes would need to rise over 12-fold, on average, to reach the global prosperity standard of $25. The region with the second-highest regional Prosperity Gap is South Asia, with a gap of 6.2 in 2024, followed closely by the Middle East and North Africa, for which the trend has been extrapolated from 2018 because of a lack of recent survey data. A breakdown by region shows that Sub-Saharan Africa accounts for 39 percent of the global gap, followed by South Asia (31 percent) and East Asia and Pacific (15 percent) (figure 2.1, panel b).

FIGURE 2.1

Sub-Saharan Africa has the highest Prosperity Gap and contributes the most to the Global Prosperity Gap, followed by South Asia

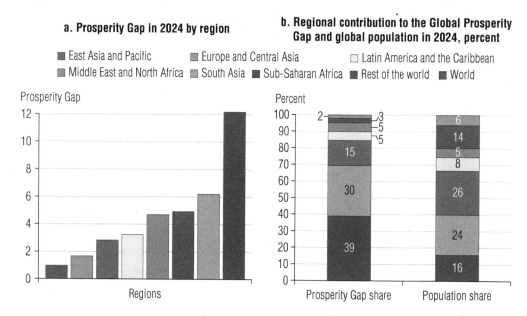

a. Prosperity Gap in 2024 by region

b. Regional contribution to the Global Prosperity Gap and global population in 2024, percent

- ■ East Asia and Pacific
- ▨ Europe and Central Asia
- ☐ Latin America and the Caribbean
- ▨ Middle East and North Africa
- ▨ South Asia
- ■ Sub-Saharan Africa
- ■ Rest of the world
- ■ World

Source: World Bank, Poverty and Inequality Platform (version September 2024), https://pip.worldbank.org.
Note: Regional Prosperity Gaps are reported in panel a, while the region's population-weighted contributions (percent) to the Global Prosperity Gap and the region's population share (percent) are shown in panel b. Regions follow the definition in the Poverty and Inequality Platform. The estimates for 2024 are projected starting in 2019 for the Middle East and North Africa, starting in 2020 for Sub-Saharan Africa, and starting in 2023 for all other regions. See annex 1A for further details on projection. The label values may not add to 100 percent due to rounding.

The COVID-19 pandemic slightly increased the Prosperity Gap, but since 2022 it has returned to prepandemic levels. The Global Prosperity Gap increased from 5.1 in 2019 to 5.3 in 2020 and then fell back to 5.1 in 2022 (figure 2.2). In 2024, the gap is estimated to be 4.9—slightly below the 2019 level. In other words, in the past five years, the Global Prosperity Gap has fallen by only 0.8 percent annually, compared with 2.1 percent annually in the five years from 2014 to 2019 (figure 2.3).

FIGURE 2.2

There has been minimal progress in reducing the Prosperity Gap since the COVID-19 pandemic

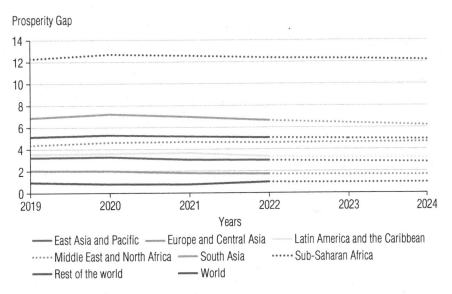

Source: World Bank, Poverty and Inequality Platform (version September 2024), https://pip.worldbank.org.
Note: The estimates for 2023 and 2024 are projected for all regions. For the Middle East and North Africa, the latest available year with enough population coverage to report the region's estimate is 2018. Estimates for all years after 2018 for the region are projected. Likewise, for Sub-Saharan Africa, estimates are projected starting in 2020. See chapter 1 for further details on population coverage. See annex table 2E.1 in annex 2E for these estimates.

In 2020, the gap rose the most in Sub-Saharan Africa and South Asia. While the gap had rebounded back to the 2019 level in South Asia by 2021, in Sub-Saharan Africa it remains almost the same as in 2019. In the Middle East and North Africa, the gap in 2024 exceeds the level before the pandemic. However, the estimate for that region has large uncertainties, as only a handful of countries in the region have reported a survey in recent years. In other regions, the changes in the Prosperity Gap have been small, signaling little progress during this period.

Over the past 30 years, the Global Prosperity Gap has fallen by more than half

Despite the recent stagnation in the Prosperity Gap, there has been substantial progress in improving shared prosperity since the 1990s (figure 2.3). In 1990, the average gap from the global prosperity standard was 10.9, meaning that incomes on average needed to be increased close to elevenfold to bring everyone around the world to $25 per day. By 2024, this gap has more than halved. During the past 30 years, the Global Prosperity Gap only increased (worsened) twice: during the Asian financial crisis (an increase of 0.7 percent from 1997 to 1998) and during the COVID-19 pandemic (an increase of 3.2 percent from 2019 to 2020).

FIGURE 2.3

There has been considerable progress in reducing the Global Prosperity Gap since 1990

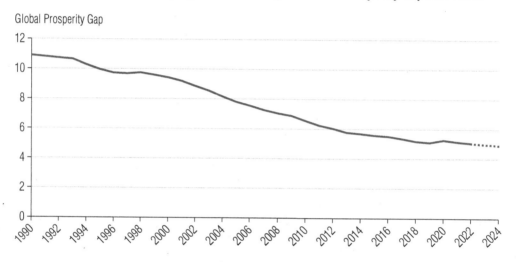

Source: World Bank, Poverty and Inequality Platform (version September 2024), https://pip.worldbank.org.
Note: The estimates in 2023 and 2024 are projected. The prosperity threshold is set at $25 per person per day in 2017 purchasing power parity dollars.

Historical trends also show the uneven progress in shared prosperity across regions and the large role of East Asia and Pacific in driving global progress over the past three decades (figure 2.4, panel a). In line with the poverty trends in chapter 1, strong progress in East Asia and Pacific has meant that the region's Prosperity Gap has decreased the most, falling from 16.5 in 1990 to 2.8 in 2024. Sub-Saharan Africa started with a similar Prosperity Gap in 1990 (17.9), and, while some progress was made over the next three decades, the Prosperity Gap still stands at 12.2 in 2024. Worryingly, progress in reducing the Prosperity Gap in Sub-Saharan Africa stalled in the last decade.

The contributions of different regions to the Global Prosperity Gap have changed significantly, driven by these differential rates of progress in shared prosperity across regions (figure 2.4, panel b). In 1990, East Asia and Pacific contributed the most (46 percent) to the total Prosperity Gap. Next came South Asia (25 percent) and Sub-Saharan Africa (16 percent). By 2024, the East Asia and Pacific contribution to the global gap is estimated to fall to just

15 percent. Progress in South Asia over the same period since 1990 reduced its absolute contribution to the Global Prosperity Gap, but since the pace of progress was slower than in East Asia and Pacific, its share has increased by 2024 to 30 percent. The contribution of Sub-Saharan Africa to the Global Prosperity Gap is estimated to have increased by 23 percentage points, reaching 39 percent in 2024. This means that more inclusive growth in Sub-Saharan Africa and South Asia is key for future reductions in the Global Prosperity Gap.

FIGURE 2.4

The East Asia and Pacific region has driven the reduction of the Global Prosperity Gap

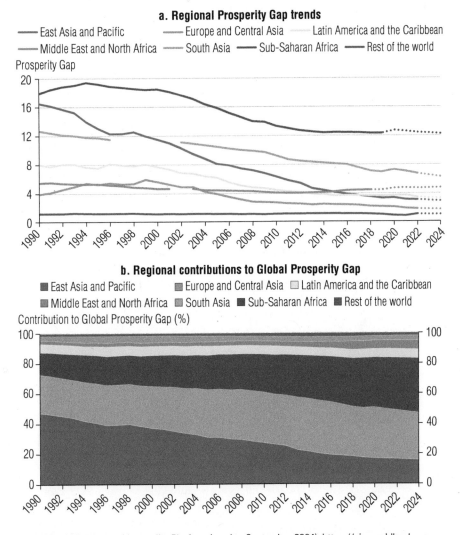

a. Regional Prosperity Gap trends

East Asia and Pacific — Europe and Central Asia — Latin America and the Caribbean — Middle East and North Africa — South Asia — Sub-Saharan Africa — Rest of the world

b. Regional contributions to Global Prosperity Gap

East Asia and Pacific — Europe and Central Asia — Latin America and the Caribbean — Middle East and North Africa — South Asia — Sub-Saharan Africa — Rest of the world

Source: World Bank, Poverty and Inequality Platform (version September 2024), https://pip.worldbank.org.
Note: Regional Prosperity Gaps are reported in panel a, while the regions' population-weighted contributions (percent) to the Global Prosperity Gap are reported in panel b. Estimates for all regions are projected after 2022, while estimates for the Middle East and North Africa are projected as of 2019 and those for Sub-Saharan Africa are projected as of 2020. Population coverage is less than 50 percent of the regions' population for the year 2002 in the Middle East and North Africa and for the years 1997–2001 in South Asia. To obtain the aggregate share of the Global Prosperity Gap, panel b includes all regional estimates whether or not there is data coverage. Regions follow the definitions in the Poverty and Inequality Platform.

Both growth and reductions in inequality contributed to increases in shared prosperity, although the role of inequality has declined in recent decades

Between 1990 and 2024, the Global Prosperity Gap improved at an annual rate of 2.3 percent, with global mean income increasing at an annual rate of 1.48 percent and global inequality declining by 0.86 percent. The changes in the Global Prosperity Gap can be exactly decomposed into growth in mean income and changes in inequality (see annex 2B and Kraay et al. [2023] for further detail). Note that overall inequality is the inequality between all citizens of the world, which captures differences both between and within countries.[9] The gains in prosperity globally over the past three decades were driven primarily by catch-up growth in populous and relatively poorer regions of the world, in particular China and other countries in East Asia and Pacific. Relatively poorer countries grew, on average, faster than higher-income countries (Mahler, Yonzan, and Lakner 2022a). The growth of these populous and relatively poorer countries led to a substantial reduction in between-country inequality, which accounts for most of global interpersonal inequality (Lakner and Milanovic 2016).

Not all periods in the last three and a half decades experienced the same rates of growth and inequality reduction, however (figure 2.5). Between 1990 and 2000, the Global Prosperity Gap improved at an annual rate of 1.5 percent, with 0.9 percent gains coming from improving

---

FIGURE 2.5

The COVID-19 pandemic abruptly slowed the gains in the Global Prosperity Gap

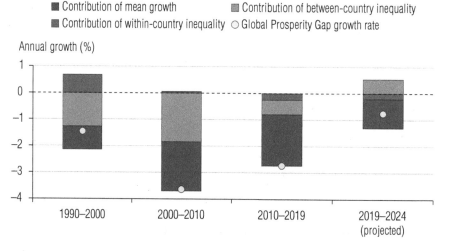

Source: World Bank, Poverty and Inequality Platform (version September 2024), https://pip.worldbank.org.
Note: A decrease in the Prosperity Gap is an improvement in welfare. Growth is calculated as the log difference. Change in the Prosperity Gap is the sum of the (negative) growth in the mean income and the decline in total inequality. Positive growth in the mean decreases (improves) the Prosperity Gap and thus, in the figure, the contribution of the mean growth is shown as the negative of mean growth. That is, for all the periods in the graph, there was positive growth in the global mean, which is displayed as a negative contribution. Inequality is measured using the inequality measure related to the Prosperity Gap. Change in total inequality is the sum of changes in between-country and within-country inequality. See annex 2B for further details.

mean income and 0.6 percent from the narrowing of overall global inequality driven by a faster decline of inequality between countries. The between-country inequality decreased by 1.3 percent, while the average within-country inequality rose by 0.7 percent, for a 0.6 percent net change in overall global inequality. The reductions in the Global Prosperity Gap were larger in the subsequent two decades (annualized reduction of 3.6 percent between 2000 and 2010, and by 2.7 percent between 2010 and 2019). These reductions were driven by strong economic growth and the narrowing of global inequality, but the contribution of inequality declined significantly after 2010. In the most recent period, between-country inequality is expected to worsen (increase), which will dampen the progress on global shared prosperity. Sluggish growth in developing economies following the pandemic is one factor affecting this trend (World Bank 2024b). It follows the largest single-year increase relative to the last three decades in global income inequality that the world experienced in 2020 (Mahler, Yonzan, and Lakner 2022a). Average within-country inequality, on the other hand, is expected to decrease (discussed in the section on within-country inequality below).

The Prosperity Gap worsens when inequality is higher

For a given level of average income, countries with greater inequality have a higher Prosperity Gap. Table 2.1 presents two examples to illustrate this point. First, Benin and Cameroon have similar mean household consumption levels, but Benin has a lower Prosperity Gap (greater shared prosperity) than Cameroon because it has lower inequality. Second, despite Colombia being significantly richer than Peru in terms of mean income, Peru has a lower Prosperity Gap (greater shared prosperity) due to its lower level of inequality. Put differently, higher inequality means that Colombia would need an average income of $22.60 per day (or 30 percent higher than its current level) to have the same Prosperity Gap as Peru. This illustrates how countries with higher inequality require higher average income to reach the same level of prosperity as countries with lower inequality. In other words, higher inequality leads to an "inequality penalty."

TABLE 2.1

An inequality penalty is built into the Prosperity Gap index

	Benin	Cameroon	Peru	Colombia
	2021	2021	2022	2022
Prosperity Gap	7.20	8.32	3.60	4.69
Mean income	5.02	5.37	12.4	17.3
Inequality	1.44	1.79	1.79	3.25

Source: World Bank, Poverty and Inequality Platform (version September 2024), https://pip.worldbank.org.
Note: The Prosperity Gap is calculated using the global prosperity standard of $25 per person per day in 2017 purchasing power parity dollars (PPP$). The table also shows the decomposition of the Prosperity Gap into the product of (25/mean income) and inequality. Inequality is measured using the inequality measure related to the Prosperity Gap—the average income multiple needed to reach the mean income (see annex 2B for details). Mean income is expressed in 2017 PPP$ per person per day. Estimates for each country are reported using the most recent survey data.

FIGURE 2.6

Inequality increases the Prosperity Gap

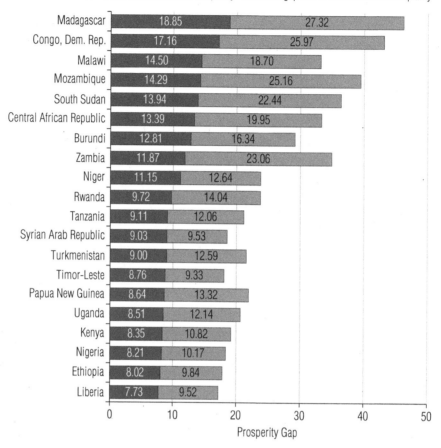

■ Prosperity Gap with benchmark inequality ■ Excess gap due to current level of inequality

Country	Prosperity Gap with benchmark inequality	Excess gap due to current level of inequality
Madagascar	18.85	27.32
Congo, Dem. Rep.	17.16	25.97
Malawi	14.50	18.70
Mozambique	14.29	25.16
South Sudan	13.94	22.44
Central African Republic	13.39	19.95
Burundi	12.81	16.34
Zambia	11.87	23.06
Niger	11.15	12.64
Rwanda	9.72	14.04
Tanzania	9.11	12.06
Syrian Arab Republic	9.03	9.53
Turkmenistan	9.00	12.59
Timor-Leste	8.76	9.33
Papua New Guinea	8.64	13.32
Uganda	8.51	12.14
Kenya	8.35	10.82
Nigeria	8.21	10.17
Ethiopia	8.02	9.84
Liberia	7.73	9.52

Prosperity Gap

Source: World Bank, Poverty and Inequality Platform (version September 2024), https://pip.worldbank.org.
Note: Each bar indicates the Prosperity Gaps with benchmark level of inequality (dark blue) and with current level of inequality (yellow) for the 20 poorest countries with data, ranked by average per capita household consumption. Countries are ranked from the poorest (top) to the richest (bottom). The benchmark inequality is the lowest observed inequality in the Poverty and Inequality Platform. Estimates are reported using the latest household survey.

To illustrate this inequality penalty further, figure 2.6 shows the 20 poorest nations in the world ranked according to their mean household per capita income (the poorest at the top to the richest at the bottom). For each country, the figure reports a hypothetical Prosperity Gap with a benchmark level of inequality equal to the lowest observed inequality in the Poverty and Inequality Platform database (dark blue bar) and the Prosperity Gap with the current level of inequality in the country (dark blue + yellow bars). The resulting difference in the Prosperity

Gaps signals the magnitude of the influence of "excess" inequality (yellow segment of the bar). For instance, Madagascar would have a Prosperity Gap of 18.8 instead of 27.3 had its inequality been at the hypothetical benchmark level. In other words, excess inequality in Madagascar is responsible for a 45 percent larger Prosperity Gap. Likewise, Tanzania—a country that is more equal than Madagascar—has a Prosperity Gap of 9.1 with a benchmark level of inequality or 12.6 with the current level of inequality, suggesting a 38 percent impact of excess inequality. Note also that when countries have the same level of inequality (as in the dark blue bars), Prosperity Gaps are largest for the poorest nation and smallest for the richest nation. However, different levels of inequality across countries change the ranking of countries. For instance, Zambia, the eighth poorest nation by mean income, is ranked the fourth-worst-off nation by the Prosperity Gap, illustrating the high level of inequality in Zambia. Put differently, while Zambia and Niger have similar levels of mean income ($2.69 and $2.53 per day, respectively), the Prosperity Gap in Zambia is almost double that in Niger (23.1 and 12.6, respectively), signaling the sizable differences in inequality.

The impact of high inequality on shared prosperity is also illustrated by the time required for individuals in each country on average to reach the prosperity standard of $25 per day.[10] Figure 2.7 plots the number of years it will take select upper-middle-income countries to reach $25 on average, assuming each country grows at 2 percent per capita annually (dark blue bars), which is slightly higher than the global average annual household income growth in the past three decades, or 4 percent per capita annually (yellow bars). In both cases, inequality within the country is kept fixed. Countries are ranked according to their mean per capita income, with the poorest on top and the richest at the bottom. Generally, it is expected that richer countries (those at the bottom) will face a shorter time than the poorer countries to reach $25 per person per day. However, this is not always the case. For example, Serbia, a country which has a lower mean income ($20) than Brazil ($21), will need about 69 years to reach $25 on average, compared to 113 years for Brazil, if both countries grow at 2 percent per capita annually. Brazil faces a time horizon close to 1.6 times longer than that of Serbia precisely because inequality in Brazil is close to 1.6 times greater than in Serbia. With a 4 percent annual per capita income growth instead, Brazilians on average will reach $25 in 57 years instead of 113 years, signaling the crucial role of income growth. A reduction of the same magnitude is also possible if the country grows annually at 2 percent per capita with half the current level of inequality. While halving inequality is an extreme ask, this thought experiment highlights that, by actively working toward reducing inequalities today, countries can pave the way for faster shared prosperity gains in the future.

FIGURE 2.7
Inequality delays prosperity

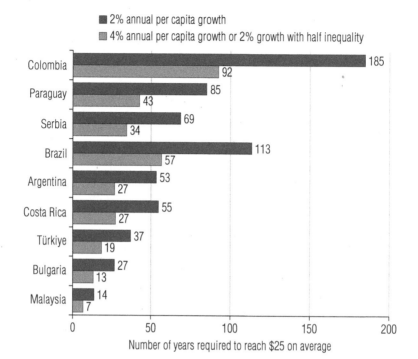

- ■ 2% annual per capita growth
- ■ 4% annual per capita growth or 2% growth with half inequality

Number of years required to reach $25 on average

Source: World Bank, Poverty and Inequality Platform (version September 2024), https://pip.worldbank.org.
Note: Only results for select upper-middle-income countries using the latest survey are reported. Countries are ranked from the poorest (top) to the richest (bottom) by average household per capita income. Each country is assumed to grow at 2 percent per capita annually (dark blue bars) or 4 percent per capita annually (yellow bars) with the current level of inequality. The number of years required to reach $25 per person on average is equivalent if countries grow at 2 percent per capita annually with a level of inequality that is half the current level or grow annually at 4 percent with the current level of inequality.

Within-country inequality: The number of economies with high inequality

The second new World Bank indicator of shared prosperity tracks the *number of economies with high inequality.* These are defined as economies with a Gini index greater than 40, based on the most recent household survey for a country. The Gini index is a measure of inequality that is bounded between 0 (a society in which everyone has the same income and hence perfect equality) and 100 (where one person has all the income and hence the most unequal society).

Looking at all economies since 2000, a Gini of 40 roughly defines the top one-third of economies with the highest levels of inequality. While no single statistic can fully convey the full picture of inequality, the Gini index has many desirable properties and it is likely the most familiar measure of inequality, known to the widest audience, and with a long history of use (Haddad et al. 2024). It is also important that most inequality measures are highly correlated with the Gini index (Haddad et al. 2024).[11] Annex 2D and chapter 4 discuss the issues that arise in the measurement of high inequality and explain why a threshold of 40 is used.

The indicator used in this report is based on either income or consumption inequality, depending on the welfare measure adopted by each country. Box 2.3 outlines the various concepts of welfare and what they mean for levels of inequality. Most high-income countries and countries in Latin America and the Caribbean use income, while the rest of the world tends to use consumption. For the same country, the inequality of income tends to be higher than the inequality of consumption, since savings increase with income.[12] Looking across countries, however, countries that use consumption—typically low-income and lower-middle-income countries—are, on average, more unequal (Haddad et al. 2024). As these differences are important, the analysis differentiates between income- and consumption-based countries wherever possible. In addition to the threshold of 40 that is used by the World Bank in its vision indicator, this chapter also splits out economies with a Gini index below 30 (World Bank, n.d.).[13]

BOX 2.3

Concepts of welfare and differences in measured inequality

The level of inequality depends on the underlying concept of welfare that is captured. Economic inequality is generally captured in one of three welfare spaces—income, consumption, or wealth—each reflecting different aspects of welfare and different observed levels of inequality. Whereas *income* signals an individual's or family's potential buying power, *consumption* expenditure is the realization of that buying power. Households generally do not consume all their income. What is left over (that is, savings), tends to be greater for richer households than for poorer households. This implies that the distribution of consumption tends to be more equal than the distribution of income (see annex 2D and chapter 4 for further detail). Whereas income and consumption both represent the flow of resources—that is, how much one earns or spends in a given time frame, typically a year—*wealth* represents a stock of resources such as accumulated assets, including property, corporate stock holdings, or savings, as well as other investments that can be inherited or acquired. For example, a house (or stock) is wealth, and the rent (or dividends) is the income generated from this asset. The distribution of wealth tends to be much more unequal than either income or consumption.[a]

(continued)

Concepts of welfare and differences in measured inequality *(continued)*

These concepts are interlinked. For instance, recent increases in income inequality have been attributed to the higher rate of return of wealth among the richest (Piketty 2014). Nevertheless, these concepts of welfare are distinct in several crucial ways. Unlike income, which can fluctuate annually, wealth tends to accumulate over time and is more resistant to short-term economic changes. This likely makes wealth a better indicator of long-term resilience and a better signal for economic opportunity or mobility. However, among the three concepts outlined here, wealth remains the most difficult to capture. This is in part due to measurement challenges that similarly plague income measurement in developing countries, along with the potential to "hide" wealth offshore that is a concern even for the countries with the most comprehensive data (Zucman 2015). Given these challenges, this report uses income or consumption, depending on the type of survey available.

a. For example, see the studies by Saez and Zucman (2020) for the United States and by Alvaredo, Atkinson, and Morelli (2018) for the United Kingdom.

See annex 2D for a more detailed discussion of the differences between income and consumption surveys. Chapter 4 expands on the challenges of measuring inequality using household surveys, including the likely underrepresentation of top incomes. Correcting for "missing" top incomes will increase the level of inequality; however, it is not clear whether the trends would be much different with or without the correction (see chapter 4 and World Bank 2016).

Economies with high inequality are concentrated in Latin America and the Caribbean and in Sub-Saharan Africa

Using the latest round of household surveys for each economy, 49 economies worldwide had a Gini index above 40. High-inequality economies are concentrated in Latin America and the Caribbean as well as Sub-Saharan Africa (map 2.1). Over 80 percent of the countries in Latin America and the Caribbean had a Gini index above 40, with Brazil and Colombia being the most unequal countries, followed by countries in Central America. Within Sub-Saharan Africa, inequality is highest in Southern, Central, and Eastern Africa and lowest in Western Africa (map 2.1). At the other end of the spectrum, the Gini index is low for Nordic, Eastern European, and ex-Soviet countries. Overall, Europe and Central Asia has one of the highest numbers of economies with relatively low inequality. Only Türkiye exhibits higher levels of inequality than the rest of the region.

High inequality is more prevalent in low- and middle-income countries as well as countries in fragile and conflict-affected situations (FCS) (figure 2.8). The high-income economies with elevated levels of inequality are Chile, Panama, the United States, and Uruguay (table 2F.1). In contrast, around two-fifths of middle-income countries and one-third of low-income countries exhibit high levels of inequality. Although data are limited, two-fifths of FCS countries have high levels of inequality, compared to only a quarter of non-FCS countries in the sample. Of the 68 International Development Association (IDA) countries with data, less than 15 percent were in the low-inequality group and more than double that (37 percent) were in the high-inequality group.[14]

MAP 2.1

The 49 economies with high inequality are concentrated in Sub-Saharan Africa and Latin America and the Caribbean

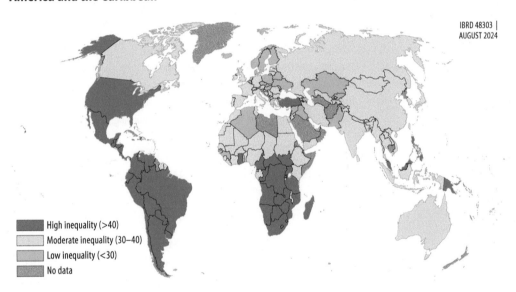

IBRD 48303 |
AUGUST 2024

High inequality (>40)
Moderate inequality (30–40)
Low inequality (<30)
No data

Sources: World Bank, Poverty and Inequality Platform (version September 2024), https://pip.worldbank.org; Haddad et al. 2024.
Note: The map presents the Gini index from the latest available survey (after 2000), which measures the inequality of income or consumption, depending on the economy. High-inequality economies have a Gini index above 40, moderate-inequality economies are those with a Gini index between 30 and 40, and low-inequality economies are those with a Gini index below 30. See annex table 2F.1 for the economy classifications, Gini indexes, year of survey, and the type of welfare—income, or consumption—used.

FIGURE 2.8

Poorer and conflict-affected economies tend to be more unequal

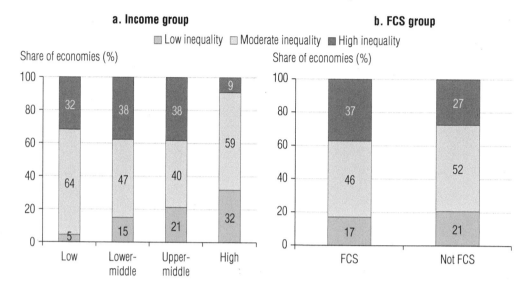

a. Income group

b. FCS group

☐ Low inequality ☐ Moderate inequality ■ High inequality

Source: World Bank, Poverty and Inequality Platform (version September 2024), https://pip.worldbank.org.
Note: FCS = fragile and conflict-affected situations. High-inequality economies have a Gini index above 40, moderate-inequality economies are those with a Gini index between 30 and 40, and low-inequality economies are those with a Gini index below 30. The data cover 166 economies, with at least one household survey in the Poverty and Inequality Platform between 2000 and 2022. The Gini index is from the latest survey year. Income group and FCS status are based on fiscal year 2024 lists. The label values may not add to 100 percent due to rounding.

The number of economies with high inequality has fallen, but the percentage of people living in high-inequality economies has not changed much in the past decade

The number of economies with high inequality declined from 74 in 2000 to 49 in 2022 (figure 2.9, panel a). This aggregate view understates the movements of economies across these groups. In a typical year, some economies see their Gini index rise above 40, while others cross the threshold in the other direction. Since 2005, in a typical year, more economies have exited the high-inequality status than have fallen into it, illustrating this progress (figure 2.9, panel b). When a household survey is not available for an economy in 2022, the high-inequality indicator uses the latest Gini index available for that economy.[15] Note that while there has been progress in the number of economies moving out of the high-inequality category, the number of people living in economies with high inequality has stayed roughly the same in the last decade, from over 23 percent (1.7 billion) of the global population in 2013 to 22 percent (1.8 billion) in 2022. The majority of the global population today (70 percent [5.6 billion]) lives in an economy with moderate inequality while relatively few (8 percent [609 million]) live in economies with low inequality (figure 2F.1).

FIGURE 2.9

There is a steady decline in the number of economies with high inequality since 2000

a. Count of high-inequality economies, 2000–22

☐ Low inequality ☐ Moderate inequality ■ High inequality

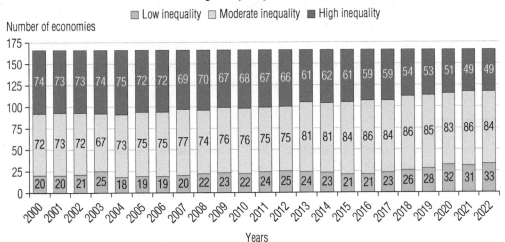

b. Change in number of high-inequality economies from prior year

■ Switched to high ☐ Switched to not-high ---- Fitted value

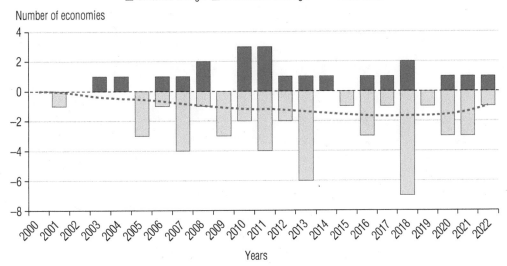

Sources: World Bank, Poverty and Inequality Platform (version September 2024), https://pip.worldbank.org; Haddad et al. 2024.

Note: High-inequality economies have a Gini index above 40, moderate are those with a Gini index between 30 and 40, and low are those with a Gini index less than 30. When no survey is available in a given year, data from the most recent survey year are used. The earliest survey is backcasted when the first survey is available only after 2000 to avoid missing values. The graph covers 166 economies with at least one household survey in the Poverty and Inequality Platform between 2000 and 2022.

The observed reduction in the number of economies with high inequality is not sensitive to small changes around the threshold value of 40. To see this, figure 2.10 shows the share of economies that had a Gini index within a 5 percent range of the threshold. Those with Gini values above 42 (5 percent over the threshold) are indicated in dark red and those with Gini values below 38 (5 percent less than the threshold) are shown in dark blue. Even with a threshold Gini value of 38 (or 42), the share of economies with high inequality would still be declining over time. This means that the trend of economies exiting high-inequality status is not due to marginal cases of inequality around the threshold.

FIGURE 2.10

The decline in the number of economies with high inequality is not driven by small changes around the threshold

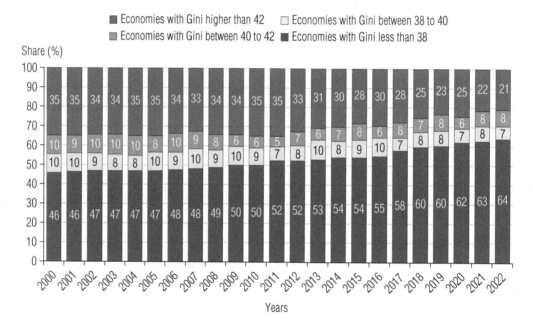

Source: World Bank, Poverty and Inequality Platform (version September 2024), https://pip.worldbank.org.
Note: This figure shows the share of economies with a Gini index below 38 (dark blue), between 38 and 40 (light blue), between 40 and 42 (yellow), and over 42 (dark red). The values of 38 and 42 are ± 5 percent from 40. When no survey is available for a given year, data from the most recent survey year are used. The earliest survey is backcasted when the first survey is available only after 2000 to avoid missing values. The graph covers 166 economies with at least one household survey in the Poverty and Inequality Platform between 2000 and 2022. The label values may not add to 100 percent due to rounding.

The falling number of high-inequality economies (74 to 49) has led to an increase in the number of both low-inequality (20 to 33) and moderate-inequality (72 to 84) economies. Figure 2.11 depicts the movement of economies into and out of all three inequality categories—high (above 40), moderate (between 30 and 40), and low (below 30)—for each five-year period between 2000 and 2020. Except during 2010–15, more economies transitioned from moderate-inequality status to low-inequality status than from moderate- to high-inequality status. In all periods, more economies exited than entered high inequality. For every two economies that moved out of the high-inequality group (23 between 2000 and 2020), one was added to the moderate-inequality group (11) and one was added to the low-inequality group (12).

FIGURE 2.11

More economies moved to a lower-inequality group than to a higher-inequality group, 2000–20

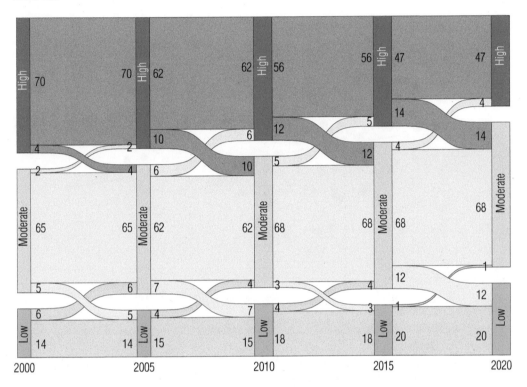

Source: World Bank, Poverty and Inequality Platform (version September 2024), https://pip.worldbank.org.
Note: High inequality is defined as economies with a Gini index above 40, moderate as those between 30 and 40, and low as those below 30. This chart shows the number of economies in each group in the start year and end year at five-year periods. When no survey is available for a given year, data from the most recent survey year are used. The earliest survey is backcasted when the first survey is available only after 2000 to avoid missing values.

Countries with high initial levels of inequality have experienced faster reductions in inequality in the last two decades, leading to some convergence of inequality levels across countries, which explains the changes in the number of economies with high inequality just described (figure 2.12). Average annual changes in inequality are close to zero among countries with a Gini index of less than 30. On average, the annual reduction in inequality has been greater for countries with larger initial Gini values. In Bolivia, for example, the Gini index of income decreased from above 58 in 2005 to 41 in 2021 (a decline of 30 percent). Similarly, Botswana, with an initial Gini index of consumption close to 65, experienced a decline of 18 percent between 2002 and 2015. The finding of inequality convergence holds for both countries with income or consumption as the measure of welfare.

FIGURE 2.12

The reduction in inequality has been faster for economies with high levels of initial inequality

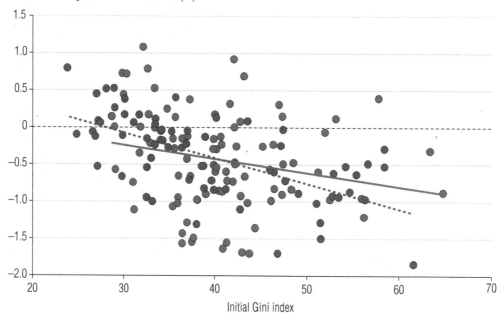

Sources: World Bank, Poverty and Inequality Platform (version September 2024), https://pip.worldbank.org; Haddad et al. 2024 (updated).

Note: Initial Gini index for each economy is for the earliest available year, starting with 2000. The vertical axis shows the (annualized) percent change between the initial Gini and its final value, obtained from the latest survey round. The sample consists of 155 economies with at least two surveys. There might be breaks in comparability over such a long period, which are not controlled for.

Inequality has declined for the typical country in recent decades, although the pandemic had disparate impacts across countries

Thus far, this analysis has focused on movements of economies around the high-inequality threshold; however, it is also important to look at the evolution of inequality more generally. To analyze the evolution of within-country inequality over the long term, figure 2.13 shows the average Gini at half-decade intervals starting with 2000 by aggregating all surveys conducted within each interval. Since many countries lack data for every year, pooling surveys at half-decade periods allows a meaningful comparison of average within-country inequality over time. On average, 123 countries are represented at each interval. Figure 2.13 provides four ways of summarizing average within-country inequality across the world over the past two decades.

Irrespective of the approach, average within-country inequality has been on a downward trend since 2000. Similar analysis had shown an increase over the preceding period before 2000 (World Bank 2016).

The average consumption Gini, after briefly rising in 2015–19 by 0.23 Gini points, returned to a long-term downward trend from 2020–22. On the other hand, the average income Gini continued to fall until 2015–19 but has somewhat plateaued in the most recent period.

Since not all countries conduct a household survey at five-year intervals, the full sample at each half-decade interval comprises different sets of countries. To examine the impact of such shifts, inequality trends are also analyzed using a smaller balanced sample that includes the same set of countries throughout. The dashed lines in figure 2.13 show averages across income and consumption Ginis, restricting the sample to 63 countries (of which 43 conduct income-based surveys) that have a survey in each period. Results based on this balanced sample of countries further confirm the downward trends in average within-country inequality around the world, with consumption Ginis falling faster than income Ginis in 2020–22.

FIGURE 2.13

Average within-country inequality has been falling in the past 20 years

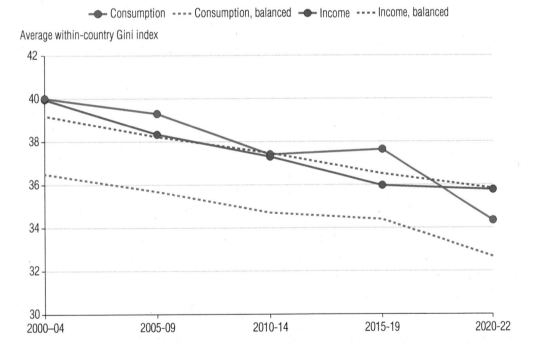

Source: Word Bank, Poverty and Inequality Platform (version September 2024), https://pip.worldbank.org.
Note: The sample comprises 121 economies in 2000–04, 131 in 2005–09, 137 in 2010–14, 133 in 2015–19, and 93 economies in 2020–22. The balanced sample comprises 63 economies, 43 of which are income-based surveys. In cases where economies conducted several survey rounds within a half-decade period, the figure uses the median Gini value for the economy across surveys within that interval. Simple averages are used, unweighted by population.

To highlight the changes since the pandemic, figure 2.14 examines shifts in within-country inequality before and after COVID-19. This analysis is based on a sample of 72 countries that reported a survey after 2020 and had comparable data from a pre-COVID-19 round.[16] For each country, the changes in inequality compare the Gini index from the most recent survey round conducted before COVID-19 (2019 or earlier) with the latest available round after the first wave of COVID-19 (2021 or later). Countries with their latest survey dating to 2020 are excluded from this analysis, as COVID-19 affected most countries during that year.

FIGURE 2.14

Most economies experienced a decline in inequality after COVID-19

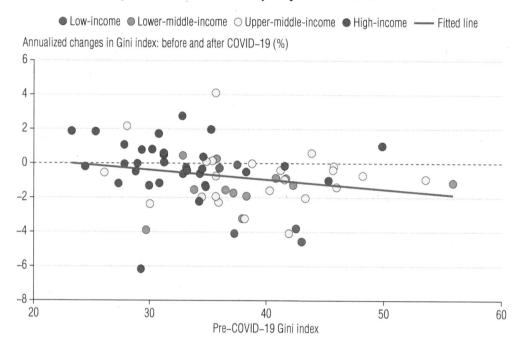

Source: World Bank, Poverty and Inequality Platform (version September 2024), https://pip.worldbank.org.
Note: Sample consists of 72 economies that reported a survey after 2020 and had comparable data from a pre-COVID-19 round (2019 or earlier). The changes in inequality are calculated by comparing the Gini value from the most recent round of survey conducted in an economy before the COVID-19 pandemic, with its latest available and comparable round after the pandemic. The trend line, reported for all economies, is not weighted by population size.

Within-country inequality is observed to have fallen in many countries, with greater reductions in countries that were more unequal before the pandemic, which is similar to the patterns observed over the longer period above (figure 2.12). In slightly more than half the cases where inequality fell, the observed reductions exceed 1 Gini point, which has previously been used as a rough adjustment for sampling errors (World Bank 2016).[17] For the countries with a reduction in inequality, the average decline was highest among low-income countries (falling by an average 2.7 Gini points), followed by lower-middle-income countries (2.2 Gini points), upper-middle-income countries (1.5 Gini points), and high-income countries (0.7 Gini points).[18] Of the 72 countries, 6 saw an increase of more than 1 Gini point and 28 saw a decline of more than 1 Gini point. Of the 28 countries with a reduction in inequality of more than 1 Gini point,

9 are in Sub-Saharan Africa, 7 are in Latin America and the Caribbean, 6 are in Europe and Central Asia, 2 each are in the East Asia and Pacific region and from the rest of the world grouping, and 1 each is from the Middle East and North Africa region and the South Asia region.

Effectively addressing inequality requires a comprehensive approach that tackles structural sources of inequality

High levels of inequality are the result of several structural factors, and the appropriate actions to address inequality will vary across countries. Policies to reduce inequality have been reviewed extensively in the literature. For example, World Bank (2016) reviewed the policy evidence at the global level. More recently, World Bank reports have highlighted factors and important policies to reduce inequality in Sub-Saharan Africa, one of the regions with the highest levels of inequality (Sinha, Inchauste, and Narayan 2024; World Bank 2024a). The Latin America and Caribbean Inequality Review focuses on inequality along various dimensions, including income, wealth, education, health, and political power (Alvaredo et al. 2023; Bancalari et al. 2023; Fernández et al. 2024; Lupu 2024). The review aims to provide evidence to understand why, despite major structural economic and social changes, inequality in Latin America and the Caribbean persists at exceptionally high levels. Given these detailed reviews on policies and inequality, this section does not aim to provide an exhaustive review of all policy options, nor does it offer universal prescriptions. Instead, this section gives a broad overview of the policy space and outlines the interlinkages between inequalities defined at various stages.

There is nothing inevitable about inequality. Policies can affect structural sources of inequality at three interrelated stages. First, they can address inequality in acquiring human capital and other assets, before individuals join the labor market, such as policies aimed at reducing differences in educational attainment. These differences oftentimes reflect an inequality of opportunity, encompassing factors that are linked to circumstances that are out of an individual's control, such as birthplace, parental income, gender, race, and others. Second, policies can address inequality in using skills and assets, which arise from market and institutional distortions in the labor, product, capital, and input markets. These distortions include anticompetitive or discriminatory practices, or policies and regulations that provide preferential treatment or restrict market access for some, while limiting access for others, thus curtailing their productive potential and limiting earning opportunities. Third, fair fiscal policies can be leveraged to improve the redistributive impact of taxes and transfers. Despite equalizing opportunities, inequality could still arise ex post simply due to bad luck or shocks. The poor and vulnerable face a greater risk due to the changing global climatic (chapter 3) and economic conditions.

Structural inequalities at each stage reinforce each other and are dynamic. For instance, differences in parental income—reflective of inequality in the previous generation—have been directly linked to inequality in building productive capacities (inequality of opportunities for the current generation) as well as the current generation's ability to utilize those capacities

(Chetty et al. 2017; Corak 2013; World Bank 2017a). The latter is what economists have termed intergenerational mobility (or persistence, in the case of lack of mobility). Recent work on Latin America has estimated that as much as one-half to two-thirds of current inequality could be due to circumstances that are out of individuals' control (Brunori, Ferreira, and Neidhöfer 2023). This means that a society with high inequality is also likely to have greater inequality of opportunity, which further leads to lower mobility across generations, which, in turn, leads to further inequality. Policies are key to break such cycles of worsening inequality. World Bank (2024b) and Sinha, Inchauste, and Narayan (2024) provide a comprehensive overview of various policies in these three stages, but some brief examples are included here.

Key actions to tackle inequalities in building productive capacities that would help equalize opportunities include the following: (a) increasing access to quality education, from early childhood through higher education, which significantly affects skill development and future earning potential; (b) supporting the accumulation of human capital within the family by expanding the opportunities and resources available for child development at home (c) reducing disparities in health and nutrition, including prenatal care and early childhood health; (d) expanding access to basic public services; (e) improving access to productive assets such as land; and (f) creating a social environment that allows for better early life experiences, such as reducing exposure to crime and improving the availability of community resources. For instance, Brazil has been successful in reducing inequality by providing public education and free universal health care (World Bank 2016).

Inequality in utilizing productive capacities arises during individuals' active participation in the labor market and is shaped by differences in employment dynamics, types of incomes, and workplace conditions. As discussed above, these ex post inequalities in outcomes are linked to ex ante inequality of opportunity, which, left unaddressed, can affect the ex ante inequalities of the following generation. Government policies to reduce inequalities in using productive capacities include fostering market-based innovations to provide better access to capital and technology, facilitating the expansion of connective infrastructure to promote access to markets, fostering participation in global value chains, tackling labor market segmentation and frictions, enhancing legal protection, promoting competition, and reducing discrimination.

Finally, government policies on taxes and transfers determine how inequality in market income is translated into the inequality in disposable income, which is what was used to measure inequality and poverty in this report. Governments can significantly reduce inequality by making tax systems more progressive and redistribute income through pro-poor transfers. Investing in adequate social protection programs, such as unemployment benefits, pensions, and health care, helps mitigate income inequality by providing support to the disadvantaged, protecting them against shocks, and delivering long-term inclusive income growth. It is important, however, to note that policy effects may vary across countries. The net effect of taxes, transfers, and subsidies substantially increases consumable income for the poorest households in high-income countries, but these measures decrease consumable income for the poorest households in low-income countries (World Bank 2022).

High-income countries deliver more fiscal redistribution while exhibiting less inequality initially because they are more effective at targeting resources and have more fiscal space

Figure 2.15 plots the Gini index of disposable income against the Gini index of market income.[19] Although we refer to income throughout this section, countries that use consumption as their main measure are also included.[20] In all countries with available estimates, inequality is reduced after direct taxes and transfers are accounted for.[21] However, how much countries redistribute varies greatly, which is indicated by the distance from the 45-degree line. At one extreme, Ireland has reduced the Gini index by 17 points (from 46.6 to 29.4 in 2018), whereas The Gambia has reduced it by 0.2 points (from 36.1 to 35.9 in 2015/16).[22]

FIGURE 2.15
Market versus disposable income

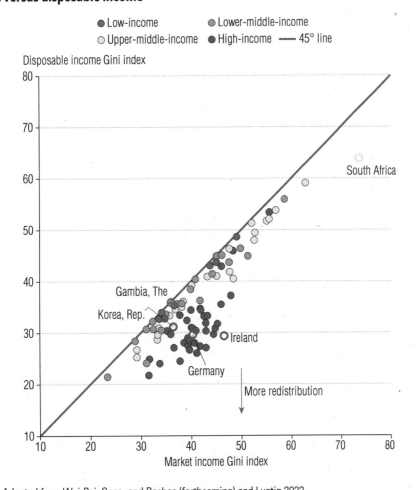

Sources: Adapted from Wai-Poi, Sosa, and Bachas (forthcoming) and Lustig 2023.
Note: The data are from the Commitment to Equity (CEQ) Institute, the Organisation for Economic Co-operation and Development (OECD), and World Bank databases, which collectively cover 96 economies over the past decade across all income groups and regions. The analysis includes the latest data point available for each country from the CEQ database and the OECD, which might differ from the latest year in the Poverty and Inequality Platform that has been used in the rest of the report. See also annex 2D and chapter 4 for discussion of the differences in inequality when income and consumption are used as the welfare aggregate.

High-income countries conduct more fiscal redistribution, but they also need to do less since they start out with a more equal distribution of market incomes. For instance, South Africa has greatly reduced its income inequality in absolute terms through taxes and transfers in the last decades. However, inequality remains high even after redistribution because South Africa's prefiscal inequality is among the highest in the world (World Bank 2022). Fiscal redistribution reduces the Gini in South Africa by around 10 points (from 73.7 to 63.8 in 2015), which is almost the same as the extent of redistribution in Germany (from 40.3 to 29.9 in 2019). However, since South Africa starts out with much greater inequality, it ends up with a Gini that is double that of Germany's level. Countries end up with the same inequality in disposable income, but in different ways. For example, the Republic of Korea's inequality of disposable income is only slightly higher than Germany's, but its redistribution is about half, since it starts out with a more equal pretax distribution.[23]

In general, high-income countries achieve greater fiscal redistribution. The extent of fiscal redistribution depends on a broad set of fiscal policies, such as taxes and transfers. High-income countries are more effective at targeting taxes and transfers and at ensuring that poor households are better-off as a result of these fiscal policies. In low-income countries, incomes of all households (including poor households) are lower after taxes, transfers, and subsidies (World Bank 2022). This is because high-income countries rely on direct taxes and transfers, while low- and middle-income countries rely more on indirect taxation and subsidies, which generate mixed and generally more muted distributional impacts. Most African households pay far more in taxes than they receive in transfers and subsidies, effectively leaving them poorer (Sinha, Inchauste, and Narayan 2024; World Bank 2024a). As a consequence, although taxes and spending reduce inequality in all economies, the magnitude is considerably lower in low-income countries.

One reason for the heterogeneity across countries is fiscal space. As countries develop, the total amount of taxes collected as a share of gross domestic product increases, leaving countries with more resources to support redistribution. Another reason is the composition of these taxes. The importance of indirect taxes (for instance, value added tax, sales taxes, and tariffs) declines and personal income taxes become more prominent as countries become richer (Bachas, Jensen, and Gadenne 2024). In fact, only the richest decile usually pays direct taxes of around 5 percent of income in low-income countries, which is slightly lower than the share paid by the poorest decile in a typical high-income country (World Bank 2022). Both of these factors limit the redistributive capacity of low-income countries. These countries have fewer resources to redistribute than high-income countries, and they raise taxes in a less progressive way because indirect taxes are broad-based taxes that do not take household income levels into account.

Improving the effectiveness of fiscal policies in poorer countries is not easy. Informality weakens the effectiveness of fiscal policy (Bachas, Jensen, and Gadenne 2024). Food subsidies and tax exemptions on food and energy do not reach the poor as intended. Although these goods and services constitute a large share of poor households' consumption baskets, the households obtain these items mainly in the informal economy, such as through small, unregistered stores and markets or directly from home production with no pass-through of consumption taxes to final prices. For example, in Rwanda, the share of the household budget spent in informal stores falls from 90 percent for the lowest income decile of households to 70 percent for the highest decile (Bachas, Gadenne, and Jensen 2023). Thus, value added tax exemptions and subsidies ultimately benefit richer households that are more able to make use of these benefits (World Bank 2022). In addition, these exemptions reduce total revenues and thus limit what can be achieved through the transfer side.

Another consideration is that prefiscal inequality is relatively low for low-income countries, at an average Gini of 36; higher for lower-middle-income (42) and upper-middle-income (48) countries; but it is lower for high-income countries, with a respective Gini index of around 40. As countries develop, their market inequality tends to increase and then fall again as they become richer (World Bank 2024d). These changes result from various structural and random shocks affecting the economies to various degrees (see related discussion in Alvaredo et al. [2023]). Additionally, this comparison is complicated by the difference between income- and consumption-based measures of inequality. The share of income-based measures increases with a country's income level. This has two major implications. First, inequality of low-income countries is likely underestimated, since consumption inequality is, on average, lower than income-based inequality. Second, most high-income countries use income-based measures, while upper-middle-income countries use both income and consumption measures. As a consequence, the described relationship is likely less steeply increasing with income at low levels of development (low-income countries) but decreasing at high levels of development (high-income countries).

Addressing inequality for low- and lower-middle-income countries requires focusing on tackling all phases of inequality; fiscal redistribution alone is not the solution

Sub-Saharan Africa actually redistributes more than non-African countries with comparable income levels, but it is not enough to offset the high market inequality (Sinha, Inchauste, and Narayan 2024; World Bank 2024a). Addressing inequality effectively requires a holistic approach that targets all three stages. Policies directly addressing inequality-reinforcing barriers at these various stages can simultaneously close opportunity gaps and boost socioeconomic mobility (Sinha, Inchauste, and Narayan 2024; World Bank 2016) (figure 2.16). In 15 of 18 countries in Sub-Saharan Africa with available data, more than half of the inequality in consumption is due to factors beyond an individual's control, such as their place of birth or ethnicity (Sinha, Inchauste, and Narayan 2024). Sub-Saharan Africa also does worse than similar countries in terms of educational mobility (Narayan et al. 2018). In some of the poorest countries in the region, only 20 percent of respondents surpass the education of their parents, compared with 80 percent in East Asia (van der Weide et al. 2024). Chapter 3 of this report also highlights the importance of building resilience, which involves many of the actions mentioned here. Building resilience is also key for reducing inequality, so households do not slide back as the result of shocks, which will become more frequent in the future.

FIGURE 2.16

Effectively addressing inequality requires a comprehensive approach that tackles all phases of inequality

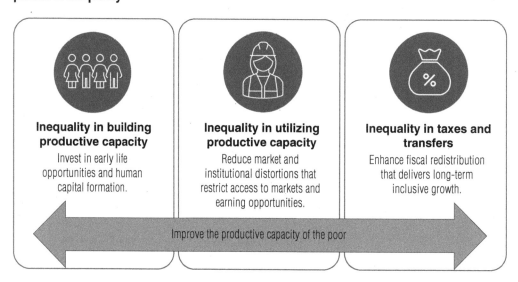

Source: World Bank.

Annex 2A. Comparing the growth in the mean of the bottom 40 percent versus the Global Prosperity Gap and the Gini index

Figure 2A.1, panel a, compares the growth in the Prosperity Gap with the growth in the mean of the bottom 40 percent of the distribution (bottom 40). It is expected that the two measures would be negatively correlated, since a greater *improvement* in the income of the poor (higher bottom 40 growth) is associated with a faster *decline* in the Prosperity Gap. The takeaway is that the changes in the bottom 40 closely align with the changes in the Prosperity Gap, and they overwhelmingly move in the same direction. In some cases, the bottom 40 change is greater (for example, for Romania), while in other cases the Prosperity Gap change is greater (such as for the Slovak Republic). This can be explained by the sensitivity of the measures to changes at different parts of the distribution of income or consumption.

FIGURE 2A.1

Old and new measures of shared prosperity track each other well

a. Growth in the bottom 40 versus growth in the Global Prosperity Gap

b. Shared prosperity premium versus Gini index

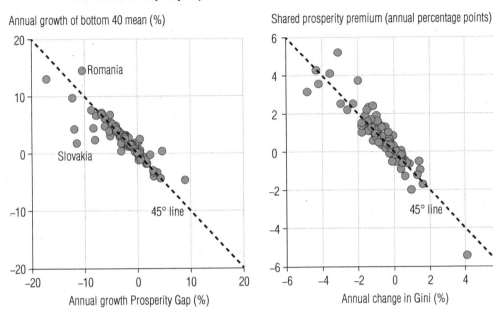

Sources: World Bank, Poverty and Inequality Platform (version September 2024), https://pip.worldbank.org; Global Database of Shared Prosperity (13th edition).

Note: The figure plots those economies with comparable data between the years spanning circa 2016 to 2021 as reported in the Global Database of Shared Prosperity, 13th edition (https://pip.worldbank.org/shared-prosperity). The estimates of Prosperity Gap, Gini index, and growth in the mean income of the bottom 40 percent are calculated using the latest available data in PIP (Poverty and Inequality Platform). The shared prosperity premium is defined as the difference between the growth in the bottom 40 mean and growth in the overall mean. A positive premium means that the mean of the bottom 40 grows faster than the overall mean.

Similarly, figure 2A.1, panel b, compares the shared prosperity premium—difference between the growth of the bottom 40 and growth of the overall mean (Lakner et al. 2022)—with the change in the Gini index. Once again, the two measures can be expected to correlate negatively, since a *larger* shared prosperity premium (that is, the poorer parts of the distribution growing faster than the overall population) leads to a *reduction* in inequality. With few exceptions, the two measures track each other well, especially when changes are small.

Annex 2B. The Global Prosperity Gap

The Global Prosperity Gap is *the average factor by which incomes need to be multiplied to bring everyone in the world to the prosperity standard of $25 per person per day.* Let y_i represent the income of individual $i = 1, \ldots, N$ and let $z = \$25$ per person per day represent the prosperity standard, then the Global Prosperity Gap (GPG) is:

$$GPG = \frac{1}{N}\sum_{i=1}^{N}\frac{z}{y_i}.$$

The Global Prosperity Gap summarizes how far the world is, on average, from achieving a prosperity standard defined at the global level. The measure was developed by Kraay et al. (2023) and has since been adopted by the World Bank (2024c). Since this number represents a shortfall, the measure falls as welfare improves. The indicator has a pro-poor weighting scheme, so that individuals who are further behind the prosperity standard contribute proportionally more to the Prosperity Gap than individuals closer to the standard. Similarly, while growth anywhere in the world contributes to reducing the gap, the indicator rewards the growth of the poorest the most.

The global prosperity standard is set at $25 per person per day, roughly equal to the average per capita household income when countries reach high-income status, according to the World Bank's income classification. Two properties of the prosperity standard are important. First, the prosperity standard is simply a scaling factor, so it does not influence the trends, growth rates, or ranking across groups as long as the same threshold is applied to everyone. In other words, the conclusion of which region in the world is driving the trend in the Global Prosperity Gap will not change regardless of whether the global standard scales upward or downward. Second, the prosperity standard can easily be adapted to specific circumstances. For example, if applying a prosperity standard that was half (double) the global standard, namely, $12.5 per day ($50 per day), then the Prosperity Gap would also be half (double) the shortfall calculated at $25 per day.

Subgroup decomposition of the Prosperity Gap

The Global Prosperity Gap can be expressed as a population-weighted average of the Prosperity Gaps for different subgroups, allowing for an assessment of which regions, countries, or population groups are driving the changes. For example, using population sizes, the Global Prosperity Gap can be easily decomposed into Prosperity Gaps of world regions, each regional gap can be divided into country gaps, and the country gaps can be separated into gaps of provinces or relevant population groups (such as ethnicity).

More formally, let each group $g = 1, \ldots, G$ have a Prosperity Gap of PG_g; then the Global Prosperity Gap can be decomposed as follows:

$$GPG = \sum_{g=1}^{G}\frac{N_g}{N} \times PG_g,$$

where N is the total population and N_g is the population of group g.

Decomposition of the Prosperity Gap into mean and inequality

The Prosperity Gap can be written as product of the shortfall of the average income from the prosperity threshold, $z/\bar{y}$, and an inequality measure, $I(y,\bar{y})$ (Kraay et al. 2023). The latter captures the average shortfall from the mean income of society and is referred to as the mean ratio deviation.

$$\textit{Prosperity Gap} = \left(\frac{z}{\bar{y}}\right) \times I(y,\bar{y}), \text{ and } I(y,\bar{y}) \equiv \frac{1}{N}\sum_{i=1}^{N}\frac{\bar{y}}{y_i}.$$

The growth in the Prosperity Gap can be decomposed into growth in mean income and growth in inequality. Formally, the growth in the Prosperity Gap, $PG(y_t, z)$, from initial period t to final period $t+1$ (approximated as the change in logarithms) can be expressed as

$$\underbrace{\ln\left(\frac{PG(y_{t+1},z)}{PG(y_t,z)}\right)}_{\textit{growth in prosperity gap}} = \underbrace{\ln\left(\frac{I(y_{t+1},\bar{y}_{t+1})}{I(y_t,\bar{y}_t)}\right)}_{\textit{growth in inequality}} - \underbrace{\ln\left(\frac{\bar{y}_{t+1}}{\bar{y}_t}\right)}_{\textit{growth in mean}}.$$

The mean ratio deviation can be multiplicatively decomposed into within-group and between-group inequalities. Formally, for mutually exclusive groups $g=1,\ldots,G$ with population N_g, income distribution y_g, and mean income $\bar{y}_g$, the mean ratio deviation is given by

$$I(y,\bar{y}) = \underbrace{\left(\sum_{g=1}^{G}\frac{N_g}{N}\frac{\bar{y}}{\bar{y}_g}\right)}_{\textit{between-group inequality}}\underbrace{\left(\sum_{g=1}^{G}w_g I(y_g,\bar{y}_g)\right)}_{\textit{within-group inequality}}, \text{ where } w_g = \frac{N_g/\bar{y}_g}{\sum_{g'=1}^{G}N_{g'}/\bar{y}_{g'}}.$$

Annex 2C. Bottom coding welfare distributions

The data at the bottom of the income and consumption distributions are known to have measurement issues due to transient factors and measurement errors (Ravallion 2016). For consumption surveys, zero and very low reported consumption are likely to be the result of measurement error, given that there is a biological minimum consumption level required to sustain life. For example, as many as 13 consumption surveys in the Poverty and Inequality Platform have observations with zero consumption. For income surveys, very low, zero, and even negative incomes are more plausible, as individuals can finance consumption by drawing down savings. Even in the case of income, however, the minimum threshold for consumption could be a satisfactory threshold to bottom code, recognizing that the consumption levels of those individuals with low income are unlikely to be lower and could well be considerably higher.[24]

Sensitivity to low income or consumption is a desirable feature of any distribution-sensitive measure. However, some welfare measures cannot incorporate negative or zero incomes. In addition, small positive values can have an extreme influence on distribution-sensitive indexes (Cowell and Victoria-Feser 2006; Cowell and Flachaire 2007), which also applies to the Prosperity Gap. Hence, income or consumption is often bottom coded at some strictly positive value.[25] For a discussion on bottom coding the Prosperity Gap, see Kraay et al. (2023).

All indicators in the Poverty and Inequality Platform were previously reported by truncating income or consumption distributions at zero (in other words, observations with a negative value were dropped). In addition, ad hoc adjustments were made for the indicators that could not accept zero values. For example, in the case of the mean log deviation, zero values were replaced with a small positive value, while zero values were dropped in the case of the Watts index.

With the September 2024 edition of the Poverty and Inequality Platform data, which is used in this report, all poverty, prosperity, and inequality indicators are calculated using income and consumption distributions that (a) do not include negative incomes (that is, they are dropped as before) and (b) replace all other observations below $0.25 per person per day with $0.25 per person per day. For details on the need to bottom code, threshold used, methods explored, and the effect on indicators, see Yonzan et al. (forthcoming).

Figure 2C.1 shows the impact of bottom coding on the Prosperity Gap. It shows the rank-rank correlation of the Prosperity Gap between bottom coding a distribution at $0.25/day and not bottom coding using the most recent survey from each country. It ranks the countries from the least prosperous (rank of 1) to the most prosperous. Most observations are close to the 45-degree line, suggesting limited reranking. Not bottom coding would mean, for example using the latest surveys, that Norway would be wrongly classified as less prosperous than Egypt (a country with an average household income more than eight times lower) because of a few very small income observations in Norway. Spain is in a similar situation. Bottom coding addresses these data issues at the country level, while it has a minimum impact on aggregate results (Yonzan et al., forthcoming).

FIGURE 2C.1

The rank-rank correlation of the Prosperity Gap between bottom coding at $0.25/day and not bottom coding

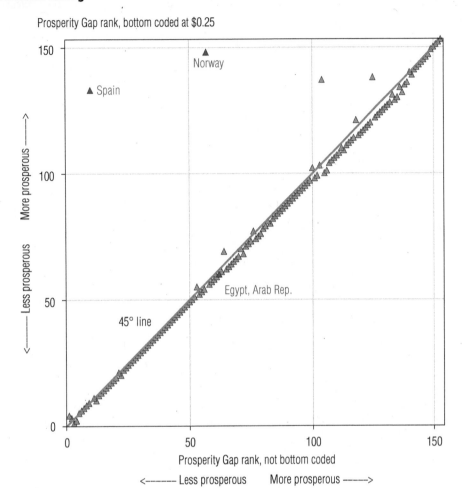

Source: Yonzan et al., forthcoming.

Note: Each observation is from the latest (post-2000) country survey ranked from the least prosperous (rank of 1) to the most prosperous. On the vertical axis, countries are ranked after bottom coding the distribution at $0.25/day in 2017 purchasing power parity dollars. Observations with zero values are not included in either sample since they are dropped in the case with no bottom code.

Annex 2D. Measuring the number of economies with high inequality

The new World Bank indicator of the *number of economies with high inequality* is defined as those with a Gini index greater than 40 based on the most recent household survey for an economy. The indicator is reported for all economies with harmonized consumption or income aggregates in the World Bank's Poverty and Inequality Platform. The indicator tracks the number of *economies*, and therefore all *economies*, regardless of population, count the same.

The indicator is based on either income or consumption inequality, depending on the welfare measure adopted by each economy. Most high-income countries and countries in Latin America and the Caribbean use income, while the rest of the world uses consumption (table 2D.1). In the latest year, only 6 percent of low-income and lower-middle-income countries have income-based surveys. This poses a challenge because income inequality is generally higher than consumption inequality for the same sample of households (Deininger and Squire 1996).[26]

TABLE 2D.1

Statistics of Gini indexes in the Poverty and Inequality Platform, post-2000

	Economy count	Survey count	Share of LICs and LMICs	Average Gini
Income-based surveys	66	1,057	0.06	37.3
Consumption-based surveys	100	570	0.71	36.2
Total	166	1,627	0.45	36.9

Source: World Bank, Poverty and Inequality Platform (version September 2024), https://pip.worldbank.org.
Note: LICs = lower-income countries; LMICs = lower-middle-income countries.

Among countries that have both income- and consumption-based surveys for the same year, the average consumption-based Gini index is 4.5 points, or 10 percent, lower than the corresponding income-based index (Haddad et al. 2024). Figure 2D.1 plots income and consumption Gini indexes for these countries. Most observations are above the 45-degree line, which suggests that for this group of countries, income-based Gini indexes are, on average, higher than consumption-based Gini indexes. Two main factors explain this difference. At the lower end, consumption is generally bounded by a subsistence level of consumption, while income can take zero and negative values in a given year. At the higher end, not all income is spent on consumption, but some is saved or invested.

The difference in observed Gini indexes between countries that use consumption and those that use income (36.2 versus 37.3, that is, a difference of 1.1 Gini points [see table 2D.1]) is considerably smaller than the observed difference for the countries that report both measures (4.5 Gini points) (Haddad et al. [2024]). This is explained by the fact that the sample of countries is fundamentally different when countries that use consumption and countries that use income are compared. Countries that use consumption—typically low- and lower-middle-income countries—are, on average, more unequal than countries that use income, many of which are high-income countries. Because these differences are challenging to account for, where possible, the analysis in chapter 2 differentiates between income- and consumption-based countries. Chapter 4 provides a broader discussion of this issue. The systematic difference also raises the question whether income and consumption inequalities should be compared against the same threshold, which is discussed further below.

FIGURE 2D.1

Relationship between income and consumption Ginis for countries with both

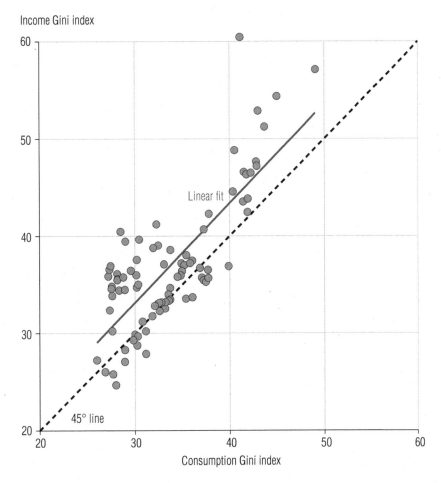

Source: World Bank, Poverty and Inequality Platform (version September 2024), https://pip.worldbank.org.
Note: Estimated relationship between income and consumption Gini indexes for countries that have surveys reporting both welfare aggregates in a given year.

Why the Gini index?

High inequality is tracked with the Gini index, which is a summary measure of inequality that is bounded between zero (a society where everyone has the same income and hence perfect equality) and 100 (where one person has all the income and hence maximum inequality). While no single statistic can fully convey the full picture of inequality, the Gini index has many desirable properties, is likely the most familiar measure of inequality, is known to the widest audience, and has enjoyed a long history of use (Haddad et al. 2024). The fact that it is bounded from 0 to 100 makes it easy to interpret. It considers everyone's income as opposed to only segments of the distribution, like income shares or ratios. It satisfies the major axioms required of a distributional measure, including the Pigou-Dalton transfer axiom.[27]

Nonetheless, it is important to acknowledge its shortcomings. First, every index has an implicit welfare judgment built in, and the Gini index is no exception. The Gini depends on ranks rather than on income levels, which makes it relatively insensitive to very large income gaps at the top of the distribution. Instead, the Gini index is more sensitive to changes in the middle of the income distribution (Atkinson 1970; Allison 1978; Jenkins 2009). Hence, transfers affecting the middle class change the measure more than equivalent transfers at the bottom or the top. Second, the index cannot be exactly additively decomposed into contributions of between-group inequality (for instance, inequality coming from the average differences between groups, such as by geographical region) and within-group inequality (Bourguignon 1979; Shorrocks 1980). Third, while the extremes are easy to interpret, a one-point change in the index is not readily interpretable.

At the same time, two things are worth noting. First, most inequality measures are highly correlated with the Gini index. The Spearman and Pearson correlations between the Gini index and four commonly used inequality measures—mean log deviation, Palma ratio, income ratio of the 90th to the 10th income percentiles (or p90/p10), and Theil (T) index—range from 0.908 to 0.999 (Haddad et al. 2024). More substantially, the high correlation across indexes means that the selection of the index does not make much practical difference in the classification of economies into low, moderate, or high inequality (Haddad et al. 2024).[28] The global patterns, therefore, are indistinguishable from each other.

Why the threshold of 40 for the Gini index?

There are no universally recognized standards for defining high levels of inequality globally. There is no consensus on a specific threshold at which inequality becomes "high" or detrimental to developmental or growth outcomes. Cross-country data fail to identify any distinct tipping points along the range of Gini indexes.

In the absence of predefined standards, the Gini index threshold of 40 was chosen on the basis of the following considerations. First, several United Nations reports define countries with Gini indexes above 40 as highly unequal. For instance, the United Nations Statistics Division classifies countries as having low inequality if their Gini index is less than 25, moderately low if it is between 25 and 30, moderately high if it is between 30 and 40, highly unequal if it is between 40 and 45, and very high if it is above 45 (United Nations 2022).[29] Further, a UNICEF report defines a Gini index above 40 as high or severe inequality (UNICEF 2018), and finally, a World Bank report on inequality in educational outcomes considered Gini indexes for earnings above 40 to be unequal and above 50 highly unequal (Porta et al. 2011). Second, a Gini threshold of 40 separates approximately the top third of all Gini indexes from surveys conducted between 2000 and 2022 (67th percentile equals 41.1), as well as the top third of the separate consumption and income distributions (67th percentile equals 40.8 and 41.6, respectively) (Haddad et al. 2024).[30] Finally, a poll conducted by Haddad et al. (2024) of World Bank experts working on poverty and inequality in various countries found that the median expert viewed inequality over 40 as high when using consumption and considered 45 high when using income.

While there are some differences when thresholds are defined for income-only and consumption-only surveys, this gap has narrowed over time. In the 1990s, the 67th percentile of consumption (income) Ginis corresponded to values of 44.1 (49.1). In comparison, using data from the latest available surveys of all economies, the 67th percentile corresponds to 39.3 (40.3).[31] Trends in the number of economies with high inequality reported in this chapter are robust to the range of thresholds reported here and those shown in figure 2.10 in the main text. With all these results in mind, the same threshold was chosen across income and consumption surveys, which is simpler to communicate and follows the practice of United Nations agencies.

Annex 2E. Prosperity Gap estimates by region

TABLE 2E.1

Prosperity Gap estimates, by region

Region	1990	1995	2000	2005	2010	2015	2019	2020	2021	2022	2023	2024
East Asia and Pacific	16.5	13.0	11.5	8.06	6.26	4.06	3.25	3.28	3.04	3.00	2.92	2.83
Europe and Central Asia	3.83	5.18	5.54	3.83	2.63	2.36	2.06	2.01	1.81	1.74	1.70	1.67
Latin America and the Caribbean	8.01	7.52	7.64	6.15	4.40	3.60	3.57	3.61	3.67	3.36	3.28	3.25
Middle East and North Africa	5.40	5.25	4.59	4.35	4.00	4.16	4.38	4.62	4.67	4.61	4.65	4.69
South Asia	12.7	11.7	--	10.4	9.19	8.05	6.88	7.22	6.97	6.64	6.43	6.21
Sub-Saharan Africa	17.9	19.2	18.5	15.8	13.3	12.4	12.3	12.7	12.6	12.4	12.3	12.2
Eastern and Southern Africa	17.0	18.7	19.0	17.0	14.4	13.5	--	14.7	14.5	14.3	14.2	14.1
Western and Central Africa	19.2	19.9	--	14.2	11.8	10.8	9.54	9.74	9.66	9.56	9.51	9.42
Rest of the world	1.15	1.15	1.09	1.10	1.07	1.11	0.98	0.83	0.80	1.01	0.98	0.98
World	10.9	9.96	9.43	7.81	6.55	5.58	5.12	5.28	5.16	5.07	5.00	4.93

Source: World Bank, Poverty and Inequality Platform (version September 2024), https://pip.worldbank.org.
Note: The estimates for Middle East and North Africa and Eastern and Southern Africa are projected starting in 2019. Western and Central Africa and Sub-Saharan Africa are projected starting in 2020. All other regions are projected in 2023 and 2024. For further details on projection, see annex 1A of chapter 1. Gray shading = projected estimate.

Annex 2F. Further results on within-country inequality

FIGURE 2F.1

Whereas the share of economies with high inequality has declined, the share of population living in economies with high inequality has barely changed in the past decade

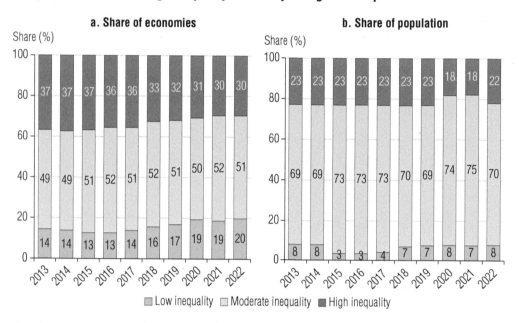

a. Share of economies

b. Share of population

■ Low inequality ☐ Moderate inequality ■ High inequality

Sources: World Bank, Poverty and Inequality Platform (version September 2024), https://pip.worldbank.org; Haddad et al. 2024.

Note: High-inequality economies are those with a Gini index above 40, moderate-inequality economies are those with a Gini index between 30 and 40, and low-inequality economies are those with a Gini index less than 30. When no survey is available in a given year, data from the most recent survey year are used. The earliest survey is backcasted when the first survey is only available after 2000 to avoid missing values. The graph covers 166 economies with at least one household survey in the Poverty and Inequality Platform. The label values may not add to 100 percent due to rounding. See also figure 2.9.

TABLE 2F.1

Gini index in latest available survey, by economy

Economy and group	Region	Survey year	Welfare type	Gini index
High inequality				
Angola	Sub-Saharan Africa	2018.17	Consumption	51.3
Argentina	Latin America and the Caribbean	2022	Income	40.7
Bolivia	Latin America and the Caribbean	2021	Income	40.9
Botswana	Sub-Saharan Africa	2015.85	Consumption	53.3
Brazil	Latin America and the Caribbean	2022	Income	52.0
Cabo Verde	Sub-Saharan Africa	2015	Consumption	42.4
Cameroon	Sub-Saharan Africa	2021.67	Consumption	42.2
Central African Republic	Sub-Saharan Africa	2021	Consumption	43.0
Chile	Latin America and the Caribbean	2022	Income	43.0
Colombia	Latin America and the Caribbean	2022	income	54.8
Comoros	Sub-Saharan Africa	2014	Consumption	45.3
Congo, Dem. Rep.	Sub-Saharan Africa	2020	Consumption	44.7
Congo, Rep.	Sub-Saharan Africa	2011.67	Consumption	48.9
Costa Rica	Latin America and the Caribbean	2023	Income	46.7
Djibouti	Middle East and North Africa	2017	Consumption	41.6
Ecuador	Latin America and the Caribbean	2023	Income	44.6
Eswatini	Sub-Saharan Africa	2016.17	Consumption	54.6
Ghana	Sub-Saharan Africa	2016.75	Consumption	43.5
Grenada	Latin America and the Caribbean	2018.36	Consumption	43.8
Guatemala	Latin America and the Caribbean	2014	Income	48.3
Haiti	Latin America and the Caribbean	2012	Consumption	41.1
Honduras	Latin America and the Caribbean	2019	Income	48.2
Jamaica	Latin America and the Caribbean	2021	Consumption	40.2
Lesotho	Sub-Saharan Africa	2017.14	Consumption	44.9
Madagascar	Sub-Saharan Africa	2012.73	Consumption	42.6
Malaysia	East Asia and Pacific	2021.46	Income	40.7
Mexico	Latin America and the Caribbean	2022	Income	43.5
Micronesia, Fed. Sts.	East Asia and Pacific	2013	Consumption	40.1
Mozambique	Sub-Saharan Africa	2019.92	Consumption	50.3
Namibia	Sub-Saharan Africa	2015.27	Consumption	59.1

(continued)

TABLE 2F.1

Gini index in latest available survey, by economy *(continued)*

Economy and group	Region	Survey year	Welfare type	Gini index
Nicaragua	Latin America and the Caribbean	2014	Income	46.2
Panama	Latin America and the Caribbean	2023	Income	48.9
Papua New Guinea	East Asia and Pacific	2009.67	Consumption	41.9
Paraguay	Latin America and the Caribbean	2022	Income	45.1
Peru	Latin America and the Caribbean	2022	Income	40.3
Philippines	East Asia and Pacific	2021	Income	40.7
Rwanda	Sub-Saharan Africa	2016.77	Consumption	43.7
São Tomé and Príncipe	Sub-Saharan Africa	2017	Consumption	40.7
South Africa	Sub-Saharan Africa	2014.83	Consumption	63.0
South Sudan	Sub-Saharan Africa	2016.5	Consumption	44.1
St. Lucia	Latin America and the Caribbean	2015.78	Consumption	43.7
Tanzania	Sub-Saharan Africa	2017.92	Consumption	40.5
Türkiye	Europe and Central Asia	2021	Income	44.4
Uganda	Sub-Saharan Africa	2019.64	Consumption	42.7
United States	Rest of the world	2022	Income	41.3
Uruguay	Latin America and the Caribbean	2022	Income	40.6
Venezuela, RB	Latin America and the Caribbean	2006	Income	44.7
Zambia	Sub-Saharan Africa	2022	Consumption	51.5
Zimbabwe	Sub-Saharan Africa	2019	Consumption	50.3
Moderate inequality				
Australia	Rest of the world	2018	Income	34.3
Austria	Rest of the world	2021	Income	30.7
Bangladesh	South Asia	2022	Consumption	33.4
Benin	Sub-Saharan Africa	2021.75	Consumption	34.4
Bosnia and Herzegovina	Europe and Central Asia	2011	Consumption	33.0
Bulgaria	Europe and Central Asia	2021	Income	39.0
Burkina Faso	Sub-Saharan Africa	2021.67	Consumption	37.4
Burundi	Sub-Saharan Africa	2020.15	Consumption	37.5
Canada	Rest of the world	2019	Income	31.7
Chad	Sub-Saharan Africa	2022	Consumption	37.4
China	East Asia and Pacific	2021	Consumption	35.7
Côte d'Ivoire	Sub-Saharan Africa	2021.75	Consumption	35.3

(continued)

TABLE 2F.1

Gini index in latest available survey, by economy *(continued)*

Economy and group	Region	Survey year	Welfare type	Gini index
Cyprus	Rest of the world	2021	Income	31.3
Dominican Republic	Latin America and the Caribbean	2022	Income	37.0
Egypt, Arab Rep.	Middle East and North Africa	2019.43	Consumption	31.9
El Salvador	Latin America and the Caribbean	2022	Income	38.8
Estonia	Europe and Central Asia	2021	Income	31.8
Ethiopia	Sub-Saharan Africa	2015.5	Consumption	35.0
Fiji	East Asia and Pacific	2019.15	Consumption	30.7
France	Rest of the world	2021	Income	31.5
Gabon	Sub-Saharan Africa	2017	Consumption	38.0
Gambia, The	Sub-Saharan Africa	2020.08	Consumption	38.8
Georgia	Europe and Central Asia	2022	Consumption	33.5
Germany	Rest of the world	2020	Income	32.4
Greece	Rest of the world	2021	Income	32.9
Guinea-Bissau	Sub-Saharan Africa	2021.75	Consumption	33.4
India	South Asia	2021.25	Consumption	32.8
Indonesia	East Asia and Pacific	2023	Consumption	36.1
Iran, Islamic Rep.	Middle East and North Africa	2022.23	Consumption	34.8
Ireland	Rest of the world	2021	Income	30.1
Israel	Rest of the world	2021	Income	37.9
Italy	Rest of the world	2021	Income	34.8
Japan	Rest of the world	2013	Income	32.9
Jordan	Middle East and North Africa	2010.24	Consumption	33.7
Kenya	Sub-Saharan Africa	2021	Consumption	38.7
Korea, Rep.	Rest of the world	2021	Income	32.9
Lao PDR	East Asia and Pacific	2018.42	Consumption	38.8
Latvia	Europe and Central Asia	2021	Income	34.3
Lebanon	Middle East and North Africa	2011.77	Consumption	31.8
Liberia	Sub-Saharan Africa	2016	Consumption	35.3
Lithuania	Europe and Central Asia	2021	Income	36.7
Luxembourg	Rest of the world	2021	Income	32.7
Malawi	Sub-Saharan Africa	2019.31	Consumption	38.5
Mali	Sub-Saharan Africa	2021.57	Consumption	35.7

(continued)

TABLE 2F.1

Gini index in latest available survey, by economy *(continued)*

Economy and group	Region	Survey year	Welfare type	Gini index
Malta	Rest of the world	2020	Income	31.4
Marshall Islands	East Asia and Pacific	2019.5	Consumption	35.5
Mauritania	Sub-Saharan Africa	2019.6	Consumption	32.0
Mauritius	Sub-Saharan Africa	2017	Consumption	36.8
Mongolia	East Asia and Pacific	2022	Consumption	31.4
Montenegro	Europe and Central Asia	2021	Income	34.3
Morocco	Middle East and North Africa	2013.5	Consumption	39.5
Myanmar	East Asia and Pacific	2017	Consumption	30.7
Nauru	East Asia and Pacific	2012.69	Consumption	32.4
Nepal	South Asia	2022.5	Consumption	30.0
Niger	Sub-Saharan Africa	2021.5	Consumption	32.9
Nigeria	Sub-Saharan Africa	2018.75	Consumption	35.1
North Macedonia	Europe and Central Asia	2019	Income	33.5
Portugal	Rest of the world	2021	Income	34.6
Qatar	Rest of the world	2017.5	Income	35.1
Romania	Europe and Central Asia	2021	Income	33.9
Russian Federation	Europe and Central Asia	2021	Income	35.1
Samoa	East Asia and Pacific	2013.25	Consumption	38.7
Senegal	Sub-Saharan Africa	2021.71	Consumption	36.2
Serbia	Europe and Central Asia	2021	Income	33.1
Seychelles	Sub-Saharan Africa	2018.08	Income	32.1
Sierra Leone	Sub-Saharan Africa	2018	Consumption	35.7
Solomon Islands	East Asia and Pacific	2012.79	Consumption	37.1
Spain	Rest of the world	2021	Income	33.9
Sri Lanka	South Asia	2019	Consumption	37.7
Sudan	Sub-Saharan Africa	2014	Consumption	34.2
Suriname	Latin America and the Caribbean	2022	Consumption	39.2
Switzerland	Rest of the world	2020	Income	33.7
Taiwan, China	Rest of the world	2021	Income	31.6
Tajikistan	Europe and Central Asia	2015	Consumption	34.0
Thailand	East Asia and Pacific	2021	Consumption	34.9

(continued)

TABLE 2F.1

Gini index in latest available survey, by economy *(continued)*

Economy and group	Region	Survey year	Welfare type	Gini index
Togo	Sub-Saharan Africa	2021.63	Consumption	37.9
Tunisia	Middle East and North Africa	2021.23	Consumption	33.7
Tuvalu	East Asia and Pacific	2010	Consumption	39.1
United Kingdom	Rest of the world	2021	Income	32.4
Uzbekistan	Europe and Central Asia	2022	Consumption	31.2
Vanuatu	East Asia and Pacific	2019.21	Consumption	32.3
Viet Nam	East Asia and Pacific	2022	Consumption	36.1
West Bank and Gaza	Middle East and North Africa	2016.75	Consumption	33.7
Yemen, Rep.	Middle East and North Africa	2014	Consumption	36.7
Low inequality				
Albania	Europe and Central Asia	2020	Consumption	29.4
Algeria	Middle East and North Africa	2011.17	Consumption	27.6
Armenia	Europe and Central Asia	2022	Consumption	27.9
Azerbaijan	Europe and Central Asia	2005	Consumption	26.6
Belarus	Europe and Central Asia	2020	Consumption	24.4
Belgium	Rest of the world	2021	Income	26.6
Bhutan	South Asia	2022	Consumption	28.5
Croatia	Europe and Central Asia	2021	Income	28.9
Czechia	Europe and Central Asia	2021	Income	26.2
Denmark	Rest of the world	2021	Income	28.3
Finland	Rest of the world	2021	Income	27.7
Guinea	Sub-Saharan Africa	2018.5	Consumption	29.6
Hungary	Europe and Central Asia	2021	Income	29.2
Iceland	Rest of the world	2017	Income	26.1
Iraq	Middle East and North Africa	2012	Consumption	29.5
Kazakhstan	Europe and Central Asia	2021	Consumption	29.2
Kiribati	East Asia and Pacific	2019.27	Consumption	27.8
Kosovo	Europe and Central Asia	2017	Consumption	29.0
Kyrgyz Republic	Europe and Central Asia	2022	Consumption	26.4
Maldives	South Asia	2019.6	Consumption	29.3
Moldova	Europe and Central Asia	2021	Consumption	25.7

(continued)

TABLE 2F.1

Gini index in latest available survey, by economy *(continued)*

Economy and group	Region	Survey year	Welfare type	Gini index
Netherlands	Rest of the world	2021	Income	25.7
Norway	Rest of the world	2019	Income	27.7
Pakistan	South Asia	2018.5	Consumption	29.6
Poland	Europe and Central Asia	2021	Income	28.5
Slovak Republic	Europe and Central Asia	2021	Income	24.1
Slovenia	Europe and Central Asia	2021	Income	24.3
Sweden	Rest of the world	2021	Income	29.8
Syrian Arab Republic	Middle East and North Africa	2022	Consumption	26.6
Timor-Leste	East Asia and Pacific	2014	Consumption	28.7
Tonga	East Asia and Pacific	2021	Consumption	27.1
Ukraine	Europe and Central Asia	2020	Consumption	25.6
United Arab Emirates	Rest of the world	2018	Income	26.4

Source: World Bank, Poverty and Inequality Platform (version September 2024), https://pip.worldbank.org.

Notes: Data include latest consumption or income surveys in the Poverty and Inequality Platform. High-inequality economies are those with a Gini index above 40, medium-inequality economies are those with a Gini index between 30 and 40, and low-inequality economies are those with a Gini index below 30. Economies are sorted by inequality group (high, moderate, or low) and alphabetically within each group. Decimal years indicate that the survey was conducted over two calendar years. The number before the decimal indicates the first year of the survey and the numbers after the decimal indicate the proportion of the survey occurring in the second year.

Notes

1. For a description of the welfare index that the Global Prosperity Gap is based on, see Kraay et al. (2023).
2. Inequalities can reflect fair differences in effort and talent, which in turn provide the incentives that generate both higher social and economic mobility. At the same time, high inequality may be symptomatic of factors that are detrimental to growth or could lead to political and social instability that weakens growth.
3. A study from the United States has found that inequality of opportunity has a negative effect on economic growth (Marrero and Rodríguez 2013). Using global data, Ferreira et al. (2018), however, did not find robust evidence of inequality of opportunity worsening growth outcomes. Combining the concepts of inequality in incomes and opportunity, Aiyar and Ebeke (2020) provide evidence that income inequality exerts a negative effect on growth, when inequality of opportunity is high.

4. The typical person refers to the individual with the median income or consumption. The reported estimates are projections for 2024 as reported in the Poverty and Inequality Platform. Bulgaria entered high-income status according to the fiscal year 2025 list (see Metreau, Young, and Eapen [2024]). Since the latest reference year with household survey data is aligned with the fiscal year 2024 classifications, this report uses the fiscal year 2024 list to classify countries.

5. The standard is also close to the median poverty line in high-income countries (Jolliffe et al. 2022). Furthermore, the choice of $25 as the threshold affects the *level* of the Prosperity Gap, but it is completely irrelevant to the ordering of countries and changes over time which are what the measure is primarily used for. Another threshold would imply rescaling the Prosperity Gap—for example, a threshold of $100 (4 × $25) would mean that the Global Prosperity Gap in 2024 is approximately 20 (4 × 5) as opposed to around 5.

6. The importance of individuals decreases exponentially with increases in income. For example, a person with $30 gets a weight of 0.83, while a person with $20 gets a weight of 1.25, or 1.5 times the weight of the person with $30, although both are $5 from the threshold. As a practical matter, the people living above $25 contributed 2 percent to the Global Prosperity Gap in 2024, while they account for 20 percent of the global population. The Prosperity Gap can be written as the product of ($25/mean income) and inequality. This formulation already shows that the index decreases (improves) as mean income increases or inequality decreases. For further details, see annex 2B.

7. Sensitivity to low incomes is a desirable feature of any distribution-sensitive measure. However, some welfare measures, including the Prosperity Gap, cannot incorporate negative or zero incomes. The underlying distributions used to calculate all welfare measures—poverty, prosperity, and inequality—in the Poverty and Inequality Platform are bottom coded at $0.25 per person per day. See annex 2C for details.

8. To report a global estimate, 50 percent of the global population needs to be covered by a recent survey and, in addition, 50 percent of the population of low- and lower-middle-income countries needs to be covered as well. Globally, this criterion is satisfied up to 2022. Estimates beyond 2022 are projected for the global estimate and all regions (for further details, see annex 1A of chapter 1). In addition, survey data for the Middle East and North Africa and Sub-Saharan Africa remain limited (see box 1.2 of chapter 1). As a result, the estimates presented starting in 2019 for the Middle East and North Africa and starting in 2020 for Sub-Saharan Africa are projected on the basis of less than half of the regional population covered by a recent survey.

9. Milanovic (2005) has proposed three ways of capturing global inequality. Concept 1 considers only the differences in mean incomes across countries, or just the inequality *between* countries. Concept 2 adjusts the former by allowing for population differences across countries. Concepts 1 and 2 do not account for inequality within countries. Concept 3, in contrast, considers the interpersonal incomes of everyone in the world and thus incorporates inequality both between and within countries. The Global Prosperity Gap captures concept 3 inequality. Note, however, that the inequality indicator related to the Prosperity Gap is multiplicatively decomposable into inequality between and within countries (see annex 2B and Kraay et al. [2023]).

10. This is similar to the idea of the average poverty exit time outlined by Morduch (1998).

11. The high correlation in rankings using various inequality indexes means that the selection of the index does not make much practical difference in the classification of economies as having low, moderate, or high inequality. The global patterns, therefore, are indistinguishable from each other. When engaging in country-level dialogue, a broader menu of indexes can be used to inform policy discussions (see annex 2D for more details on this).

12. For instance, the Philippines had a consumption Gini index of 37.3 and an income Gini index of 40.7 in 2021. The survey preferred by the World Bank country expert is used when both income and consumption surveys are available.

13. A Gini index of less than 30 is defined as low inequality, following previous United Nations reports (see annex 2D for details). While any threshold is somewhat arbitrary, it is useful to study progress against high inequality, as well as progress toward low inequality.

14. The IDA, a part of the World Bank Group, provides grants and concessional loans to the world's poorest countries. As of 2024, there are 75 countries (of which 68 are accounted for in the Gini data set) eligible for support from IDA, with 75 percent of total commitments concentrated in Sub-Saharan Africa. For more information, see https://ida.worldbank.org/en/ida-financing.

15. Not all economies have a survey in every year. To compare the same set of economies throughout, the latest Gini index is used. The finding of declining high inequality could be confounded by the fact that the number of economies with updated data has risen over time. One way to check the trends in declining within-country inequality while accounting for the differences in reporting standards across economies is to compute average inequality estimates for each economy at a 10-year interval. This ensures that the compositions of economies during 2000–09 and 2010–19 remain largely similar (142 of 166 economies had at least one survey in both the 2000–09 and 2010–19 periods). Economies are then assigned to a high-inequality status if their decadal average Gini exceeds 40. This analysis confirms the drop in the number of economies with high inequality: falling from 61 during the first decade of 2000 to 48 in the subsequent one.

16. Survey comparability depends on various characteristics such as the sampling process, questionnaire, methodological changes in the construction of welfare aggregates, consistent price deflation over time and space, and so on. The Poverty and Inequality Platform contains metadata on the comparability of poverty estimates within countries over time. For further detail on the comparability assessment, see Castaneda Aguilar et al. (2019) and the *Poverty and Inequality Platform Methodological Handbook* (https://datanalytics.worldbank.org/PIP-Methodology/).

17. Based on Alvaredo and Gasparini (2015), World Bank (2016) used a change in 1 Gini point as a rough check on statistical significance due to lack of confidence intervals.

18. Mahler, Yonzan, and Lakner (2022) attribute changes in inequality among richer countries in 2020 to the extensive social protection measures that were put in place during the pandemic.

19. See the Commitment to Equity (CEQ) Institute (https://commitmentoequity.org/datacenter/) for data. Data for the 96 economies include 8 low-income countries, 20 lower-middle-income countries, 24 upper-middle-income countries, 7 high-income countries that are not members of the Organisation for Economic Co-operation and Development (OECD), and 37 OECD high-income countries (for the 6 countries for which both CEQ and OECD data are available, OECD data are used). The OECD studies include direct taxes and transfers but not indirect taxes and subsidies or in-kind health and education spending. The disposable income-based Gini index here is the closest measure to the Gini index used in the rest of this chapter, although it is important to recognize that it comes from different sources, leading to some differences. For methodological details, see Lustig (2023). Likewise, note that the difference between the gross and disposable income distribution in most developing countries is extremely fuzzy. In general, surveys inform on "disposable" incomes. Getting back gross incomes requires identifying informality features to impute social security and health insurance contributions, which is often challenging. On the other hand, fully accounting for redistribution would require including indirect taxation and subsidies as well as in-kind public spending, which is also nontrivial.

20. In countries that use consumption data to estimate poverty and inequality, household consumption from the survey is equated with disposable income. After equating consumption to disposable income, a backward calculation is conducted by adding employee and employer nonpension contributions, such as unemployment benefits, disability, and health, and direct personal income taxes (excluding all contributions to social security) (Lustig 2022). In a next step, benefits from the nonpension contributions and government direct transfers (cash and near-cash) are subtracted (Lustig 2022). Note that disposable income is market income after income taxes and nonpension contributions are deducted and direct cash transfers and social pensions are added. In contrast, market income is wages and salaries, contributor pension payments, income from capital and private transfers before taxes and transfers. In this approach, savings are not accounted for.

21. The CEQ methodology, which goes beyond the income concepts used here, focuses on direct taxes on household income and indirect taxes on household consumption, as well as direct transfers to households, spending on health and education, and energy and food subsidies. Agriculture subsidies are occasionally included, as is employer-paid health insurance. However, active labor market policies, corporate income tax, infrastructure spending, and many tax incentives are excluded.

22. World Bank (2022) draws on the CEQ approach also to estimate inequality for these broader concepts that include indirect taxes and subsidies, as well as in-kind transfers and user fees. This report, however, discusses only disposable income, since this offers the greatest country coverage. The broader concepts are not available for the advanced economies. For details, see Lustig (2023). Note that the difference between market, or pretax, and disposable, or post-tax or transfer, income is often used to assess by how much government policies impact inequality. While this is a very useful measure, it is important to stress that this does not capture all government policies, notably the policies that impact premarket inequality and in-market inequality as described above and which are fundamental. Furthermore, even within the space of fiscal policies, disposable income does not provide the full picture (World Bank 2022): for example, indirect taxes (such as sales taxes) and indirect subsidies (for instance, subsidized prices for electricity) are not captured in disposable income. Similarly, in-kind transfers, such as government health and education, spending are not accounted for.

23. In Korea (2020), the Gini index of market income is 36.5 and the Gini index of disposable income is 31.2, which implies fiscal redistribution of 5.3 Gini points. In Germany (2019), the respective figures are 40.3 (market Gini), 29.9 (disposable Gini), and 10.4 (redistribution).

24. There are 20 income surveys in the Poverty and Inequality Platform database in which measured incomes are zero in the lowest percentiles of the income distribution and a consumption survey is available for the same year. These countries are all upper-middle-income or high-income countries in Eastern Europe. Pooling across all surveys, median consumption over those percentiles for which reported incomes are zero is $2.64 per day, with the lowest consumption percentile being $0.84 per day.

25. For example, the Luxembourg Income Study bottom (and top) codes the distribution of log income at three times the interquartile range below (above) the first (third) quartile when reporting inequality measures (Neugschwender 2020).

26. There are other differences in how countries measure well-being. For instance, prices are generally lower in rural than in urban areas—meaning that real income or consumption expenditure values can be sensitive to the use of appropriate spatial deflators. However, these deflators vary considerably across countries (Mancini and Vecchi 2022). Income can further be defined in various ways (market, pretax, post-tax, and pretransfer, disposable), and each has various levels of inequality. The household surveys reported in the Poverty and Inequality Platform capture mostly disposable (post-tax and transfer) income. See also chapter 4.

27. This transfer axiom means that a transfer from a richer person to a poorer person always reduces inequality. Income shares are insensitive to such transfers if they occur within the quantile group. Other properties include symmetry (if people swapped incomes, the measure remains unchanged) and scale invariance (if everyone's income increases tenfold, the measure is unchanged).

28. Only with the p90/p10 ratio are there notable rerankings of economies compared with the Gini index. Because the p90/p10 ratio discards information contained in other percentiles, it has fewer theoretically desirable properties, which in turn could explain the observed patterns.

29. The report uses the same harmonized cross-country survey data as in this report and does not distinguish between income- and consumption-based measures of welfare. If using a data set with systematically higher Gini indexes for countries, for example, the World Inequality Database, which corrects for missing incomes at the very top of the income distribution and which thus has higher Gini indexes on average, then the appropriate threshold to use for high inequality would potentially be higher than 40. See also chapter 4 for a related discussion.

30. Haddad et al. (2024) used all surveys in the Poverty and Inequality Platform starting in 2000. This report does the same. Furthermore, for years where no survey is available, following Haddad et al., this report uses the Gini index from the last available survey for the economy. For years prior to the first survey year, the Gini index from the first survey is backcasted. For instance, if the economy's first survey was conducted in 2005, all years prior to 2005 have the same Gini index as in 2005.

31. There have also been efforts to transform the consumption-based measures to income and vice versa to address any systematic differences between countries that use consumption and those that use income (see discussion above). Haddad et al. (2024) found that the 67th percentile threshold, when the available consumption surveys, as well as income surveys converted to consumption, are considered, is between 39.3 and 40.1. The same threshold when consumption surveys are converted to income and pooled with the available income surveys range between 45.3 and 45.5.

References

Aiyar, Shekhar, and Christian Ebeke. 2020. "Inequality of Opportunity, Inequality of Income and Economic Growth." *World Development* 136: 105115. https://doi.org/10.1016/j.worlddev.2020.105115.

Allison, Paul D. 1978. "Measures of Inequality." *American Sociological Review* 43 (6): 865. https://doi.org/10.2307/2094626.

Alvaredo, Facundo, Anthony B. Atkinson, and Salvatore Morelli. 2018. "Top Wealth Shares in the UK Over More Than a Century." *Journal of Public Economics* 162: 26–47.

Alvaredo, Facundo, François Bourguignon, Francisco H. G. Ferreira, and Nora Lustig. 2023. "Seventy-five Years of Measuring Income Inequality in Latin America." *IDB Publications* [preprint]. https://doi.org/10.18235/0005211.

Alvaredo, Facundo, and Leonardo Gasparini. 2015. "Chapter 9—Recent Trends in Inequality and Poverty in Developing Countries." In *Handbook of Income Distribution*, edited by A. B. Atkinson and F. Bourguignon, 697–805. Amsterdam, The Netherlands: Elsevier. https://doi.org/10.1016/B978-0-444-59428-0.00010-2.

Amendola, Adalgiso, Roberto Dell'Anno, and Lavinia Parisi. 2019. "Happiness and Inequality in European Countries: Is It a Matter of Peer Group Comparisons?" *Economia Politica* 36 (2): 473–508. https://doi.org/10.1007/s40888-018-0130-6.

Atkinson, Anthony B. 1970. "On the Measurement of Inequality." *Journal of Economic Theory* 2 (3): 244–63. https://doi.org/10.1016/0022-0531(70)90039-6.

Atkinson, Anthony B. 2015. *Inequality: What Can Be Done?* Cambridge: Harvard University Press.

Bachas, Pierre, Lucie Gadenne, and Anders Jensen. 2023. "Informality, Consumption Taxes, and Redistribution." *Review of Economic Studies* rdad095. https://doi.org/10.1093/restud/rdad095.

Bachas, Pierre, Anders Jensen, and Lucie Gadenne. 2024. "Tax Equity in Low- and Middle-Income Countries." *Journal of Economic Perspectives* 38 (1): 55–80. https://doi.org/10.1257/jep.38.1.55.

Bancalari, Antonella, Samuel Berlinski, Giancarlo Buitrago, María Fernanda García, Dolores de la Mata, and Marcos Vera-Hernández. 2023. "Health Systems and Health Inequalities in Latin America." *IDB Publications* [preprint]. https://doi.org/10.18235/0005243.

Banerjee, Abhijit V., and Esther Duflo. 2003. "Inequality and Growth: What Can the Data Say?" *Journal of Economic Growth* 8 (3): 267–99. https://doi.org/10.1023/A:1026205114860.

Baselgia, Enea, and Reto Foellmi. 2022. "Inequality and Growth: A Review on a Great Open Debate in Economics." WIDER Working Paper 2022, UNU-WIDER, Helsinki, Finland. https://doi.org/10.35188/UNU-WIDER/2022/136-5.

Bergstrom, Katy. 2022. "The Role of Income Inequality for Poverty Reduction." *The World Bank Economic Review* 36 (3): 583–604. https://doi.org/10.1093/wber/lhab026.

Bourguignon, Francois. 1979. "Decomposable Income Inequality Measures." *Econometrica: Journal of the Econometric Society* 47 (4): 901–20.

Bourguignon, Francois. 2003. "The Growth Elasticity of Poverty Reduction: Explaining Heterogeneity across Countries and Time Periods." In *Inequality and Growth: Theory and Policy Implications,* edited by T. S. Eicher and S. J. Turnovsky, 326. Cambridge: MIT Press. https://doi.org/10.7551 /mitpress/3750.003.0004.

Brueckner, Markus, and Daniel Lederman. 2018. "Inequality and Economic Growth: The Role of Initial Income." *Journal of Economic Growth* 23 (3): 341–66. https://doi.org/10.1007/s10887-018-9156-4.

Brunori, Paolo, Francisco H. G. Ferreira, and Guido Neidhöfer. 2023. "Inequality of Opportunity and Intergenerational Persistence in Latin America." WIDER Working Paper 2023/39, UNU-WIDER, Helsinki, Finland. https://doi.org/10.35188/UNU-WIDER/2023/347-5.

Brunori, Paolo, Francisco H. G. Ferreira, and Vito Peragine. 2013. "Inequality of Opportunity, Income Inequality, and Economic Mobility: Some International Comparisons." In *Getting Development Right: Structural Transformation, Inclusion, and Sustainability in the Post-Crisis Era,* edited by E. Paus, 85–115. New York: Palgrave Macmillan. https://doi.org/10.1057/9781137333117_5.

Cagé, Julia. 2023. "Political Inequality." Working Paper 2023/22 [preprint], World Inequality Lab, Paris. https://wid.world/document/political-inequality-wid-world-working-paper-2023-22/.

Card, David, Alexandre Mas, Enrico Moretti, and Emmanuel Saez. 2012. "Inequality at Work: The Effect of Peer Salaries on Job Satisfaction." *American Economic Review* 102 (6): 2981–3003. https://doi .org/10.1257/aer.102.6.2981.

Castaneda Aguilar, R. Andres, Aziz Atamanov, Carolina Diaz-Bonilla, Dean Jolliffe, Christoph Lakner, Jose Montes, Daniel Gerszon Mahler, et al. 2019. "September 2019 PovcalNet Update: What's New." Global Poverty Monitoring Technical Note 10. https://doi.org/10.1596/32478.

Chetty, Raj, David Grusky, Maximilian Hell, Nathaniel Hendren, Robert Manduca, and Jimmy Narang. 2017. "The Fading American Dream: Trends in Absolute Income Mobility Since 1940." *Science* 356 (6336): 398–406. https://doi.org/10.1126/science.aal4617.

Corak, Miles. 2013. "Income Inequality, Equality of Opportunity, and Intergenerational Mobility." *Journal of Economic Perspectives* 27 (3): 79–102. https://doi.org/10.1257/jep.27.3.79.

Cowell, Frank A., and Emmanuel Flachaire. 2007. "Income Distribution and Inequality Measurement: The Problem of Extreme Values." *Journal of Econometrics* 141 (2): 1044–72. https://doi.org/10.1016/j .jeconom.2007.01.001.

Cowell, Frank A., and Maria-Pia Victoria-Feser. 2006. "Distributional Dominance with Trimmed Data." *Journal of Business & Economic Statistics* 24 (3): 291–300.

Cruces, Guillermo, Ricardo Perez-Truglia, and Martin Tetaz. 2013. "Biased Perceptions of Income Distribution and Preferences for Redistribution: Evidence from a Survey Experiment." *Journal of Public Economics* 98: 100–12. https://doi.org/10.1016/j.jpubeco.2012.10.009.

Deininger, Klaus, and Lyn Squire. 1996. "A New Data Set Measuring Income Inequality." *The World Bank Economic Review* 10 (3): 565–91.

Erikson, Robert S. 2015. "Income Inequality and Policy Responsiveness." *Annual Review of Political Science* 18 (2015): 11–29. https://doi.org/10.1146/annurev-polisci-020614-094706.

Fernández, Raquel, Carmen Pagés, Miguel Szekely, and Ivonne Acevedo. 2024. "Education Inequalities in Latin America and the Caribbean." NBER Working Paper 32126, National Bureau of Economic Research, Cambridge, Mass. https://doi.org/10.3386/w32126.

Ferreira, Francisco H. G., Christoph Lakner, Maria Ana Lugo, and Berk Özler. 2018. "Inequality of Opportunity and Economic Growth: How Much Can Cross-Country Regressions Really Tell Us?" *Review of Income and Wealth* 64 (4): 800–27. https://doi.org/10.1111/roiw.12311.

Forbes, Kristin J. 2000. "A Reassessment of the Relationship between Inequality and Growth." *American Economic Review* 90 (4): 869–87. https://doi.org/10.1257/aer.90.4.869.

Gründler, Klaus, and Philipp Scheuermeyer. 2018. "Growth Effects of Inequality and Redistribution: What Are the Transmission Channels?" *Journal of Macroeconomics* 55: 293–313. https://doi.org/10.1016/j .jmacro.2017.12.001.

Haddad, Cameron Nadim, Daniel Gerszon Mahler, Carolina Diaz-Bonilla, Ruth Hill, Christoph Lakner, and Gabriel Lara Ibarra. 2024. "The World Bank's New Inequality Indicator: The Number of Countries with High Inequality (English)." Policy Research Working Paper WPS 10796, World Bank, Washington, DC. https://documents.worldbank.org/en/publication/documents-reports /documentdetail/099549506102441825/IDU1bd155bac16d78143af188331f87564a9d6c8.

Hvidberg, Kristoffer B., Claus T. Kreiner, and Stefanie Stantcheva. 2023. "Social Positions and Fairness Views on Inequality." *The Review of Economic Studies* 90 (6): 3083–118. https://doi.org/10.1093/restud /rdad019.

Jenkins, Stephen P. 2009. "Distributionally-Sensitive Inequality Indices and the GB2 Income Distribution." *Review of Income and Wealth* 55 (2): 392–98. https://doi.org/10.1111/j.1475-4991.2009.00318.x.

Jolliffe, Dean Mitchell, Daniel Gerszon Mahler, Christoph Lakner, Aziz Atamanov, and Samuel Kofi Tetteh-Baah. 2022. "Assessing the Impact of the 2017 PPPs on the International Poverty Line and Global Poverty (English)." Policy Research Working Paper Series 9941, World Bank, Washington, DC. https:// documents.worldbank.org/en/publication/documents-reports/documentdetail/353811645450974574 /Assessing-the-Impact-of-the-2017-PPPs-on-the-International-Poverty-Line-and-Global-Poverty.

Kraay, Aart C., Christoph Lakner, Berk Ozler, Benoit Marie A. Decerf, Dean Mitchell Jolliffe, Olivier Christian Brigitte Sterck, and Nishant Yonzan. 2023. "A New Distribution Sensitive Index for Measuring Welfare, Poverty, and Inequality (English)." Policy Research Working Paper WPS 10470, World Bank, Washington, DC. https://documents.worldbank.org/en/publication/documents-reports /documentdetail/099934305302318791/IDU0325015fc0a4d6046420afe405cb6b6a87b0b.

Lakner, Christoph, Daniel Gerszon Mahler, Mario Negre, and Espen Beer Prydz. 2022. "How Much Does Reducing Inequality Matter for Global Poverty?" *The Journal of Economic Inequality* 20 (3): 559–85. https://doi.org/10.1007/s10888-021-09510-w.

Lakner, Christoph, and Branko Milanovic. 2016. "Global Income Distribution: From the Fall of the Berlin Wall to the Great Recession." *The World Bank Economic Review* 30 (2): 203–32. https://doi.org/10.1093 /wber/lhv039.

Li, Hongyi, and Heng-fu Zou. 1998. "Income Inequality Is Not Harmful for Growth: Theory and Evidence." *Review of Development Economics* 2 (3): 318–334. https://doi.org/10.1111/1467-9361.00045.

Lupu, Noam. 2024. "Weak Parties and the Inequality Trap in Latin America [preprint]." Washington, DC: IDB Publications. https://doi.org/10.18235/0012891.

Lustig, Nora, ed. 2022. *Commitment to Equity Handbook,* 2nd ed. *Fiscal Incidence Analysis: Methodology, Implementation, and Applications,* vol. 1. Washington, DC: Brookings Institution. https://www .brookings.edu/wp-content/uploads/2017/04/CEQ-Handbook-2022-Vol-1.pdf.

Lustig, Nora, ed. 2023. *Commitment to Equity Handbook: Estimating the Impact of Fiscal Policy on Inequality and Poverty.* Washington, DC: Brookings Institution Press.

Mahler, Daniel Gerszon, Nishant Yonzan, and Christoph Lakner. 2022. "The Impact of COVID-19 on Global Inequality and Poverty." Policy Research Working Paper 10198, World Bank, Washington, DC. https://doi.org/10.1596/1813-9450-10198.

Mancini, Giulia, and Giovanni Vecchi. 2022. "On the Construction of a Consumption Aggregate for Inequality and Poverty Analysis." World Bank Group, Washington, DC.

Marrero, Gustavo A., and Juan G. Rodríguez. 2013. "Inequality of Opportunity and Growth." *Journal of Development Economics* 104: 107–22. https://doi.org/10.1016/j.jdeveco.2013.05.004.

Metreau, Eric, Kathryn Elizabeth Young, and Shwetha Grace Eapen. 2024. "World Bank Country Classifications by Income Level for 2024–2025." *World Bank Blogs*, July 1, 2024. https://blogs .worldbank.org/en/opendata/world-bank-country-classifications-by-income-level-for-2024-2025.

Milanovic, Branko. 2005. *Worlds Apart: Measuring International and Global Inequality.* Princeton, NJ: Princeton University Press. https://doi.org/10.1515/9781400840816.

Morduch, Jonathan. 1998. "Poverty, Economic Growth, and Average Exit Time." *Economics Letters* 59 (3): 385–90. https://doi.org/10.1016/S0165-1765(98)00070-6.

Narayan, Ambar, Roy Van der Weide, Alexandru Cojocaru, Christoph Lakner, Silvia Redaelli, Daniel Gerszon Mahler, Rakesh Gupta N. Ramasubbaiah, and Stefan Thewissen. 2018. *Fair Progress? Economic Mobility across Generations around the World.* Washington, DC: World Bank. http://hdl .handle.net/10986/28428.

Neugschwender, Jörg. 2020. "Top and Bottom Coding at LIS." LIS Technical Working Paper Series No. 9, LIS Cross-National Data Center in Luxembourg.

Piketty, Thomas. 2014. *Capital in the Twenty-First Century*. Cambridge: Harvard University Press. https://www.jstor.org/stable/j.ctt6wpqbc.

Porta, Emilio, Gustavo Arcia, Kevin Macdonald, Sergiy Radyakin, and Misha Lokshin. 2011. *Assessing Sector Performance and Inequality in Education: Streamlined Analysis with ADePT Software*. Washington, DC: World Bank.

Ravallion, Martin. 2016. "Are the World's Poorest Being Left Behind?" *Journal of Economic Growth* 21 (2): 139–64. https://doi.org/10.1007/s10887-016-9126-7.

Saez, Emmanuel, and Gabriel Zucman. 2020. "The Rise of Income and Wealth Inequality in America: Evidence from Distributional Macroeconomic Accounts." *Journal of Economic Perspectives* 34 (4): 3–26.

Shorrocks, A. F. 1980. The Class of Additively Decomposable Inequality Measures. *Econometrica: Journal of the Econometric Society* 48 (3): 613–25.

Sinha, N., G. Inchauste, and A. Narayan. 2024. *Leveling the Playing Field: Addressing Structural Inequalities to Accelerate Poverty Reduction in Africa*. 2024. Washington, DC: World Bank.

UNICEF (United Nations International Children's Emergency Fund). 2018. *Economic and Social Development Atlas 2018*. New York: UNICEF.

United Nations. 2022. "Sustainable Development Goals Progress Chart: Technical Note." New York: United Nations Statistics Division (UNSD).

van der Weide, Roy, Christoph Lakner, Daniel Gerszon Mahler, Ambar Narayan, and Rakesh Gupta. 2024. "Intergenerational Mobility around the World: A New Database." *Journal of Development Economics* 166: 103167. https://doi.org/10.1016/j.jdeveco.2023.103167.

Wai-Poi, M., M. Sosa, and P. Bachas. Forthcoming. "Taxes, Spending and Equity: International Patterns and Lessons for Developing Countries." World Bank, Washington, DC.

World Bank. 2016. *Poverty and Shared Prosperity 2016: Taking on Inequality*. Washington, DC: World Bank. https://doi.org/10.1596/978-1-4648-0958-3.

World Bank. 2017a. "Global Mobility Report 2017: Tracking Sector Performance (English)." Washington, DC: World Bank. https://documents.worldbank.org/en/publication/documents-reports/documentdetail/920101508269072500/Global-mobility-report-2017-tracking-sector-performance.

World Bank. 2017b. *Monitoring Global Poverty: Report of the Commission on Global Poverty (English)*. Washington, DC: World Bank. doi: 10.1596/978-1-4648-0961-3.

World Bank. 2022. *Poverty and Shared Prosperity 2022: Correcting Course*. Washington, DC: World Bank. https://www.worldbank.org/en/publication/poverty-and-shared-prosperity.

World Bank. 2024a. "Africa's Pulse, no. 29, April 2024: Tackling Inequality to Revitalize Growth and Reduce Poverty in Africa." Washington, DC: World Bank. https://doi.org/10.1596/978-1-4648-2109-7.

World Bank. 2024b. "Global Economic Prospects, June 2024." https://www.worldbank.org/en/publication/global-economic-prospects.

World Bank. 2024c. *New World Bank Group Scorecard FY24–FY30: Driving Action, Measuring Results (English)*. Washington, DC: World Bank. https://documents.worldbank.org/en/publication/documents-reports/documentdetail/099121223173511026/BOSIB1ab32eaff0051a2191da7db5542842.

World Bank. 2024d. *World Development Report 2024: The Middle-Income Trap*. Washington, DC: World Bank.

World Bank. n.d. "Translating Our Vision." World Bank Group Scorecard, accessed June 6, 2024. https://scorecard.worldbank.org/en/scorecard/home.

Yonzan, Nishant, Minh Cong Nguyen, Christoph Lakner, Aart Kraay, Dean Mitchell Jolliffe, Haoyu Wu, and Gabriel Lara Ibarra. Forthcoming. "Bottom-Coding for the Measurement of Global Poverty and Inequality." World Bank, Washington, DC.

Zucman, Gabriel. 2015. *The Hidden Wealth of Nations: The Scourge of Tax Havens*. Chicago: University of Chicago Press. https://www.degruyter.com/document/doi/10.7208/9780226245560/html.

Livable Planet

Protecting People from Extreme Weather Events

3

Summary

- *Today, one in five people is at risk from an extreme weather event in their lifetime. This means they are likely to face severe setbacks in their livelihoods, significantly hindering poverty reduction efforts.*

- *Protecting people from extreme weather events requires acting on two fronts: (a) lowering vulnerability by enhancing risk management and (b) preventing the escalation of future climate hazards by accelerating transformations to reduce the emissions intensiveness of growth.*

- *To inform decisions, it is important to understand the trade-off between growing incomes and lowering greenhouse gas (GHG) emissions, find ways to scale up synergistic policies that can help advance on multiple fronts or reduce trade-offs, and manage transition costs of climate mitigation policies to specific groups and communities.*

- *Priorities should consider where countries stand on the interlinked goals.*

- *Poverty reduction by fostering investments in human, physical, and financial capital needs to be prioritized in low-income settings.*

- *Middle-income countries need to prioritize income growth that reduces vulnerability and synergies such as cutting air pollution.*

- *Upper-middle- and high-income countries account for four-fifths of global GHG emissions. These countries need to act fast in transitioning to low-carbon-intense economies, while managing transition costs particularly for the poor and vulnerable.*

- *Fostering international cooperation and closing financing gaps for sustainable development are critical to enable the transition toward more sustainable, low-carbon, and resilient economies. Achieving a world free of poverty on a livable planet is possible but requires serious and immediate efforts.*

The concept of a livable planet

The goals of ending extreme poverty, boosting shared prosperity, and ensuring a livable planet are closely interlinked. The World Bank's vision recognizes this and tracks the multidimensional concept of a livable planet along three dimensions: climate mitigation and adaptation, biodiversity and nature, and life essentials (figure 3.1) (World Bank, n.d.). These three areas underscore that to sustain a livable planet, action on various aspects, such as reducing the risks from climate-related hazards; preserving healthy ecosystems; and ensuring access to life essentials such as food, water, and low air pollution, is necessary.

This chapter concentrates on one aspect of the complex relationship between poverty, shared prosperity, and livable planet: the need to protect people from the worsening impacts of climate-related hazards. Acting on this front is fundamental to support the goals of ending poverty and increasing shared prosperity on a livable planet.[1]

FIGURE 3.1
Livable planet dimensions

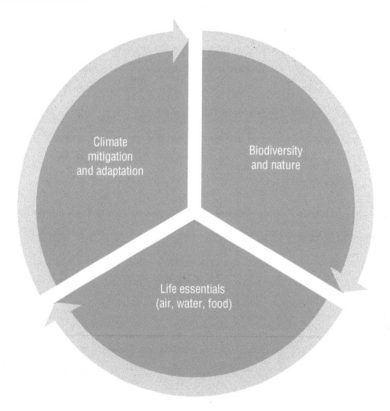

Source: Original figure for this publication (World Bank, n.d.).

Every year, extreme weather events have a negative impact on millions of households (Baquié and Fuje 2020; Hallegatte and Walsh 2021; Hill and Porter 2017; Kochhar, Knippenberg, and Leon 2023; Pape and Wollburg 2019). Hallegatte, Bangalore et al. (2016) estimate that tropical storms, floods, droughts, and earthquakes push 26 million people into poverty every year.

The poor are more likely to be adversely affected by hazardous events than the nonpoor. For example, while wealthier people can save parts of their income in formal financial institutions and diversify their portfolio, the poorest often hold only in-kind assets such as livestock or housing, which are more likely to be destroyed by natural disasters (Dercon 2004; Hallegatte and Walsh 2021).[2] Two-thirds of the global extreme poor also work in the agricultural sector and are more likely to rely on other forms of natural capital for income generation and food security, making them more vulnerable to extreme weather events, rising temperatures, and environmental degradation (Angelsen et al. 2014; Azzarri and Signorelli 2020; Castaneda et al. 2016; Dang, Hallegatte, and Trinh 2024; Fedele et al. 2021; Ortiz-Bobea et al. 2021). This creates a vicious cycle: vulnerability traps the poor in poverty and pushes others into poverty, while poverty exacerbates vulnerability to climate-related hazards (Hallegatte, Fay, and Barbier 2018; Triyana et al. 2024). Evidence shows that resilience is generally lower for poorer people because of several interconnected factors (Hill and Narayan 2020).

Poorer countries and people will suffer stronger negative consequences from climate-related hazards, leading to increases in poverty (Cevik and Jalles 2023; Dang, Cong Nguyen, and Trinh 2023; Diffenbaugh and Burke 2019; Gilli et al. 2023; Tol 2018). The setbacks that climate shocks can cause for poverty reduction are well-documented by many country-level assessments, with various degrees of severity (Dang, Hallegatte, and Trinh 2024; World Bank Group 2023). If global warming surpasses critical thresholds, impacts will likely be magnified beyond current projections (IPCC 2023a).

Climate-related hazards also have negative impacts on nonmonetary aspects of welfare that will undermine future incomes and poverty reduction. Higher temperatures affect people's health and lead to excess mortality rates, especially in poorer and hotter countries and older populations, diminishing productivity and welfare (Acevedo et al. 2020; Carleton et al. 2022). Heat exposure also significantly reduces education outcomes, with long-term consequences for the livelihoods of children and broader economic development (Park, Behrer, and Goodman 2021; Randell and Gray 2019). Lower agricultural output caused by warming and extreme weather events exacerbates food insecurity (Barrett 2021; Hasegawa et al. 2018). Undernourishment and undernutrition reduce educational attainment (Glewwe and Miguel 2007). Annex 3A discusses progress and challenges in food and nutrition security in recent years. The increased frequency and severity of natural disasters are also expected to be important drivers of both internal and cross-border migration (World Bank 2023i). These events can displace millions of people, often forcing them to move to safer areas within their own countries. For example, in 2022, floods in Pakistan displaced around 8 million people (Beyer and Milan 2023).[3]

To effectively manage climate risks, especially for poorer populations, it is essential to understand the determining factors of these risks now and in the future. The first part of this chapter describes the elements that lead to climate risk, with a focus on extreme weather events and people's well-being, and highlights the fact that protecting people from extreme weather events requires action to reduce their vulnerability to and the likelihood of hazards. First, reducing vulnerability calls for improving risk management by investing in the capacity to prepare for shocks and the ability to cope afterward. Second, there must be a significant reduction of GHG emissions to prevent the escalation of hazards associated with global warming. Failure to act now will exacerbate development challenges in the future.

The second part of this chapter discusses how advances in development and climate action require understanding and managing of trade-offs between inclusive economic growth and lowering emissions, transition costs, and identifying synergistic actions that can be scaled up. The chapter ends with a discussion on policy priorities depending on where economies stand on the interlinked goals of eradicating poverty, boosting shared prosperity, and reducing GHG emissions.

The importance of protecting people from extreme weather events

Unpacking climate risks

Risk depends on three elements: hazard, exposure, and vulnerability (figure 3.2). Climate-related hazards are characterized by natural or human-made physical events or trends occurring with a sufficiently high possibility that can result in death, harm, or other health effects, as well as destruction and loss to property, infrastructure, livelihoods, service provision, and other resources. Exposure is defined as the presence of people and livelihoods in places and settings that could be adversely affected by one or more hazards. For example, in the case of a flood hazard, those exposed would be the people who could be adversely affected by floodwaters. Vulnerability is the propensity or predisposition to be adversely affected. Continuing the flood example, not everyone who is exposed to a flood hazard may be vulnerable, because some are sufficiently resilient to not experience any adverse effects. People who are sufficiently vulnerable and are exposed to one or more hazards are deemed at risk for climate-related hazards.

FIGURE 3.2

Risks depend on hazard, exposure, and vulnerability

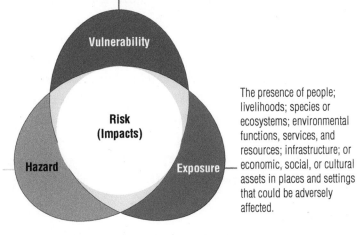

The propensity or predisposition to be adversely affected. Vulnerability encompasses a variety of concepts and elements, including sensitivity or susceptibility to harm and lack of capacity to cope and adapt.

Vulnerability

The potential occurrence of a natural or human-induced physical event or trend that may cause loss of life, injury, or other health impacts, as well as damage and loss to property, infrastructure, livelihoods, service provision, ecosystems, and environmental resources.

Risk (Impacts)

Hazard

Exposure

The presence of people; livelihoods; species or ecosystems; environmental functions, services, and resources; infrastructure; or economic, social, or cultural assets in places and settings that could be adversely affected.

Source: IPCC 2023a.

Nearly one in five people is likely to experience a severe weather shock in their lifetime that they will struggle to recover from

The World Bank has developed an indicator that tracks the number of people at high risk for climate-related hazards across the world (World Bank, n.d.). Nearly one in five people (18 percent) is at high risk from climate-related hazards globally, meaning that they are likely to experience a severe climate shock in their lifetime that they are going to struggle to recover from. This measure combines information on people's exposure to extreme weather hazards (specifically floods, heat, drought, and cyclones) with information on their vulnerability to severe impacts from these events when they occur. Vulnerability reflects the propensity to be adversely affected or unable to cope with the effects. Those at risk are people both exposed to a severe weather event and vulnerable to its impact. Box 3.1 summarizes how the indicator was constructed, and annex 3B provides more details.

About 60 percent of the world population was exposed to extreme floods, droughts, cyclones, or heat waves in 2021 (figure 3.3). In other words, more than 4 billion people in the world live in areas likely to experience an extreme weather event. Globally, 42 percent of people are exposed to heat waves, 10 percent to floods, 18 percent to droughts, and 7 percent to cyclones. These exposure numbers are expected to increase as climate change is increasing the frequency and intensity of these events (IPCC 2023a).

Exposure to these four hazards varies by region (figure 3.3). The South Asia region has the largest share of population that is exposed to shocks (88 percent), followed by East Asia and Pacific (68 percent). The global exposure to heat waves is driven by East Asia and Pacific, where half of the population is exposed, and South Asia, where four of five people are exposed. More than 1 in 10 people in East Asia and Pacific, South Asia, and the Middle East and North Africa are exposed to floods. Exposure to droughts, among all hazards, is highest in Europe and Central Asia, Latin America and the Caribbean, North America, and Sub-Saharan Africa.

For individuals in low-income countries, droughts are the leading hazard (figure 3.3). Exposure to heat waves is greater in lower-middle- and upper-middle-income countries. Individuals in high-income countries are most often exposed to droughts. Overall, the share of population exposed to any type of hazard follows an inverted U-shaped curve with country income levels, with the highest share of exposure in lower-middle-income countries (73 percent), followed by upper-middle-income countries (55 percent). Exposure rates in low-income and high-income countries are lower (41 percent and 32 percent, respectively). Behind these aggregate numbers lie substantive within-country differences. For instance, greater exposure to floods is concentrated in urban areas, where poorer households settle in more flood-prone locations because of land scarcity and lower cost (Rentschler, Salhab, and Jafino 2022).

BOX 3.1

Measuring climate risks: The percentage of people at high risk from climate-related hazards globally

The *percentage of people at high risk from climate-related hazards globally* is defined as the number of people who are both exposed to a set of key climate-related hazards (floods, droughts, cyclones, and heat waves) and highly vulnerable (that is, they have a propensity to be significantly affected or unable to cope with the impacts) as a share of the world population. People are counted as at high risk from climate-related hazards if they are exposed to at least one hazard and are identified as highly vulnerable in at least one dimension of vulnerability (see figure B3.1.1). Annex 3B provides a full list of aspects used and more details on how the indicator is constructed.

This indicator follows the traditional risk framework in which risk is the combination of hazard, exposure, and vulnerability. Hazard is the potential occurrence of an extreme event, exposure is the scope of people affected in the location of the hazard, and vulnerability is the propensity or predisposition of these people to be adversely affected. Here, vulnerability is proxied by a set of indicators measuring (a) the physical propensity to experience severe losses (proxied by the lack of mobility and access to basic infrastructure services, such as water and electricity) and (b) the inability to cope with and recover from losses (proxied by low income, not having education, not having access to financial services, and not having access to social protection).

(continued)

Measuring climate risks: The percentage of people at high risk from climate-related hazards globally (continued)

The indicator is based on a sample of 103 economies with data on all vulnerability dimensions and spans 86 percent of the world population.[a] Despite this broad coverage, note that data availability is insufficient for some climate-vulnerable economies. For instance, this is the case for most Small Island States, which are at risk from intensifying climate change (Thomas et al. 2020; Vousdoukas et al. 2023). The latest available data within three years before or after 2021 are used. The indicator currently takes into account a subset of climate hazards using historical data, a subset of vulnerability dimensions, and an aggregation methodology similar to approaches used for multidimensional poverty measures. The methodology will be revised over time as new data are collected and new methodologies are developed. Chapter 4 discusses in more detail measurement challenges with respect to the indicator and some areas in which the indicator will be updated in future rounds.

FIGURE B3.1.1

Counting people at high risk from climate-related hazards

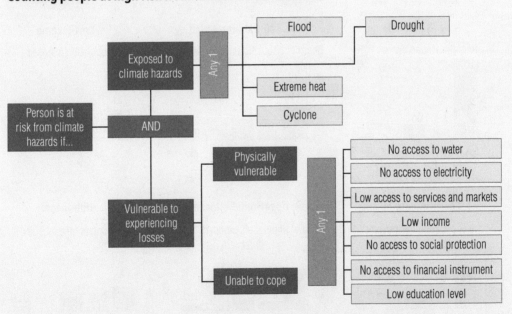

Source: World Bank Group Scorecard indicator, https://scorecard.worldbank.org/en/scorecard/home.

a. The coverage by region is 89 percent for East Asia and Pacific, 95 percent for Europe and Central Asia, 87 percent for Latin America and the Caribbean, 45 percent for the Middle East and North Africa, 100 percent for North America, 98 percent for South Asia, and 65 percent for Sub-Saharan Africa.

FIGURE 3.3

South Asia and lower-middle-income countries have the highest exposure rates to extreme weather hazards

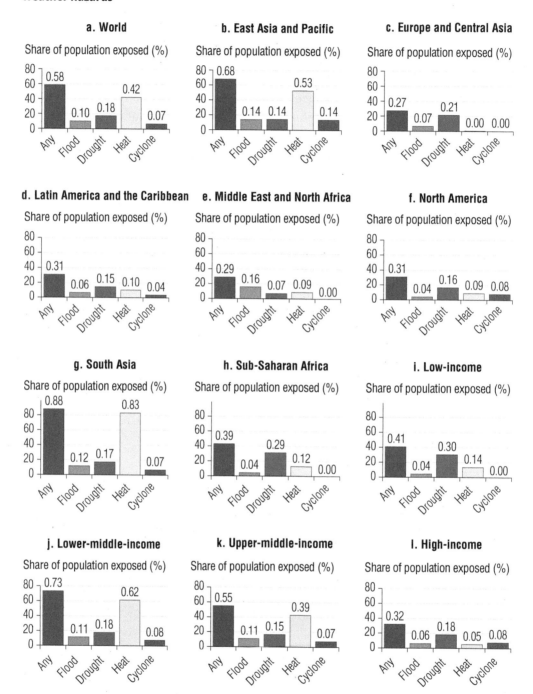

Source: World Bank Group Scorecard indicator: the percentage of people at high risk of climate-related hazards globally, https://scorecard.worldbank.org/en/scorecard/home.

Note: See box 3.1 and annex 3B for more details on the calculation of the share of population exposed. For low-income countries and the Middle East and North Africa region, the indicator covers less than 50 percent of the population.

Being at high risk is defined as being exposed to hazards and also being vulnerable to their impacts. Nearly one in five people (17.9 percent) is at high risk from climate-related hazards globally. Sub-Saharan Africa has the largest share of people at high risk from extreme weather events (map 3.1). In Sub-Saharan Africa, nearly the same proportion of people exposed to an extreme weather event is also at high risk (39.2 percent and 37.3 percent, respectively, of the total population). In Latin America and the Caribbean and the Middle East and North Africa, 13.2 percent and 13.9 percent of the population is at risk, respectively. In East Asia and Pacific, less than one-tenth of people are at risk. The share of people at risk is lowest in North America, where less than 1 percent of the population is at high risk, despite 31 percent of the population being exposed to any weather shock. In absolute terms, South Asia has the largest total population at high risk from extreme weather events (594 million people, or 32 percent of the sample population).

MAP 3.1

Large populations are exposed to extreme weather events in South Asia and East Asia and Pacific, and vulnerability is high in Sub-Saharan Africa

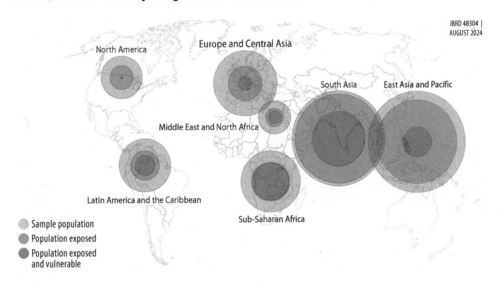

Source: World Bank Group Scorecard indicator: the percentage of people at high risk of climate-related hazards globally, https://scorecard.worldbank.org/en/scorecard/home.

Note: Gray circles depict the overall population in the sample in the data, blue circles show the population exposed to any type of hazard, and red circles indicate the population exposed to any type of hazard and vulnerable along at least one dimension. The placement of circles is for illustrative purposes only and reflects populations for the respective region as a whole. The blue circle for Sub-Saharan Africa is barely visible because almost everyone in Sub-Saharan Africa who is exposed is also vulnerable. For the Middle East and North Africa region, the indicator covers less than 50 percent of the population.

Figure 3.4 shows that economies can have similar levels of exposure but different levels of risk and vice versa. For economies along the 45-degree line, vulnerability is high, since everyone who is exposed is also at risk. In economies that are further away from the line, people are less vulnerable, since the share of population that is at risk can be significantly smaller than the share of the population exposed. The figure shows that low-income and some lower-middle-income countries are very close to the 45-degree line. Economies with higher incomes have much lower levels of risk at similar levels of exposure.

FIGURE 3.4

For similar levels of exposure, risks vary

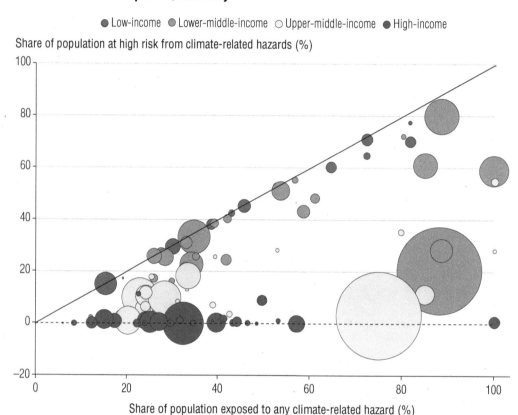

Sources: World Bank Group Scorecard indicator: the percentage of people at high risk of climate-related hazards globally, https://scorecard.worldbank.org/en/scorecard/home, and World Development Indicators, https://databank .worldbank.org/source/world-development-indicators.
Note: Bubble size indicates population. Exposure refers to the population exposed to floods, droughts, cyclones, or heat waves. Risk refers to the population exposed and vulnerable along at least one of the seven dimensions of vulnerability (see box 3.1 and annex 3B for more details on the construction of the indicators).

The comparisons between exposure and risk highlight that risks can be mitigated. While exposure in Sub-Saharan Africa is not as great as in other regions, high levels of vulnerability keep people at high risk. This is explained by people in Sub-Saharan Africa having a greater propensity or predisposition to be adversely affected. The region lags in factors that are important to management and coping, such as access to basic infrastructure services (for example, water and electricity, income, education, and financial services). For instance, in Sub-Saharan Africa, only 50 percent of the population has access to electricity and 65 percent of the population has access to basic drinking water (see annex 3C for a discussion on the livable planet dimension of water and sanitation and chapter 1 for a discussion of multidimensional poverty), making them more vulnerable to adverse shocks. Box 3.2 depicts climate risks in countries that are part of the International Development Association.

BOX 3.2

Climate risks in IDA countries are high because of slow progress in growing incomes and limited improvements in other key dimensions of vulnerability

Countries eligible to borrow from the International Development Association (IDA) account for about three-quarters of the global extreme poor.[a] While IDA countries are different in many respects, they have common challenges from low per capita incomes, widespread extreme poverty, and heightened fragility (World Bank 2024b).

Vulnerability to climate change–related and other natural disasters is a pressing concern for IDA countries (World Bank 2024b). Natural disasters are occurring with increasing frequency in these settings, causing significant damage already. Between 2011 and 2022, they caused an average loss of 1.3 percent of gross domestic product, which is considerably higher than that of other lower-income countries (World Bank 2024b). Low-income countries and Small States are particularly vulnerable to the effects of climate change, due to lack of resilience and adaptive capacity (Jafino et al. 2020; World Bank 2024a). Extreme weather events are also significantly affecting food security in IDA countries, especially those in fragile and conflict-affected situations (FAO et al. 2023; World Bank 2024b).

Of the population in IDA countries covered by the data on risks from extreme weather events used for this report, 56 percent are exposed to extreme weather hazards and 47 percent are at risk (figure B3.2.1, panel a). This means that 84 percent of those who are exposed are also at risk. In comparison, while a larger share of people is exposed to extreme weather events in non-IDA countries (59 percent), only 11 percent are at risk. Vulnerability is high along several dimensions in IDA countries. Lack of social protection is the most common deprivation, followed by lack of financial inclusion, access to electricity, and education.

Climate risks are increasing in IDA countries. Between 2010 and 2019, the number of people exposed to extreme weather events rose in both IDA and non-IDA countries but twice as fast in IDA countries (figure B3.2.1, panel b). For this calculation, the probability of experiencing a hazard is kept constant over time, and the changes are therefore driven by population growth and people settling in more exposed areas (Doan et al. 2023). However, despite the increase in the exposed population, non-IDA countries were able to significantly reduce the number of people at risk over this period. This is not the case for IDA countries,

(continued)

Climate risks in IDA countries are high because of slow progress in growing incomes and limited improvements in other key dimensions of vulnerability *(continued)*

in which the number of people at risk rose almost one to one with the population exposed. These differences are also apparent when the share of people at risk is examined. Whereas in IDA countries it fell by 5 percent, it fell by 22 percent in non-IDA countries.[b] In non-IDA countries, the population at risk dropped because of the large gains in income and financial access, developments from which people in IDA countries did not benefit as much.

Risks from extreme weather in IDA countries are high and reductions in vulnerability have been limited

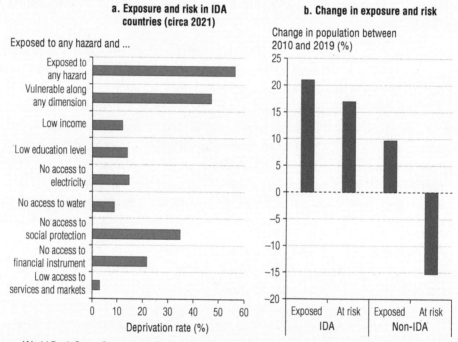

a. Exposure and risk in IDA countries (circa 2021)

b. Change in exposure and risk

Sources: World Bank Group Scorecard indicator: the percentage of people at high risk of climate-related hazards globally, https://scorecard.worldbank.org/en/scorecard/home, in panel a and data from Doan et al. 2023 in panel b.
Note: IDA = International Development Association. Exposure refers to the population exposed to floods, droughts, cyclones, or heat waves. Risk refers to the population exposed and vulnerable in at least one of seven aspects (see box 3.1 and annex 3B for more details on the construction of the indicators). In panel b, the sample consists of 45 countries that have data for both 2010 and 2019. These countries represent 52 percent of the population in IDA countries and 63 percent of the population in non-IDA countries. The variables used to compute the risk indicator for 2010 and 2019 differ slightly from the risk indicator for the year 2021 used in other parts of the report.

a. The IDA, a part of the World Bank, provides grants and concessional loans to the world's poorest countries. As of 2024, there are 75 countries eligible for support from IDA, with 75 percent of total commitments concentrated in Sub-Saharan Africa. For more information, see https://ida.worldbank.org/en/ida-financing.
b. The fact that the population at risk grew but the share of population at risk fell in IDA countries is explained by population growth.

Small States and Small Island States are particularly vulnerable to the effects of climate change due to high levels of exposure and lack of resilience and adaptive capacity (see box 3.3 for a discussion of climate risks in Small States). However, most of these countries are not included in the risk indicator because of lack of data on all vulnerability dimensions. Furthermore, there are various factors that shape vulnerability and risk that cannot be considered in the vulnerability index, one of which is gender (chapter 4 discusses some measurement challenges in more detail). Women are employed predominantly in agriculture in low-income countries, the sector most affected by climatic shocks, and female farmers are more vulnerable than male farmers (Erman et al. 2021). Access to and control of assets are important determinants in the vulnerability to climate-related hazards, with women highly disadvantaged within households (Lankes et al. 2024). Extreme weather events have been shown to increase domestic violence against women (Abiona and Koppensteiner 2018; Sekhri and Storeygard 2014). Women still shoulder the majority of domestic work, which becomes even more pronounced after disasters, hindering their ability to pursue or resume employment (Eastin 2018; Erman et al. 2021). Not being able to engage in income-generating activities further reduces long-run opportunities and exacerbates vulnerabilities. Eastin (2018) shows that climate shocks and natural disasters are associated with declines in women's economic and social rights and that this decline is more pronounced in poorer and more agricultural societies. Therefore, natural disasters disproportionally affect women in terms of income, employment, and life expectancy (Erman et al. 2021).

BOX 3.3

Small States face significant economic and climate-related challenges

Small States—those with a population of 1.5 million or less—face multiple challenges. Since 2000, per capita growth rates have been slower in Small States than in other emerging market and developing economies (EMDEs) and advanced economies (World Bank 2024a). Small States were hit hard by the COVID-19 pandemic; in 2020, GDP per capita contracted by 11 percent in Small States, seven times as much as in other EMDEs (World Bank 2023e).

Small States are particularly vulnerable to extreme weather events. Since 1990, natural disasters have caused an average annual loss of 4.8 percent of GDP per year in Small States, compared with less than 0.5 percent in other EMDEs (World Bank 2023e). Many Small States are Small Island States, which are exposed to large storms and floods that cause significant welfare losses (Heinen, Khadan, and Strobl 2019). The slow onset of challenges induced by climate change, mainly rising temperatures and sea levels, will heavily affect these economies under current trajectories (Vousdoukas et al. 2023).

(continued)

BOX 3.3

Small States face significant economic and climate-related challenges *(continued)*

For example, in the Maldives, sea levels could rise 0.5 to 0.9 meters by 2100 (World Bank 2024c). At least 80 percent of the land mass lies less than 1 meter above mean sea level, and more than 40 percent of the population resides within 100 meters of the coastline. Without adaptation, a 1-in-10-year coastal flood could damage 3.3 percent of total assets in the country by 2050 (World Bank 2024c). In addition, ocean pollution from significant amounts of per capita waste and coastal infrastructure development negatively affects island and marine ecosystems, adding to the stress from sea level rise and higher ocean temperatures (World Bank 2024d). These issues are not specific to the Maldives; other Small Island States face similar concerns (Thomas et al. 2020; Vousdoukas et al. 2023; World Bank 2023d). Rising sea levels and extreme weather events degrade coral reefs, beaches, and land and as a result pose a severe threat to tourism and agriculture, which are important sectors for most Small Island States (Thomas et al. 2020).

Yet many Small States have limited fiscal space to invest in risk management and climate adaptation. Forty percent of the EMDEs that are Small States are at high risk of debt distress or already in it, roughly twice the share for other EMDEs, and more than half are at least at moderate risk of debt distress (World Bank 2024a). The pandemic further diminished available fiscal space. All these factors pose significant challenges, and Small States need to improve institutional capacity, enhance competitiveness, and boost education to tackle them. Small Island States, in particular, urgently need to invest in adaptation measures to address sea level rise, coastal flooding, and cyclones, as well as heat stress (Thomas et al. 2020; World Bank 2023d). Adaptation will require a combination of natural-based solutions and an expansion of climate-resilient infrastructure (Vousdoukas et al. 2023; World Bank 2024c).

Without faster action, climate-related hazards will likely intensify

In 2022, the three main anthropogenic GHGs—carbon dioxide (CO_2), methane, and nitrous oxide—reached record levels, trapping nearly 50 percent more heat than in 1990.[4] There is overwhelming scientific consensus that human activities are responsible for increases in GHG emissions, which have led to the warming of the atmosphere, ocean, and land (Cook et al. 2016). The Sixth Assessment Report of the Intergovernmental Panel on Climate Change (IPCC) determined that observed global warming over the past 200 years is nearly fully attributable to human activities (Eyring et al. 2021;

Matthews and Wynes 2022).[5] These rising temperatures are linked to the occurrence and severity of extreme weather events (IPCC 2023c). Since the 1970s, floods and storms, as well as droughts and heat waves, have been occurring more often (figure 3.5). Without reduction in GHG emissions, climate risks will increase.

GHG emission levels and trends vary significantly across regions. Since 2000, total annual GHG emissions in East Asia and Pacific have surpassed annual emissions in Europe and Central Asia, making East Asia and Pacific the highest-emitting region (figure 3.6, panel a). At the other end of the spectrum, Sub-Saharan Africa is responsible for only 5 percent of global emissions. Between 2000 and 2022, only Europe and Central Asia and North America reduced total GHG emissions. GHG emissions in upper-middle-income countries have surpassed those of high-income countries since 2004 (figure 3.6, panel b). In North America, despite maintaining the largest carbon footprint per person, emissions per capita declined by almost 30 percent (figure 3.6, panel c). Emissions per person also dropped in Sub-Saharan Africa (28 percent), Latin America and the Caribbean (21 percent), and Europe and Central Asia (11 percent). In contrast, per capita emissions have almost doubled in East Asia and Pacific (surpassing per capita emissions of all regions except North America), increased by 50 percent in South Asia, and increased by 22 percent in the Middle East and North Africa.

FIGURE 3.5

Extreme weather events are occurring more frequently since 1970

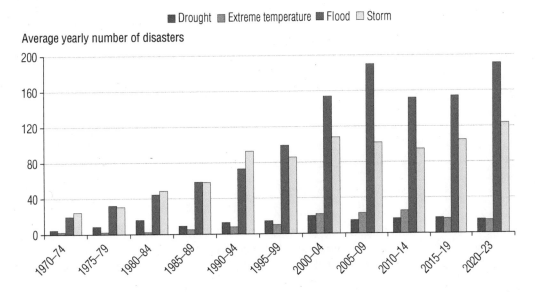

Source: International Disasters Database 2023.

FIGURE 3.6

Growth of total GHG emissions has continued but economic activity has become less emissions intensive over the past two decades

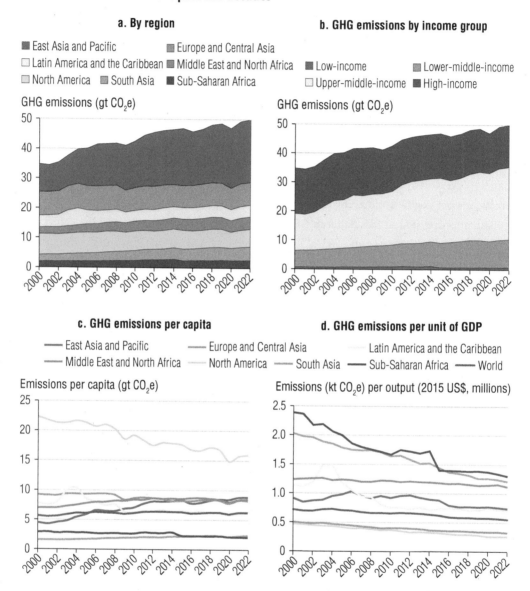

a. By region

- ■ East Asia and Pacific
- ■ Europe and Central Asia
- □ Latin America and the Caribbean
- ■ Middle East and North Africa
- □ North America
- ■ South Asia
- ■ Sub-Saharan Africa

b. GHG emissions by income group

- ■ Low-income
- ■ Lower-middle-income
- □ Upper-middle-income
- ■ High-income

c. GHG emissions per capita

d. GHG emissions per unit of GDP

- —— East Asia and Pacific
- —— Europe and Central Asia
- —— Latin America and the Caribbean
- —— Middle East and North Africa
- —— North America
- —— South Asia
- —— Sub-Saharan Africa
- —— World

Sources: Emissions Database for Global Atmospheric Research, Grassi et al. 2023, and World Development Indicators, https://databank.worldbank.org/source/world-development-indicators.

Note: CO₂e = carbon dioxide equivalent; GDP = gross domestic product; GHG = greenhouse gases. CO₂e values are indicated in gigatons (gt), tons (t), or kilotons (kt) and millions of 2015 US dollars. In panel b, fixed income group classifications from 2022 are used. Increases in GHG emission intensities between 2002 and 2004 in Latin America and the Caribbean are driven by Brazil. The drop in emissions in Sub-Saharan Africa (panels c and d) in 2015 comes from the Democratic Republic of Congo, where land use, land use change, and forestry emissions declined substantially after 2014.

Relating GHG emissions to country-level output gives an approximate measure of emission intensity (figure 3.6, panel d) and speaks to advances in energy efficiency and the adoption of renewable energy sources in making economic growth less carbon intensive. Since 2000, economic growth has become less carbon intensive across all regions, but progress has slowed down recently. The rate of reduction in emissions intensity has plateaued in recent years in Sub-Saharan Africa, the Middle East and North Africa, Latin America and the Caribbean, and East Asia and Pacific.

Protecting people from extreme weather events

Lowering vulnerability by enhancing risk management

Vulnerability depends on two important factors: (a) the physical propensity to experience a severe income, asset, or health loss and (b) the inability to cope with and recover from the shock. By strengthening household coping capacity and access to basic support systems, vulnerability to the same hazard levels can be lowered significantly.

The *World Development Report 2014* (World Bank 2013) and a large body of evidence of risks and development highlight the important role that risk management can play in increasing resilience to negative shocks. Risk management must integrate the ability to prepare for risks with the capacity to respond effectively afterward. Building on the foundational work of Ehrlich and Becker (1972), preparation should encompass three proactive measures: self-insurance, market insurance, and self-protection. In addition to these measures, a comprehensive risk management strategy includes support for sensible coping measures. Better knowledge can lead to more informed decisions about allocating resources between insurance and protection. Similarly, improved insurance and protection can make coping less challenging and less costly. How to best promote resilience to climate risks is discussed in more detail in a forthcoming World Bank Policy Research report. Box 3.4 summarizes the upcoming report's main findings.

BOX 3.4

How to best promote climate resilience

An upcoming World Bank Policy Research report on resilient development aims to contribute to debates about how best to promote climate resilience. The report advocates for a broad perspective, emphasizing that resilience to climate change hinges significantly on the adaptation choices made by millions of individuals, households, farms, and businesses.

The report highlights that government-led top-down approaches are essential, for instance, collective adaptation measures such as protective infrastructure or large-scale irrigation. However, they will struggle to reach all vulnerable populations. Empowering individuals to act and invest in measures suitable

(continued)

BOX 3.4

How to best promote climate resilience *(continued)*

for improving their resilience given their specific circumstances is crucial. This approach requires well-informed policies grounded in robust evidence.

The report finds that some reasons that households, farmers, and firms are not adapting quickly enough are lack of information, lack of access to finance, no or few markets for adaptation tools or services, or unclear or distorted public policies. These problems can be solved by helping people become adaptation pragmatists, by providing them with proper information and access to the required tools and resources.

The report proposes specific reforms as well as several broad principles to guide policy, such as the following. (a) Adaptation measures with general-purpose benefits such as information provision and/or financial inclusion must be a priority. Promote self-help first, leverage markets where possible, and involve governments where necessary. (b) More broadly, the complexity of the problem suggests bundling adaptation policy instruments ("risk layering"), building on a hierarchy of resilience instruments: improved knowledge and information as a solid base. (c) Better access to savings and credit would improve welfare overall and act as self-insurance. (d) More formal insurance would spread risk and speed up recovery. (e) Social protection would be the insurance of last resort.

Investments in education and infrastructure are fundamental for risk management

Development strategies that bolster households' productivity and income-generating capacities often concurrently enhance their ability to manage climate risks by enhancing prevention and coping (Doan et al. 2023; Hallegatte and Rozenberg 2017; Pörtner et al. 2022) and should be prioritized in poorer and more vulnerable countries.

Investing in education is fundamental to increasing incomes, but it also allows households to better prepare for and cope with shocks. One important part of risk management is knowledge, and more education helps on that front. There is evidence that households with higher levels of education have a better understanding and ability to process risk information such as weather forecasts and early warnings (Hoffmann and Muttarak 2017; Muttarak and Lutz 2014; Muttarak and Pothisiri 2013). In addition, households with more education are less likely to engage in negative coping strategies (Dimitrova 2021; Hill and Mejía-Mantilla 2017; Le and Nguyen 2023). Recent research by Dobermann (2023) provides robust evidence on the importance of education to adapting to climate change in India.

Improving infrastructure not only increases access to markets and productivity but also supports risk management and resilience. For example, better access to roads in remote areas increases access to markets, goods, and services. When a drought reduces local food availability, improved access to markets reduces the impact on local food prices (Burgess and Donaldson 2010). Moreover, better infrastructure can improve access to energy, water, and communication, which can allow households to better cope with shocks when they occur. Infrastructure improvements are beneficial for both economic development and resilience, but unlocking synergies depends on how infrastructure is built. Infrastructure investments need to account for future risks, such as rising occurrences and intensities of flooding (Hallegatte, Bangalore et al. 2016; Hallegatte, Rentschler, and Rozenberg 2019). Stress-testing and simulating how climate shocks propagate through road networks is an example of assessing where improvements to infrastructure are needed to make its functionality resilient (Hallegatte, Rentschler, and Rozenberg 2019). Consider that constructing infrastructure in a resilient manner improves its cost-effectiveness in the long run, and higher up-front investment costs can reduce damages and repair costs in the future (Hallegatte, Rentschler, and Rozenberg 2019).[6]

Expanding insurance is also key

Beyond these foundational investments in human capital and infrastructure, it is important to strengthen insurance mechanisms that protect individuals from severe poverty and prevent deeper hardship during crises (Gill, Revenga, and Zeballos 2016).

Financial development is important to enable access to credit, formal insurance, and other financial products that can help households and businesses manage climate risk. One of the primary objectives of financial inclusion is to enhance households' capacity to manage common but unpredictable events that entail financial expenses. Mobile money is an example: when a weather crisis strikes, mobile money can allow households to quickly receive transfers or remittances from relatives or migrant family members who live elsewhere (Batista and Vicente 2023; Jack and Suri 2014). For instance, Sub-Saharan Africa has shown significant growth in financial inclusion driven by mobile money account adoption. Yet a large share of adults still conducts transactions in cash, suggesting opportunities to increase financial inclusion through continued payment digitalization (Demirgüç-Kunt et al. 2022). Many people exposed to severe climate risk are not financially included (figure 3.7). These issues are particularly prevalent in Sub-Saharan Africa and the Middle East and North Africa regions, where about one in three people exposed to extreme weather events does not have a financial account (including mobile money).

Developing insurance markets and increasing the demand for insurance is central. In 2023, the estimated global economic losses due to natural disasters were $380 billion,[7] only about one-third of which was covered by insurance. In low-income countries, less than 10 percent of losses was covered by insurance, forcing governments to redirect limited development funds toward disaster recovery. Despite its importance for risk management, access to insurance remains insufficient, leaving billions unprotected. For example, household demand for insurance is constrained by a number of factors. One important challenge is affordability, as the demand for insurance is price sensitive (Cai, de Janvry, and Sadoulet 2020; Cole et al. 2013; Hill et al. 2019; Karlan et al. 2014; McIntosh, Sarris, and Papadopoulos 2013). Interventions to reduce prices (for example, reducing reinsurance costs, increasing efficiency of marketing, or reducing taxes on insurance products) can increase demand.

Moreover, insurance is a more complex financial product than savings or credit products. Financial literacy training increases demand for insurance (Cai and Song 2017; Vasilaky et al. 2020). Liquidity constraints also limit its use; moving payment of the insurance to the end of the coverage period can increase demand (Casaburi and Willis 2018; Liu, Chen, and Hill 2020).

Noncontributory social assistance programs, or social safety nets, aimed at those who are chronically or extremely poor also serve as insurance of last resort. The use of adaptive social protection can help vulnerable people to manage risks from climate-related hazards by timely transferring of resources to disaster victims (World Bank Group 2023). Postdisaster transfers have a benefit-cost ratio above 1.3 (Hallegatte, Bangalore et al. 2016). For example, the Philippines supported recipients of its flagship social safety net program, Pantawid Pamilyang Pilipino Program, when they were hit by the Yolanda Typhoon in 2013 (World Bank 2022c). In Kenya, the Hunger Safety Net Programme provided aid to over 100,000 additional households in response to drought during 2015 and issued a special transfer to 200,000 households in anticipation of expected droughts (Hallegatte, Bangalore et al. 2016). Anticipatory cash transfers before the traditional humanitarian response would normally arrive can have a significant additional welfare impact (Pople et al. 2021). Yet in Sub-Saharan Africa, 71.2 percent of the people exposed to severe cyclone, flood, drought, and heat waves are neither covered nor contributing to social protection and are unlikely to receive public support when one of these severe events occurs (figure 3.7). Additionally, not all of those covered will have their climate risk fully covered by public safety nets.

FIGURE 3.7

A large share of the population in Sub-Saharan Africa exposed to extreme weather events does not have access to social protection or a financial account

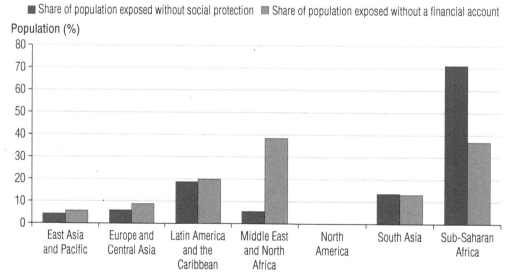

Source: World Bank Group Scorecard indicator: the percentage of people at high risk of climate-related hazards globally, https://scorecard.worldbank.org/en/scorecard/home.

Note: The figure shows the share of population exposed to any hazard who neither receives social protection benefits nor contributes to social insurance and the share of population exposed to any hazard who does not have a financial account (including mobile money). For North America, the share of population exposed to any climate-related hazard and without social protection or access to a financial account is zero. See annex 3B in chapter 3 for more details.

While safety nets serve as insurance of last resort, they need to be complemented by social insurance programs designed to protect a broader segment of the population from falling back into poverty because of individual or systemic shocks. Additionally, global insurance mechanisms are essential to help countries manage the impacts of large-scale natural disasters affecting multiple nations or pandemics.

Basic systems to deliver timely information on climate risk are fundamental

The evidence shows that climate risk management can be enhanced through expanded early warning systems, hazard maps, and climate knowledge. In Bangladesh, Cyclone Bhola caused 300,000 deaths in 1970, and Cyclone April killed 138,000 in 1991. Since then, investments in resilient infrastructure, road networks, and early warning systems have significantly reduced fatalities. Cyclone Sidr in 2007 resulted in 3,363 deaths, while Cyclone Fani in 2019 caused five, and in 2020, Bangladesh evacuated 2.4 million people for Cyclone Amphan, with 20 fatalities. Yet one-fifth of the world's population is not covered by an early warning system, even though these systems save lives and greatly reduce climate-related disaster losses in developing countries (United Nations, n.d.).

Faster economic transformations to reduce the emissions intensiveness of growth

Faster transformations of the global economy are necessary to limit global warming and reduce climate risks.[8] Since 2015, when the Paris Agreement was adopted, GHG emissions were expected to rise by 16 percent until 2030 on the basis of existing policies. Today, the expected increase is 3 percent, showcasing that transformations have already occurred over the past years. However, figure 3.8 shows that with current policies, temperatures are projected to increase close to 2°C. Even if currently pledged Nationally Determined Contributions (NDCs)[9] were to be enacted, emissions would not fall enough to limit global warming to below 1.5°C (IPCC 2023b). Only a Net Zero 2050 scenario, which is shaped by stringent climate policies and innovation, would have the chance to limit warming to around 1.5°C.[10] A net-zero path would require emissions to decline by 80 percent in advanced economies and by 60 percent in emerging-market and developing economies by 2035 compared with the 2022 level (IEA 2023a).[11]

It is necessary to continue expanding the use of renewable energy and improving energy efficiency. The energy sector produces three-quarters of global emissions. Electricity and heat generation alone accounted for 29 percent of all emissions in 2022; transportation was responsible for 14 percent, followed by manufacturing and construction (13 percent).[12] Despite progress, in 2022, renewable sources added up to just 7 percent of total global energy, up from 4 percent in 1990 (figure 3.9). Petroleum (with other liquid fuels) and coal remain the largest sources of energy (32 percent each), although natural gas is catching up and accounted for one-quarter of energy production in 2022 (figure 3.9, panel b). To reduce GHG emissions, the reliance on coal and oil will need to be brought down substantially. Yet the share of coal in energy production has increased globally and in absolute terms has declined only in today's high-income countries. Doubling the pace of progress in energy efficiency could cut energy bills by one-third and could constitute 50 percent of CO_2 reductions by 2030 (IEA et al. 2023).

FIGURE 3.8

Projections of emissions and temperatures to 2050 show that with current policies, temperatures would increase close to 2°C

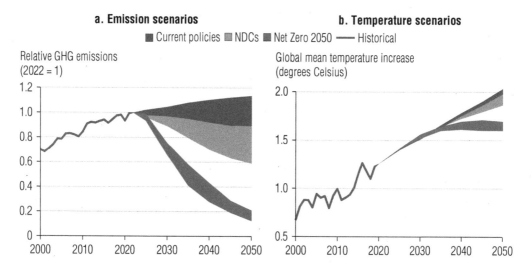

Sources: Panel a: Network for Greening the Financial System (NGFS) 2023, harmonized to historical 2022 emissions estimations from EDGAR data. Panel b: World Bank calculations using projections from NGFS 2023, harmonized to historical 2020 temperature estimations from IPCC 2021.

Note: GHG = greenhouse gas; NDCs = Nationally Determined Contributions. Ranges for each policy scenario are based on four different projection models: GCAM 6.0, MESSAGEix-GLOBIOM 1.1-M-R12, REMIND-MAgPIE 3.2-4.6 Integrated Physical Damages (95th-high), and REMIND-MAgPIE 3.2-4.6 Integrated Physical Damages (median). In panel b, temperature increases are relative to the average global surface temperature of the period 1850–1900 (preindustrial) (IPCC 2021). Temperature projections refer to the AR6 surface temperature increase (50th percentile) from the MAGICC 7.5.3 model.

FIGURE 3.9

Energy production mix by income group remains largely based on coal and petroleum

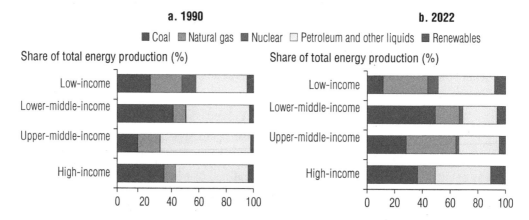

Source: US Energy Information Administration.

Note: Energy is measured in quadrillion (10^{15}) British thermal units. Income classifications are fixed at 2022 definitions.

Further advancements and adoption of technology have the potential to speed up the necessary transformations (Millward-Hopkins et al. 2020). In many contexts, it is already more economical to use renewable energy than energy from other sources. While the price of generating energy from fossil fuels has been relatively stable and jumped in 2022, the cost of solar photovoltaic energy has fallen by 89 percent and the cost of wind energy dropped by 69 percent between 2010 and 2022. Without the growth of key clean energy technologies since 2019 (for example, solar photovoltaic, wind power, heat pumps, and electric cars), growth in emissions would have been three times larger (IEA 2023b).

Carbon pricing policies are key to incorporate the environmental externalities of GHG emissions, incentivize efficiency gains, reduce the reliance on fossil fuels, and spur innovation in less emission-intense technologies. (World Bank 2024e). The coverage of carbon taxes and emission trading systems has increased from 0.15 percent of global emissions in 1990 to 24 percent in 2024. Despite the progress, three-quarters of global emissions remain unaccounted for, and many emissions have negative effective prices because of pervasive fossil fuel subsidies. Thus, while coverage is increasing, the global total carbon price—which takes into account the additional net effect of indirect pricing from fossil fuel taxes and subsidies—has not increased much since 1994 (Agnolucci et al. 2023). Repurposing fossil fuel subsidies is thus important to remove market distortions and also to help move resources to sustainable projects (Damania, Balseca et al. 2023). Investing in research and development and digitalization is crucial to spur innovation and transitions.

Priorities for advancing on the interlinked goals

Ending extreme poverty and boosting shared prosperity on a livable planet require actions in two areas: delivering faster and inclusive growth (that is, growing labor incomes by delivering more and better jobs and investing in the productive capacity of the poor) and protecting people from climate shocks (namely, enhancing risk management and accelerating climate change mitigation). Solutions to advance on these fronts are not always simple. Fundamental changes in how countries approach their national development strategies and their contribution to global public goods are required.

With limited budgets, high uncertainty, and conflicting interests, policy makers may need to prioritize and make difficult choices. To inform decisions, it is important to understand the trade-off between growing incomes and lowering GHG emissions, find ways to scale up synergistic policies that can help advance on multiple fronts or reduce trade-offs, and manage short-term transition costs of climate mitigation policies to specific groups and communities.

The trade-off between growing incomes and lowering emissions

Past economic growth and poverty reduction have been associated with high GHG emissions. This marks an apparent tension between advancing on poverty reduction and growing people's incomes and reducing emissions. Unsurprisingly, research suggests that additional emissions attributed to moving individuals out of *extreme* poverty do not counteract climate goals, as emissions of low-income households are miniscule (Bruckner et al. 2022). Wollburg, Hallegatte, and Mahler (2023) calculated the additional economic growth that would be required to eradicate extreme poverty and the additional emissions implied using historical emission intensities (from 2010–19). Eradicating extreme poverty would entail 4.7 percent more emissions than in 2019 (figure 3.10). However, this number becomes larger at higher poverty lines. At $6.85 per day, additional emissions would reach 46 percent, with historical emission intensities. This trade-off is different across countries depending on their levels of poverty and the sources of economic growth and emission levels. Yet it is clear that the foregone reduction in GHG emissions from extreme poverty eradication is minimal.

FIGURE 3.10

Additional emissions associated with poverty alleviation increase with the level of ambition

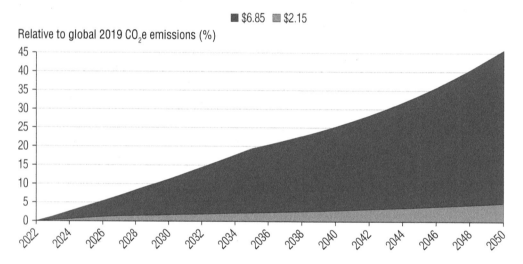

Source: Wollburg, Hallegatte, and Mahler 2023.

Note: CO_2e = carbon dioxide equivalent. The figure shows additional emissions relative to 2019 if poverty were to be alleviated at the $2.15 and $6.85 per person per day poverty lines (expressed in 2017 purchasing power parity dollars) using historical emission intensities.

Synergistic policies can ameliorate the trade-offs

Investing in renewable energy and energy efficiency can offer multiple benefits beyond reducing emissions

Investment in renewable energy and energy efficiency offers multiple benefits beyond reducing emissions. Studies show that renewable energy investments not only help lower emissions but also meet growing energy demands and improve energy security (World Bank Group 2023). For many countries with little energy access in particular, it can be more cost-effective to develop renewable energy infrastructure than to expand fossil fuel generation (World Bank Group 2023).[13] Solar and wind energy are particularly efficient for connecting sparsely populated areas, from which lower-income regions can benefit directly. For example, in countries such as Côte d'Ivoire and Uzbekistan, where gas supplies are decreasing and electricity demand is rising, transforming power systems to renewable energy is the most cost-efficient solution (World Bank Group 2023).

These investments are also synergistic in the sense that they can ease the trade-off between economic growth, poverty reduction, and emissions. Simulations indicate that investing in renewable energy and energy efficiency combined would in fact lower the additional emissions that accompany the economic growth needed to reduce poverty by more than half (figure 3.11) (Wollburg, Hallegatte, and Mahler 2023).

FIGURE 3.11

Lower emissions from poverty alleviation projected with energy efficiency and decarbonization

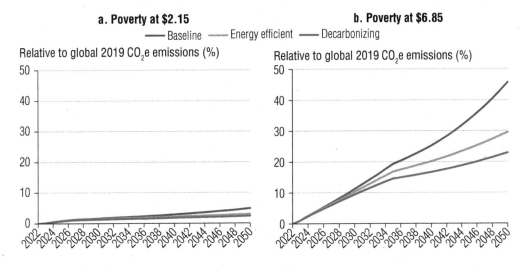

Source: Wollburg, Hallegatte, and Mahler 2023.

Note: CO_2e = carbon dioxide equivalent. The figure shows additional emissions relative to 2019 if poverty were to be alleviated at the $2.15 and $6.85 per person per day poverty lines (expressed in 2017 purchasing power parity dollars). The baseline scenario uses historical emission intensities. Energy-efficient and decarbonizing scenarios assume that all countries achieve the top 10 percent historical performance in energy efficiency and decarbonization.

Relatedly, electrified heating presents another synergy between climate change mitigation and rising incomes by significantly enhancing energy efficiency. For instance, heat pumps are three to five times more energy efficient than gas boilers (IEA 2022). Their usage can reduce running and maintenance costs, as well as exposure to fluctuating fuel prices. Which heating solution ultimately has the lowest cost for households is highly context specific, depending on existing infrastructure, the cost of energy fuels, and the availability of affordable renewable resources (World Bank and ESMAP 2023).

Tackling air pollution is a clear win-win strategy and should be prioritized

Air pollution is a leading environmental risk to people's health (World Bank 2022f). Air pollution is estimated to be responsible for a staggering 6.7 million deaths[14] annually worldwide, almost the total number of deaths due to COVID-19 (Coronavirus) to date[15] or an amount roughly equivalent to one-third of the combined deaths due to communicable, maternal, neonatal, and nutritional diseases in 2021.[16] Air pollution carried a global health cost representing 6.1 percent of the global GDP in 2019 (World Bank 2022f). Besides the enormous impact that the lack of clean air has on health, air pollution can also harm productivity, cognitive performance, decision-making, and human capital accumulation (Aguilar-Gomez et al. 2022).

Most people breathe air polluted above World Health Organization (WHO) maximum recommended levels.[17] As of 2019, all countries experienced (on average) unhealthy air quality. This does not imply that everyone is exposed to harmful pollution levels, since exposure can be heterogeneous, but it does indicate that a lack of clean air is a problem affecting all countries. From 1960 to 2009, global mean population-weighted air pollution concentrations rose by 38 percent, driven largely by increases in China and India. Consequently, attributable deaths surged globally by 89 percent to 124 percent during this period (Butt et al. 2017).

For some countries, particularly those in South Asia and Sub-Saharan Africa, annual exposure levels are particularly high, exceeding 10 times the recommended levels. Indeed, South Asia is home to 37 of the 40 most polluted cities in the world (World Bank 2023g). While the population-weighted air pollution exposure is 2.8 times the recommended levels in high-income countries, in upper-middle-, lower-middle-, and low-income countries the exposure rates are 6.8, 12.5, and 8.1 times the recommended levels, respectively. In South Asia, air pollution causes an estimated 2 million premature deaths each year and imposes significant economic costs.

Cleaner air is a large co-benefit of lowering GHG emissions. The burning of fuels that feeds climate change is also a source of some of the ultrafine particles that degrade air quality. Methane emissions, for example, are one of the main precursors to ground-level ozone, a major source of premature death. The solid fuels that pollute the indoor air of many homes also significantly contribute to global human-made black carbon emissions (Klimont et al. 2017). While some air pollutants also contribute to climate *cooling* (Fuller et al. 2022), synergies between the reduction of air pollutants and the mitigation of GHG emissions exist and should be promoted. In cities such as Tbilisi, where the impact of vehicle traffic and industrial emissions on outdoor air pollution is substantial, policies enacted to curb such emissions would have considerable co-benefits in the form of public health and economic outcomes. In such a context, a carbon tax could lead to significant reductions of particulate matter (PM) (Baquié et al. 2024). Urban development that focuses on mass transit systems can lower both CO_2 emissions and air pollution levels (Mukim and Roberts 2023).

World Bank (2023g) has shown that cost-effective strategies to lower air pollution in South Asia not only can save lives but also can bring important climate benefits. For example, reduction of concentrations to WHO Interim Target 1 on air pollution by 2030 would reduce CO_2 by 22 percent and methane by 21 percent.[18]

Several other actions can help, depending on the context

Another area with sizable synergies between lowering emissions, increasing resilience, and increasing incomes is improvement of agricultural productivity through climate-smart practices, especially for low-income countries (Sutton, Lotsch, and Prasann 2024). These practices, such as crop diversification and soil conservation, not only mitigate risks from climate-related hazards but also enhance crop yields and farmer incomes, especially in vulnerable regions (Aker and Jack 2021; World Bank 2012).

In regions where agriculture is an important contributor to emissions, such as Latin America and the Caribbean and Sub-Saharan Africa, such practices will be crucial. For instance, in Colombia, agriculture accounts for 22 percent of the country's GHG emissions, and agricultural expansion over the past two decades has occurred primarily at the expense of forests and natural ecosystems. Climate-smart agriculture increases agricultural productivity, spurring economic growth without deforestation. However, only 15 percent of farms in Colombia use innovative technologies, and most climate-smart agricultural initiatives have remained in the pilot stage. Public policy is crucial in promoting these practices more widely. This can be achieved by redirecting agricultural support, strengthening innovation systems, facilitating financing services, and improving land information systems and administration (World Bank 2023c). In Cambodia, which could suffer one of the largest losses in rice yields in Southeast Asia due to climate change, analysis indicates that the negative impacts of droughts can be entirely mitigated through irrigation or crop rotation practices (World Bank 2023b).

Repurposing agricultural subsidies to climate-smart and productivity-enhancing practices can reduce overall agricultural emissions by more than 40 percent and the land footprint of agriculture by 2.2 percent, and greater productivity could reduce global extreme poverty by about 1 percent (Laborde et al. 2022). This is relevant not only for lower-income countries—removing inefficient subsidies alleviates market distortions and reduces deforestation and biodiversity loss in high-income countries as well (Damania, Balseca et al. 2023). Agricultural and energy subsidies constitute around 3 percent of GDP in lower-middle-income and low-income countries, but only 20 percent of spending on subsidies reaches the bottom 40 percent of the populations (World Bank 2022e).

Sustainable forest management initiatives not only protect biodiversity and reduce emissions but also provide livelihood opportunities for local communities, thereby reducing poverty and enhancing resilience to climate-related disasters (Barbier 2010; Damania, Polasky et al. 2023; Grosset, Papp, and Taylor 2023). In Peru, transitioning to a zero-carbon forest sector could generate employment opportunities, yield $3.5 billion in benefits from restored ecosystem services, and increase the sector's value added sevenfold by 2050 (World Bank 2022b). More efficient land use could sequester an additional 85.6 billion metric tons of CO_2 equivalent without adverse economic impacts—an amount equivalent to approximately 1.7 years' worth of global emissions (Damania, Polasky et al. 2023).[19] Land degradation affects an estimated 3.2 billion people worldwide, and the poorest are most often exposed (IPBES 2019). Forest loss also has important ramifications for public health. More than 30 percent of new diseases reported since 1960 have been linked to land use change, including deforestation (FAO 2022). These diseases (for example, Ebola and severe acute respiratory syndrome) often emerge when wildlife habitats are altered or destroyed, which can force wildlife closer to humans and increase the likelihood of disease transmission (FAO 2022). This underscores the importance of maintaining healthy forest ecosystems to reduce the risk of future pandemics and protect both environmental and human health.[20] Annex 3D summarizes some elements related to healthy ecosystems focused on forests.

It is important to identify and remove constraints to scale up synergistic policies

While synergistic strategies exist across different geographical contexts and sectors, challenges may still arise in their implementation. For instance, agroforestry may require a fundamental shift in traditional farming techniques, necessitating new skills or knowledge that farmers may not initially possess. Risk aversion can also be a challenge; farmers might be hesitant to adopt new practices because of uncertainty about the outcomes or fear of initial yield reductions. Financial constraints are another common barrier, as up-front costs for resources or training can be prohibitive for lower-income households. Moreover, cultural and social norms can influence the willingness to adopt new methods, as practices deeply ingrained in community identity may not be easily altered. Lastly, the lack of supportive policies or incentives from governments can impede widespread adoption, as can inadequate access to markets or resources necessary to implement these new practices effectively. Addressing these barriers through finance, comprehensive support systems, education, and community engagement is essential for successful adoption and long-term sustainability of synergic strategies.

Managing transition costs is important for the poor and vulnerable

Transitioning toward a low-carbon, climate-resilient economy may involve a trade-off between a cost today and benefits in the future, as well as opportunity costs between different priorities. These transitions bring future climate benefits by altering the probability distribution of climate-related hazards, but they can be costly for specific people now.

Transitioning to green industries may lead to or accelerate job displacement in traditional industries that rely heavily on fossil fuels. Reductions in coal production are likely to not have substantial impacts on national employment and output in many economies because of the industry's low labor share. For example, in Indonesia, the world's second-largest coal exporter, the coal industry's share of the GDP is less than 2 percent and it employs only 0.2 percent of the workforce (World Bank Group 2023). However, impacts on local communities can be substantial in some instances (World Bank Group 2023). Challenges arise as displaced workers may face difficulties transitioning to alternative employment because of differences in skills, wages, and geographic locations (World Bank 2023a). For instance, in six South Asian countries (Bangladesh, India, Maldives, Nepal, Pakistan, and Sri Lanka), workers in pollution-intensive jobs are systematically less educated and are often informally employed; the opposite applies to workers in green jobs. Going beyond educational levels to consider foundational skills, analysis in Poland shows that people in green jobs on average have higher numeracy, literacy, and problem-solving skills. There are also major gender differences in green employment across all major occupation groups, with women tending to have browner jobs (World Bank 2022d). As noted above, with renewable energy becoming cheaper than coal and other energy sources in many contexts, it is not only through climate policies that solutions for changes in employment demand will be needed.

Workers in carbon-intensive sectors can be affected not only by local energy transition policies but also by the global consequences of carbon mitigation policies on trade flows. Changes in goods and labor demand may originate from abroad. Take, for example, the Carbon Border Adjustment Mechanism (CBAM), a carbon tariff that penalizes high-carbon exports to the European Union. If industries in certain countries fail to decarbonize, such systems may redirect demand to producers elsewhere (Haddad, Hansl, and Pechevy 2024). While CBAM is not likely to have a large impact on countries' GDP or trade balances, it may negatively impact workers in some sectors in lower-income countries (World Bank Group 2022).

Consumers, especially those with less purchasing power or who allocate a significant portion of their budget to food and energy, may encounter challenges from policies aimed at reducing emissions that affect prices. For example, carbon pricing schemes and the removal of fossil fuel subsidies could lead to short-term increases in poverty in several low- and middle-income countries if the policies are not carefully designed (World Bank Group 2022).

Removing and repurposing inefficient subsidies are key to reduce emissions and free up significant fiscal space for many countries, which can be repurposed (Damania, Balseca et al. 2023). Abolishing inefficient and emission-inducing policies such as fossil fuel subsidies would result in a larger decrease in consumption among the wealthiest households than among the poorest ones in absolute terms (Klaiber, Rentschler, and Dorband 2023). However, indirect subsidies, like those for energy, often constitute a greater share of the market income for poorer households (World Bank Group 2022). Energy costs can also comprise a large share of the budget of poor and vulnerable households, as they tend to be inefficient users of energy because of outdated appliances and poorly insulated housing. This is particularly the case for poor households in high- and upper-middle-income countries. In contrast, in low- and lower-middle-income countries, poor households use very little energy and therefore they may not be strongly exposed to fuel price changes (Hallegatte et al. 2023).

For example, evidence shows that a fuel tax would disproportionately affect low-income households in Cape Town, South Africa, as they lack the means to change their modes of transportation or housing. In Kinshasa, the Democratic Republic of Congo, the lower-middle-income class is more affected because the poorest people are excluded from energy-intensive services and have limited access to areas with a high concentration of jobs (Hallegatte et al. 2023; Liotta, Avner, and Hallegatte 2023). Research by Steckel et al. (2021) demonstrates that the impact of carbon pricing varies importantly across the income distribution among eight low- and middle-income Asian economies.

The short-term costs of climate mitigation policies and how to manage them will vary depending on each country's context. These challenges will also depend on how policies are implemented and how political and economic institutions align to support a just transition (Lankes et al. 2024; Rizk and Slimane 2018). Short-term costs, such as higher energy prices or job losses in carbon-intensive sectors, can be particularly hard for poorer people to manage. Therefore, assessing how the green transition affects poor and vulnerable people and designing policies to reduce negative impacts are essential.

Policies that invest in skills and reskilling can play a vital role in facilitating the transition of workers affected by industry changes. Active labor market programs, for instance, not only help workers acquire the skills needed for this transition but also ensure a workforce ready to meet the demand in green industries. Programs supporting internal migration can be particularly valuable (Rigolini 2021). To support communities most affected by job losses, targeted policies are essential. These include initiatives to promote job creation, especially in areas facing employment challenges, and support for climate-smart agricultural practices, job training, and skills development. Such measures are crucial for facilitating the transition to low-carbon and sustainable livelihoods.

It is also important to implement compensatory measures in order to not disproportionately affect poor households. Well-designed redistribution measures can mitigate the impacts on households, especially those with lower incomes (Blanchard, Gollier, and Tirole 2023). According to the findings of Steckel et al. (2021), even redistributing revenues generated from carbon pricing to all individuals, not just the poor, results in a net income gain for poor households. Similarly, redistributing domestic carbon revenues as an equal-per-capita climate dividend more than offsets the negative effects of higher prices, lifting approximately 6 million people out of poverty globally.

To counteract the adverse effects of fuel price hikes on the poor, governments have various policy tools beyond cash transfers at their disposal. For instance, in urban areas, making public transportation more affordable or providing subsidies to assist low-income households in securing housing closer to job opportunities can help mitigate these impacts (Liotta, Avner, and Hallegatte 2023). Such incentives also align with emission reduction objectives.

Doing what matters where it matters most

The pathways presented above involve difficult trade-offs in objectives and transition costs. It is important to recognize that low growth, high debt servicing and limited financing, and high uncertainty severely constrain the ability of many countries to act. In this polycrisis, there is an urgent need to focus on and prioritize the actions that will have the highest return for development and that can allow the world to make significant progress on the interlinked goals.

A key guiding element to setting priorities is where the poor and vulnerable live and where the emissions are generated. Going forward, as shown in chapter 1, extreme poverty will be concentrated increasingly in Sub-Saharan Africa and in fragile and conflict-affected countries (in Sub-Saharan Africa and elsewhere). The poorest countries are also the most at risk from climate hazards.

Yet, emissions are generated largely by high-income and upper-middle-income countries. High-income and upper-middle-income countries account for 32 percent and 52 percent of global CO_2 emissions, while constituting only 15 percent and 35 percent of the global population, respectively. Ten economies emit two-thirds of global emissions annually (figure 3.12, panel b). The next 30 economies by total emissions contribute 24 percent of global emissions. The 140 least-emitting economies, which comprise 12 percent of the total population, produce less than 5 percent of GHG emissions.[21]

FIGURE 3.12

Positive relationship between income levels and GHG emissions

a. Emissions per capita are converging between high- and upper-middle-income economies

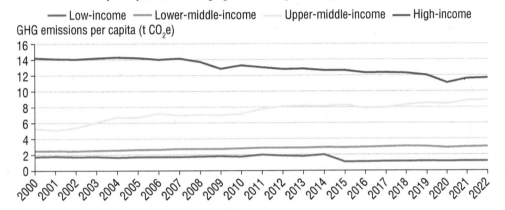

b. Ten economies produce two-thirds of global GHG emissions

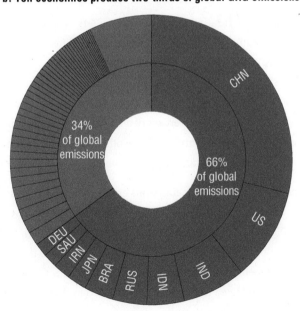

(continued)

FIGURE 3.12

Positive relationship between income levels and GHG emissions *(continued)*

c. High-income and upper-middle-income countries are responsible for 90 percent of historical emissions

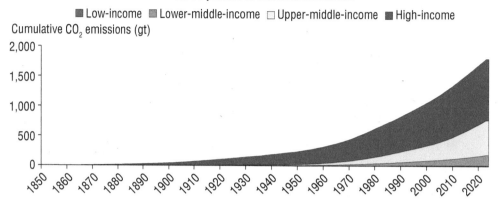

Sources: Emissions Database for Global Atmospheric Research, Grassi et al. 2023, and World Development Indicators (panels a and b); and PRIMAP-hist data from Gütschow, Pflüger, and Busch 2024 (panel c).
Note: CO_2e = carbon dioxide equivalent; GHG = greenhouse gas; LULUCF = land use, land use change, and forestry. Panel a: Emissions per capita are in tons of CO_2e. Panel b: The 10 economies are Brazil (BRA), China (CHN), Germany (DEU), India (IND), Indonesia (IDN), the Islamic Republic of Iran (IRN), Japan (JPN), the Russian Federation (RUS), Saudi Arabia (SAU), and the United States (US). Data are from 2022. Panel c: CO_2 emissions are cumulative, in gigatons (gt), and do not include emissions from LULUCF. Panels a and c: Country income groups are fixed at 2022 definitions. In panel a, the drop in emissions from low-income countries in 2015 comes from the Democratic Republic of Congo, where LULUCF emissions declined substantially after 2014.

The stock of GHG emissions in the atmosphere is what matters for warming (Eyring et al. 2021; IPCC 2023a). Considering cumulative historical emissions, the differences between income groups become even more apparent. Today's high-income countries have emitted large amounts of CO_2 since the mid-19th century, and upper-middle-income countries have been catching up quickly over the last 40 years (figure 3.12, panel c). As of 2022, high-income and upper-middle-income countries were responsible for 90 percent of all historical CO_2 emissions, of which roughly two-thirds came from high-income countries. On the other hand, low-income countries have contributed less than 1 percent of historical CO_2 emissions.

In prioritizing mitigating emissions, how emissions are evolving should also be considered. Figure 3.13 shows how emissions per capita are projected to evolve under current policies and under the Net Zero 2050 scenario between income groups (NGFS 2023). GHG emissions from high- and upper-middle-income countries emissions are projected to decline under current policies, but not nearly fast enough to limit warming to around 1.5°C. To reach this goal, additional CO_2 emissions will need to fall to practically zero in these countries. In addition, lower-middle-income countries do not contribute much to emissions today but without action, they will have a significant role in total emissions in a few decades.

FIGURE 3.13

Projected movement toward Net Zero 2050 by country income groups shows that high-income and upper-middle-income countries must lead the transition

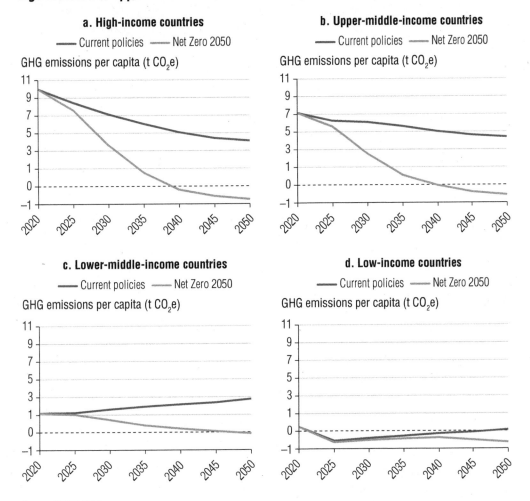

a. High-income countries

—— Current policies —— Net Zero 2050

GHG emissions per capita (t CO_2e)

b. Upper-middle-income countries

—— Current policies —— Net Zero 2050

GHG emissions per capita (t CO_2e)

c. Lower-middle-income countries

—— Current policies —— Net Zero 2050

GHG emissions per capita (t CO_2e)

d. Low-income countries

—— Current policies —— Net Zero 2050

GHG emissions per capita (t CO_2e)

Source: NGFS 2023.

Note: GHG = greenhouse gas; NGFS = Network for Greening the Financial System; t CO_2e = tons of carbon dioxide equivalent. Emissions per capita are shown in tons (t) of CO_2e. Emissions from NGFS (2023) are adjusted to match levels in 2020 in figure 3.6. Emissions come from the NGFS Net Zero 2050 scenario.

Figure 3.14 brings these considerations together and illustrates a simplified way to identify priorities. Importantly, each unique situation requires its own tailored solutions, and the results from this report do not aim to be prescriptive for a specific country. Country-specific studies are recommended to guide prioritization at that level (for example, World Bank Country Climate and Development reports). The following discussion aims to shed light on where attention should be placed from a broader global perspective.

FIGURE 3.14

Priorities to advance on the interlinked goals

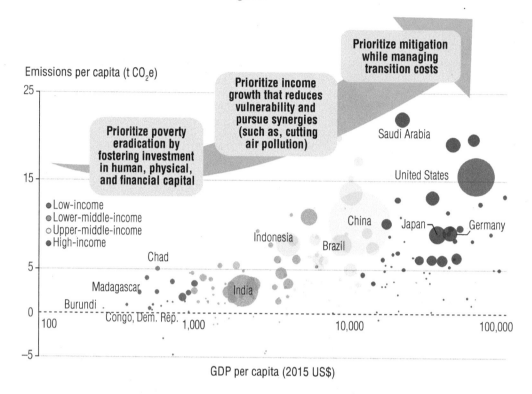

Source: Emissions Database for Global Atmospheric Research, Grassi et al. 2023, and World Development Indicators, https://databank.worldbank.org/source/world-development-indicators.

Note: GDP = gross domestic product; GHG = greenhouse gas; t CO_2e = tons of carbon dioxide equivalent. The sizes of the bubbles indicate total GHG emissions. Negative emissions occur when ecosystems absorb more carbon than the country emits. A few small countries with very high per capita emissions (Bahrain, Guyana, Iceland, Kuwait, Oman, Palau, Qatar, Trinidad and Tobago, and the United Arab Emirates) and countries with very low per capita emissions (the Central African Republic and Vanuatu) are omitted for visual purposes. The horizontal axis uses a logarithmic scale.

Low-income settings: Prioritize poverty reduction by fostering investments in human, physical, and financial capital

Economic growth has been neither large enough nor inclusive enough to reduce poverty significantly in low-income settings, as discussed in chapter 1. In these settings, greater economic growth is an essential foundation to support poverty reduction and build resilience. To successfully translate growth into gains in poverty reduction, efforts need to be focused on creating opportunities for those at the bottom of the income distribution and reducing high inequality. It is also important to reduce vulnerability to shocks by enhancing risk management (knowledge, protection, insurance, and coping; discussed in part 1 of this chapter). Fast growth that creates jobs and improves the productive capacity of poorer households (for instance, investing in human capital) is important to serve the dual function of increasing incomes and improving resilience. Yet investments in education in low-income countries remain very low.[22] Supporting stability, economic and spatial transformation, and the well-functioning of urban labor markets will be key.

For low-income countries, this process should not come with high GHG emissions. Low-income countries barely contribute to emissions, and emissions are not expected to grow significantly under current policies (figures 3.6, panel b, and 3.13, panel d). Still, low-income countries must be careful to avoid locking into carbon-intensive technologies and growth paths that will become more costly and less efficient in the future, and they must aim to pursue synergic polices (Hallegatte, Rentschler, and Rozenberg 2019). As discussed above, today low carbon is most often also the lowest cost option, and there are synergies between renewable energy and economic growth. The initial financing costs of infrastructure and electrical grids and limited regulatory environments remain the largest barriers for a green energy transition in low-income countries (World Bank 2023f). This is where international financing plays a key role in enabling such countries to invest in future-oriented technologies now and to not lock in on a pathway that will leave them with inefficient and stranded assets in the future (Hallegatte, Rentschler, and Rozenberg 2019).

Middle-income countries: Prioritize income growth that reduces vulnerability and synergies such as cutting air pollution

Growth in middle-income countries needs to continue and accelerate to lift people above the poverty lines of $3.65 and $6.85 per day, but many countries in this group are stuck in a middle-income trap (World Bank 2024g). As for low-income countries, fast growth that creates jobs and investments to increase the productive capacity of the poorer households are important. This needs to be complemented with measures to improve risk management.

At the same time, the GHG emissions of many middle-income countries cannot be neglected. Even though lower-middle-income countries contribute less than higher-income countries to GHG emissions now (19 percent of total emissions in 2022), with current policies their emissions will increase over the next decades (figure 3.13, panel c) and will surpass those of upper-middle-income countries in the 2040s and higher-income countries by 2030 in absolute terms. Therefore, it is essential that lower-middle-income countries start transitioning to a less carbon-intensive pathway soon (figure 3.15 shows primary energy and electricity generation pathways under the NGFS Net Zero 2050 scenario).

Since growth needs to be less carbon intensive, it is vital to identify some synergistic policies that can make a significant contribution to all goals and scale them up. For example, tackling air pollution is a clear area with multiple gains. In countries where agriculture is important, climate-smart agriculture and repurposing agricultural subsidies could be important areas of action. Investing early in renewable energy investments, which would significantly reduce emissions going forward, reduce transition costs in the future, and help meet the growing energy demand and energy security needs, is also key.

High-income and upper-middle-income countries: Accelerate mitigation while managing transition costs

The quickest way to reduce future climate risks is for high-income and upper-middle-income countries with high emissions to drastically cut their emissions while managing transition costs. Wealthier nations accelerating actions to reduce current emissions could significantly affect global emissions and alter the distribution of future environmental risks worldwide. Upper-middle-income countries also have significant populations at risk from extreme weather events, so it is in their own populations' interest to act on reducing GHG emissions.

High-income and upper-middle-income countries need to prioritize and accelerate the shift away from primary energy generated by fossil fuels, which would have to fall by around 60 percent by 2035 and by 90 percent by 2050 in comparison to 2020 levels (figure 3.15, panel a). The use of energy will also need to become more efficient.[23] Recent evidence indicates that countries with significant renewable potential, such as Brazil, can fully decarbonize their power systems without higher costs or compromising resilience.

In contrast to lower-income countries, high- and upper-middle-income countries are in a better position to leverage funds and technology to transition to net zero. Research and development are needed to spur technological innovation to accelerate progress in fully decoupling economic growth from GHG emissions. Several countries have already managed to decouple growth from emissions, and more need to follow. Fostering technology infusion and innovation in upper-middle-income countries will be decisive for those countries to raise incomes while lowering emissions and to transition to high-income status (see World Bank 2024g). These processes can catalyze a widespread adoption of renewable energy, the deployment of which requires a higher level of technological sophistication. Furthermore, middle-income countries need to reduce barriers to the expansion of renewables, for instance, by ensuring that power dispatch follows the lowest marginal cost, which is not the case in many countries (World Bank 2024g). However, it will be important to manage transition costs to protect their more vulnerable populations.

Swift and coordinated global action is essential to meet these critical goals

There are pressing needs for more and better alignment of funding and stronger international cooperation to meet the escalating challenges posed by climate change and development goals. International cooperation to achieve the Sustainable Development Goals (SDGs) and climate goals is ongoing but faces significant challenges and requires urgent action and increased investment. The United Nations *World Economic Situation and Prospects 2024* report highlights the need for robust global cooperation to tackle economic vulnerabilities, rising interest rates, and climate disasters. The report stresses that without significant investments in sustainable development and climate action, achieving the SDGs will remain elusive (United Nations 2024; United Nations and Inter-Agency Task Force on Financing for Development 2024).

The financing gap for sustainable development is growing, with many developing countries lacking access to affordable finance and facing high debt burdens, which hinder their ability to invest in both development and climate resilience (United Nations and Inter-Agency Task Force on Financing for Development 2024; World Bank 2024b). Estimates suggest that an additional annual investment of $4 trillion is needed to meet the SDGs by 2030 (United Nations and Inter-Agency Task Force on Financing for Development 2024). Despite reaching the $100 billion climate finance goal in 2022, significant gaps remain. More financing is needed for adaptation and building resilient infrastructure in the first place. Climate adaptation costs alone for developing countries are expected to be between $160 billion and $340 billion annually by 2030 (UNEP 2022).

FIGURE 3.15

Amounts of primary energy and generation of electricity from fossil sources need to decline massively to reach net zero by 2050

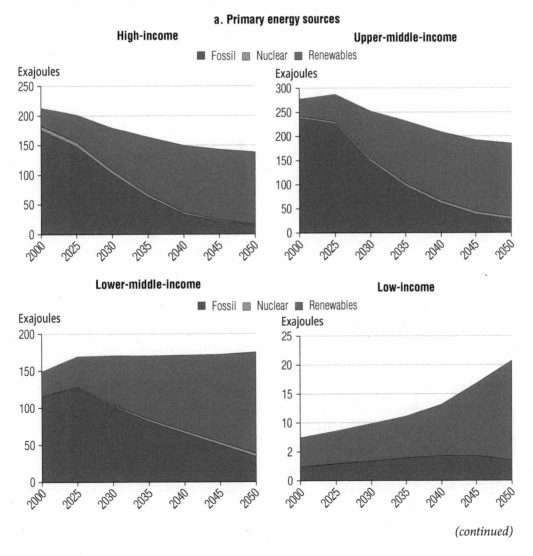

a. Primary energy sources

(continued)

FIGURE 3.15

Amounts of primary energy and generation of electricity from fossil sources need to decline massively to reach net zero by 2050 *(continued)*

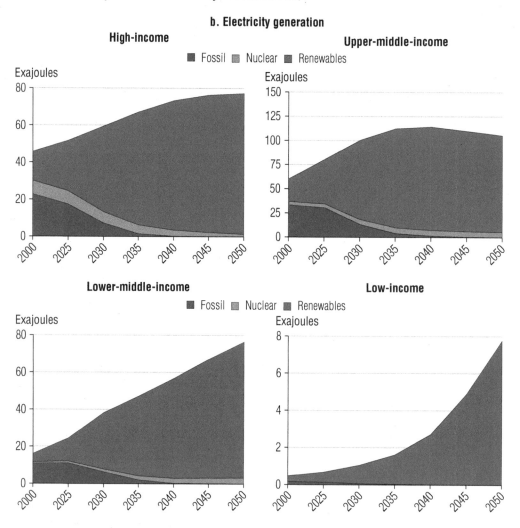

b. Electricity generation

Source: NGFS 2023.

Note: NGFS = Network for Greening the Financial System. Primary energy and the generating of electricity (in exajoules) are plotted and come from the NGFS Net Zero 2050 scenario.

In particular, lower-income countries will need substantial and immediate investment in both adaptation and mitigation actions (World Bank 2024b). For instance, there is a significant gap between the required and actual funding for climate adaptation and mitigation in Sub-Saharan Africa. Current international adaptation finance flows are estimated to be 5 to 10 times below the needed levels. Current adaptation costs in Africa are estimated to be in the range of $7 billion to $15 billion per year, with projections suggesting that this could rise to $35 billion annually by the 2040s and up to $200 billion per year by the 2070s if warming exceeds 2°C. If no adaptation measures are implemented, costs could escalate to 7 percent of Africa's GDP by 2100 (UNEP 2022).

The implementation of development and climate policy solutions requires a robust financial framework capable of navigating the fragmented global aid landscape— effectively incorporating domestic resource mobilization with external funding sources, including concessional funding. In particular, it is crucial to promote a greater balance and complementarity between leveraged and unleveraged approaches to aid delivery (see box 3.5 for a discussion of the current challenges in the aid ecosystem). Scaling up both public and private financing for SDGs and climate investments also entails closing policy gaps, enhancing international cooperation, and reforming financial institutions to provide more substantial and sustainable support.

BOX 3.5

The increased fragmentation of aid

The global aid system has evolved significantly in the last two decades, leading to challenges for recipient countries. The difficulties include increased complexity due to more than 200 donor agencies, fragmentation of financial flows, limited direct funding through national budgets (only 40 percent), and ineffective leveraging of resources. These trends, driven by donor preferences and geopolitical factors, complicate the alignment of national development goals with global challenges, with no clear framework for resource allocation. The impact is most severe in the poorest countries, which struggle with institutional capacity and face inefficiencies in managing multiple donor relationships (World Bank 2024f).

The increased fragmentation of aid is evident in the growing number of donor-funded transactions and the financial scale of aid commitments. From 2000 to 2021, official financial flows (OFFs) grew by 218 percent in real terms, with transactions surging 427 percent. During this period, the average size of official development assistance grants decreased by half, from $1.7 million to $0.8 million, which disproportionately burdens countries with weaker capacities because of higher transaction costs (World Bank 2024f).

Despite a more than threefold increase in OFFs to developing countries, there has been a notable shift away from channeling funds through recipient government budgets. By 2021, 80 percent of projects were implemented by nongovernmental entities, primarily through project-type interventions, with about one-fourth of transactions in the last decade channeled through nongovernmental organizations (NGOs). Over two-thirds of these transactions were executed by donor-based NGOs. More than half of the funds bypass country budgets, using channels such as donor governments, multilateral organizations, and NGOs, challenging the effectiveness of aid. Conversely, the International Development Association (IDA) directly allocated 92 percent of its funds to government agencies (World Bank 2024f).

(continued)

BOX 3.5
The increased fragmentation of aid *(continued)*

There has been significant growth in aid earmarked for specific sectors or themes, especially through vertical platforms. These funding approaches have both benefits and drawbacks. Vertical approaches, effective in addressing specific issues such as human immunodeficiency virus (HIV)/acquired immune deficiency syndrome (AIDS) or climate change, achieve economies of scale but typically pass donor funds directly to recipients, limiting resource mobilization. In contrast, horizontal platforms such as IDA amplify every donor dollar into four times the financing, enabling greater resource mobilization and potentially larger long-term impacts (World Bank 2024f).

To address these challenges, a balance between leveraged and unleveraged approaches to aid delivery is essential. This involves combining the advantages of both approaches through cofinancing and partnerships between vertical funds and multilateral development banks (MDBs). Collaboration and partnerships are crucial in an increasingly fragmented global aid landscape to mobilize scarce concessional funds. One potential solution is to optimize earmarked funds through the country-based model of MDBs, such as IDA, which can leverage each donor dollar by a multiple of three or four, expanding the resources available to developing countries (World Bank 2024f).

Annex 3A. Progress on food and nutrition security

There have been remarkable gains in food and nutrition security (FNS) over the past decades. Figure 3A.1, panel a, illustrates that the global prevalence of undernourishment was reduced by more than one-third, dropping from 13 percent in 2000 to below 8 percent in 2018 (FAO et al. 2023). Between 2000 and 2022, global stunting rates have improved by similar amounts (figure 3A.1, panel b), in part driven by improvements in the quantity and quality of calories consumed, as monetary poverty has rapidly declined over the same period (see chapter 1 of this report). These gains in FNS have made important contributions to improving immediate and lifelong outcomes for both children and adults (UNICEF 2022b).

However, global events over the past decade threaten the sustainability of those gains and illustrate the urgency with which FNS needs to be supported globally. Increasing numbers of prolonged conflicts across the world have increased the number of people living in food emergencies (FSIN and Global Network Against Food Crises 2024); countries across the world have not fully recovered from the significant job losses associated with the COVID-19 pandemic (World Bank 2022a); high global food price inflation has adversely affected net consumers of food, particularly those in urban areas (FAO et al. 2023); conflicts—including Russia's invasion of Ukraine—have affected significant producers of food on which much of the world relies (FAO et al. 2023); and incomes of poor agricultural producers worldwide are already in decline because of a changing climate and are stretched in the short term by the need to invest in more sustainable production techniques (Barrett, Ortiz-Bobea, and Pham 2023).

Figure 3A.1, panel a, illustrates that the prevalence of undernourishment is already on the rise globally and has been close to 10 percent since 2021. There is a stark regional imbalance in undernourishment. Of the countries with available data, the prevalence is particularly high in Sub-Saharan Africa (22 percent) and South Asia (16 percent). Fragility and conflict aggravate limited access to food and nutrition, with 21 percent of the population in fragile and conflict-affected situations being undernourished. Similarly, the global prevalence of the population that is either moderately or severely food insecure has risen from 22 percent in 2015 to 29 percent in 2023 (figure 3A.1, panel c). Chapter 4 discusses the measurement of food and nutrition insecurity in more detail.

Governments across the world and international organizations recognize this challenge and are working together to increase momentum to support FNS and to achieve SDG 2 (no hunger). For example, between April 2022 and June 2023, the World Bank Group Global Crisis Response Framework made available $45 billion to respond to the global FNS crisis, striking a balance between emergency needs and long-term investments in resilience across multiple sectors for lower- and middle-income client countries (World Bank 2022a). Building on this experience, FNS is also one of the six newly announced World Bank Global Challenge Programs, which will leverage existing and new financing and partnerships, amplify knowledge and learning, and streamline processes (World Bank 2023h). Continued action across the world is needed to achieve SDG 2, where achieving the goal was unlikely even before recent setbacks (FAO et al. 2023).

FIGURE 3A.1

The evolution of World Bank Vision and Scorecard indicators for food and nutrition security

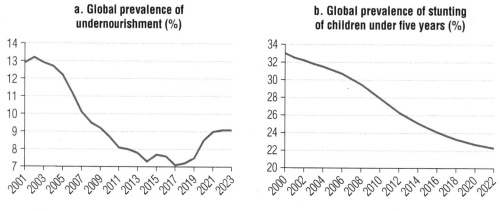

a. Global prevalence of undernourishment (%)

b. Global prevalence of stunting of children under five years (%)

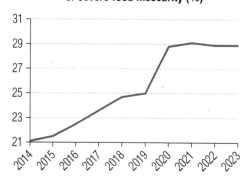

c. Global prevalence of moderate or severe food insecurity (%)

Sources: Panels a and c are reported by the Food and Agriculture Organization (FAO); panel b is reported by the United Nations Children's Fund, the World Health Organization, and the World Bank, all accessed through the FAOSTAT database.

Annex 3B. Measuring climate risks: The percentage of people at high risk from climate-related hazards globally

Measuring risk from climate hazards is a complex and data-intensive endeavor. Background work by Doan et al. (2023) developed a methodology to estimate the *percentage of people at high risk from climate-related hazards globally*. This indicator builds on the IPCC (2023b) framework in which risk is the combination of hazard, exposure, and vulnerability. People are considered at high risk from climate-related hazards if they are exposed to at least one of four hazards (floods, droughts, heat waves, and cyclones) and are identified as highly vulnerable on at least one of seven dimensions of vulnerability (that is, if they have a propensity to be adversely affected or unable to cope with the impacts). See figure B3.1.1 in this chapter for an overview of the indicator. Chapter 4 discusses in more detail measurement challenges with respect to the indicator and some areas in which the indicator will be updated in future rounds.

Measuring hazards and exposure

A hazard is the potential occurrence of an extreme event. Evidence shows that weather hazards are key for determining climate risk (Hallegatte, Fay, and Barbier 2018; Hallegatte, Vogt-Schilb et al. 2016). While this measure does not cover all climate-related events, the four hazards considered have been documented to significantly affect livelihoods and hinder economic growth and people's welfare in the past (Azzarri and Signorelli 2020; Dang, Cong Nguyen, and Trinh 2023; Hill and Porter 2017; Hsiang 2010). Climate change will exacerbate the frequency and severity of hazardous events, increasing climate risks to people going forward. Focusing on these hazards enables the combination of data from 168 economies to produce a global indicator.

Defining the population exposed to climate-related hazards requires specifying an intensity threshold and return period for each type of event. The first threshold specifies an intensity (in physical units) that must be exceeded for a particular location to be considered exposed. The return period specifies a minimum frequency of above-threshold events for a location to be considered exposed. The intensity threshold helps focus the indicator on the population exposed to events that have the potential to cause significant impacts. The return period focuses the indicator on exposure to events that are relatively likely to occur.

Table 3B.1 lists the intensity thresholds used to define the exposed population. The return period used is 100 years (except for droughts; see chapter 4), which means that people have a greater than 50 percent chance of experiencing the respective shock in their lifetime (using average global life expectancy).

TABLE 3B.1

Hazard thresholds

Hazard	Intensity threshold
Agricultural drought	> 30% cropland or grassland affected by severe drought
Flood	> 50-cm maximum inundation depth
Heat wave	> 33°C maximum 5-day average of daily maximum WBGT
Tropical cyclone	> 37.6-m/s 10-minute average sustained wind speed or equivalent ≥ Category 2 on the Saffir-Simpson scale

Source: World Bank Group Scorecard indicator: the percentage of people at high risk of climate-related hazards globally, https://scorecard.worldbank.org/en/scorecard/home.
Note: C = Celsius; cm = centimeter; m/s = meters per second; WBGT = wet bulb globe temperature.

The selected intensity levels are based on the literature and are levels above which an event is considered to have severe effects on people. In the case of drought, the cutoff used follows the severe drought definition by the FAO. In the case of flood, inundation depths of at least 50 centimeters indicate a high risk that bring disruptions to livelihoods and economic activity, as well as risk to life for select locations and vulnerable groups (Rentschler, Salhab, and Jafino 2022). For a fluvial and marine flood depth of 0.5 meters, Huizinga, de Moel, and Szewczyk (2017) estimate that the average share of residential assets lost ranges from 0.22 to 0.49. Cyclone damage functions also indicate direct economic damage in the range of 0.2 to 0.5 for category 2 wind speeds for most regions, which defines the cutoff used for cyclones (Eberenz, Lüthi, and Bresch 2021). A wet bulb globe temperature threshold of 33°C corresponds to the reference upper limit for healthy, acclimatized humans at rest to keep a normal core temperature, based on international standard ISO 7243 used to assess heat stress on workers (ISO 2017). Heat-related mortality and hospital visits increase significantly around this level.

Measuring vulnerability

Vulnerability is the propensity or predisposition of people to be adversely affected by hazards. Here, vulnerability is proxied by seven indicators measuring (a) the physical propensity to experience severe losses (proxied by the lack of mobility and access to basic infrastructure services, such as water and electricity) and (b) the inability to cope with and recover from losses (proxied by low income, not having education, not having access to financial services, and not having access to social protection). Table 3B.2 summarizes the different dimensions.

TABLE 3B.2

Extreme vulnerability definitions and sources

Vulnerability dimension		Extreme vulnerability cutoff	Source
Inability to cope with losses	Income	People who live below $2.15/day	World Bank GSAP (2024)
	Education	No adults in the households have completed primary education	World Bank GMD
	Social protection	Household neither receives social transfers nor contributes to social insurance	World Bank ASPIRE
	Financial inclusion	Household does not have an account (bank, other financial institution, mobile money)	World Bank Global Findex
Physical propensity to experience severe loss	Water	Do not have access to improved water	World Bank GMD with JMP
	Energy	Do not have access to electricity	World Bank GMD with GED
	Transport	Do not live within 2 km of an all-season road (if in a rural area)	RAI—UN Sustainable Development Center indicator

Source: World Bank Group Scorecard indicator: the percentage of people at high risk of climate-related hazards globally, https://scorecard.worldbank.org/en/scorecard/home.
Note: ASPIRE = Atlas of Social Protection Indicators of Resilience and Equity; GED = Global Electrification Database; GMD = Global Monitoring Database; GSAP = Global Subnational Atlas of Poverty; km = kilometers; JMP = Joint Monitoring Programme; RAI = Rural Access Index.

Proxying ability to cope

The first dimension of inability to cope is not having income to manage the impact of shocks. The aim of this measure is to identify individuals who have incomes that are too low to be able to meet basic needs if a shock to incomes occurs. The second dimension is educational attainment. This measure captures both a household's ability to understand and respond to risk information such as weather forecasts and early warnings and their ability to switch livelihoods when facing climate-related shocks. The third dimension is access to public support, or social protection. There is considerable evidence that cash transfers help households manage shocks. For this dimension, households are identified as highly vulnerable if they neither receive social transfers nor contribute to social insurance. The final dimension of the ability to cope is access to financial services. There is a strong body of evidence showing that households borrow after a disaster to meet basic consumption needs, and transfers of money between family and friends in the aftermath of a disaster are also central to household risk management. Access to a bank account is used to indicate whether households have access to financial services to smooth consumption in the face of a shock.

Physical propensity to experience severe losses

 The first dimension of physical propensity to experience severe losses is a lack of access to an improved water source. When shocks hit, access to improved drinking water can protect households from contaminated water due to flooding and storms, as well as lessen the impact of droughts. The second dimension is access to electricity. During shocks such as heat waves, households with electricity are much more likely to have assets such as fans that can alleviate the impact. The third dimension is access to services and markets. Access to transport networks plays a pivotal role in enhancing resilience, increasing access to health and other services, and ensuring that households can access alternate employment opportunities and markets for goods.

Combining hazards, exposure, and vulnerability

First, gridded population data (GHS-POP) are overlaid with urbanization data (GHSL) and the hazard data as defined in table 3B.1. Hazard data are resampled to match the population grids, so that each cell is classified exclusively as rural or urban and exposed or not exposed. Agricultural drought is defined to occur only in rural areas. Similarly, the transport indicator is considered to be relevant only for rural areas. Second, most of the vulnerability indicators are representative at subnational units, such as regions. The grids with exposed populations are aggregated to these subnational boundaries. The final indicator of the population at high risk from extreme hazards is calculated by multiplying the share of vulnerable people with the population exposed in the subnational unit, which is aggregated to the national level (see chapter 4 for more details on the imputation process).

Annex 3C. Enabling access to safe water and sanitation is crucial for well-being and helps reduce vulnerability

Unsafe water and sanitation are leading risk factors for child mortality (Global Burden of Disease Collaborative Network 2022) and early-childhood stunting worldwide (Danaei et al. 2016), affecting human capital and economic growth. Climate change is shifting rainfall patterns and increasing the frequency and intensity of floods and droughts. Without radical change, problems of too much, too little, or too polluted water will only increase.

There are still important gaps in access to safe drinking water, with rural areas and Sub-Saharan Africa lagging behind. While 9 in 10 people across the world have access to basic drinking water, only 7 in 10 people have access to safely managed drinking water. In particular, Sub-Saharan Africa lags behind other regions, with only two-thirds of people having access to at least basic drinking water (figure 3C.1, panel a) and only one-fifth of people having access to safely managed drinking water services.[24] For almost 30 percent of the region's population, it takes more than 30 minutes to fetch water (limited water access), or water comes from unprotected wells or springs (unimproved water access). For 6 percent of the region's population, surface water is the only source of drinking water (WHO/UNICEF Joint Monitoring Programme 2024). Gaps in access to basic drinking water are significantly larger in rural areas (figure 3C.1, panel b).

Regional differences in access to basic sanitation are even starker than for drinking water. In Sub-Saharan Africa, only one-third of the population has an improved sanitation facility not shared with other households, while 18 percent uses shared facilities, 31 percent relies on unimproved sanitation facilities, and 17 percent does not have access to any sanitation facility. In the other regions, at least three-quarters of the population is able to access improved sanitation facilities not shared with other households. In South Asia, 9 percent has no facilities and 12 percent shares facilities.

About 450 million people globally live in areas where poverty is high and water access is low, and about 1 billion people live in areas where poverty is high and sanitation access is low (Zhang and Borja-Vega 2024). Water for everyone can help reduce poverty and improve well-being while making populations more able to cope with negative climate effects. Drinking water is vital for human survival, and that water must be clean for a healthy and productive life. Clean water and safe sanitation have an impact on all phases of human development, especially for children's health and education, which shape their future economic prospects (Andres et al. 2018; Gould, Lavy, and Paserman 2011). Safe water and sanitation are also important for fostering gender equality and social inclusion, as it is often women and girls who bear the responsibility of collecting water, and lack of clean water and safe sanitation facilities reduces girls' school attendance (Adukia 2017; Koolwal and van de Walle 2013).

FIGURE 3C.1

Regional and urban-rural differences in access to water

a. Regional differences

■ Access to basic drinking water (%)　　■ Access to basic sanitation services (%)

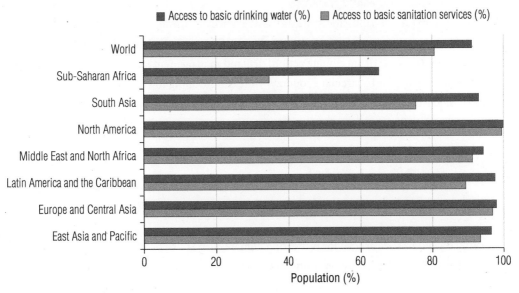

b. Urban-rural differences

— Rest of the world　　— Sub-Saharan Africa　　● Rural　　○ Urban

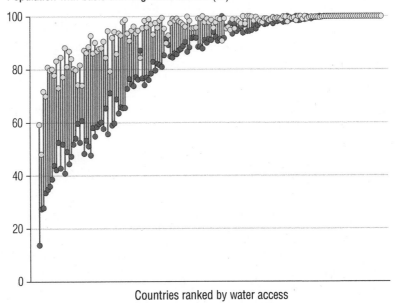

Source: WHO/UNICEF Joint Monitoring Programme 2024 data, accessed through the World Development Indicators, https://databank.worldbank.org/source/world-development-indicators.

Note: Panel a shows the population with access to basic drinking water and basic sanitation services. Panel b shows the share of urban and rural populations with access to basic drinking water by country. Solid red lines indicate that the country is located in Sub-Saharan Africa. Blue lines indicate that the country is outside Sub-Saharan Africa.

Actions on water and sanitation also need to consider impacts on GHG emissions. Wastewater accounts for 5 percent to 8 percent of human-caused methane emissions, and modern sanitation infrastructure and wastewater treatment can help reduce overall GHG emissions (Ocko et al. 2021; Song et al. 2023). A recent study in Kampala, Uganda, showed that high emissions from on-site sanitation systems (used extensively throughout cities in lower-middle-income countries) constituted more than half the city's total emissions (Johnson et al. 2022). Moreover, prioritizing climate action, demand management strategies, reductions in nonrevenue water,[25] and a circular economy while transitioning toward energy-efficient water utilities alongside sustainable and effective water management can substantially contribute to climate change mitigation and adaptation.

Annex 3D. Healthy ecosystems—zooming in on the importance of forests

Healthy ecosystems are crucial for mitigating climate change by absorbing CO_2 and acting as carbon sinks. Terrestrial ecosystems not only reduce annual anthropogenic CO_2 emissions by around one-third (IPCC 2023b), but also provide numerous economic opportunities and reduce vulnerability. Forests support food and nutrition security and materials that are essential to sustain livelihoods (Razafindratsima et al. 2021). Grasslands aid water consumption and agricultural activity by helping filter and purify water and by contributing to soil health by preventing erosion, enhancing soil fertility, and supporting nutrient cycling; furthermore, forested watersheds and wetlands supply 75 percent of the world's accessible freshwater (FAO 2019). Mangroves act as natural barriers against coastal storms and flooding, reducing the impact of natural disasters on vulnerable communities (Menéndez et al. 2020). At the same time, poor populations are also more concentrated in ecologically fragile areas, underscoring the importance of ending environmental deterioration and preserving a healthy ecosystem (Angelsen et al. 2014; Barbier 2010).

Land use change, especially when forest related, can cause significant GHG emissions. Forests are important in absorbing CO_2 emissions from the atmosphere. On the flip side, deforestation is a key cause of GHG emissions and can contribute to climatic risks locally. In the Amazon, for example, deforestation reduces the amount of moisture released into the air by trees and plants, which increases temperatures, and it decreases overall rainfall (World Bank 2023a). Deforestation and forest degradation currently account for 12 percent of global GHG emissions (IPCC 2019).

The world lost 2.6 percent of its forest cover between 2000 and 2021, but there are considerable differences between countries, with 100 of them having *increased* and 91 having *decreased* their net forest cover.[26] Sub-Saharan Africa and Latin America and the Caribbean had larger forest area loss rates during this period. Côte d'Ivoire, for example, suffered the largest decline of forest cover (46 percent), and Brazil, while losing a relatively smaller share (10 percent), experienced the largest decline in total area, given its large forest cover. On the other hand, some countries have managed to partially reverse past deforestation. China has made significant progress, increasing its forest land area by 25 percent, and Europe and Central Asia as a region also increased tree cover. Deforestation is particularly problematic in Sub-Saharan Africa, in Latin America and the Caribbean, and in East Asia and Pacific, where deforestation significantly hinders the positive effect that forests have on emissions (figure 3D.1).

FIGURE 3D.1

Greenhouse gas emissions and capture from LULUCF, 2022

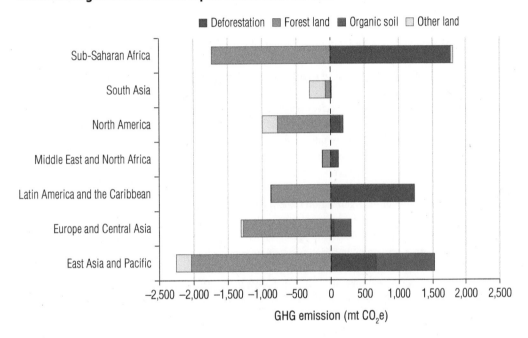

Source: Emissions Database for Global Atmospheric Research and Grassi et al. 2023.
Note: Values shown are from 2022. CO_2e = carbon dioxide equivalent; GHG = greenhouse gas; LULUCF = land use, land use change, and forestry; mt = megaton.

Tree cover loss results largely from commodity-driven agriculture, shifting agriculture, forestry, and wildfires. Commodity-driven agriculture refers to the permanent removal of forests to produce agricultural commodities or to extract minerals, and it is responsible for 21 percent of tree cover loss. In comparison, urbanization contributes to only 1 percent of tree cover loss. Temporary clearing of trees accounts for three-quarters of total tree cover loss. Wildfires, which are categorized as temporary clearing, alone are responsible for 28 percent of tree cover loss. Despite trees regrowing, this releases significant GHG emissions. Wildfires also significantly contribute to pollution, mortality, and negative health effects (Qiu et al. 2024). Protecting ecosystems will require limiting of land degradation and more efficient agricultural production to secure sustainable food production (Benke and Tomkins 2017; Smith et al. 2014).

Healthy ecosystems are foundational for healthy economies, yet economic growth in the past has come at the cost of declining natural capital. Low-income countries have many opportunities to improve both economic output and environmental outcomes (Damania, Polasky et al. 2023). This balance is important, as the poor rely much more on natural capital for income generation and food security, making them more vulnerable to extreme weather events, rising temperatures, and environmental degradation (Angelsen et al. 2014; Azzarri and Signorelli 2020; Castaneda et al. 2016; Damania et al. 2017; Dang, Hallegatte, and Trinh 2024; Fedele et al. 2021; Ortiz-Bobea et al. 2021).

Notes

1. The other livable planet dimensions are presented as part of the narrative linked to special annexes and will be explored in more detail in upcoming World Bank flagship reports.
2. Differences also exist in the quality of assets, such as housing material, making poorer households more vulnerable to asset loss even at exposure levels similar to those of richer households (Hallegatte, Vogt-Schilb et al. 2016).
3. In addition, slow-onset changes such as sea level rise, desertification, and water scarcity are making some regions less habitable and will also intensify migration. For instance, shrinking freshwater supplies and advancing deserts are pushing communities in regions like the Sahel and the dry corridor of Central America to migrate in search of better living conditions (Clement et al. 2021; Rigaud et al. 2018). However, climate hazards take a toll on household income, which makes it difficult for poor populations to find the means to migrate (Martínez Flores et al. 2024; Zaveri et al. 2021).
4. See World Meteorological Organization (2022); NOAA (2022).
5. The main GHGs that are emitted from human activities and have spurred global warming are CO_2, methane, nitrous oxide, and fluorinated gases. GHGs contribute to warming in different ways. CO_2 has a long lifetime, remaining in the atmosphere on average for hundreds of years. Emissions of CO_2 have historically been the main driver of current temperature rise; hence, reducing CO_2 emissions is essential for the long-term mitigation of global warming (Eyring et al. 2021). Methane is the second largest driver of global warming. Methane does not remain in the atmosphere as long as CO_2 (around 12 years), but it is more potent in absorbing energy and causing warming per unit of mass. The global warming potential enables comparison of the emissions of the different gases and their expression in CO_2 equivalent (CO_2e) terms. CO_2 emissions contribute almost three-quarters of the total annual GHG emissions, and methane contributes about one-sixth.
6. Hallegatte, Rentschler, and Rozenberg (2019) estimated that improving infrastructure resilience of assets exposed to hazards would cost less than 0.1 percent of the GDP of low- and middle-income countries.
7. Please see the following website for more information on losses due to natural disasters: https://www .statista.com/statistics/612561/natural-disaster-losses-cost-worldwide-by-type-of-loss/#:~:text=In%20 2023%2C%20there%20was%20a,to%20118%20billion%20U.S.%20dollars.
8. Warming beyond 1.5°C will increase the magnitude and the share of people substantially exposed to climate hazards (IPCC 2023c).
9. NDCs are climate action plans to cut emissions and adapt to climate change. All parties to the Paris Agreement are required to establish one and update it every five years (https://www.un.org/en /climatechange/all-about-ndcs#:~:text=Simply%20put%2C%20an%20NDC%2C%20or,update%20 it%20every%20five%20years).
10. Note that some, but not all, Network for Greening the Financial System (NGFS) countries are projected to have no GHG emissions in 2050 in the Net Zero 2050 scenario. Moreover, the Net Zero 2050 scenario refers to net-zero CO_2 emissions only, while total GHG emissions are not net zero across all countries. There is also heterogeneity between the models used by NGFS as to when net-zero emissions need to be reached in order to limit warming to 1.5°C.

11. The emission figures presented in this chapter are production based. Looking only at produced emissions neglects the fact that while some countries may not produce a lot of emissions, they may well consume products that are very emission intensive. East Asia and Pacific, the Middle East and North Africa, and Sub-Saharan Africa produce more emissions than they consume, while North America and Europe and Central Asia have bigger carbon footprints in consumption than in production. Despite richer countries importing slightly more emission-intensive goods, there is little empirical evidence for widespread global outsourcing of carbon production and carbon leakage resulting from climate regulations to date (Franzen and Mader 2018; Friedlingstein et al. 2020; Levinson 2023). Over time, the composition of imports from higher-income countries has shifted toward industries that are less air polluting, while the CO_2 intensity of these industries has remained at roughly same levels (Levinson 2023).

12. The nonenergy sectors, particularly agriculture, emit mostly methane and contribute about 13 percent of total GHG emissions. Land use, land use change, and forestry (LULUCF) reduced global GHG emissions by 5 percent in 2022. While deforestation causes massive GHG emissions, existing forest area and reforestation lead to a net withdrawal of GHG (emissions from LULUCF are discussed in further detail in annex 3D). While the energy sector is key, the focus of actions should depend on the region and country. In Sub-Saharan Africa and Latin America and the Caribbean, for example, agriculture and land use change contribute more to emissions than in other regions, making up almost 40 percent of total emissions. Agriculture produces a large part of methane and nitrous oxide emissions, coming mostly from cattle and other livestock (Poore and Nemecek 2018), and these gases make up 36 percent of emissions in Latin America and the Caribbean and half of emissions in Sub-Saharan Africa. The transportation sector is responsible for one-third of emissions in North America but less than 20 percent in all other regions, while manufacturing and construction are strong factors in East Asia and Pacific, with a share of 18 percent of emissions. Fugitive emissions—GHGs that are unintentionally released into the atmosphere because of leaks or evaporation during the exploration, processing, storage, or transportation of oil, gas, and coal—are comparably high in the Middle East and North Africa. These leaks are often methane emissions, leading to an overall contribution of 26 percent of CO_2 equivalent emissions in the region.

13. See, for example, World Bank Climate Change and Development reports for Benin, Brazil, Cameroon, or Tunisia.

14. For more information, see the World Health Organization website at https://www.who.int/news -room/fact-sheets/detail/household-air-pollution-and-health.

15. As of May 17, 2024, data obtained from https://data.who.int/dashboards/covid19/deaths?n=o.

16. Data from Institute for Health Metrics and Evaluation (https://vizhub.healthdata.org/gbd-results/).

17. Air pollution here refers to finer PM (less than 2.5 micrometers in aerodynamic diameter), hence PM2.5, which is particularly damaging to health as it can remain airborne for longer, can lodge deep in the respiratory tract, and is hard to avoid since it can easily travel from outdoors to indoors (Aguilar-Gomez et al. 2022). WHO established that PM2.5 annual exposure above 5 micrograms per cubic meter is harmful (Bruce et al. 2015).

18. WHO Interim Target 1 refers to a PM2.5 level of 35 micrograms per cubic meter.

19. The mitigation potential estimates indicate total amount mitigated over time (with a 20-year time horizon) through changes in land use and land management.

20. Ecosystems play many other important roles in reducing climate-related risks. For example, Beck et al. (2018) estimate that annual worldwide damage from coastal flooding would double without coral reefs.

21. Emissions are unequal not only between countries, but also between individuals. Estimates suggest that the richest 10 percent of the population is responsible for about half of world emissions. Furthermore, the richest 1 percent accounts for about 17 percent of global emissions (Chancel 2022). Conversely, the bottom half of the world's population contributes only 12 percent of global emissions. Within-country inequality in emissions is estimated to be larger than between-country inequality (Chancel, Bothe, and Voituriez 2023). By reducing their emissions, wealthier people could ease the burden on the rest of society to curb total emissions.

22. Though there is a consensus of spending at least 4 percent to 6 percent of GDP or 15 percent to 20 percent of public expenditure on education, only 1 in 10 countries and territories meets the 20 percent benchmark, and only 4 in 10 meet the 15 percent benchmark (UNICEF 2022a). In 2021, the average low-income country spent $56 per student, compared with around $1,000 in upper-middle-income and around $8,500 in high-income countries (Bend et al. 2023).

23. The availability of technology for carbon capture and storage is also assumed to increase under the Net Zero 2050 scenario of NGFS, though only at a limited scale. See, for example, the NGFS scenarios portal: https://www.ngfs.net/ngfs-scenarios-portal/explore/.

24. These indicators are published by the WHO/UNICEF Joint Monitoring Programme. Definitions of drinking water, sanitation, and hygiene indicators are based on the WHO/UNICEF Joint Monitoring Programme. Access to drinking water considers the following degrees of access: (a) safely managed access: improved water source is accessible on premise, available when needed, and free from contamination; (b) basic access: does not meet improved access criteria, but round trip to collect water from an improved water source takes 30 minutes or less; (c) limited access: improved water source that is more than 30 minutes away (round trip); (d) unimproved access: water source is not "safe," that as unprotected wells or springs; (e) surface water: the only water source is surface water from a river, dam, lake, stream, or irrigation canal. Access to basic sanitation refers to improved facilities that are not shared with other households.

25. Nonrevenue water refers to water that has been produced and is lost before reaching the consumers.

26. Based on the Forest Extent Indicator from the Global Forest Review. This indicator aims to monitor the total area of forest worldwide, including unmanaged and managed natural forests. The most recently available indicator currently measures tree cover extent in the year 2020 as a best-available proxy for forest. Note that tree cover extent includes planted forests, such as orchards, agricultural tree crops, and monoculture pulp or timber plantations—forms of tree cover that are not considered forests under some definitions. There are hundreds of definitions of "forest" based on factors including land use, patch size, species composition, legal designation, canopy density, height, and more. This indicator relies on the biophysical indicator of tree cover as measured by tree height and canopy density because it can be measured consistently with satellite imagery at a global scale. The tree height data used in this report are based on Potapov et al. (2022), which define tree cover as woody vegetation with a height of at least five meters and a canopy density of at least 20 to 25 percent at 30-meter resolution. This definition includes unmanaged and managed natural forests, tree plantations, and urban forests. A minimum patch size, such as excluding tree cover of less than 0.5 hectares, is also included in many forest definitions but is not applied in this indicator. For more information, see https://research.wri.org/gfr/data-methods.

References

Abiona, O., and M. F. Koppensteiner. 2018. "The Impact of Household Shocks on Domestic Violence: Evidence from Tanzania." IZA Discussion Paper 11992, IZA Institute of Labor Economics, Rochester, NY. https://doi.org/10.2139/ssrn.3301756.

Acevedo, Sebastian, Mico Mrkaic, Natalija Novta, Evgenia Pugacheva, and Petia Topalova. 2020. "The Effects of Weather Shocks on Economic Activity: What Are the Channels of Impact?" *Journal of Macroeconomics* 65: 103207. https://doi.org/10.1016/j.jmacro.2020.103207.

Adukia, Anjali. 2017. "Sanitation and Education." *American Economic Journal: Applied Economics* 9 (2): 23–59. https://doi.org/10.1257/app.20150083.

Agnolucci, Paolo, Carolyn Fischer, Dirk Heine, Mariza Montes de Oca Leon, Joseph Pryor, Kathleen Patroni, and Stéphane Hallegatte. 2023. "Measuring Total Carbon Pricing." *The World Bank Research Observer* 39 (2): 227–58. https://?/doi.org/10.1093/wbro/lkad009.

Aguilar-Gomez, Sandra, Holt Dwyer, Joshua S. Graff Zivin, and Matthew J. Neidell. 2022. "This Is Air: The 'Non-Health' Effects of Air Pollution." Working Paper 29848, National Bureau of Economic Research, Cambridge, MA. https://www.nber.org/system/files/working_papers/w29848/w29848.pdf.

Aker, Jenny C., and Kelsey Jack. 2021. "Harvesting the Rain: The Adoption of Environmental Technologies in the Sahel." Working Paper Series, National Bureau of Economic Research, Cambridge, MA. https://doi.org/10.3386/w29518.

Andres, Luis A., Claire Chase, Yue Chen, Richard Damania, George Joseph, Regassa Namara, Jason Russ, et al. 2018. "Water and Human Capital: Impacts Across the Lifecycle." Preprint. Washington, DC: World Bank.

Angelsen, Arild, Pamela Jagger, Ronnie Babigumira, Brian Belcher, Nicholas J. Hogarth, Simone Bauch, Jan Börner, et al. 2014. "Environmental Income and Rural Livelihoods: A Global-Comparative Analysis." *World Development* 64 (S1): S12–S28. https://doi.org/10.1016/j.worlddev.2014.03.006.

Azzarri, Carlo, and Sara Signorelli. 2020. "Climate and Poverty in Africa South of the Sahara." *World Development* 125: 104691. https://doi.org/10.1016/j.worlddev.2019.104691.

Baquié, Sandra, Arnold Patrick Behrer, Xinming Du, Alan Fuchs Tarlovsky, and Natsuko Kiso Nozaki. 2024. *Air Pollution in Tbilisi. Poverty and Distributional Consequences (English)*. Washington, DC: World Bank. http://documents.worldbank.org/curated/en/099032624150522292 /P1786931ff62000c71b32e1353319683c42.

Baquié, Sandra, and Habtamu Neda Fuje. 2020. "Vulnerability to Poverty following Extreme Weather Events in Malawi." Preprint. Policy Research Working Paper 9435, World Bank, Washington, DC.

Barbier, Edward B. 2010. "Poverty, Development, and Environment." *Environment and Development Economics* 15 (6): 635–60. https://doi.org/10.1017/S1355770X1000032X.

Barrett, Christopher B. 2021. "Overcoming Global Food Security Challenges through Science and Solidarity." *American Journal of Agricultural Economics* 103 (2): 422–47. https://doi.org/10.1111/ajae.12160.

Barrett, Christopher B., Ariel Ortiz-Bobea, and Trinh Pham. 2023. "Structural Transformation, Agriculture, Climate, and the Environment." *Review of Environmental Economics and Policy* 17 (2): 195–216. https://doi.org/10.1086/725319.

Batista, Cátia, and Pedro C. Vicente. 2023. "Is Mobile Money Changing Rural Africa? Evidence from a Field Experiment." *The Review of Economics and Statistics* 1–29. https://doi.org/10.1162/rest_a_01333.

Beck, Michael W., Iñigo J. Losada, Pelayo Menéndez, Borja G. Reguero, Pedro Díaz-Simal, and Felipe Fernández. 2018. "The Global Flood Protection Savings Provided by Coral Reefs." *Nature Communications* 9: 2186. https://doi.org/10.1038/s41467-018-04568-z.

Bend, May, Yitong Hu, Yilin Pan, Harry Anthony Patrinos, Thomas Poulsen, Angelica Rivera-Olvera, Noboyuki Tanaka, et al. 2023. *Education Finance Watch 2023 (English)*. Washington DC: World Bank. https://documents.worldbank.org/en/publication/documents-reports/documentdetail/0991031231637 55271/P17813506cd84f07a0b6be0c6ea576d59f8.

Benke, Kurt, and Bruce Tomkins. 2017. "Future Food-Production Systems: Vertical Farming and Controlled-Environment Agriculture." *Sustainability: Science, Practice and Policy* 13 (1): 13–26. https://doi.org/10.1080/15487733.2017.1394054.

Beyer, Robert, and Andrea Milan. 2023. *Climate Change and Human Mobility: Quantitative Evidence on Global Historical Trends and Future Projections*. Berlin: International Organization for Migration and Global Data Institute.

Blanchard, Olivier, Christian Gollier, and Jean Tirole. 2023. "The Portfolio of Economic Policies Needed to Fight Climate Change." *Annual Review of Economics* 15 (1): 689–722. https://doi.org/10.1146 /annurev-economics-051520-015113.

Bruce, Nigel, Dan Pope, Eva Rehfuess, Kalpana Balakrishnan, Heather Adair-Rohani, and Carlos Dora. 2015. "WHO Indoor Air Quality Guidelines on Household Fuel Combustion: Strategy Implications of New Evidence on Interventions and Exposure–Risk Functions." *Atmospheric Environment* 106: 451–57. https://doi.org/10.1016/j.atmosenv.2014.08.064.

Bruckner, Benedikt, Klaus Hubacek, Yuli Shan, Honglin Zhong, Kuishuang Feng. 2022. "Impacts of Poverty Alleviation on National and Global Carbon Emissions." *Nature Sustainability* 5 (4): 311–20. https://doi.org/10.1038/s41893-021-00842-z.

Burgess, Robin, and Dave Donaldson. 2010. "Can Openness Mitigate the Effects of Weather Shocks? Evidence from India's Famine Era." *American Economic Review* 100 (2): 449–53. https://doi.org /10.1257/aer.100.2.449.

Butt, E. W., S. T. Turnock, R. Rigby, C. L. Reddington, M. Yoshioka, J. S. Johnson, L. A. Regayre, et al. 2017. "Global and Regional Trends in Particulate Air Pollution and Attributable Health Burden over the Past 50 Years." *Environmental Research Letters* 12 (10): 104017.

Cai, Jing, Alain de Janvry, and Elisabeth Sadoulet. 2020. "Subsidy Policies and Insurance Demand." *American Economic Review* 110 (8): 2422–53. https://doi.org/10.1257/aer.20190661.

Cai, Jing, and Changcheng Song. 2017. "Do Disaster Experience and Knowledge Affect Insurance Take-Up Decisions?" *Journal of Development Economics* 124: 83–94. https://doi.org/10.1016/j.jdeveco.2016.08.007.

Carleton, Tamma, Amir Jina, Michael Delgado, Michael Greenstone, Trevor Houser, Solomon Hsiang, Andrew Hultgren, et al. 2022. "Valuing the Global Mortality Consequences of Climate Change Accounting for Adaptation Costs and Benefits." *The Quarterly Journal of Economics* 137 (4): 2037–105. https://doi.org/10.1093/qje/qjac020.

Casaburi, Lorenzo, and Jack Willis. 2018. "Time versus State in Insurance: Experimental Evidence from Contract Farming in Kenya." *American Economic Review* 108 (12): 3778–813. https://doi.org/10.1257/aer.20171526.

Castaneda Aguilar, Raul Andres, Dung Thi Thuy Doan, David Locke Newhouse, Minh Cong Nguyen, Hiroki Uematsu, and Joao Pedro Wagner De Azevedo. 2016. "Who Are the Poor in the Developing World (English)." Preprint. Policy Research Working Paper 7844, World Bank, Washington, DC. http://documents.worldbank.org/curated/en/187011475416542282/Who-are-the-poor-in-the-developing-world.

Cevik, Serhan, and João Tovar Jalles. 2023. "For Whom the Bell Tolls: Climate Change and Income Inequality." *Energy Policy* 174: 113475. https://doi.org/10.1016/j.enpol.2023.113475.

Chancel, Lucas. 2022. "Global Carbon Inequality over 1990–2019." *Nature Sustainability* 5 (11): 931–8. https://doi.org/10.1038/s41893-022-00955-z.

Chancel, Lucas, Philippe Bothe, and Tancrède Voituriez. 2023. "Climate Inequality Report 2023: Fair Taxes for a Sustainable Future in the Global South." *World Inequality Lab Study* 2023/1.

Clement, Viviane, Kanta Kumari Rigaud, Alex de Sherbinin, Bryan Jones, Susana Adamo, Jacob Schewe, Nian Sadiq, et al. 2021. *Groundswell, Part 2: Acting on Internal Climate Migration*. Washington, DC: World Bank.

Cole, Shawn, Xavier Giné, Jeremy Tobacman, Petia Topalova, Robert Townsend, and James Vickery. 2013. "Barriers to Household Risk Management: Evidence from India." *American Economic Journal: Applied Economics* 5 (1): 104–35. https://doi.org/10.1257/app.5.1.104.

Cook, John, Naomi Oreskes, Peter T. Doran, William R. L. Anderegg, Bart Verheggen, Ed W. Maibach, J. Stuart Carlton, et al. 2016. "Consensus on Consensus: A Synthesis of Consensus Estimates on Human-Caused Global Warming." *Environmental Research Letters* 11 (4): 048002. https://doi.org/10.1088/1748-9326/11/4/048002.

Damania, Richard, Esteban Balseca, Charlotte de Fontaubert, Joshua Gill, Kichan Kim, Jun Rentschler, Jason Russ, et al. 2023. *Detox Development: Repurposing Environmentally Harmful Subsidies*. Washington, DC: World Bank. http://hdl.handle.net/10986/39423.

Damania, Richard, Sébastien Desbureaux, Marie Hyland, Asif Islam, Aude-Sophie Rodella, Jason Russ, and Esha Zaveri. 2017. *Uncharted Waters: The New Economics of Water Scarcity and Variability*. Washington, DC: World Bank Group.

Damania, Richard, Stephen Polasky, Mary Ruckelshaus, Jason Russ, Markus Amann, Rebecca Chaplin-Kramer, James Gerber, et al. 2023. *Nature's Frontiers: Achieving Sustainability, Efficiency, and Prosperity with Natural Capital*. Washington, DC: World Bank.

Danaei, Goodarz, Kathryn G. Andrews, Christopher R. Sudfeld, Günther Fink, Dana Charles McCoy, Evan Peet, Ayesha Sania, et al. 2016. "Risk Factors for Childhood Stunting in 137 Developing Countries: A Comparative Risk Assessment Analysis at Global, Regional, and Country Levels." *PLOS Medicine* 13 (11): e1002164. https://doi.org/10.1371/journal.pmed.1002164.

Dang, Hai-Anh H., Stephane Hallegatte, and Trong-Anh Trinh. 2024. "Does Global Warming Worsen Poverty and Inequality? An Updated Review (English)." https://documents.worldbank.org/en/publication/documents-reports/documentdetail/099455202082432489/IDU1f816eef91ee7914e9f1ac0216dd1d09d0264.

Dang, Hai-Anh H., M. Cong Nguyen, and Trong-Anh Trinh. 2023. "Does Hotter Temperature Increase Poverty and Inequality? Global Evidence from Subnational Data Analysis." Policy Research Working Paper 104, World Bank, Washington, DC. https://doi.org/10.1596/1813-9450-10466.

Demirgüç-Kunt, Asli, Leora Klapper, Dorothe Singer, and Saniya Ansar. 2022. *The Global Findex Database 2021: Financial Inclusion, Digital Payments, and Resilience in the Age of COVID-19 (English).* Washington, DC: World Bank Group.

Dercon, Stefan. 2004. "Growth and Shocks: Evidence from Rural Ethiopia." *Journal of Development Economics* 74 (2): 309–29. https://doi.org/10.1016/j.jdeveco.2004.01.001.

Diffenbaugh, Noah S., and Marshall Burke. 2019. "Global Warming Has Increased Global Economic Inequality." *Proceedings of the National Academy of Sciences* 116 (20), 9808–13. https://doi.org/10.1073/pnas.1816020116.

Dimitrova, Anna. 2021. "Seasonal Droughts and the Risk of Childhood Undernutrition in Ethiopia." *World Development* 141: 105417. https://doi.org/10.1016/j.worlddev.2021.105417.

Doan, Miki Khanh, Ruth Hill, Stephane Hallegatte, Paul Corral, Ben Brunckhorst, Minh Nguyen, Samuel Freije-Rodriguez, et al. 2023. "Counting People Exposed to, Vulnerable to, or at High Risk from Climate Shocks: A Methodology." Policy Research Working Paper 10619, World Bank, Washington, DC. https://doi.org/10.1596/1813-9450-10619.

Dobermann, Tim. 2023. "How Building Up the Human Capital of the World's Poor Can Help Lessen the Climate Crisis." Preprint. *LSE Business Review* (blog).

Eastin, Joshua. 2018. "Climate Change and Gender Equality in Developing States." *World Development* 107: 289–305. https://doi.org/10.1016/j.worlddev.2018.02.021.

Eberenz, Samuel, Samuel Lüthi, and David N. Bresch. 2021. "Regional Tropical Cyclone Impact Functions for Globally Consistent Risk Assessments." *Natural Hazards and Earth System Sciences* 21 (1): 393–415. https://doi.org/10.5194/nhess-21-393-2021.

Ehrlich, Isaac, and Gary S. Becker. 1972. "Market Insurance, Self-Insurance, and Self-Protection." *Journal of Political Economy* 80 (4): 623–48. https://doi.org/10.1086/259916.

Erman, Alvina, Sophie Anne De Vries Robbé, Stephan Fabian Thies, Kayenat Kabir, and Mir Maruo. 2021. *Gender Dimensions of Disaster Risk and Resilience: Existing Evidence.* Technical Report. Washington, DC: World Bank. https://mars.gmu.edu/handle/1920/12777.

Eyring, Veronika, Nathan P. Gillett, Krishna Achutarao, Rondrotiana Barimalala, Marcelo Barreiro Parrillo, Nicolas Bellouin, Christophe Cassou, et al. 2021. "Human Influence on the Climate System." In *Climate Change 2021: The Physical Science Basis. Working Group I Contribution to the Sixth Assessment Report of the Intergovernmental Panel on Climate Change,* edited by V. Masson-Delmotte et al. IPCC Sixth Assessment Report. Cambridge, UK: Cambridge University Press. https://www.ipcc.ch/report/sixth-assessment-report-working-group-i/.

FAO (Food and Agriculture Organization of the United Nations). 2019. *Forests: Nature-Based Solutions for Water,* no. 251. vol. 70 2019/1. Unasylva 251. Rome, Italy: FAO. https://doi.org/10.4060/CA6842EN.

FAO (Food and Agriculture Organization of the United Nations). 2022. *In Brief to The State of the World's Forests 2022. Forest Pathways for Green Recovery and Building Inclusive, Resilient and Sustainable Economies.* Rome, Italy: FAO. https://doi.org/10.4060/cb9363en.

FAO (Food and Agriculture Organization of the UN), IFAD (International Fund for Agricultural Development), UNICEF, WFP (World Food Programme), and WHO (World Health Organization). 2023. *The State of Food Security and Nutrition in the World 2023: Urbanization, Agrifood Systems Transformation and Healthy Diets across the Rural-Urban Continuum.* Rome: FAO. https://doi.org/10.4060/cc3017en.

Fedele, Giacomo, Camila I. Donatti, Ivan Bornacelly, and David G. Hole. 2021. "Nature-Dependent People: Mapping Human Direct Use of Nature for Basic Needs across the Tropics." *Global Environmental Change* 71: 102368. https://doi.org/10.1016/j.gloenvcha.2021.102368.

Franzen, Axel, and Sebastian Mader. 2018. "Consumption-Based versus Production-Based Accounting of CO_2 Emissions: Is There Evidence for Carbon Leakage?" *Environmental Science & Policy* 84: 34–40. https://doi.org/10.1016/j.envsci.2018.02.009.

Friedlingstein, Pierre, Michael O'Sullivan, Matthew W. Jones, Robbie M. Andrew, Judith Hauck, Are Olsen, Glen P. Peters, et al. 2020. "Global Carbon Budget 2020." *Earth System Science Data* 12 (4): 3269–340. https://doi.org/10.5194/essd-12-3269-2020.

FSIN and Global Network Against Food Crises. 2024. *2024 Global Report on Food Crises.* Rome, Italy: GRCF. https://www.fsinplatform.org/grfc2024.

Fuller, Richard, Philip J. Landrigan, Kalpana Balakrishnan, Glynda Bathan, Stephan Bose-O'Reilly, Michael Brauer, et al. 2022. "Pollution and Health: A Progress Update." *The Lancet Planetary Health* 6 (6): e535–47. https://doi.org/10.1016/S2542-5196(22)00090-0.

Gill, Indermit S., Ana Revenga, and Christian Zeballos. 2016. "Grow, Invest, Insure: A Game Plan to End Extreme Poverty by 2030." Policy Research Working Paper 7892, World Bank, Washington, DC. https://papers.ssrn.com/abstract=2870160.

Gilli, Martino, Matteo Calcaterra, Johannes Emmerling, and Francesco Granella. July 25, 2023. "Climate Change Impacts on the Within-Country Income Distributions." https://doi.org/10.2139/ssrn.4520461.

Glewwe, Paul, and Edward A. Miguel. 2007. Chapter 56: "The Impact of Child Health and Nutrition on Education in Less Developed Countries." In *Handbook of Development Economics,* edited by T. Paul Schultz and John Strauss, 3561–606. Amsterdam, The Netherlands: Elsevier. https://doi.org/10.1016/S1573-4471(07)04056-9.

Global Burden of Disease Collaborative Network. 2022. "Global Burden of Disease Study 2021 (GBD 2021) Results." Seattle, WA: Institute for Health Metrics and Evaluation (IHME). https://vizhub.healthdata.org/gbd-results/.

Gould, Eric D., Victor Lavy, and M. Daniele Paserman. 2011. "Sixty Years after the Magic Carpet Ride: The Long-Run Effect of the Early Childhood Environment on Social and Economic Outcomes." *The Review of Economic Studies* 78 (3): 938–73. https://doi.org/10.1093/restud/rdq038.

Grassi, Giacomo, Clemens Schwingshackl, Thomas Gasser, Richard A. Houghton, Stephen Sitch, Josep G. Canadell, Alessandro Cescatti, et al. 2023. "Harmonising the Land-Use Flux Estimates of Global Models and National Inventories for 2000–2020." *Earth System Science Data* 15 (3): 1093–114. https://doi.org/10.5194/essd-15-1093-2023.

Grosset-Touba, Florian, Anna Papp, and Charles Taylor. January 27, 2023. "Rain Follows the Forest: Land Use Policy, Climate Change, and Adaptation." https://doi.org/10.2139/ssrn.4333147.

Gütschow, Johannes, Mika Pflüger, and Daniel Busch. 2024. "The PRIMAP-hist national historical emissions time series (1750-2022) v2.5.1." Zenodo, February 27, 2024. https://doi.org/doi:10.5281/zenodo.10705513.

Haddad, M., B. Hansl, and A. Pechevy. 2024. "Trading in a New Climate: How Mitigation Policies Are Reshaping Global Trade Dynamics" (blog), February 13, 2014. https://blogs.worldbank.org/en/developmenttalk/trading-new-climate-how-mitigation-policies-are-reshaping-global-trade-dynamics.

Hallegatte, Stephane, Mook Bangalore, Laura Bonzanigo, Tamaro Kane, Marianne Fay, Ulf Narloch, David Treguer, et al. 2016. *Shock Waves: Managing the Impacts of Climate Change on Poverty.* Washington, DC: World Bank.

Hallegatte, Stephane, Adriene Camille Vogt-Schilb, Mook Bangalore, and Julie Rozenberg. 2016. *Unbreakable: Building the Resilience of the Poor in the Face of Natural Disasters (English).* Washington, DC: World Bank Publications.

Hallegatte, Stéphane, Catrina Godinho, Jun Rentschler, Paolo Avner, Ira Irina Dorband, Camilla Knudsen, Jana Lemke, et al. 2023. *Within Reach: Navigating the Political Economy of Decarbonization.* Climate Change and Development Series. Washington, DC: World Bank Group. http://hdl.handle.net/10986/40601.

Hallegatte, Stephane, Marianne Fay, and Edward B. Barbier. 2018. "Poverty and Climate Change: Introduction." *Environment and Development Economics* 23 (3): 217–33. https://doi.org/10.1017/S1355770X18000141.

Hallegatte, Stephane, Jun Rentschler, and Julie Rozenberg. 2019. *Lifelines: The Resilient Infrastructure Opportunity.* Washington, DC: World Bank. http://hdl.handle.net/10986/31805.

Hallegatte, Stephane, and Julie Rozenberg. 2017. "Climate Change through a Poverty Lens." *Nature Climate Change* 7 (4): 250–56. https://doi.org/10.1038/nclimate3253.

Hallegatte, Stéphane, and Brian Walsh. 2021. "Natural Disasters, Poverty and Inequality: New Metrics for Fairer Policies." In *The Routledge Handbook of the Political Economy of the Environment*. Milton Park, UK: Routledge.

Hasegawa, Tomoko, Shinichiro Fujimori, Petr Havlík, Hugo Valin, Benjamin Leon Bodirsky, Jonathan C. Doelman, Thomas Fellmann, et al. 2018. "Risk of Increased Food Insecurity under Stringent Global Climate Change Mitigation Policy." *Nature Climate Change* 8 (8): 699–703. https://doi.org/10.1038/s41558-018-0230-x.

Heinen, Andréas, Jeetendra Khadan, and Eric Strobl. 2019. "The Price Impact of Extreme Weather in Developing Countries." *The Economic Journal* 129 (619): 1327–42. https://doi.org/10.1111/ecoj.12581.

Hill, Ruth, and Carolina Mejía-Mantilla. 2017. "With a Little Help: Shocks, Agricultural Income, and Welfare in Uganda." Poverty and Equity Global Practice Working Paper 095 [Preprint], World Bank, Washington, DC.

Hill, Ruth Vargas, Neha Kumar, Nicholas Magnan, Simrin Makhija, Francesca di Nicola, David J. Spielman, and Patrick S. Ward. 2019. "Ex Ante and Ex Post Effects of Hybrid Index Insurance in Bangladesh." *Journal of Development Economics* 136: 1–17. https://doi.org/10.1016/j.jdeveco.2018.09.003.

Hill, Ruth Vargas, and Ambar Narayan. 2020. "Covid-19 and Inequality: A Review of the Evidence on Likely Impact and Policy Options." Working Paper 3, Centre for Disaster Protection, London.

Hill, Ruth Vargas, and Catherine Porter. 2017. "Vulnerability to Drought and Food Price Shocks: Evidence from Ethiopia." *World Development* 96: 65–77. https://doi.org/10.1016/j.worlddev.2017.02.025.

Hoffmann, Roman, and Raya Muttarak. 2017. "Learn from the Past, Prepare for the Future: Impacts of Education and Experience on Disaster Preparedness in the Philippines and Thailand." *World Development* 96: 32–51. https://doi.org/10.1016/j.worlddev.2017.02.016.

Hsiang, Solomon M. 2010. "Temperatures and Cyclones Strongly Associated with Economic Production in the Caribbean and Central America." *Proceedings of the National Academy of Sciences* 107 (35): 15367–72. https://doi.org/10.1073/pnas.1009510107.

Huizinga, Jan, Hans de Moel, and Wojciech Szewczyk. 2017. "Global Flood Depth-Damage Functions: Methodology and the Database with Guidelines." Preprint. *JRC Research Reports JRC105688*, Joint Research Centre, Brussels, Belgium. https://ideas.repec.org//p/ipt/iptwpa/jrc105688.html.

IEA (International Energy Agency). 2022. *The Future of Heat Pumps*. Paris: International Energy Agency. https://www.iea.org/reports/the-future-of-heat-pumps.

IEA (International Energy Agency). 2023a. *Net Zero Roadmap: A Global Pathway to Keep the 1.5 °C Goal in Reach. 2023 Update*. Paris: IEA. https://www.iea.org/reports/net-zero-roadmap-a-global-pathway-to-keep-the-15-0c-goal-in-reach.

IEA (International Energy Agency). 2023b. *Energy Efficiency 2023*. Paris: IEA. https://www.iea.org/reports/energy-efficiency-2023.

IEA (International Energy Agency), IRENA (International Renewable Energy Agency), UNSD (United Nations Statistics Division), World Bank, and WHO (World Health Organization). 2023. *Tracking SDG7: The Energy Progress Report, 2023*. Washington, DC: World Bank.

IPBES (Intergovernmental Science-Policy Platform on Biodiversity and Ecosystem Services). 2019. *Global Assessment Report on Biodiversity and Ecosystem Services of the Intergovernmental Science-Policy Platform on Biodiversity and Ecosystem Services*. Bonn, Germany: IPBES Secretariat. https://doi.org/10.5281/zenodo.6417333.

IPCC (Intergovernmental Panel on Climate Change). 2019. *Climate Change and Land: An IPCC Special Report on Climate Change, Desertification, Land Degradation, Sustainable Land Management, Food Security, and Greenhouse Gas Fluxes in Terrestrial Ecosystems*, edited by P. R. Shukla et al. Geneva: IPCC.

IPCC (Intergovernmental Panel on Climate Change). 2021. *Climate Change 2021—The Physical Science Basis: Working Group I Contribution to the Sixth Assessment Report of the Intergovernmental Panel on Climate Change*, 1st ed. Cambridge University Press. https://doi.org/10.1017/9781009325844.

IPCC (Intergovernmental Panel on Climate Change). 2023a. *Climate Change 2022—Impacts, Adaptation and Vulnerability: Working Group II Contribution to the Sixth Assessment Report of the Intergovernmental Panel on Climate Change*, 1st ed. Cambridge, UK: Cambridge University Press. https://doi.org/10.1017/9781009325844.

IPCC (Intergovernmental Panel on Climate Change). 2023b. *Climate Change 2022—Mitigation of Climate Change: Working Group III Contribution to the Sixth Assessment Report of the Intergovernmental Panel on Climate Change*, 1st ed. Cambridge, UK: Cambridge University Press. https://doi.org/10.1017/9781009157926.

IPCC (Intergovernmental Panel on Climate Change). 2023c. *Climate Change 2023: Synthesis Report. Contribution of Working Groups I, II and III to the Sixth Assessment Report of the Intergovernmental Panel on Climate Change*, edited by H. Lee and J. Romero. Geneva: IPCC. https://10.59327/IPCC/AR6-9789291691647.

ISO (International Organization for Standardization). 2017. *Ergonomics of the Thermal Environment—Assessment of Heat Stress Using the WBGT (Wet Bulb Globe Temperature) Index*. ISO Standard 7243:2017. Geneva, Switzerland: ISO.

Jack, William, and Tavneet Suri. 2014. "Risk Sharing and Transactions Costs: Evidence from Kenya's Mobile Money Revolution." *American Economic Review* 104 (1): 183–223. https://doi.org/10.1257/aer.104.1.183.

Jafino, Bramka Arga, Brian Walsh, Julie Rozenberg, and Stephane Hallegatte. 2020. "Revised Estimates of the Impact of Climate Change on Extreme Poverty by 2030." Preprint. Policy Research Working Paper 9417, World Bank, Washington, DC.

Johnson, Jake, Fiona Zakaria, Allan G. Nkurunziza, Celia Way, Miller A. Camargo-Valero, and Barbara Evans. 2022. "Whole-System Analysis Reveals High Greenhouse-Gas Emissions from Citywide Sanitation in Kampala, Uganda." *Communications Earth & Environment* 3 (1): 1–10. https://doi.org/10.1038/s43247-022-00413-w.

Karlan, Dean, Robert Osei, Isaac Osei-Akoto, and Christopher Udry. 2014. "Agricultural Decisions after Relaxing Credit and Risk Constraints." *The Quarterly Journal of Economics* 129 (2): 597–652. https://doi.org/10.1093/qje/qju002.

Klaiber, Christoph Michael, Jun Erik Maruyama Rentschler, and Ira Irina Dorband. 2023. "Distributional and Health Co-Benefits of Fossil Fuel Subsidy Reforms—Evidence from 35 Countries (English)." Policy Research Working Paper 10398, World Bank, Washington, DC.

Klimont, Zbigniew, Kaarle Kupiainen, Chris Heyes, Pallav Purohit, Janusz Cofala, Peter Rafaj, Jens Borken-Kleefeld, et al. 2017. "Global Anthropogenic Emissions of Particulate Matter Including Black Carbon." *Atmospheric Chemistry and Physics* 17 (14): 8681–723. https://doi.org/10.5194/acp-17-8681-2017.

Kochhar, Nishtha, Erwin Willem Knippenberg, and Yvonnick Leon. 2023. "Droughts and Welfare in Afghanistan (English)." Preprint. Policy Research Working Paper 10272, World Bank, Washington, DC.

Koolwal, Gayatri, and Dominique van de Walle. 2013. "Access to Water, Women's Work, and Child Outcomes." *Economic Development and Cultural Change* 61 (2): 369–405. https://doi.org/10.1086/668280.

Laborde, David, Madhur Gautam, Abdullah Mamun, Valeria Pineiro, Will Martin, and Rob Vos. 2022. *Repurposing Agricultural Policies and Support: Options to Transform Agriculture and Food Systems to Better Serve the Health of People, Economies, and the Planet*. Washington, DC: World Bank Group.

Lankes, Hans Peter, Rob Macquarie, Éléonore Soubeyran, and Nicholas Stern. 2024. "The Relationship between Climate Action and Poverty Reduction." *The World Bank Research Observer* 39 (1): 1–46. https://doi.org/10.1093/wbro/lkad011.

Le, Kien, and My Nguyen. 2023. "Rainfall Shocks, Health and Well-Being in Rural Vietnam." *Studies in Microeconomics* 23210222221144873. https://doi.org/10.1177/23210222221144873.

Levinson, Arik. 2023. "Are Developed Countries Outsourcing Pollution?" *Journal of Economic Perspectives* 37 (3): 87–110. https://doi.org/10.1257/jep.37.3.87.

Liotta, Charlotte, Paolo Avner, and Stéphane Hallegatte. 2023. "Efficiency and Equity in Urban Flood Management Policies: A Systematic Urban Economics Exploration." Policy Research Working Paper 10292, World Bank, Washington, DC. https://doi.org/10.1596/1813-9450-10292.

Liu, Yanyan, Kevin Chen, and Ruth V. Hill. 2020. "Delayed Premium Payment, Insurance Adoption, and Household Investment in Rural China." *American Journal of Agricultural Economics* 102 (4): 1177–97. https://doi.org/10.1002/ajae.12038.

Martínez Flores, Fernanda, Sveta Milusheva, Arndt R. Reichert, and Ann-Kristin Reitmann. 2024. "Climate Anomalies and International Migration: A Disaggregated Analysis for West Africa." *Journal of Environmental Economics and Management* 126: 102997. https://doi.org/10.1016/j.jeem.2024.102997.

Matthews, H. Damon, and Seth Wynes. 2022. "Current Global Efforts Are Insufficient to Limit Warming to 1.5°C." *Science* 376 (6600): 1404–9. https://doi.org/10.1126/science.abo3378.

McIntosh, Craig, Alexander Sarris, and Fotis Papadopoulos. 2013. "Productivity, Credit, Risk, and the Demand for Weather Index Insurance in Smallholder Agriculture in Ethiopia." *Agricultural Economics* 44 (4–5): 399–417. https://doi.org/10.1111/agec.12024.

Menéndez, Pelayo, Iñigo J. Losada, Saul Torres-Ortega, Siddharth Narayan, and Michael W. Beck. 2020. "The Global Flood Protection Benefits of Mangroves." *Scientific Reports* 10 (1): 4404. https://doi.org/10.1038/s41598-020-61136-6.

Millward-Hopkins, Joel, Julia K. Steinberger, Narasimha D. Rao, and Yannick Oswald. 2020. "Providing Decent Living with Minimum Energy: A Global Scenario." *Global Environmental Change* 65: 102168.

Mukim, Megha, and Mark Roberts, ed. 2023. *Thriving: Making Cities Green, Resilient, and Inclusive in a Changing Climate*. Washington, DC: World Bank. http://hdl.handle.net/10986/38295.

Muttarak, Raya, and Wolfgang Lutz. 2014. "Is Education a Key to Reducing Vulnerability to Natural Disasters and Hence Unavoidable Climate Change?" *Ecology and Society* 19 (1). https://www.jstor.org/stable/26269470.

Muttarak, R. and Wiraporn Pothisiri. 2013. "The Role of Education on Disaster Preparedness: Case Study of 2012 Indian Ocean Earthquakes on Thailand's Andaman Coast." *Ecology and Society* 18 (4). https://www.jstor.org/stable/26269420.

NGFS (Network for Greening the Financial System). 2023. *NGFS Scenarios Technical Documentation*, v.4.2. Paris: NGFS.

NOAA (National Oceanic and Atmospheric Administration). 2022. "NOAA Research News: Greenhouse Gas Pollution Trapped 49% More Heat in 2021 than in 1990, NOAA Finds." May 23, 2022.

Ocko, Ilissa B., Tianyi Sun, Drew Shindell, Michael Oppenheimer, Alexander N. Hristov, Stephen W. Pacala, Denise L. Mauzerall, et al. 2021. "Acting Rapidly to Deploy Readily Available Methane Mitigation Measures by Sector Can Immediately Slow Global Warming." *Environmental Research Letters* 16 (5): 054042. https://doi.org/10.1088/1748-9326/abf9c8.

Ortiz-Bobea, Ariel, Toby R. Ault, Carlos M. Carrillo, Robert G. Chambers, and David B. Lobell. 2021. "Anthropogenic Climate Change Has Slowed Global Agricultural Productivity Growth." *Nature Climate Change* 11 (4): 306–12. https://doi.org/10.1038/s41558-021-01000-1.

Pape, Utz Johann, and Philip Randolph Wollburg. 2019. "Impact of Drought on Poverty in Somalia." Preprint. Policy Research Working Paper 8698, World Bank, Washington, DC.

Park, R. Jisung, A. Patrick Behrer, and Joshua Goodman. 2021. "Learning Is Inhibited by Heat Exposure, Both Internationally and within the United States." *Nature Human Behaviour* 5 (1): 19–27. https://doi.org/10.1038/s41562-020-00959-9.

Poore, J., and T. Nemecek. 2018. "Reducing Food's Environmental Impacts through Producers and Consumers." *Science* 360 (6392): 987–992. https://doi.org/10.1126/science.aaq0216.

Pople, Ashley, Ruth Hill, Stefan Dercon, and Ben Brunckhorst. 2021. "Anticipatory Cash Transfers in Climate Disaster Response." CSAE Working Paper Series 2021-07, Centre for the Study of African Economies, University of Oxford, Oxford, UK.

Pörtner, Hans-Otto, Debra C. Roberts, Melinda M. B. Tignor, Elvira Poloczanska, Katja Mintenbeck, Andrés Alegría, Marlies Craig, et al. (ed.). 2022. "Climate Change 2022: Impacts, Adaptation and Vulnerability. Working Group II Contribution to the Sixth Assessment Report of the Intergovernmental Panel on Climate Change." Cambridge University Press, Cambridge, UK.

Potapov, Peter, Matthew C. Hansen, Amy Pickens, Andres Hernandez-Serna, Alexandra Tyukavina, Svetlana Turubanova, Viviana Zalles, et al. 2022. "The Global 2000-2020 Land Cover and Land Use Change Dataset Derived from the Landsat Archive: First Results." *Frontiers in Remote Sensing* 3. https://doi.org/10.3389/frsen.2022.856903.

Qiu, Minghao, Jessica Li, Carlos F. Gould, Renzhi Jing, Makoto Kelp, Marissa Childs, Mathew Kiang, et al. 2024. "Mortality Burden from Wildfire Smoke under Climate Change." Working Paper 32307, National Bureau of Economic Research, Cambridge, MA. https://doi.org/10.3386/w32307.

Randell, Heather, and Clark Gray. 2019. "Climate Change and Educational Attainment in the Global Tropics." *Proceedings of the National Academy of Sciences* 116 (18): 8840–5. https://doi.org/10.1073/pnas.1817480116.

Razafindratsima, Onja H., Judith F.M. Kamoto, Erin O. Sills, Doris N. Mutta, Conghe Song, Gillian Kabwe, Sarah E. Castle, et al. 2021. "Reviewing the Evidence on the Roles of Forests and Tree-Based Systems in Poverty Dynamics." *Forest Policy and Economics* 131: 102576. https://doi.org/10.1016/j.forpol.2021.102576.

Rentschler, Jun, Melda Salhab, and Bramka Arga Jafino. 2022. "Flood Exposure and Poverty in 188 Countries." *Nature Communications* 13 (1): 3527. https://doi.org/10.1038/s41467-022-30727-4.

Rigaud, Kanta Kumari, Alex de Sherbinin, Bryan Jones, Jonas Bergmann, Viviane Clement, Kayly Ober, Jacob Schewe, et al. 2018. *Groundswell: Preparing for Internal Climate Migration.* Washington, DC: World Bank.

Rigolini, Jamele 2021. "Social Protection and Labor: A Key Enabler for Climate Change Adaptation and Mitigation." Washington, DC: World Bank.

Rizk, Reham, and Mehdi Ben Slimane. 2018. "Modelling the Relationship between Poverty, Environment, and Institutions: A Panel Data Study." *Environmental Science and Pollution Research* 25 (31): 31459–73. https://doi.org/10.1007/s11356-018-3051-6.

Sekhri, Sheetal, and Adam Storeygard. 2014. "Dowry Deaths: Response to Weather Variability in India." *Journal of Development Economics* 111: 212–23. https://doi.org/10.1016/j.jdeveco.2014.09.001.

Smith, P., H. Clark, H. Dong, E. A. Elsiddig, H. Haberl, R. Harper, J. House, et al. 2014. "Agriculture, Forestry and Other Land Use (AFOLU)." In *Climate Change 2014: Mitigation of Climate Change. IPCC Working Group III Contribution to AR5,* 811–922. Cambridge, UK: Cambridge University Press,.

Song, Cuihong, Jun-Jie Zhu, John L. Willis, Daniel P. Moore, Mark A. Zondlo, and Zhiyong Jason Ren. 2023. "Methane Emissions from Municipal Wastewater Collection and Treatment Systems." *Environmental Science & Technology* 57 (6): 2248–61. https://doi.org/10.1021/acs.est.2c04388.

Steckel, Jan C., Ira I. Dorband, Lorenzo Montrone, Hauke Ward, Leonard Missbach, Fabian Hafner, Michael Jakob, et al. 2021. "Distributional Impacts of Carbon Pricing in Developing Asia." *Nature Sustainability* 4 (11): 1005–14. https://doi.org/10.1038/s41893-021-00758-8.

Sutton, William R., Alexander Lotsch, and Ashesh Prasann. 2024. *Recipe for a Livable Planet: Achieving Net Zero Emissions in the Agrifood System.* Agriculture and Food Series. Washington, DC: World Bank.

Thomas, Adelle, April Baptiste, Rosanne Martyr-Koller, Patrick Pringle, and Kevon Rhiney. 2020. "Climate Change and Small Island Developing States." *Annual Review of Environment and Resources* 45: 1–27. https://doi.org/10.1146/annurev-environ-012320-083355.

Tol, Richard S. J. 2018. "The Economic Impacts of Climate Change." *Review of Environmental Economics and Policy* 12 (1): 4–25. https://doi.org/10.1093/reep/rex027.

Triyana, Margaret Maggie, Andy Jiang Turk, Yurui Hu, and Md Shah Naoaj. 2024. "Climate Shocks and the Poor: A Review of the Literature (English)." Preprint. Policy Research Working Paper 10742, World Bank, Washington, DC.

UNEP (United Nations Environment Programme). 2022. *Adaptation Gap Report 2022: Too Little, Too Slow—Climate Adaptation Failure Puts World at Risk.* Nairobi. https://www.unep.org/adaptation-gap-report-2022.

UNICEF (United Nations Children's Fund). 2022a. *Financing Education Recovery: A Piece of Cake?* New York: UNICEF. https://www.unicef.org/reports/financing-education-recovery-piece-cake.

UNICEF (United Nations Children's Fund). 2022b. *Global Annual Results Report 2022: Every Child Survives and Thrives.* New York: UNICEF. https://www.unicef.org/media/143436/file/Global%20 annual%20results%20report%202022%20:%20Goal%20Area%201.pdf.

United Nations. 2024. *World Economic Situation and Prospects 2024.* New York: United Nations.

United Nations. n.d. "Early Warning for All," webpage, accessed August 30, 2024. https://www.un.org/en /climatechange/early-warnings-for-all.

United Nations and Inter-Agency Task Force on Financing for Development. 2024. *Financing for Sustainable Development Report 2024: Financing for Development at a Crossroads.* New York: United Nations. https://doi.org/10.18356/9789213588635.

Vasilaky, Kathryn, Rahel Diro, Michael Norton, Geoff McCarney, and Daniel Osgood. 2020. "Can Education Unlock Scale? The Demand Impact of Educational Games on a Large-Scale Unsubsidised Index Insurance Programme in Ethiopia." *The Journal of Development Studies* 56 (2): 361–83. https://doi.org/10.1080/00220388.2018.1554207.

Vousdoukas, Michalis I., Panagiotis Athanasiou, Alessio Giardino, Lorenzo Mentaschi, Alessandro Stocchino, Robert E. Kopp, Pelayo Menéndez, et al. 2023. "Small Island Developing States under Threat by Rising Seas even in a 1.5 °C Warming World." *Nature Sustainability* 6 (12): 1552–64. https://doi .org/10.1038/s41893-023-01230-5.

WHO/UNICEF Joint Monitoring Programme. 2024. "Water Supply, Sanitation and Hygiene." https://washdata.org.

Wollburg, Philip, Stephane Hallegatte, and Daniel Gerszon Mahler. 2023. "Ending Extreme Poverty Has a Negligible Impact on Global Greenhouse Gas Emissions." *Nature* 623 (7989): 982–86. https://doi .org/10.1038/s41586-023-06679-0.

World Bank. 2012. *Carbon Sequestration in Agricultural Soils (English).* Washington, DC: World Bank.

World Bank. 2013. *World Development Report 2014: Risk and Opportunity—Managing Risk for Development.* Washington, DC: World Bank. https://doi.org/10.1596/978-0-8213-9903-3.

World Bank. 2022a. *Navigating Multiple Crises, Staying the Course on Long-Term Development: The World Bank Group's Response to the Crises Affecting Developing Countries (English).* Washington, DC: World Bank. http://documents.worldbank.org/curated/en/099640108012229672 /IDU09002cbf10966704fa00958a0596092f2542c.

World Bank. 2022b. *Peru Country Climate and Development Report.* Washington, DC: World Bank.

World Bank. 2022c. *Philippines Country Climate and Development Report.* Washington, DC: World Bank.

World Bank. 2022d. *Poland Country Economic Memorandum: The Green Transformation in Poland— Opportunities and Challenges for Economic Growth.* Washington, DC: World Bank. http://hdl.handle .net/10986/38116.

World Bank. 2022e. *Poverty and Shared Prosperity 2022: Correcting Course.* Washington, DC: World Bank. https://www.worldbank.org/en/publication/poverty-and-shared-prosperity.

World Bank. 2022f. *The Global Health Cost of PM 2.5 Air Pollution: A Case for Action beyond 2021 (English).* Washington, DC: World Bank. https://doi.org/10.1596/978-1-4648-1816-5.

World Bank. 2023a. *Brazil Country Climate and Development Report.* Washington, DC: World Bank.

World Bank. 2023b. *Cambodia Country Climate and Development Report (English).* Washington, DC: World Bank.

World Bank. 2023c. *Colombia Country Climate and Development Report.* Washington, DC: World Bank.

World Bank. 2023d. *Dominican Republic Country Climate and Development Report.* Washington, DC: World Bank.

World Bank. 2023e. *Global Economic Prospects, January 2023.* Washington, DC: World Bank. https://doi .org/10.1596/978-1-4648-2017-5.

World Bank. 2023f. *Scaling Up to Phase Down: Financing Energy Transitions in the Power Sector.* Washington, DC: World Bank. https://www.worldbank.org/en/topic/energy/publication/scaling -up-to-phase-down.

World Bank. 2023g. "Striving for Clean Air: Air Pollution and Public Health in South Asia." World Bank, Washington, DC.

World Bank. 2023h. *World Bank Annual Report 2023*. Washington, DC: World Bank.

World Bank. 2023i. *World Development Report 2023: Migrants, Refugees, and Societies*. Washington, DC: World Bank.

World Bank. 2024a. *Global Economic Prospects, January 2024*. Washington, DC: World Bank. https://doi.org/10.1596/978-1-4648-2017-5.

World Bank. 2024b. *The Great Reversal: Prospects, Risks, and Policies in International Development Association Countries*. Washington, DC: World Bank. https://www.worldbank.org/en/research/publication/prospects-risks-and-policies-in-IDA-countries.

World Bank. 2024c. *Maldives Country Climate and Development Report*. Washington, DC: World Bank.

World Bank. 2024d. *Maldives: Country Environmental Analysis: Towards a More Sustainable and Resilient Blue Economy*. Washington, DC: World Bank.

World Bank. 2024e. *State and Trends of Carbon Pricing 2024*. Washington, DC: World Bank. https://openknowledge.worldbank.org/entities/publication/b0d66765-299c-4fb8-921f-61f6bb979087.

World Bank. 2024f. *Trends and Policy Options to Effectively Fight Global Poverty and Hunger*. Washington, DC: World Bank. https://www.gov.br/planalto/pt-br/agenda-internacional/forca-tarefa-para-alianca-contra-a-fome-e-a-pobreza/forca-tarefa-para-alianca-global-contra-a-fome-e-a-pobreza.

World Bank. 2024g. *World Development Report 2024: The Middle-Income Trap*. Washington, DC: World Bank.

World Bank. n.d. "Translating Our Vision." World Bank Group Scorecard online resource. https://scorecard.worldbank.org/en/scorecard/home.

World Bank and ESMAP. 2023. *Toward a Framework for the Sustainable Heating Transition in Europe and Central Asia (English)*. Washington, DC: World Bank Group. http://documents.worldbank.org/curated/en/099092023140527206/P1777440fed3230ce089060ff8ce59c9f5e.

World Bank Group. 2022. *Climate and Development: An Agenda for Action—Emerging Insights from World Bank Group 2021–22 Country Climate and Development Reports*. Washington, DC: World Bank. http://hdl.handle.net/10986/38220.

World Bank Group. 2023. *The Development, Climate, and Nature Crisis: Solutions to End Poverty on a Livable Planet—Insights from World Bank Country Climate and Development Reports Covering 42 economies*. https://doi.org/10.1596/40652.

World Meteorological Organization. 2022. Greenhouse Gas Bulletin. https://community.wmo.int.

Zaveri, Esha, Jason Russ, Amjad Khan, Richard Damania, and Edoardo Borgomeo. 2021. *Ebb and Flow, volume 1. Water, Migration, and Development*. Washington, DC: World Bank Group. http://hdl.handle.net/10986/36089.

Zhang, Fan, and Christian Borja-Vega. 2024. *Water for Shared Prosperity (English)*. Washington, DC: World Bank. https://www.worldbank.org/en/publication/water-for-shared-prosperity.

Monitoring the Interlinked Goals

4

Summary

- *Data are the infrastructure for policy and should therefore be prioritized. Eradicating poverty and boosting shared prosperity on a livable planet requires a solid foundation of evidence.*

- *The analysis presented in this report relies to a large extent on household survey data. While data availability has improved in many countries, less than one-half of the countries in the world had a household survey available for poverty monitoring in 2020 or later. This reflects issues of coverage and accessibility.*

- *The expanded vision of the World Bank, with a new measure on shared prosperity and the inclusion of a livable planet, calls for substantial improvements to the quality of data. New indicators require good coverage of the entire global distribution of income and consumption, granular exposure to climate-related risks, and multidimensional poverty.*

- *In light of the data revolution, significant investments are needed to modernize surveys and accelerate the integration and standardization of various sources of data. At the same time, efforts should focus on leveraging machine learning and artificial intelligence (AI) models to close data gaps and enable more timely monitoring.*

Advancing on these global challenges requires a solid foundation of evidence

Eradicating poverty and boosting shared prosperity on a livable planet requires decisive actions informed by solid evidence. Decisions must be made with a clear understanding of both the trade-offs and the complementarities across objectives. Across the board, more and better data are needed to design solutions to address these complex policy goals and to monitor and manage the impacts on vulnerable populations.

This chapter summarizes key points regarding data availability and measurement challenges to properly monitor the World Bank's vision. Table 4.1 presents the set of indicators selected to track this progress, encompassing three key dimensions: poverty, prosperity, and a livable planet. The first part of the chapter focuses broadly on household surveys, stressing the value that they have for the monitoring of the Sustainable Development Goals (SDGs) and highlighting ways to modernize and enhance these surveys in light of the fast-changing ecosystem. The second part of the chapter focuses on measurement challenges related to the indicators presented in this report.

TABLE 4.1

World Bank's Vision indicators

Chapter	Vision indicators
1. Poverty	Percentage of global population living in poverty (measured at two poverty lines: less than $2.15 per day and less than $6.85 per day)
2. Prosperity	Global average income shortfall from a prosperity standard of $25 per day
	Number of economies with high inequality
3. Livable Planet	Global greenhouse gas emissions (gigatons of carbon dioxide equivalent [CO_2e])
	Percentage of people at high risk from climate-related hazards globally
	Millions of hectares of key ecosystems globally
	Percentage of people facing food and nutrition insecurity globally
	Percentage of people with access to basic drinking water, sanitation services, or hygiene globally

Source: World Bank, n.d.
Note: $ = 2017 purchasing power parity dollars.

Household surveys are at the core of SDG monitoring but need to be adapted to a new data ecosystem

Household survey data continue to be at the core of the monitoring of the SDGs, as well as the World Bank's vision. Several SDGs rely heavily on survey data to monitor progress, assess needs, and evaluate the effectiveness of policies and interventions.[1] These surveys are behind the construction of more than one-third of the 234 SDG indicators (Carletto et al. 2022). For this report, household income and expenditure survey data are needed to track poverty, multidimensional poverty, shared prosperity, and high inequality and are also the basis for quantifying the share of people at risk to extreme weather events. In addition, these data are foundational for modeling and projecting the potential impacts of climate change on welfare and for understanding trade-offs and short-term costs related to climate policies for people.

Despite progress in the availability of household survey data, challenges remain, particularly for the poorest countries

Although significant strides have been made in improving the availability and quality of household surveys over the past decade, challenges remain. They include persistent issues with availability, coverage, accuracy, timeliness, affordability, policy relevance, and usability, particularly in low-income countries that would gain the most from enhanced survey data (Carletto et al. 2022).

One clear example relevant to this report is household income and expenditure surveys. Overall, there has been substantial progress in the availability of household survey data containing information on income, consumption, or both that allows tracking of SDG 1 (no poverty) and SDG 10 (reduced inequalities). Globally, between 1998 and 2022, the average number of available survey data sets per country increased from 2.1 to 9.9, almost a fivefold increase (figure 4.1). Upper-middle- and high-income countries drove this progress. However, more survey data have also become available for lower-income countries, with improvements in data quality, frequency, and processing time.[2]

This progress is manifested in the reduction in the time lag in survey-based global poverty figures (SDG 1). For example, this report has only a two-year lag in reporting baseline global estimates, compared with three years for previous editions.[3] Despite the COVID-19 (Coronavirus) pandemic, there has been sufficient survey data coverage for the world for this report to present baseline poverty data and shared prosperity data through 2022.

FIGURE 4.1

The number of household budget surveys has increased in all regions, 1998–2022

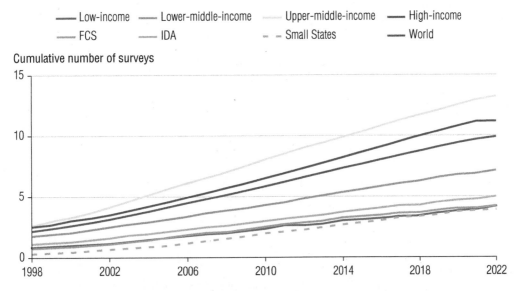

Source: World Bank, Poverty and Inequality Platform (version September 2024), https://pip.worldbank.org.
Note: FCS = fragile and conflict-affected situations; IDA = International Development Association. The classification of countries by FCS, by inclusion in the World Bank's IDA, and by income status is based on the data for 2022. IDA countries are those eligible for grants and concessionary loans from the IDA, which provides support to the poorest countries in the world (consisting of low-income countries and some countries in other income groups).

Despite progress, fewer than one-half of the countries around the world had a survey available for 2020 or later for global SDG 1 monitoring (figure 4.2). This limited availability of data reflects issues of limited or infrequent data collection, the lack of statistical capacity, fragility, or reluctance and delay in sharing data because such data are politically sensitive. Less than one-half of low-income or fragile countries and Small States have a survey since 2020 available. These countries have consistently had the least amount of survey data since 1998, and the pace of progress is slow compared with that of richer countries.[4] For this report, two key regions (Sub-Saharan Africa and the Middle East and North Africa) do not have sufficient data coverage for global poverty monitoring and therefore rely on nowcasts based largely on data from before the COVID-19 pandemic. For the most populated countries (for example, the Arab Republic of Egypt, Ethiopia, Mozambique, and Nigeria), survey microdata are available but have not been released in time for this report. The limited number of recent survey data has important implications for the reliability of global poverty estimates, especially for these data-deprived regions and country groups.

FIGURE 4.2

Less than one-half of the countries in the world have data available for global monitoring of poverty in 2020 or later

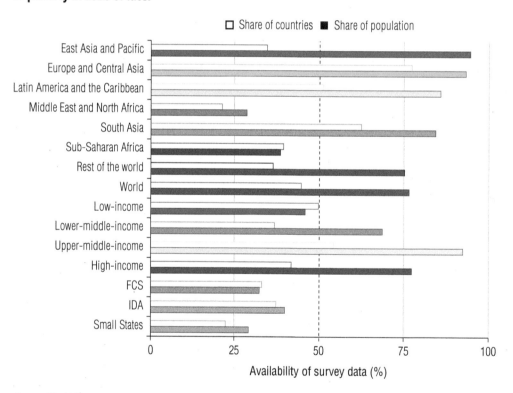

Source: World Bank, Poverty and Inequality Platform (version September 2024), https://pip.worldbank.org.
Note: FCS = fragile and conflict-affected situations; IDA = International Development Association. The figure shows the share of countries and share of population that is covered by a survey for 2020 or later. The classification of countries by FCS, by inclusion in the World Bank's IDA, and by income status is based on the data for 2022. IDA countries are those eligible for grants and concessionary loans from the IDA, which provides support to the poorest countries in the world (consisting of low-income countries and some countries in other income groups).

Surveys need to be modernized and adapted to a new data ecosystem

The data ecosystem has dramatically changed, and household surveys need to be adapted. Urbanization and higher income levels tend to make data collection harder and reduce response rates (Carletto et al. 2022). The COVID-19 pandemic also disrupted statistical systems. Between 2020 and 2022, data openness improved only marginally and data availability did not grow for the first time in six years (Open Data Watch 2023). These developments reflect the impact of the pandemic disruptions, particularly in countries without experience in remote data collection, signaling a strong need for increased investment to build resilient data systems. Moreover, the world is undergoing a data revolution with an increasing number of data sources, big data, and more powerful modeling, as well as new technologies to engage users and producers of data. Keeping current with these trends requires thinking about how surveys can be modernized to respond to challenges and leverage new opportunities.

At the technical level, an assessment done by the World Bank's Living Standards Measurement Study and the United Nations Statistics Division, under the guidance of the Inter-Secretariat Working Group on Household Surveys, identified eight key technical priorities for household surveys in the coming decade. These priorities were selected on the basis of three main criteria: (a) areas that have demonstrated success or hold significant potential for medium-term impact, (b) areas that strengthen the data foundation while advancing research and development, and (c) areas most likely to benefit low- and middle-income countries, where improvements are most urgently needed. The priorities are as follows: (a) enhancing the interoperability and integration of household surveys; (b) designing and implementing more inclusive, respondent-focused surveys; (c) improving sampling efficiency and coverage; (d) expanding the use of objective measurement technologies; (e) building capacity for computer-assisted personal interviewing, phone, web, and mixed-mode surveys; (f) systematizing the collection, storage, and use of paradata and metadata; (g) incorporating machine learning and AI for data quality control and analysis; and (h) improving data access, discoverability, and dissemination (Carletto et al. 2022).

While increased funding for data is essential, surveys must also become more efficient and nimbler, with a strong emphasis on data integration

Collecting traditional survey data can be very expensive, which is one reason why these surveys are usually undersupplied (Chin 2021).[5] With constrained budgets, it is hard to prioritize data investments vis-à-vis other development needs.[6] Lower-income countries experience a funding gap, which is partially filled by multilateral and bilateral donors. In 2021, the annual funding required by countries eligible for International Development Association (IDA) or International Bank for Reconstruction and Development financing to produce core statistics was estimated at $6.2 billion, with $1.4 billion sourced externally.[7]

The Atkinson Commission report on global poverty recommends greater financial investments in data and data systems, as well as international coordination and accountability for data (World Bank 2017).

However, as budgets are always tight, investing in making data collection more efficient and nimbler is also key. With the ongoing data revolution, enhancing the interoperability and integration of household surveys with censuses, geospatial data, administrative records, and nontraditional sources, such as satellite data and call-detail records, can increase the cost-effectiveness and relevance of survey data. This interoperability can improve accuracy and granularity in both spatial and temporal resolution, but it is possible only through data integration. One successful application is the linkage of survey data and census data with geospatial data for poverty mapping (Corral et al. 2022; Corral, Henderson, and Segovia 2023; Elbers, Lanjouw, and Lanjouw 2003; Hentschel et al. 2000).[8]

For example, georeferencing is key for integrating data with spatial features and enhancing the granularity of information. Georeferenced survey data can help validate and calibrate machine learning models that combine these data with satellite imagery and geospatial data to derive estimates of poverty, asset wealth, and agricultural outcomes at high spatial resolution. This integration allows for more detailed analyses, which are crucial for policy making and resource allocation. Georeferencing is crucial for measuring vulnerability to climate hazards where hazard information needs to be linked with household surveys to identify populations at risk. This is discussed in more detail below.

Another important step for improving data integration is to standardize key variables across core surveys, which enhances the ability to bridge information between various surveys effectively. For example, one of the challenges of the World Bank's current Multidimensional Poverty Measure (MPM) is precisely the difficulty in combining poverty data with nonmonetary dimensions of well-being, such as basic services, collected in other surveys. As a result of these difficulties, the global population covered by the MPM lags behind the monetary poverty measures (see chapter 1). Similarly, the livable planet indicator (in table 4.1) of the percentage of people with access to basic drinking water, sanitation services, or hygiene globally is not comparable with the indicator of water and sanitation in the MPM because of differences in definitions of these variables across surveys. By standardizing key variables, such as demographic information (for example, age, gender, and income), geographic location, and basic services indicators, it becomes easier to link and compare data from various surveys. This enables more comprehensive analyses and facilitates the combination of data sets to generate richer, more detailed insights.

Furthermore, including common variables facilitates the use of advanced analytical techniques, such as machine learning and AI, to identify patterns and correlations across larger, more diverse data sets. This can lead to more accurate predictive models and better-informed decision-making.

Beyond funding and technical improvements, the challenge in many settings is to make data available more broadly and in a timely manner

Development data that have been collected are not always shared or made available to others in a timely fashion and at low cost. The Open Data Inventory (ODIN) provides a way for monitoring global progress on the availability and accessibility of official statistics. The ODIN overall score on the state of official statistics for 2022 was lowest for low-income countries, with significant gaps between upper-middle- and high-income countries (figure 4.3, panel a). The differences are smaller for poverty and income data, marking progress made in data collection in these areas. Data openness is a pressing concern for low-income and lower-middle-income countries (figure 4.3, panel b). The gap relative to upper-middle- and high-income countries in data openness is significantly larger than for data coverage, indicating that in several countries data exist but are not accessible. In the Middle East and North Africa, openness looks worse than suggested by the ODIN scores when assessed by microdata access (Ekhator-Mobayode and Hoogeveen 2022).

FIGURE 4.3

Data accessibility scores for countries by income categories

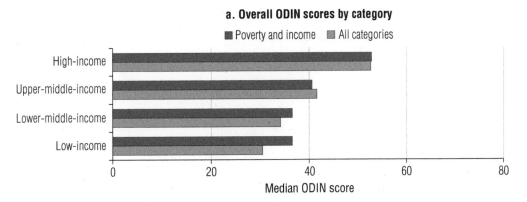

a. Overall ODIN scores by category

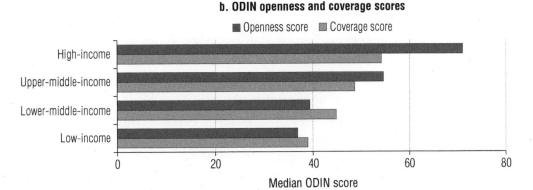

b. ODIN openness and coverage scores

Source: Open Data Watch 2023.
Note: ODIN = Open Data Inventory. Panel a shows the median ODIN overall scores for all categories and the poverty and income categories. Panel b shows the median ODIN openness and coverage scores for all categories. ODIN score goes from 0 to 100. Fixed income group classifications from 2022 are used.

Improving access requires actions on several fronts. More effective data governance is key to creating an environment where data can be produced, made available for use, and shared safely, while ensuring that the benefits of data are shared equitably (World Bank 2021). Within the wide range of competing policy interests, strengthening the independence and technical capacity of national statistical systems should be prioritized more than ever before.

Household surveys should also leverage modeling to fill information gaps and support more timely monitoring

Welfare monitoring provides a clear illustration of the need for more data. Because official measures of poverty are derived from household surveys that are costly and time-intensive, the information is not produced frequently enough to meet the needs of many policy makers, especially in low-income and FCS settings.

Modeling approaches, including recent AI and machine learning models, could help overcome this limited availability of survey data to provide more timely information. This could be done by integrating additional big data sources, such as geospatial data or call detail record data, to estimate and predict poverty more frequently. In essence, these types of models explore patterns between poverty estimates from survey data and covariates from nonsurvey data (such as satellite imagery) to predict poverty rates in nonsurvey years. Note that the accuracy of such models hinges on the availability and quality of recent survey data. These approaches cannot substitute for investment in traditional surveys (such as household budget surveys or censuses). When no recent survey data are available, using these models is not feasible or will produce low-quality estimates.

At the same time, evidence suggests that predicting welfare changes over time using these models is still difficult, especially on a global scale, and therefore more research is needed. For instance, Marty and Duhaut (2024) compared various models and data sources to predict poverty and found that models explain only 4 percent to 6 percent of the variation in asset wealth over time (26 percent being the maximum in one country). So far, predicting nonmonetary welfare indicators such as food security over time has been found to be more feasible than predicting monetary or asset-based welfare indicators (see, for example, Andree et al. [2020] and Tang, Liu, and Matteson [2022]). Mahler, Castañeda Aguilar, and Newhouse (2022) found that on the country level, using data from national accounts to nowcast poverty outperforms more complex models using a variety of geospatial variables. More research on how to enhance the accuracy of machine learning models in estimating changes in monetary poverty and other welfare metrics using big data sources is needed.

Household surveys need to be improved to support the growth of more advanced analytics for monitoring. This would require investments in comprehensive metadata documentation and the adoption of standardized, interoperable data practices. Detailed descriptions for all variables, along with clear documentation of data collection methodologies, are essential for ensuring that AI algorithms understand the context and nature of the data.

Provenance information, including data sources and processing history, helps maintain reliability and allows for replicable studies. Standardized data formats and metadata, as well as application programming interfaces (APIs) for seamless data access, enhance interoperability with various AI tools and platforms. Using ontologies and taxonomies to classify and relate data elements further aids AI systems in interpreting and analyzing the data.

A broadened World Bank vision calls for a more holistic and multifaceted approach to measuring well-being and risks

The rest of this chapter shifts the focus from data to measurement across four areas that pertain to the indicators discussed in this report. The first area deals with measuring inequality—discussing challenges such as differences between consumption and income data, the underreporting of top incomes in household surveys, and discrepancies between household surveys and national accounts data. The second area concerns nonmonetary measures and delves into the measurement of food insecurity, given the complexity of the concept and measurement challenges of the selected indicator. The third area focuses on capturing vulnerability and climate risks more accurately. The final area reflects on the challenges in forecasting the impacts of global warming on poverty, given the discussions presented in chapter 3.

These selected measurement areas are prioritized because of the content of this report, yet other measurement topics remain important. For instance, within-household inequality, although not discussed here, is crucial for capturing individual-level poverty and accurately disaggregating poverty by gender. In addition, this report does not discuss in detail measurement challenges related to water, sanitation, and hygiene (WASH) or healthy ecosystems. For WASH, the indicator is clear, and the main challenge is advancing coverage of the hygiene dimension. For key ecosystems, at the time this report was being completed, the World Bank's vision indicator was not yet finalized. Therefore, this indicator will be discussed in future editions of this report as well as in other upcoming World Bank reports on the planet indicators.

The added focus on inequality and the Prosperity Gap requires better measurement of the entire distribution of income or consumption

The World Bank's current methods for assessing monetary well-being have been designed over the years to measure primarily poverty. With the added focus on inequality and the Prosperity Gap, the World Bank's methods need to evolve and expand from focusing on the bottom of the distribution to considering the entire distribution (Haddad et al. 2024; Kraay et al. 2023).

The difference between using income or consumption is a challenge for monitoring inequality

Chapter 2 discussed the rationale for monitoring inequality and described the indicators. While inequality is a broad concept and should be studied with a wide range of measures to capture its multiple dimensions, this report focuses on indicators of inequality based on income (or consumption) using household surveys.[9] One key challenge is how to deal with the fact that some surveys collect income data and others collect consumption data.

The temporal smoothing behavior of consumption, particularly for the poorest households, tends to make it the preferred aggregate for measuring poverty.[10] This is especially the case in developing economies, which typically depend more on agriculture and have a larger informal sector—both factors that can make income hard to measure and seasonal. In advanced countries, however, it is much easier to capture individuals' incomes, so income surveys are more common.[11] The upshot is that most countries in Latin America and the Caribbean and all high-income countries report income surveys, while most other countries report consumption surveys. Of 170 countries with survey data in the World Bank's Poverty and Inequality Platform (PIP), the latest survey for 103 was based on consumption.

Despite these differences, the two aggregates are currently used interchangeably in the measurement of progress toward the World Bank goals; this is done to maximize the number of countries monitored. Although this creates issues of comparability in the measurement of poverty, it allows the coverage of the global goals to be expanded. The distinction becomes more problematic, however, in the analysis of prosperity and inequality where larger parts of the income distribution matter. A clear issue is that countries in Latin America and the Caribbean typically use income data, while in Sub-Saharan Africa consumption data are more readily available. These two regions stand out as having high levels of inequality, but the differences in their underlying welfare measures make it difficult to compare their levels of inequality.

Earlier studies indicate that while levels of inequality may differ, the changes in inequality and country rankings are relatively consistent regardless of whether income or consumption measures are used.[12] Figure B4.4.1 of World Bank (2016) compares income- and consumption-based Gini indexes across several countries in Eastern Europe and Central Asia for the same years. Figure 4.4, panel a, replicates this exercise with updated data. It plots the income Gini value (right axis) against the consumption Gini value (left axis) for all the countries where such a comparison is possible using the latest survey available. For readability, data are limited to surveys conducted after 2015. It is evident that consumption-based Gini indexes are almost always considerably lower than income-based Gini indexes. However, the country rankings remain relatively similar. Figure 4.4, panel b, examines whether inequality trends differ when consumption is used instead of income. For economies with data spanning the decade 2008 to 2018, inequality changes go in the same direction for the two measures, although the magnitudes vary (figure B4.4.2 of World Bank [2016] depicts similar results for the 2008 to 2013 period).

Even so, significantly more work in collecting both income and consumption data and assessing the implications of using one or the other to monitor shared prosperity and inequality is needed. In particular, the comparison in figure 4.4 is currently possible for only a limited set of countries covering selected regions.

FIGURE 4.4

Using income and consumption does not change rankings and trends dramatically for countries where both measures exist

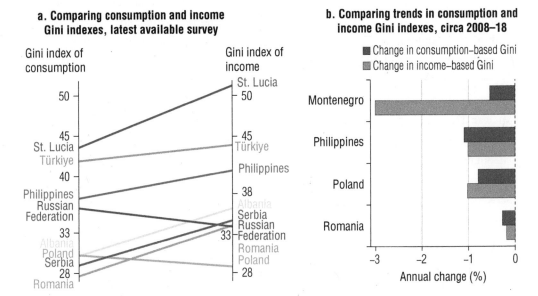

a. Comparing consumption and income Gini indexes, latest available survey

b. Comparing trends in consumption and income Gini indexes, circa 2008–18

Source: World Bank, Poverty and Inequality Platform (version September 2024), https://pip.worldbank.org.
Note: Panel a shows the Gini indexes of consumption and income for all countries using the latest available survey between 2015 and 2022. Panel b shows the annual percent change in the Gini index between circa 2008 (±4 years) and circa 2018 (±4 years) for countries that have both types of surveys that are comparable. See also figures B4.4.1 and B4.4.2 in *Poverty and Shared Prosperity 2016: Taking on Inequality* (World Bank 2016).

Another challenge for measuring inequality is capturing top incomes

The World Bank indicator for high inequality is derived from household surveys, which often underrepresent the richest individuals because of issues such as underreporting and nonresponse (Atkinson and Piketty 2007; Haddad et al. 2024). The small sample size of the very rich combined with their large income, which can affect measured aggregates, exacerbates this problem. Additionally, surveys typically fail to adequately capture entrepreneurial and capital income (Burkhauser, Hahn, and Wilkins 2015; Flachaire, Lustig, and Vigorito 2023; Piketty, Yang, and Zucman 2019; Yonzan et al. 2022).[13] As a result, inequality measured by using survey data is generally lower than when data that includes the very top income earners, such as administrative tax records, are used (Piketty and Saez 2006; Saez and Zucman 2016).

While tax data are not specifically designed to measure inequality, they better capture the incomes of the rich in countries where there is a comprehensive taxation of personal income. This leads to inequality estimates higher than those derived from surveys alone. Efforts to "correct" the top end of survey data have been made for many countries (for example, see Burkhauser, Hahn, and Wilkins 2015; Flachaire, Lustig, and Vigorito 2023; Jenkins 2017; and Piketty, Yang, and Zucman 2019). However, outside high-income countries, tax data are limited and often provide an incomplete picture because of the lack of comprehensive personal income taxes (van der Weide, Lakner, and Ianchovichina 2018). Moreover, the best method to combine survey data with administrative records remains unclear. The approach taken to merge these data sources can significantly affect inequality estimates (Alvaredo et al. 2023; Auten and Splinter 2024; Flachaire, Lustig, and Vigorito 2023; Lustig 2020). Recently, Ferreira (2023) summarized the current state of the research by suggesting that there are "inequality bands," with true inequality falling somewhere between the survey-based estimates and the more extreme upward-correction methods.

Hence, a comprehensive adjustment to data from all countries around the world for underreporting at the top is still not feasible. The World Inequality Database (WID) systematically adjusts survey data for missing top incomes, using a range of sources, including tax data where available but also national accounts (Blanchet and Chancel 2016; World Inequality Lab 2024). As expected, the adjusted Gini index (taken from WID) is greater than the survey-based Gini index (using World Bank's PIP data), as indicated by the upward sloping lines in figure 4.5, panel a. One reason for the higher Gini index in WID is better measurement of incomes at the top. This is also clear from figure 4.5, panel b, which shows the income share captured by the top 10 percent of income earners in PIP and WID. The shares reported in WID are almost always larger than those reported in PIP, indicating that an adjustment for underreporting at the top would have direct implications for measuring the number of economies with high inequality. However, it is important to bear in mind that the threshold value for high inequality would also have to be adjusted if adjusted Gini indexes were used. The threshold of 40 was set at approximately the top one-third of economies, using survey-based Gini indexes (for details, see chapter 2 and Haddad et al. 2024).

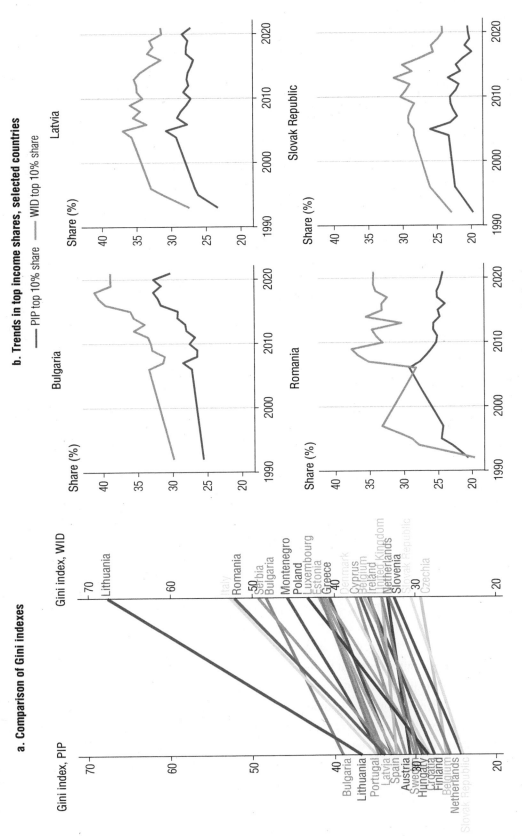

FIGURE 4.5

Comparison of inequality estimates derived from household surveys and other methods

a. Comparison of Gini indexes

b. Trends in top income shares, selected countries

Sources: World Bank, Poverty and Inequality Platform (version September 2024), https://pip.worldbank.org; World Inequality Database.

Note: PIP = Poverty and Inequality Platform; WID = World Inequality Database. Panel a compares Gini indexes between PIP and WID for 2021, which is the latest year with comparable sets for countries in both databases. Panel b compares income shares of the top 10 percent earners for select countries in Europe and Central Asia. The income concept used in PIP is per capita household income, and that used in WID is equal-split adult post-tax disposable income. See also Atkinson and Piketty (2007) for rich countries.

Direct comparisons between PIP and WID are difficult, given the differences in data sources. PIP uses data based exclusively on household surveys, while WID combines data from household surveys, administrative sources (like tax records), and national accounts.[14] Beyond this, the income concept used and the unit of measurement considered—individuals, households, or tax unit—potentially complicate comparisons (Yonzan et al. 2022). PIP uses *per capita household income or consumption* equivalent to the disposable (or after tax and transfer) income concept. To make it as comparable as possible, figure 4.5 uses the *post-tax disposable income* concept available in WID. However, PIP uses *per capita household* as the unit of analysis, whereas WID uses *income split equally among adults age 20 or over*. This discrepancy in definitions is not easily remedied and thus is not corrected for in figure 4.5, which adds to the differences. The income concepts used here also mean that comparisons between PIP and WID are possible only for rich countries and some Eastern European countries.[15] Furthermore, comparability between countries (and over time) is an important focus for these databases. PIP harmonizes data across countries and identifies cases in which surveys within a country might not be comparable across time.[16] On the other hand, given the mixture of sources used for WID, cross-country and time comparisons can be problematic. WID acknowledges that the data are not the same quality in all countries (World Inequality Lab 2024).[17] Even in well-established cases, there is an ongoing debate on which factors have driven changes across time, such as real changes in incomes at the top or changes in tax reporting rules.[18]

Regardless of the level differences, it is reassuring to know that the trends in inequality across time remain largely similar when data from PIP and WID are compared. Figure 4.5, panel b, shows that the two series, especially in the more recent period, track reasonably well. Another way to summarize this difference in trends across countries is to systematically test for any differences in year-over-year changes, that is, whether the two series report similar year-over-year changes on average. Figure 4.6 compares the year-over-year changes in the two databases for all the countries and years where such a comparison is possible.[19] The first step is to estimate the year-over-year changes in the Gini index for the list of countries with an observation in both databases. Then the difference between these annual changes is computed across the two databases. Figure 4.6 shows that the difference between the two series is close to zero on average, suggesting that the two databases track fairly closely. For all countries in the sample, the difference in annual changes between PIP and WID is not statistically significantly different from zero. In other words, the levels might be different (as indicated in figure 4.5), but the changes in the trends are comparable, whether or not top incomes are incorporated. In a recent review of the evidence for Latin America and the Caribbean, Alvaredo et al. (2023) similarly found wide differences in levels of inequality but a broadly robust dynamic pattern.

FIGURE 4.6

Differences in trends of the Gini index between PIP and WID

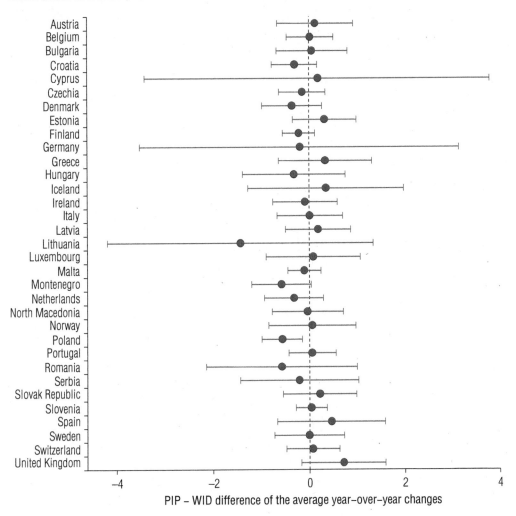

Sources: World Bank, Poverty and Inequality Platform (version September 2024), https://pip.worldbank.org; World Inequality Database.

Note: PIP = Poverty and Inequality Platform; WID = World Inequality Database. This figure illustrates the percentage points difference between the average year-over-year percent change in the Gini index in PIP and WID. The average differences (dots) and the 95 percent confidence intervals (bars) are shown. The income concept used in PIP is per capita household income, and that in WID is equal-split adult post-tax disposable income.

Rescaling using national accounts can be problematic

Income and consumption measurement challenges are not limited to the top of the distribution. Household surveys routinely omit certain spending, such as spending on durable goods or housing, and at times do not capture all relevant food consumption because of limitations in the questionnaires or because of poor data quality (Foster and Daylan 2024). Partly for these reasons, large gaps between mean income and consumption from household surveys and national accounts have been observed (Deaton 2005; Prydz et al. 2022; Ravallion 2003).

Some researchers have responded to this misalignment between surveys and national accounts by arguing that mean income or consumption in household surveys should be scaled up to match mean national income or household expenditure as measured in national accounts (Sala-i-Martin and Pinkovskiy 2016). More sophisticated methods such as the WID approach (figures 4.4 and 4.5) also distribute national accounts aggregates to create a distribution of income or consumption (Piketty et al. 2018).

This rescaling can be problematic, and more research on this area is needed. National accounts are not immune to measurement error themselves (Ravallion 2003). National accounts data have been found to change dramatically when the base year is changed (*The Economist* 2014), to be overestimated by autocrats (Martinez 2022), underestimated to get more foreign assistance (Kerner, Jerven, and Beatty 2017), or to have ample room for improvement in developing countries (Angrist et al. 2021). Furthermore, the literature that scales up to national accounts typically ignores the issue of how to adjust the poverty lines, which have been set with a survey-based distribution in mind. In addition, national accounts and household surveys do not measure identical concepts. For example, some spending from consumption aggregates is deliberately excluded because it is deemed less relevant for households' welfare (Mancini and Vecchi 2022).

For these reasons, the Atkinson Commission report on global poverty argued that a more nuanced approach to deal with measurement challenges in household survey data is to adjust for these concerns rather than to introduce new ones with national accounts data (World Bank 2017).

It is also key to broaden the scope of multidimensional poverty and expand the use of nonmonetary measures of well-being

Monetary measures alone do not capture all dimensions of welfare that are relevant to inform policies. This report presents results from the MPM in chapter 1. The MPM aims to understand poverty beyond just monetary deprivations by also considering access to education and basic infrastructure, in addition to the monetary headcount ratio at the $2.15 per person per day international poverty line. This measure draws inspiration from prominent global multidimensional indexes, particularly the Multidimensional Poverty Index developed by the United Nations Development Programme and Oxford University.[20] Unlike the Multidimensional Poverty Index, the MPM includes monetary poverty (less than $2.15 per person per day at 2017 purchasing power parity) as one of its dimensions.

To construct a global MPM, data have to be harmonized across various dimensions. Unfortunately, not all countries have current and comparable data for all relevant dimensions. The requirement of a global MPM for standardized household indicators across many countries necessarily limits indicator choice to the relatively few that are consistently measured. As noted in the 2018 *Poverty and Shared Prosperity* report, the MPM could be expanded with additional dimensions (such as health and security), but, importantly, this depends on the availability of such data (World Bank 2018). Improvements in data quality, data standardization, and data integration can significantly help enhance multidimensional poverty monitoring across time and regions.

The inclusion of the planet indicators brings more explicit recognition of these nonmonetary dimensions, and many of the same variables are also used to construct the climate risk indicator. The work behind the climate risk indicator highlights the challenges and potential of data integration for constructing a comprehensive multidimensional vulnerability measure. This is discussed later in this chapter.

In addition, the World Bank's new vision monitors progress on food and nutrition security. While food security is not discussed at length in this report, annex 4A discusses some key measurement challenges to keep in mind to inform follow-up work in this area.

Food security is described through four dimensions: (a) food availability, or the existence of enough food for people to eat; (b) food access, or the ability of individuals to financially afford and physically access food that is available to eat; (c) food utilization, or the ability of individuals to properly absorb the micro- and macronutrients in the foods that they eat; and (d) stability, or individuals being food secure in all dimensions at all times (Barrett 2010). Therefore, ideally it would be good to track the four dimensions to obtain a complete picture of food security.

The new World Bank Corporate Scorecard (World Bank, n.d.) proposes to measure food and nutrition security with the Food Insecurity Experience Scale (FIES) and highlights another critical food security outcome to be tracked separately: the share of children under age five who are stunted. These two measures correspond to measures of food access and food utilization. Although best practices suggest using multiple food access metrics at the household level to validate changes in food access, the FIES is the only household-level indicator that is currently available globally. The only other indicator available is the Prevalence of Undernourishment (PoU), which is calculated from a combination of national accounts data, food balance sheets, and household surveys (FAO et al. 2023).

In interpreting changes in the FIES, it is important to consider that it captures one aspect of food security and to complement findings by looking at changes in the PoU. It is also advisable to corroborate changes using closely aligned measures, including extreme poverty (Lain, Tandon, and Vishwanath 2023).[21] Annex 4A describes in more detail the complexity of the concept of food and nutrition security, how the approach proposed in the World Bank Scorecard might align with best measurement practices, and ongoing efforts to improve global measurement.

Measuring climate risks for people also involves integrating multiple dimensions of hazards and vulnerabilities

The new World Bank livable planet indicator for the percentage of people at high risk from climate-related hazards globally is defined as the share of the world's population that is both exposed to a set of key climate-related hazards (floods, droughts, cyclones, and heat waves) and highly vulnerable (that is, has a propensity to be adversely affected or unable to cope with the impacts). Specifically, people are counted as at high risk from climate-related hazards if they are exposed to at least one hazard and are identified as highly vulnerable in at least one dimension of vulnerability. Annex 4B summarizes key data sources related to hazards and ongoing work to improve the estimates. More information can be found in Doan et al. (2023).

Measuring the risk from climate-related hazards is a complex task. Each of the three components of the indicator—hazards, exposure, and vulnerability—has multiple dimensions, and the combination of the three further adds to the complexity. This section discusses some key limitations and areas for future improvement.

Effective measurement of climate risks requires focusing on hazards and dimensions of vulnerability that are relevant to people and can be measured globally

The hazards selected for the indicator are based on evidence that they are highly likely to affect people. With this in mind, the indicator produced by Doan et al. (2023) used in this report considers four climate-related hazard events that have significant impacts on livelihoods: floods, droughts, heat waves, and cyclones (IPCC 2023).[22] On the other hand, the indicator does not consider geophysical hazards and environmental factors (such as earthquakes or air pollution) or climate trends such as sea level rise. It also omits some climate-related hazards such as wildfires, which rising temperatures make more devastating (IPCC 2023).[23] Furthermore, the measurement of hazard distributions is based on historical data and does not account for increasing occurrences and geographic ranges of hazards in the future. Thus, the resulting measure is a lower bound of the population at risk from climate hazards.

The same applies for the selection of vulnerability dimensions. Vulnerability captures household deprivations along seven dimensions (see annex 3B of chapter 3 for more details).[24] For a variety of reasons, a range of additional factors that could matter for households' coping and adaptive capacity—such as the type of assets that households hold, insurance (for example, health or home insurance), or gender—is currently not included in the vulnerability index.[25] In some cases, these variables are not available or comparable for a large enough global sample, and in other cases variables are not considered to add sufficient information on vulnerability.

Measuring risk of and vulnerability to climate hazards needs further investments in data coverage for vulnerable regions and data integration of various relevant dimensions

To derive populations that are exposed to hazards, Doan et al. (2023) overlaid and resampled urbanization data (Global Human Settlement Layer) with gridded population data. Hazard intensities and probabilities were then matched with these cells to define the shares of urban and rural populations exposed to various hazard types. A key constraint is the different spatial resolution of indicators. Hazard data are resampled to match the population grids, so that each cell is classified exclusively as rural or urban and exposed or not exposed.[26] Resampling different spatial resolutions can introduce measurement error. For instance, floods are measured with a resolution close to 90 meters, whereas the spatial resolution is about 11 kilometers for cyclones and 30 kilometers for heat waves. Work is under way to develop a more fine-grained spatial resolution for heat waves, which, however, tend to be less localized than floods, for example.

In contrast to the availability of global gridded data on hazards, data on vulnerability come mostly from household surveys and are (a) much more spatially aggregated for several of the dimensions and (b) not available in surveys for all countries. As data on vulnerability are typically only representative or available at subnational administrative regions, assumptions on the distribution of characteristics along exposed and nonexposed grids within the region need to be made. For the risk indicator, it is assumed that populations in exposed and nonexposed areas do not differ along vulnerability characteristics. While this might be a strong assumption, Doan et al. (2023) tested assigning different vulnerability characteristics to exposed and nonexposed areas, and found that this approach would lead to a difference in results of less than one percentage point in most areas.

A person is considered vulnerable if they belong to a household deprived in any of the vulnerability dimensions. If all vulnerability indicators were collected for all countries in one survey, it is reasonable to directly infer whether a person is vulnerable along at least one dimension. While most data are available in the Global Monitoring Database (GMD), data on social protection, financial inclusion, and some of the nonincome dimensions missing in GMD for a particular country are based on other surveys, censuses, or administrative data sets.[27] Data from other sources are fused into the data from the GMD by randomly assigning households as vulnerable or nonvulnerable on the basis of the rate of vulnerability observed in the strata that the household belongs to (strata are based on information on rural versus urban area, welfare quintile, and subnational level, if available).[28] The share of vulnerable people (at least one dimension) is then calculated for the region for which the data are representative. These steps are repeated 100 times to account for household heterogeneity within each subgroup, and the final number is the average share of vulnerable households among these repetitions. This approach preserves the share of those who are vulnerable across data sets; however, inevitably, this imputation approach introduces some inaccuracy. The population at high risk from extreme hazards is then calculated by multiplying the share of vulnerable people by the population exposed.[29] Another important area for future research is whether being at risk already changes populations' behavior and welfare without the materialization of shocks.

A further caveat is that survey data are not available for every year across all countries, which affects this indicator as well as the monetary and nonmonetary poverty indicators. For instance, only 4 of the 40 countries that the World Bank classifies as Small States have all data required to construct the risk indicator, which mirrors their low survey data coverage mentioned above. Therefore, most Small Island States are not included in the sample, despite being at high risk from climate change (Thomas et al. 2020; Vousdoukas et al. 2023). In addition, within one country, data sources can be from different years, which could introduce measurement error into the imputation process. For some countries, the last available survey is too old to be included in the indicator. For income and consumption, there are well-founded methods of extrapolating and interpolating across years, but such methods are not available for the other indicators. Therefore, countries for which surveys are too old are excluded from the vulnerability indicator.

The best option to improve the measurement of vulnerability is to have better and more frequent household surveys. Including all indicators in comparable manners in household surveys across countries would reduce biases from the imputation process. Consultations on such harmonization are under way. More frequent surveys would offer a more accurate and up-to-date picture of vulnerability.

There is a trade-off between global and context-specific numbers, and the indicator does not capture indirect effects

One essential part of the measurement process of the risk indicator involves addressing the intensity and probability of hazards. For each hazard, an intensity level that corresponds to an extreme event and the probability that such an event occurs need to be selected to define the population exposed. The choice of intensity thresholds draws on literature to define what constitutes a severe event with potential to cause significant impacts to the welfare of the exposed population (World Bank 2024a). A limitation may be that there is a trade-off between global and context-specific numbers, because the impact of intensity levels can vary between contexts. The probability of occurrence for events is given by its return period, which reflects the likelihood that a hazard occurs at or above a specific intensity in a year. For all hazards except drought, a return period of 100 years is used. That period reflects a greater than 50 percent chance of experiencing an event during a person's lifetime.[30] For droughts, data go back only 39 years, and there is ongoing work to generate probabilistic scenarios.

In addition, the final measure of risk currently does not differentiate between populations that are more or less frequently affected by hazard events above respective thresholds or by various levels of intensity above the threshold. Furthermore, the cumulative effects of low-intensity but high-frequency events can also be sizable for people's welfare (Hallegatte et al. 2020). The effects of some hazards (for example, flooding and cyclones) are immediate, whereas others are slower (for instance, heat waves), and the costs of different types of hazards are likely to differ. The indicator thus reflects the extensive rather than intensive margin of impacts. Furthermore, probability distributions of hazards will likely change in the future because of climate change, and the most significant hazards for human welfare today are not necessarily the same as those that will matter most in the future. Doan et al. (2023) provide analyses of choosing different return periods for hazards. How climate change will affect return periods and how this will determine exposure rates of populations are areas of ongoing research.

A globally comparable indicator also implies that it may not be relevant to the same extent in all countries. For example, in the current measure, a household is considered vulnerable if no adult has primary education. Outside low-income countries, this threshold may not be relevant. Furthermore, some vulnerability dimensions may be more relevant to certain hazards than to others. Access to electricity makes the use of fans more likely, which reduces the impacts of heat waves (Carleton et al. 2022), but floods or storms may destroy electricity infrastructure. These interconnections between hazards and vulnerability remain an area for future work.

Also note that the indicator considers only the localized impact of the hazards. It does not reflect the indirect effects and spillovers of hazards, such as changes in prices or demand spurred by shocks in other regions (Cevik and Gwon 2024; Hallegatte et al. 2016). Capturing these indirect effects and transmission channels would require vast data, including localized input-output data. Exposure to extreme weather events through location can also be endogenous to hazards, as people affected by a weather shock once or multiple times will likely try to move (World Bank 2023).[31] Accounting for indirect effects is not feasible at this stage for a global indicator because of data requirements and the fact that they vary across settings (Cevik and Gwon 2024; Somanathan et al. 2021).

The measurement challenges for poverty, prosperity, and planetary indicators are amplified when future outcomes are projected

Challenges when future outcomes are projected can be broadly grouped into two categories. The first is the uncertainty of modeling what will happen to future poverty and planetary indicators when considered in isolation. Figure 4.7 shows projections of gross domestic product (GDP) per capita from five scenarios of the Shared Socioeconomic Pathways (SSPs) and the models of the Organisation for Economic Co-operation and Development (OECD) and the International Institute of Applied Systems Analysis (IIASA) (Crespo Cuaresma 2017; Dellink et al. 2017). These scenarios are used extensively, for instance, by the Intergovernmental Panel on Climate Change (IPCC) and are useful in depicting various scenarios of how the world could evolve in the future and how the scenarios could lead to different emission and global warming paths (IPCC 2023). As can be seen in figure 4.7, projected GDP per capita varies substantially across scenarios and models, depending on assumptions about how the global economy will evolve and the model used. If countries' incomes grow in accordance with the most optimistic scenarios, then global extreme poverty, and even poverty at higher lines, will be eliminated within decades.[32] These projections have been criticized for being misaligned from historical experiences (Welch 2024). This is most relevant for low-income countries, where projected growth rates in the next decades exceed experienced growth rates by several orders of magnitude. If historical growth performances continue in the coming decades, then extreme poverty is unlikely to fall drastically in the coming decades (see chapter 1). Global emissions may likewise evolve on very different paths, depending on the use of fossil fuels and the adoption of mitigation policies. See annex 4C for more details on how greenhouse gas (GHG) emissions are tracked.

FIGURE 4.7

Projections of GDP per capita vary significantly between Shared Socioeconomic Pathways

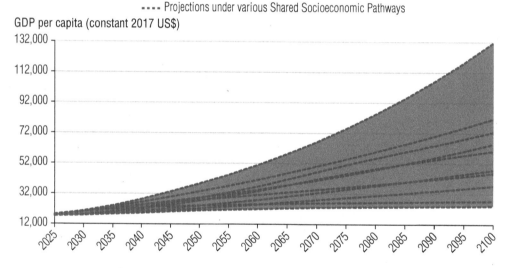

Source: Shared Socioeconomic Pathways (SSPs projection data, accessed through the IIASA SSP Scenario Explorer 3.0.1).
Note: GDP = gross domestic product; IIASA = International Institute of Applied Systems Analysis; OECD = Organisation for Economic Co-operation and Development; SSPs = Shared Socioeconomic Pathways. Each line represents GDP per capita projection from one of the five SSPs from either the IIASA model (Crespo Cuaresma 2017) or the OECD model (Dellink et al. 2017).

The second category of uncertainty emerges when the interdependence of poverty, prosperity, and planetary indicators is analyzed. There is broad consensus that global warming (due to anthropogenic [human-caused] emissions) will have negative consequences for economic growth and poverty reduction in the future and that rising temperatures and climate hazards are already affecting large populations (Dang,

Cong Nguyen, and Trinh 2023; Hallegatte and Walsh 2021). However, there is considerable uncertainty around the exact extent of future economic damages caused by climate change. Burke, Hsiang, and Miguel (2015) found that global GDP could be reduced by 20 to 30 percent by the end of the century, while Nordhaus (1992) suggests a reduction of 2 to 3 percent in a no-abatement scenario. Newell et al. (2021) ran 800 plausible models linking temperature to GDP and found that in the best-performing models, global GDP changes due to warming at the end of the century range from 84 percent losses to 359 percent gains. To these uncertainties should be added the uncertainties regarding the within-country distributional impact of temperature changes, as well as the many other impacts of climate change related to extreme weather events, such as tipping points and sea level rise. Predicting human behavior and adaptation, as well as changes in policies, is nearly impossible but will have a crucial impact on planetary outcomes and on how these planetary factors translate into poverty or prosperity.

When these two uncertainties are compounded—the uncertainties related to what will happen to poverty and emissions in the future and uncertainty in modeling the interaction between them—the range of possible future outcomes is massive. According to one paper that addressed parts of these uncertainties, the additional number of people in extreme poverty in 2070 due to the impacts of climate change could be anywhere from 4 million to 306 million (Moyer et al. 2023). A direct result of this uncertainty is a large variance in the social cost of carbon, which is a frequent input to loss and damage calculations and cost-benefit analysis of current mitigation policies. Work must continue to reduce the range of these uncertainties.

Data underpin the development process and should be prioritized

Data are the foundation for impactful, evidence-based policy making. Without data, understanding and acting to improve the welfare of people are impossible. Policy makers working to alleviate poverty, build resilience, and promote sustainable well-being need accurate data to make informed decisions, particularly in an environment with increasing uncertainty, misinformation, and limited budgets.

The value of data to facilitate development and ensure that no one is left behind—as encapsulated in the SDGs—can be enhanced if data are reliable and timely and can be disaggregated by key demographic characteristics. Data not only help governments with service delivery, preparing for and responding to emergencies, and prioritizing marginalized, underserved population subgroups, but also provide the populace with the information they need to hold governments accountable and to make better political decisions, for example, during elections (Jolliffe et al. 2023; World Bank 2015, 2021).

The good news is that the world is facing a data revolution brought about by the explosion of data generation and the advancement of technologies to collect, store, process, and analyze large volumes of data. This revolution has been fueled by the proliferation of digital devices, social media, sensors, and other technologies that generate vast amounts of data in real time. The key is to determine how to turn data into information and information into insights that can enable better decision-making and ultimately help people.

While data availability has improved in many countries, less than one-half of the poorest countries in the world had a household survey from 2020 or later available for global monitoring. More investment is needed to produce reliable, granular, and timely information. This requires foundational efforts to strengthen national statistical systems and innovative approaches to advance the frontier of data and modeling for welfare analysis. Collaborative efforts to develop and promote best practices and AI-driven solutions that enhance every stage of the entire data life cycle are essential. As the lived experience of poverty goes well beyond what can be captured by monetary measures, it is important to ensure that data efforts are also invested in understanding other dimensions of well-being, such as deprivations in access to and the quality of services, health, or food security.

Annex 4A. Measuring food security

The most commonly used definition of food security was agreed upon by stakeholders at the 1996 World Food Summit, with the original formulation stating that food security is "a situation that exists when all people, at all times, have physical, social and economic access to sufficient, safe and nutritious food that meets their dietary needs and food preferences for an active and healthy life" (FAO 1996). In practice, food security is described through four dimensions: (a) food availability, or the existence of enough food for people to eat; (b) food access, or the ability of individuals to financially afford and physically access food that is available to eat; (c) food utilization, or the ability of individuals to properly absorb the micro- and macronutrients in the foods that they eat; and (d) stability, or individuals being food secure in all dimensions at all times (Barrett 2010).

The dimensions of food security are hierarchical in the order listed above, where adequacy in a food security dimension requires adequacy in the previous dimension. For example, adequate food availability is necessary, but not sufficient, for adequate food access. The chain continues all the way through food stability. Furthermore, each dimension of food security is itself multidimensional. For example, food access includes both the consumption of an adequate number of calories and a sufficient quality of food consumed (Barrett 2010).

As described above, the food security outcomes tracked in the Corporate Scorecard—the FIES and the share of children under age five who are stunted—correspond to measures of food access and food utilization, respectively. Although these are important indicators, a more complete assessment of changes in food and nutrition security requires measures of the four separate dimensions of food and nutrition security.

Food access dimensions are particularly difficult to measure precisely. There are two separate sources of measurement error introduced in the measurement of food access. First, it is difficult to precisely measure the caloric and nutritional content of all food consumed. Although there are several ways to estimate these figures, the methods that produce the most precise estimates involve individual-level surveys that are complex, expensive, difficult to analyze, and nearly impossible to perform on a large scale (Fiedler, Martin-Prével, and Moursi 2013; Gibson 2005).[33] In the absence of these difficult-to-collect and expensive data, researchers often turn to household consumption and expenditure surveys (HCESs) to measure the quantity and quality of foods consumed (Wiesmann et al. 2009).

Using HCESs provides a solution, but it brings challenges in measuring the caloric and nutritional content of each food item consumed (Haytowitz et al. 2019). It is also difficult with these surveys to identify the nutritional content of many processed foods and food consumed outside the household that are becoming increasingly important to modern diets (Subramanian and Deaton 1996). These issues compound other traditional sources of measurement error that affect the measurement of expenditure in HCESs, such as recall biases, impacts of different questionnaire formats, and a wide variety of other concerns (Beegle et al. 2012). The variance in estimates of the quantity and quality of food consumption is therefore large and is potentially increasing over time as households consume more processed foods and meals outside the household (Tandon and Landes 2011, 2014).[34]

Given these difficulties and the need to obtain estimates of food access in real time and in data-poor environments, practitioners and researchers have increasingly relied on metrics that are relatively easy to implement, while also approximating the degree of food access in its many dimensions (Maxwell and Caldwell 2008; Swindale and Bilinksy 2006; World Food Programme 2009). Two common approaches include (a) measuring dietary diversity and the frequency with which individuals and households consume certain food groups, such as with the Food Consumption Score and the Household Dietary Diversity Score (Swindale and Bilinksy 2006; World Food Programme 2009), and (b) measuring food coping strategies often associated with consuming too little or consuming a poor-quality diet, such as the Coping Strategies Index and the Reduced Coping Strategies Index (Maxwell and Caldwell 2008).

Others have argued that additional psychological aspects related to food access should be captured in standard metrics (Webb et al. 2006). An additional set of experiential measures of food access—such as the Food Insecurity Experience Scale, the Latin America and Caribbean Food Security Scale, and the Household Food Insecurity Access Scale—extend food access measurement to these dimensions by asking about food coping strategies and anxiety over insufficient food access (Maxwell, Vaitla, and Coates 2014). However, there are significant additional challenges to incorporating anxiety regarding poor food access and other subjective measures. In particular, answers to subjective welfare questions depend on respondent-specific scales that (a) may not be comparable across individuals or stable over time, (b) are potentially subject to frame-of-reference effects, and (c) suffer from measurement errors, over and above those affecting traditional welfare metrics (Benjamin et al. 2023; Ravallion 2012; Tandon 2024).

Using multiple measures can be useful for obtaining a more complete picture. There is a growing body of literature illustrating that many of the food access metrics described above lead to different conclusions when collected from the same household (Broussard and Tandon 2016; Maxwell, Vaitla, and Coates 2014). Because of these factors, it is often recommended that food access be captured using more than one measure and that improvement in food access should be validated across each broad category of food access metrics, using at least one dietary diversity-based indicator and at least one coping-strategy-based indicator (IPC 2023; Vaitla et al. 2017). Using evidence from 10 West African countries, Lain, Tandon, and Vishwanath (2023) illustrated that there are similar prevalences of food insecurity among segments of the population that are likely undernourished and segments that are likely not undernourished in 4 of 10 countries, according to the FIES. Furthermore, they found that there is a relatively large prevalence of food insecurity in the segments of the population that are least likely to be undernourished in 5 of the 10 countries according to the FIES. Although the work cannot identify exactly why these differences exist between the FIES and other food access metrics for several countries, one possibility highlighted is the difficulty in interpreting the subjective questions on food access that are a significant component of the measure.

Although best practices suggest using multiple food access metrics at the household level to validate changes in food access, the FIES is the only household-level indicator that is currently available globally. The only other indicator available is the PoU, which is calculated from a combination of national accounts data, food balance sheets, and household surveys (FAO et al. 2023). Thus, it is important to interpret changes in the FIES along with changes in the PoU and to corroborate changes by using closely aligned measures, including extreme poverty (Lain, Tandon, and Vishwanath 2023).[35]

These challenges of using multiple food access metrics also exist at the country level, so it is important to aim to collect multiple measures. A recent stock-taking exercise of the statistical system across regions found significant gaps in the types of information available for measuring progress in improving food access (Maxwell, Vishwanath, and Tandon 2024). For example, in the East Asia and Pacific region, of 16 countries covered by World Bank global poverty databases,[36] only one collected more than a single food access metric in the most recent household survey from which monetary poverty was estimated. Furthermore, of these countries, eight collected only the FIES and six collected no food security information at all (Maxwell, Vishwanath, and Tandon 2024). Given the difficulties in following best practices within individual countries regarding the measurement of changes in food access, the same caveats that apply at the global level also apply to the vast majority of individual countries.

Efforts are under way to improve global and country monitoring of food access. In particular, Maxwell, Vishwanath, and Tandon (2024) identified how existing information contained in the detailed food consumption modules in the extensive collection of household consumption surveys from across the world can be used. Their work illustrates for a set of West African countries that existing data can be used to construct measures of calorie consumption, undernourishment, and diet quality and that these indicators all align well with more standard and existing food access metrics. Their work further offers guidance on how best to improve food access measurement in national statistical systems going forward, including multiple food access metrics in each survey, use of more of the consumption data to refine existing food security statistics, and ways that might reduce some of the noise in trying to infer the calorie content of consumption quantified using nonstandard units.

Annex 4B. Data used for climate hazards

The new World Bank livable planet indicator on the percentage of people at high risk from climate-related hazards globally is defined as the share of the world's population that is both exposed to a set of key climate-related hazards (floods, droughts, cyclones, and heat waves) and highly vulnerable (that is, have a propensity to be adversely affected or unable to cope with the impacts). Specifically, people are counted as at high risk from climate-related hazards if they are exposed to at least one hazard and are identified as highly vulnerable in at least one dimension of vulnerability. The remainder of this section summarizes key data sources related to hazards and ongoing work to improve the estimates. More information can be found in Doan et al. (2023).

Droughts

The new indicator uses historic agricultural drought frequency data from the Food and Agriculture Organization depicting the annual frequency of severe drought events from 1984 to 2022. These events are defined according to the Agricultural Stress Index (ASI), based on remote sensing vegetation (Landsat Normalized Difference Vegetation Index) and land surface temperature (BT4) data, combined with historical agricultural cropping cycles. Severe drought is identified when a Vegetation Health Index falls below 35 percent over a growing season. The ASI value represents the percentage of affected crop or grassland pixels within each administrative unit. Annual frequencies are converted into approximate return periods, with any location recording at least one severe drought from 1984 to 2022 considered exposed to a 39-year return period event.[37] The data set, restricted to rural areas, maps regions where more than 30 percent or 50 percent of cropland or grassland was affected in any growing season, with return periods ranging from 5 years to 39 years based on historical frequency. An area of ongoing work is to generate probabilistic estimates of drought using this data, to derive 100-year return periods which are used for the other hazards.

Floods

The indicator uses modeled pluvial and fluvial flood maps from the 2019 Fathom Global 2.0 flood hazard data set. Fluvial floods result from rivers overflowing because of intense precipitation or snowmelt, while pluvial floods occur from heavy rainfall leading to saturated soil or overwhelmed drainage systems. The Fathom data set provides maximum inundation depths for these floods at a resolution of approximately 90 meters, covering return periods from 5 years to 1,000 years. Note that the data assume no flood defenses, which might overestimate exposure in some regions, particularly those with effective flood protection.

For coastal flooding, the indicator uses a separate data set by Deltares (2021), which models flooding caused by tides and storm surges at the same resolution and using the same digital elevation model as Fathom 2.0. The coastal flood data depict maximum depths for return periods from 0 to 250 years. The Fathom flood maps for 231 countries were merged to create global fluvial and pluvial maps for each return period, which were then combined with the global coastal flood maps to produce a comprehensive global flood hazard map. This map, covering return periods from 5 years to 100 years, shows the maximum inundation depth of any flood type. An update to Fathom 3.0 is planned for the coming year.

Heat waves

The indicator uses modeled five-day heat wave maps from the World Bank Climate Change Knowledge Portal. This probabilistic data set shows the maximum five-day average of the daily maximum Environmental Stress Index (ESI) at a resolution of approximately 30 kilometers for return periods between 5 years and 100 years. The ESI approximates the wet bulb globe temperature using temperature, relative humidity, and solar radiation, adjusted for systematic underestimation from solar radiation. Derived from hourly ERA5[38] climate reanalysis data, the maximum five-day average was calculated for each year from 1950 through 2022, detrended, and fit to generalized extreme value distributions to estimate return levels for a five-day heat wave event. Ongoing work aims to develop a more spatially detailed measure of heat, to increase measurement accuracy and align with other indicators.

Cyclones

The indicator uses global modeled tropical cyclone maps from Bloemendaal et al. (2020). The tropical cyclone data set is created using the Synthetic Tropical cyclOne geneRation Model (STORM), which resamples 38 years of historical cyclone track data from the International Best Track Archive for Climate Stewardship (IBTrACS). This extends the data set to represent 10,000 years of cyclone activity, covering all tropical cyclone basins except the South Atlantic (because of insufficient historical data). The results were validated against historical observations and previous studies. The STORM data set shows the maximum 10-minute average sustained wind speed at a resolution of approximately 11 kilometers for return periods from 10 years to 10,000 years. While it does not include storm surge and heavy precipitation, these factors are considered in modeled flood maps and included in the multihazard analysis.

Annex 4C. Tracking GHG emissions

Greenhouse gas (GHG) emissions from stationary sources, such as power plants and industrial processes, can be estimated with a high degree of precision by using Continuous Emissions Monitoring Systems (CEMS), automated tools to constantly track and analyze various pollutants. Specialized satellites equipped with imaging spectrometers designed to measure vertical-column abundances of GHGs also play a crucial role in providing GHG data from stationary sources. Modern satellite systems can achieve spatial resolutions of approximately 30 meters, allowing for detailed mapping of emissions sources, including from specific emission facilities and individual gas fields and oil wells. Yet they can also cover large areas, with some systems having a field of up to 35 square kilometers. Data gaps in coverage due to infrequent passes, insufficient spatial resolution, and atmospheric interference introduce challenges, however. Data from satellite systems such as GHGSat and the National Aeronautic and Space Administration's EMIT mission, when combined with airborne and ground-based measurements, can create a comprehensive GHG monitoring picture.

Emissions of CO_2 from combustion activities (representing 71 percent of global emissions in 2022) are estimated by using CEMS and, where such systems are absent, supplemented with Fuel Analysis Methods (FAM) and Emission Factors and Default Values Methods (EFDVM). These methods combine estimates of (a) the quantities of fuels that are combusted to support human activities and (b) the pollutant content of those fuels, per the 2006 IPCC guidelines for GHG inventories (IPCC 2006), to arrive at volumes of GHGs emitted. While FAM and EFDVM are less accurate than CEMS, the estimated accuracy of emissions from fossil fuel combustion and industrial processes combined is deemed high, since the quantities of fossil fuels and other emissive materials produced (such as cement and steel) are well known (Crippa et al. 2023). Global total GHG emissions are estimated with an accuracy of approximately ±10 percent and at the country level are estimated with an accuracy of between ±4 and ±35 percent (Crippa et al. 2023).

Estimating noncombustion GHG emissions, including methane (22 percent of global emissions in 2022), nitrous oxide (5 percent of global emissions in 2022), and fluorinated gases (F-gases) (3 percent of global emissions in 2022), requires more nuanced methods. For non-land use sectors, emission estimates are generally based on estimates of specific activities, the mixture of technologies used to support the activities, country-specific emissions factors, and reduction factors that reflect levels of abatement equipment installed.

Estimating GHG emissions from land use, land use change, and forestry (LULUCF) is challenging because of the complexity of terrestrial ecosystems and the difficulties of disentangling natural from anthropogenic fluxes. Net emissions from managed lands can vary substantially, depending on the type and age of vegetation and human activities, and uniform global data for these components are not available. There are also often discrepancies between measurement approaches (Friedlingstein et al. 2020; Grassi et al. 2023). Differences arise from the definition of land use (change): for instance, whether absorbed carbon from managed forests is counted in national emissions. See Crippa et al. (2023), European Commission (n.d.), IPCC (2006), and National Academies of Sciences, Engineering, and Medicine (2022).

The primary sources of GHG emissions data include national inventories, national statistical offices, satellite observations, country reports, and sector-specific measurements. National activities and inventories, compiled and submitted to international bodies such as the United

Nations Framework Convention on Climate Change (UNFCCC) and the United Nations Food and Agricultural Organization, directly provide country-and sector-level emissions data or activity data that may be used to impute emissions. However, there are different GHG reporting requirements set for Annex I (industrialized) and non-Annex I (nonindustrialized) economies under the Kyoto protocol, which has led to different qualities and reliabilities of data between these countries.[39] Sector-specific measurements focus on key emission sources such as energy production, transportation, and agriculture.

Secondary providers synthesize data from original providers such as the UNFCCC and national statistical offices, using standardized IPCC methodologies to present GHG data that can be useful to the research community and analysts and for rapid visualization. These organizations, which include Climate Watch, Global Carbon Budget, Our World in Data, the Joint Research Center's Emissions Database for Global Atmospheric Research (EDGAR), and the Pacific Northwest National Laboratory Community Emissions Data System, among others, often count sources differently, which may lead to some divergence in imputed emissions, but which often is not of concern since the source of discrepancy is typically known or can be identified.

Despite advancements in technology and data integration, challenges in achieving comprehensive real-time global coverage of emissions, standardizing measurement methodologies, and ensuring data accuracy and transparency remain. Ongoing efforts aim to address these challenges and improve the timeliness, precision, and reliability of GHG emissions data.

The World Bank's new indicator of global GHG emissions is based on EDGAR, augmented by preliminary estimates for LULUCF using a hybrid-inventory approach developed for the Joint Research Center's annual report, *GHG Emissions of All World Countries: 2023* (Crippa et al. 2023). For more highly disaggregated, country-level non-LULUCF emissions, the new indicator uses a more granular EDGAR data set (EDGAR v8.0), which includes national estimates of annual emissions disaggregated by 37 subsectors and all GHGs included in the Kyoto protocol—CO_2, methane, and nitrous oxide, as well as 25 different fluorinated gases—from 1970 to 2022.[40] These data, when aggregated to the global level, are nearly identical to the EDGAR Report data. To account for the discrepancy in global EDGAR values and the aggregation of national LULUCF data from Grassi et al. (2023), the new indicator includes a small residual factor by sector and gas.

While GHG emissions started to accelerate during the nineteenth century, when industrialization began, this report depicts more recent trends in emissions because disaggregated data—for example, data disaggregated by type of GHG or economic sector (including LULUCF)—are available only since 1990; for all sectors for most countries, they have been available only since 2000. Some GHG emissions remain in the atmosphere for centuries.[41] Reducing emissions going forward is essential to limit future impacts of climate change (Eyring et al. 2021; IPCC 2023).[42] Recent scientific evidence points to a linear relationship between cumulative emissions and average global temperatures, underscoring the importance of tracking countries' efforts to lower GHG emissions.

Notes

1. Several SDGs rely on survey data, including SDGs 1 (no poverty), 2 (zero hunger), 3 (good health and well-being), 4 (quality education), 5 (gender equality), 6 (clean water and sanitation), 7 (affordable and clean energy), 8 (decent work and economic growth), 10 (reduced inequalities), 11 (sustainable cities and communities), 16 (peace, justice, and strong institutions), and 17 (partnerships for the goals).

2. For example, the World Bank, in collaboration with the West African Economic and Monetary Union Commission, has contributed to two rounds of comparable and high-quality survey data sets for member countries in 2018/19 and 2021/22 (Castañeda Aguilar et al. 2022, 2024).

3. Previous versions of this report—which were called *Poverty and Shared Prosperity Reports*—typically had a three-year lag in reporting baseline (based on surveys) global poverty and shared prosperity estimates. More recent data ensure that at least one-half of the population globally, and in low- and lower-middle-income countries, is covered by a recent survey, which is the coverage threshold required for reporting the global poverty aggregate (World Bank 2024b).

4. For example, about one-half of the 26 economies in East Asia and Pacific are islands with small populations and have infrequent surveys. A similar reason explains the difference in country- and population-coverage for high-income countries, although survey data are also unavailable for some large high-income countries, such as Japan. Hence, population-weighted coverage rates in high-income countries are less than those of upper-middle-income countries.

5. The potential benefits of data are almost limitless. There are direct benefits to individuals and indirect benefits or spillovers to society. Data can be used, reused, shared, and reshared for several purposes, both intended and unintended (World Bank 2021). However, like all public goods, because data are nonrivalrous and nonexcludable in consumption, private producers are unable to charge commensurate prices to cover the huge cost of production and reflect the marginal benefits accruing to all consumers. As a result, unless governments intervene, data will remain scarce.

6. Since the introduction of the Data for Policy initiative in 2020, the World Bank has loaned $2 billion to 40 countries for related work, mostly in Sub-Saharan Africa (Dabalen, Himelein, and Castelan 2020).

7. For more information, see the investment case "Multiplying Progress through Data Ecosystems" at https://www.data4sdgs.org/sites/default/files/file_uploads/Investment%2Bcase_Multiplying%2Bprogress%2Bthrough%2Bdata%2Becosystems_vFINAL.pdf.

8. Poverty mapping tries to overcome the limited sample size of household surveys by combining their data with other data sets that allow for a finer spatial disaggregation, such as census data (for example, see Elbers et al. [2003]).

9. While harmonized income and consumption distributions are available for the majority of countries, wealth distributions are not. Understanding the distribution of wealth is critical to get a comprehensive picture of material inequality. See box 2.3 in chapter 2 for further details.

10. Consumption typically fluctuates less than income across time, since individuals borrow or draw from their savings when income is lower and save when income is higher, making consumption less volatile.

11. Conceptually, income is a measure of the potential purchasing power for all goods and services, while consumption is a direct measure of the goods and services that the individual or household has actually obtained. Richer households tend to save more than poorer households. This means that, on average, the inequality of consumption (realized outcomes) is usually lower than the inequality of income for the same set of households. In addition, while consumption tends to fluctuate less over time, income is generally more volatile in the sense that it may be influenced greatly by seasonal factors or by interruptions in employment—particularly in the agricultural and informal sectors. Households can also declare zero and even negative income on a survey but exhibit a positive consumption level by drawing from savings. Sudden losses of employment can reduce income dramatically, but changes in consumption depend on the availability of factors such as safety nets and

within- and between-household transfers and on whether shocks are transitory or permanent (Jappelli and Pistaferri 2010). Other issues, such as consumption of home-produced foods, also tend to be difficult to capture in surveys, leading to low measured income.

12. All comparisons of consumption and income in PIP are based on separate surveys conducted using income and consumption. Hence, even in the same year, they may not use the same survey design and most likely capture results for different households.

13. While most of the literature has focused on income data, there is also evidence that expenditure surveys underestimate the top because of incomplete coverage of spending on durables (Aguiar and Bils 2015).

14. Note that for many high-income countries, PIP uses European Union Statistics on Income and Living Conditions surveys, which in some cases make adjustments to the survey data using administrative data.

15. For countries in Latin America and the Caribbean, the post-tax disposable income series is not available in WID. Other regions in PIP primarily use consumption surveys.

16. Survey comparability depends on various characteristics such as the sampling process, questionnaire, methodological changes in the construction of welfare aggregates, consistent price deflation over time and space, and so on. PIP contains metadata on the comparability of poverty estimates within countries over time. For further details on the comparability assessment, see Atamanov et al. (2019) and the PIP *Methodological Handbook* (https://datanalytics.worldbank.org/PIP-Methodology/).

17. For details, refer to https://wid.world/transparency/.

18. For a summary of the recent debate on the top income shares in the United States, see Gale et al. (2023).

19. The comparison includes data for all years that are available in both sources. To maximize the sample, comparability breaks in PIP are not accounted for. WID does not report comparability breaks.

20. For details, refer to https://ophi.org.uk/.

21. Under plausible and empirically supported assumptions, undernourishment is concentrated among the extreme poor. Thus, the degree of overlap between the FIES and extreme poverty is informative on whether those who are moderately or severely food insecure are most likely to be undernourished.

22. See World Bank (n.d.) for further details on data sources and measurement for the included hazards and vulnerability indicators (https://scorecard.worldbank.org/en/scorecard/home).

23. Wildfires are also direct consequences of human activity, such as arson or negligence, and global data availability limits the accuracy of predictions, for instance, because effects can be felt in different locations than where fires themselves are (think of smoke and air pollution) (Qiu et al. 2024).

24. The dimensions are income, education, social protection, financial inclusion, water, energy, and transport.

25. Natural disasters disproportionally affect women in terms of income, employment, and life expectancy (Erman et al. 2021). Power dynamics and traditional gender roles influence how women are affected by natural disasters and how they are able to cope in the aftermath (Lankes et al. 2024). Extreme weather events have been shown to increase domestic violence against women (Abiona and Koppensteiner 2018; Sekhri and Storeygard 2014). Access to assets and control of them are important determinants of vulnerability to climate change, according to which women are highly disadvantaged within households. Women still shoulder the majority of domestic work—a situation that becomes even more pronounced after disasters, hindering their ability to pursue or resume employment (Eastin 2018; Erman et al. 2021). Not being able to engage in income-generating activities further reduces long-run opportunities and exacerbates vulnerabilities. Eastin (2018) showed that climate shocks and natural disasters are associated with declines in women's economic and social rights and that this decline is more pronounced in poorer and more agricultural societies.

26. Note that the urban versus rural distinction is relevant for drought hazards and transport as a physical propensity to experience severe loss (vulnerability). Both are measured only for rural areas.

27. Other data sources include World Bank ASPIRE (Atlas of Social Protection Indicators of Resilience and Equity) (social protection), World Bank Findex (financial inclusion), World Bank Global

Electrification Database (energy), the WHO/UNICEF (World Health Organization/United Nations Children's Fund) Joint Monitoring Programme (water), and the United Nations Sustainable Development Center indicator (transport).

28. For countries that have some missing data but near-universal values for certain variables (such as electricity, water, or social protection access), the near-universal value is assumed for the whole population.

    The definition of variables can vary across surveys. For example, surveys in the GMD typically include a variable for "improved water access." The relevant variable for the SDGs and for the World Bank Scorecard indicator, however, is access to "basic drinking water, sanitation services, or hygiene," which could make comparisons between indicators difficult. Please see World Bank (n.d.) for further details.

29. Note that to aggregate grid-level exposure to subnational regions, the population count in grid cells that are partially covered by administrative units is weighted by the fraction of the grid cell covered by the statistical region.

30. A 100-year return period means that, on average, a specific event occurs once every 100 years. Naturally, this means that it can occur more often than once in 100 years. With an average global life expectancy of around 70 years, the probability of experiencing an extreme weather event with a 100-year return period is about 50 percent.

31. The effect of climate shocks on migration is complex where household responses depend on levels of assets and risks of staying and where rapid-onset shocks (such as floods) have stronger effects than slow-onset changes (Kaczan and Orgill-Meyer 2020).

32. The SSPs are a set of five scenarios developed by the climate research community that depict various pathways of how global society, demographics, and economics might change over the next century and how these changes could affect GHG emissions and global warming (Riahi et al. 2017).

33. For example, one method is observed-weighted food record data. See Gibson (2005) for details.

34. In addition to the difficulty of measuring the nutritional content of food consumed, the second source of measurement error in measuring food access is driven by the fact that many of the dietary needs of individuals are unobservable and based on individual choices and activities (Institute of Medicine 2006). Although many studies make assumptions regarding caloric needs of individuals based on their age, sex, and assumed activity level (FAO et al. 2023), such uncertainties further add to the extensive measurement error in food access metrics.

35. Under plausible and empirically supported assumptions, undernourishment is concentrated among the extreme poor. Thus, the degree of overlap between the FIES and extreme poverty is informative concerning whether those who are moderately or severely food insecure are most likely to be undernourished.

36. These figures omit countries in which the most recent household survey was fielded before the FIES was developed in 2014.

37. A return period refers to the average time it takes for an event at a specific intensity level to occur or, put differently, the probability of an event occurring every year.

38. ERA5 is the fifth generation of the European Centre for Medium-Range Weather Forecasts atmospheric reanalysis of the global climate (covering 1940 to the present).

39. See, for example, reporting requirements for Annex I countries (https://unfccc.int/process-and-meetings/transparency-and-reporting/reporting-and-review-under-the-convention/greenhouse-gas-inventories-annex-i-parties/reporting-requirements), and for a classification of countries under the Kyoto protocol, see https://unfccc.int/parties-observers#:~:text=Non%2DAnnex%20I%20Parties%20are,prone%20to%20desertification%20and%20drought.

40. EDGAR v8.0's GHG estimates for combustion and industrial processes are based on the application of IPCC GHG accounting methodology across all countries. EDGAR uses data from the IEA, Energy Institute, UNFCCC, Food and Agriculture Organization, and other reputable sources to derive GHG emissions at subnational and subsectoral levels based on activity and emission factors. (European Commission. n.d.)

41. CO_2 remains in the atmosphere on average for hundreds of years, whereas methane remains in the atmosphere for around 12 years, but methane is more potent in absorbing energy and causing warming per unit of mass.
42. Cumulative historical emissions are shown in chapter 3 with data from PRIMAP-hist (Gütschow, Pflüger, and Busch 2024).

References

Abiona, Olukorede, and Martin Foureaux Koppensteiner. 2018. "The Impact of Household Shocks on Domestic Violence: Evidence from Tanzania." Discussion Paper 11992, IZA, Rochester, NY. https://doi.org/10.2139/ssrn.3301756.

Aguiar, Mark, and Mark Bils. 2015. "Has Consumption Inequality Mirrored Income Inequality?" *American Economic Review* 105 (9): 2725–56. https://doi.org/10.1257/aer.20120599.

Alvaredo, Facundo, François Bourguignon, Francisco H. G. Ferreira, and Nora Lustig. 2023. "Seventy-Five Years of Measuring Income Inequality in Latin America." III Working Paper 111, International Inequalities Institute, London. https://www.lse.ac.uk/International-Inequalities/Publications/Working-Papers.

Andrée, Bo Peter Johannes, Andres Chamorro, Aart Kraay, Phoebe Spencer, and Dieter Wang. 2020. "Predicting Food Crises." Policy Research Working Paper 9412, World Bank, Washington, DC.

Angrist, Noam, Pinelopi K. Goldberg, and Dean Jolliffe. 2021. "Why Is Growth in Developing Countries So Hard to Measure?" *Journal of Economic Perspectives* 35 (3): 215–42. https://doi.org/10.1257/jep.35.3.215.

Atkinson, Anthony B., and Thomas Piketty, eds. 2007. *Top Incomes Over the Twentieth Century: A Contrast Between European and English-Speaking Countries.* New York: Oxford University Press.

Auten, Gerald, and David Splinter. 2024. "Income Inequality in the United States: Using Tax Data to Measure Long-Term Trends." *Journal of Political Economy* 132 (7): 2179–2227. https://doi.org/10.1086/728741.

Barrett, Christopher B. 2010. "Measuring Food Insecurity." *Science* 327 (5967): 825–28.

Beegle, Kathleen, Joachim De Weerdt, Jed Friedman, and John Gibson. 2012. "Methods of Household Consumption Measurement through Surveys: Experimental Results from Tanzania." *Journal of Development Economics* 98 (1): 3–18.

Benjamin, Daniel J., Jakina Debnam Guzman, Marc Fleurbaey, Ori Heffetz, and Miles Kimball. 2023. "What Do Happiness Data Mean? Theory and Survey Evidence." *Journal of the European Economic Association* 21 (6): 2377–412. https://doi.org/10.1093/jeea/jvad026.

Blanchet, Thomas, and Lucas Chancel. 2016. "National Accounts Series Methodology." WID.world Working Paper Series no. 2016/1, Wealth & Income Database.

Bloemendaal, Nadia, Ivan D. Haigh, Hans de Moel, Sanne Muis, Reindert J. Haarsma, and Jeroen C. J. H. Aerts. 2020. "Generation of a Global Synthetic Tropical Cyclone Hazard Dataset using STORM." *Scientific Data* 7 (1): 40. https://doi.org/10.1038/s41597-020-0381-2.

Broussard, Nzinga H., and Sharad Tandon, ed. 2016. *Food Insecurity Measures: Experience-Based Versus Nutrition-Based Evidence From India, Bangladesh, and Ethiopia.* Economic Research Report 220. Washington, DC: US Department of Agriculture. https://doi.org/10.22004/ag.econ.262189.

Burke, Marshall, Solomon M. Hsiang, and Edward Miguel. 2015. "Global Non-linear Effect of Temperature on Economic Production." *Nature* 527: 235–39. https://doi.org/10.1038/nature15725.

Burkhauser, Richard V., Markus H. Hahn, and Roger Wilkins. 2015. "Measuring Top Incomes Using Tax Record Data: A Cautionary Tale from Australia." *The Journal of Economic Inequality* 13 (2): 181–205. https://doi.org/10.1007/s10888-014-9281-z.

Carletto, Calogero, Haoyi Chen, Talip Kilic, and Francesca Perucci. 2022. "Positioning Household Surveys for the Next Decade." *Statistical Journal of the IAOS* 38: 923–46.

Castañeda Aguilar, R. Andrés, Aziz Atamanov, Carolina Diaz-Bonilla, Dean Jolliffe, Christoph Lakner, Jose Montes, Daniel Gerszon Mahler, et al. 2019. "September 2019 PovcalNet Update: What's New." Global Poverty Monitoring Technical Note 10, World Bank, Washington, DC. https://doi.org/10.1596/32478.

Castañeda Aguilar, R. Andrés, Adriana Castillo, Nancy P. Devpura, Reno Dewina, Carolina Diaz-Bonilla, Ifeanyi Edochie, Maria G. Farfan Bertran, et al. 2024. "March 2024 Update to the Poverty and Inequality Platform (PIP): What's New." Global Poverty Monitoring Technical Note 36, World Bank, Washington, DC. https://doi.org/10.1596/41341.

Castañeda Aguilar, R. Andrés, Reno Dewina, Carolina Diaz-Bonilla, Ifeanyi N. Edochie, Tony H. M. J. Fujs, Dean M. Jolliffe, et al. 2022. "April 2022 Update to the Poverty and Inequality Platform (PIP): What's New." Global Poverty Monitoring Technical Note 20, World Bank, Washington, DC. https://ideas.repec.org//p/wbk/wbgpmt/20.html.

Cevik, Serhan, and Gyowon Gwon. 2024. "This is Going to Hurt: Weather Anomalies, Supply Chain Pressures and Inflation." IMF Working Paper 2024/079, International Monetary Fund, Washington, DC. https://doi.org/10.5089/9798400273292.001.

Chin, Moya. 2021. "What Are Global Public Goods?" Finance & Development, December 2021. https://www.imf.org/en/Publications/fandd/issues/2021/12/Global-Public-Goods-Chin-basics.

Corral, Paul, Isabel Molina, Alexandru Cojocaru, and Sandra Carolina Segovia Juarez. 2022. "Guidelines to Small Area Estimation for Poverty Mapping." Working Paper [preprint], World Bank, Washington, DC.

Corral, Paul, Heath Henderson, and Sandra Segovia. 2023. "Poverty Mapping in the Age of Machine Learning." Policy Research Working Paper 10429, World Bank, Washington, DC.

Crespo Cuaresma, Jesús. 2017. "Income Projections for Climate Change Research: A Framework Based on Human Capital Dynamics." Global Environmental Change 42: 226–36. https://doi.org/10.1016/j.gloenvcha.2015.02.012.

Crippa, M., D. Guizzardi, F. Pagani, M. Banja, M. Muntean, E. Schaaf, W. Becker, et al. 2023. GHG Emissions of All World Countries: 2023. Luxembourg: Publications Office of the European Union. https://data.europa.eu/doi/10.2760/953322.

Dabalen, Andrew L., Kristen Himelein Kastelic, and Carlos Rodriguez Castelan. 2020. "Data for Policy (D4P) Initiative." Report 21, World Bank, Washington, DC.

Dang, Hai-Anh H., Minh Cong Nguyen, and Trong-Anh Trinh. 2023. "Does Hotter Temperature Increase Poverty and Inequality? Global Evidence from Subnational Data Analysis." Policy Research Working Paper 10466, World Bank, Washington, DC. https://doi.org/10.1596/1813-9450-10466.

Deaton, Angus. 2005. "Measuring Poverty in a Growing World (or Measuring Growth in a Poor World)." The Review of Economics and Statistics 87 (1): 1–19. https://doi.org/10.1162/0034653053327612.

Dellink, Rob, Jean Chateau, Elisa Lanzi, and Bertrand Magné. 2017. "Long-Term Economic Growth Projections in the Shared Socioeconomic Pathways." Global Environmental Change 42: 200–14. https://doi.org/10.1016/j.gloenvcha.2015.06.004.

Deltares. 2021. Planetary Computer and Deltares Global Data: Flood Hazard Maps. https://ai4edatasetspublicassets.blob.core.windows.net/assets/aod_docs/11206409-003-ZWS-0003_v0.1-Planetary-Computer-Deltares-global-flood-docs.pdf.

Doan, Miki Khanh, Ruth Hill, Stephane Hallegatte, Paul Corral, Ben Brunckhorst, Minh Nguyen, Samuel Freije-Rodriguez, et al. 2023. "Counting People Exposed to, Vulnerable to, or at High Risk From Climate Shocks: A Methodology." Policy Research Working Paper 10619, World Bank, Washington, DC. https://doi.org/10.1596/1813-9450-10619.

Eastin, Joshua. 2018. "Climate Change and Gender Equality in Developing States." World Development 107: 289–305. https://doi.org/10.1016/j.worlddev.2018.02.021.

Ekhator-Mobayode, Uche E., and Johannes Hoogeveen. 2022. "Microdata Collection and Openness in the Middle East and North Africa." Data & Policy 4: e31. https://doi.org/10.1017/dap.2022.24.

Elbers, Chris, Jean O. Lanjouw, and Peter Lanjouw. 2003. "Micro-Level Estimation of Poverty and Inequality." Econometrica 71 (1): 355–64.

Erman, Alvina, Sophie Anne De Vries Robbe, Stephan Fabian Thies, Kayenat Kabir, and Mirai Maruo. 2021. "Gender Dimensions of Disaster Risk and Resilience: Existing Evidence." Technical Report, World Bank, Washington, DC. https://mars.gmu.edu/handle/1920/12777.

European Commission. n.d. EDGAR—Emissions Database for Global Atmospheric Research: Methodology. https://edgar.jrc.ec.europa.eu/methodology.

Eyring, Veronika, Nathan P. Gillett, Krishna Achuta Rao, Rondrotiana Barimalala, Marcelo Barreiro Parrillo, Nicolas Bellouin, Christophe Cassou, et al. 2021. "Human Influence on the Climate System." In *Climate Change 2021: The Physical Science Basis. Contribution of Working Group I to the Sixth Assessment Report of the Intergovernmental Panel on Climate Change,* edited by V. Masson-Delmotte et al., 423–521. Cambridge, UK and New York: Cambridge University Press. https://www.ipcc.ch/report/sixth-assessment-report-working-group-i/.

FAO (Food and Agriculture Organization). 1996. "World Food Summit: Plan of Action." Food and Agricultural Organization. http://www.fao.org/docrep/003/w3613e/w3613e00.htm.

FAO (Food and Agriculture Organization), IFAD (International Fund for Agricultural Development), UNICEF (UN Children's Fund), WFP (World Food Programme), and WHO (World Health Organization). 2023. *The State of Food Security and Nutrition in the World.* Rome: FAO. https://openknowledge.fao.org/items/445c9d27-b396-4126-96c9-50b335364d01.

Ferreira, Francisco H. G. 2023. "Is There a 'New Consensus' on Inequality?" IZA Discussion Paper 16422, Institute of Labor Economics, Rochester, NY. https://doi.org/10.2139/ssrn.4561620.

Fiedler, John L., Yves Martin-Prével, and Mourad Moursi. 2013. "Relative Costs of 24-Hour Recall and Household Consumption and Expenditures Surveys for Nutrition Analysis." *Food and Nutrition Bulletin* 34 (3): 318–30.

Flachaire, Emmanuel, Nora Lustig, and Andrea Vigorito. 2023. "Underreporting of Top Incomes and Inequality: A Comparison of Correction Methods using Simulations and Linked Survey and Tax Data." *Review of Income and Wealth* 69 (4): 1033–59. https://doi.org/10.1111/roiw.12618.

Foster, Elizabeth, and Daylan Gomez. 2024. "Poverty Measurement Database." World Bank, Washington, DC.

Friedlingstein, Pierre, Michael O'Sullivan, Matthew W. Jones, Robbie M. Andrew, Judith Hauck, Are Olsen, Glen P. Peters, et al. 2020. "Global Carbon Budget 2020." *Earth System Science Data* 12 (4): 3269–340. https://doi.org/10.5194/essd-12-3269-2020.

Gale, William G., John Sabelhaus, and Samuel I. Thorpe. 2023. "Measuring Income Inequality: A Primer on the Debate." *Brookings,* December 21, 2023. https://www.brookings.edu/articles/measuring-income-inequality-a-primer-on-the-debate/.

Gibson, Rosalind S. 2005. *Principles of Nutritional Assessment.* Oxford, UK: Oxford University Press.

Grassi, Giacomo, Clemens Schwingshackl, Thomas Gasser, Richard A. Houghton, Stephen Sitch, Josep G. Canadell, Alessandro Cescatti, et al. 2023. "Harmonising the Land-Use Flux Estimates of Global Models and National Inventories for 2000–2020." *Earth System Science Data* 15 (3): 1093–114. https://doi.org/10.5194/essd-15-1093-2023.

Gütschow, Johannes, Mika Pflüger, and Daniel Busch. 2024. The PRIMAP-hist National Historical Emissions Time Series (1750–2022) v2.5.1. Zenodo, February 27, 2024. https://doi.org/doi:10.5281/zenodo.10705513.

Haddad, Cameron Nadim, Daniel Gerszon Mahler, Carolina Diaz-Bonilla, Ruth Hill, Christoph Lakner, and Gabriel Lara Ibarra. 2024. "The World Bank's New Inequality Indicator: The Number of Countries with High Inequality (English)." Policy Research Working Paper 10796 [preprint], World Bank, Washington, DC.

Hallegatte, Stéphane, Adrien Camille Vogt-Schilb, Mook Bangalore, and Julie Rozenberg. 2016. *Unbreakable: Building the Resilience of the Poor in the Face of Natural Disasters (English).* Washington, DC: World Bank.

Hallegatte, Stéphane, Adrien Vogt-Schilb, Julie Rozenberg, Mook Bangalore, and Chloé Beaudet. 2020 "From Poverty to Disaster and Back: A Review of the Literature." *Economics of Disasters and Climate Change* 4 (1): 223–47. https://doi.org/10.1007/s41885-020-00060-5.

Hallegatte, Stéphane, and Brian Walsh. 2021. "Natural Disasters, Poverty and Inequality: New Metrics for Fairer Policies." In *The Routledge Handbook of the Political Economy of the Environment*. Chapter 8. Milton Park, UK: Routledge.

Haytowitz, David B., Jaspreet K.C. Ahuja, Xianli Wu, Meena Somanchi, Melissa Nickle, Quyen A. Nguyen, Janet M. Roseland, et al. 2019. USDA National Nutrient Database for Standard Reference. USDA. https://doi.org/10.15482/USDA.ADC/1529216.

Hentschel, Jesko, Jean Olson Lanjouw, Peter Lanjouw, and Javier Poggi. 2000. "Combining Census and Survey Data to Trace the Spatial Dimensions of Poverty: A Case Study of Ecuador." *The World Bank Economic Review* 14 (1): 147–65. https://doi.org/10.1093/wber/14.1.147.

Institute of Medicine. 2006. *Dietary Reference Intakes: The Essential Guide to Nutrient Requirements*. Washington, DC: The National Academies Press. https://doi.org/10.17226/11537.

IPC (Integrated Food Security Phase Classification). 2023. *Technical Manual: Evidence and Standards for Better Food Security and Nutrition Decisions*. Rome: IPC.

IPCC (Intergovernmental Panel on Climate Change). 2006. *2006 IPCC Guidelines for National Greenhouse Gas Inventories*. Hayama, Japan: Institute for Global Environmental Strategies. https://www.ipcc.ch /report/2006-ipcc-guidelines-for-national-greenhouse-gas-inventories/.

IPCC (Intergovernmental Panel on Climate Change). 2023. *Climate Change 2022—Impacts, Adaptation and Vulnerability: Working Group II Contribution to the Sixth Assessment Report of the Intergovernmental Panel on Climate Change*. Cambridge, UK: Cambridge University Press. https://doi .org/10.1017/9781009325844.

Jappelli, Tullio, and Luigi Pistaferri. 2010. "The Consumption Response to Income Changes." *Annual Review of Economics* 2: 479–506. https://doi.org/10.1146/annurev.economics.050708.142933.

Jenkins, Stephen P. 2017. "Pareto Models, Top Incomes and Recent Trends in UK Income Inequality." *Economica* 84 (334): 261–89. https://doi.org/10.1111/ecca.12217.

Jolliffe, Dean, Daniel Gerszon Mahler, Malarvizhi Veerappan, Talip Kilic, and Philip Wollburg. 2023. "What Makes Public Sector Data Valuable for Development?" *The World Bank Research Observer* 38 (2): 325–46. https://doi.org/10.1093/wbro/lkad004.

Kaczan, David J., and Jennifer Orgill-Meyer. 2020. "The Impact of Climate Change on Migration: A Synthesis of Recent Empirical Insights." *Climatic Change* 158 (3): 281–300. https://doi.org/10.1007 /s10584-019-02560-0.

Kerner, Andrew, Morten Jerven, and Alison Beatty. 2017. "Does It Pay To Be Poor? Testing for Systematically Underreported GNI Estimates." *The Review of International Organizations*, 12 (1): 1–38. https://doi.org/10.1007/s11558-015-9239-3.

Kraay, Aart, Christoph Lakner, Berk Özler, Benoit Decerf, Dean Jolliffe, Olivier Sterck, and Nishant Yonzan. 2023. *"A New Distribution Sensitive Index for Measuring Welfare, Poverty, and Inequality."* Policy Research Working Paper 10470, World Bank, Washington, DC. https://doi .org/10.1596/1813-9450-10470.

Lain, Jonathan, Sharad Tandon, and Tara Vishwanath. 2023. "How Much Does the Food Insecurity Experience Scale Overlap with Poor Food Consumption and Monetary Poverty? Evidence from West Africa." *The World Bank Economic Review* 38 (2): 422–42. https://doi.org/10.1093/wber/lhad031.

Lankes, Hans Peter, Rob Macquarie, Éléonore Soubeyran, and Nicholas Stern. 2024. "The Relationship between Climate Action and Poverty Reduction." *The World Bank Research Observer* 39 (1): 1–46. https://doi.org/10.1093/wbro/lkad011.

Lustig, Nora. 2020. "The 'Missing Rich' in Household Surveys: Causes and Correction Approaches." Working Paper 08, Stone Center on Socio-Economic Inequality, New York. https://stonecenter.gc.cuny .edu/research/the-missing-rich-in-household-surveys-causes-and-correction-approaches/.

Mahler, Daniel Gerszon, R. Andrés Castañeda Aguilar, and David Newhouse. 2022. "Nowcasting Global Poverty." *The World Bank Economic Review* 36 (4): 835–56. https://doi.org/10.1093/wber /lhac017.

Mancini, Giulia, and Giovanni Vecchi. 2022. "On the Construction of a Consumption Aggregate for Inequality and Poverty Analysis." [preprint]. World Bank Group, Washington, DC.

Martinez, Luis R. 2022. "How Much Should We Trust the Dictator's GDP Growth Estimates?" *Journal of Political Economy* 130 (10): 2731–69. https://doi.org/10.1086/720458.

Marty, Robert, and Alice Duhaut. 2024. "Global Poverty Estimation using Private and Public Sector Big Data Sources." *Scientific Reports* 14 (1): 3160. https://doi.org/10.1038/s41598-023-49564-6.

Maxwell, Daniel, and Richard Caldwell. 2008. *The Coping Strategies Index Field Methods Manual: A Tool for Rapid Measurement of Household Food Security and the Impact of Food Aid Programs in Humanitarian Emergencies.* Washington, DC: US Agency for International Development. https://pdf.usaid.gov/pdf_docs/Pnads360.pdf.

Maxwell, Daniel, Bapu Vaitla, and Jennifer Coates. 2014. "How Do Indicators of Household Food Insecurity Measure Up? An Empirical Comparison from Ethiopia." *Food Policy* 47: 107–16. https://doi.org/10.1016/j.foodpol.2014.04.003.

Maxwell, Daniel, Tara Vishwanath, and Sharad Tandon. Forthcoming. *Better Using Food Consumption Data in Global Food Security Monitoring.* World Bank, Washington, DC.

Moyer, Jonathan D., Audrey Pirzadeh, Mohammod Irfan, José Solórzano, Barbara Stone, Yutang Xiong, Taylor Hanna, and Barry B. Hughes. 2023. "How Many People Will Live in Poverty because of Climate Change? A Macro-Level Projection Analysis to 2070." *Climatic Change* 176 (10): 137. https://doi.org/10.1007/s10584-023-03611-3.

National Academies of Sciences, Engineering, and Medicine. 2022. *Greenhouse Gas Emissions Information for Decision Making: A Framework Going Forward.* Washington, DC: National Academies Press. https://doi.org/10.17226/26641.

Newell, Richard G., Brian C. Prest, and Steven E. Sexton. 2021. "The GDP-Temperature Relationship: Implications for Climate Change Damages." *Journal of Environmental Economics and Management* 108: 102445. https://doi.org/10.1016/j.jeem.2021.102445.

Nordhaus, W. D. 1992. "An Optimal Transition Path for Controlling Greenhouse Gases." *Science* 258 (5086): 1315–19. https://doi.org/10.1126/science.258.5086.1315.

Open Data Watch. 2023. *Open Data Inventory 2022/23 Biennial Report.* https://odin.opendatawatch.com/Report/biennialReport2022.

Piketty, Thomas, and Emmanuel Saez. 2006. "The Evolution of Top Incomes: A Historical and International Perspective." *American Economic Review* 96 (2): 200–05. https://doi.org/10.1257/000282806777212116.

Piketty, Thomas, Emmanuel Saez, and Gabriel Zucman. 2018. "Distributional National Accounts: Methods and Estimates for the United States." *The Quarterly Journal of Economics* 133 (2): 553–609. https://doi.org/10.1093/qje/qjx043.

Piketty, Thomas, Li Yang, and Gabriel Zucman. 2019. "Capital Accumulation, Private Property, and Rising Inequality in China, 1978–2015." *American Economic Review* 109 (7): 2469–96. https://doi.org/10.1257/aer.20170973.

Pinkovskiy, Maxim, and Xavier Sala-i-Martin. 2016. "Lights, Camera… Income! Illuminating the National Accounts-Household Surveys Debate." *The Quarterly Journal of Economics*, 131(2), 579-631.

Prydz, Espen B., Dean Jolliffe, and Umar Serajuddin. 2022. "Disparities in Assessments of Living Standards Using National Accounts and Household Surveys." *Review of Income and Wealth* 68 (S2): S385–S420. https://doi.org/10.1111/roiw.12577.

Qiu, Minghao, Jessica Li, Carlos F. Gould, Renzhi Jing, Makoto Kelp, Marissa Childs, Mathew Kiang, et al. 2024. "Mortality Burden from Wildfire Smoke under Climate Change." NBER Working Paper 32307, National Bureau of Economic Research, Cambridge, MA. https://doi.org/10.3386/w32307.

Ravallion, Martin. 2003. "Measuring Aggregate Welfare in Developing Countries: How Well Do National Accounts and Surveys Agree?" The Review of Economics and Statistics 85 (3): 645–52. https://doi.org/10.1162/003465303322369786.

Ravallion, Martin. 2012. "Poor, or Just Feeling Poor? On Using Subjective Data in Measuring Poverty." Policy Research Working Paper 5968, World Bank, Washington DC.

Riahi, Keywan, Detlef P. van Vuuren, Elmar Kriegler, Jae Edmonds, Brian C. O'Neill, Shinichiro Fujimori, Nico Bauer, et al. 2017. "The Shared Socioeconomic Pathways and Their Energy, Land Use, and

Greenhouse Gas Emissions Implications: An Overview." *Global Environmental Change* 42: 153–68. https://doi.org/10.1016/j.gloenvcha.2016.05.009.

Saez, Emmanuel, and Gabriel Zucman. 2016. "Wealth Inequality in the United States since 1913: Evidence from Capitalized Income Tax Data." *The Quarterly Journal of Economics* 131 (2): 519–78. https://doi.org/10.1093/qje/qjw004.

Sekhri, Sheetal, and Adam Storeygard. 2014. "Dowry Deaths: Response to Weather Variability in India." *Journal of Development Economics*, 111: 212–23. https://doi.org/10.1016/j.jdeveco.2014.09.001.

Somanathan, E., Rohini Somanathan, Anant Sudarshan, and Meenu Tewari. 2021. "The Impact of Temperature on Productivity and Labor Supply: Evidence from Indian Manufacturing." *Journal of Political Economy* 129 (6): 1797–1827. https://doi.org/10.1086/713733.

Subramanian, Shankar, and Angus Deaton. 1996. "The Demand for Food and Calories." *Journal of Political Economy* 104 (1): 133–62. https://doi.org/10.1086/262020.

Swindale, Anne, and Paula Bilinksy. 2006. "Household Dietary Diversity Score (HDDS) for Measurement of Household Food Access: Indicator Guide, version 2." Washington, DC: USAID. https://www.fantaproject.org/sites/default/files/resources/HDDS_v2_Sep06_0.pdf.

Tandon, Sharad. 2024. "How Difficult Is It to Interpret Subjective Well-Being Questions during Crises? Evidence from the Onset of Conflict in Yemen." *Oxford Economic Papers* 76 (2): 291–313. https://doi.org/10.1093/oep/gpad028.

Tandon, Sharad, and Maurice Landes. 2014. "India Continues to Grapple With Food Insecurity." *Amber Waves: The Economics of Food, Farming, Natural Resources, and Rural America* 1: 1-1.

Tandon, Sharad, and Rip Landes. 2011. "The Sensitivity of Food Security in India to Alternate Estimation Methods." *Economic and Political Weekly* 46 (22): 92–9.

Tang, Binh, Yanyan Liu, and David S. Matteson. 2022. "Predicting Poverty with Vegetation Index." *Applied Economic Perspectives and Policy* 44 (2): 930–45. https://doi.org/10.1002/aepp.13221.

The Economist. 2014. "Step Change." April 12, 2014. https://www.economist.com/finance-and-economics/2014/04/12/step-change.

Thomas, Adelle, April Baptiste, Rosanne Martyr-Koller, Patrick Pringle, and Kevon Rhiney. 2020. "Climate Change and Small Island Developing States." *Annual Review of Environment and Resources* 45: 1–27. https://doi.org/10.1146/annurev-environ-012320-083355.

Vaitla, Bapu, Jennifer Coates, Laura Glaeser, Christopher Hillbruner, Preetish Biswal, and Daniel Maxwell. 2017. "The Measurement of Household Food Security: Correlation and Latent Variable Analysis of Alternative Indicators in a Large Multi-Country Dataset." *Food Policy* 68: 193–205. https://doi.org/10.1016/j.foodpol.2017.02.006.

van der Weide, Roy, Christoph Lakner, and Elena Ianchovichina. 2018. "Is Inequality Underestimated in Egypt? Evidence from House Prices." *Review of Income and Wealth* 64 (s1): S55–S79. https://doi.org/10.1111/roiw.12338.

Vousdoukas, Michalis I., Panagiotis Athanasiou, Alessio Giardino, Lorenzo Mentaschi, Alessandro Stocchino, Robert E. Kopp, Pelayo Menéndez, et al. 2023. "Small Island Developing States under Threat by Rising Seas Even in a 1.5 °C Warming World." *Nature Sustainability* 6 (12): 1552–64. https://doi.org/10.1038/s41893-023-01230-5.

Webb, Patrick, Jennifer Coates, Edward A. Frongillo, Beatrice Lorge Rogers, Anne Swindale, Paula Bilinsky, et al. 2006. "Measuring Household Food Insecurity: Why It's So Important and Yet So Difficult to Do." *The Journal of Nutrition* 136 (5): 1404S-8S. https://doi.org/10.1093/jn/136.5.1404S.

Welch, Ivo. 2024. "The IPCC Shared Socioeconomic Pathways (SSPs): Explained, Evaluated, Replaced." Working Paper 32178, National Bureau of Economic Research, Cambridge, MA.

Wiesmann, Doris, Lucy Bassett, Todd Benson, and John Hoddinott. 2009. "Validation of the World Food Programme's Food Consumption Score and Alternative Indicators of Household Food Security." IFPRI Discussion Paper 00870, International Food Policy Research Institute, Washington, DC.

World Bank. 2015. "World Bank's New End-Poverty Tool: Surveys in Poorest Countries," Press release, World Bank, Washington, DC. https://www.worldbank.org/en/news/press-release/2015/10/15/world-bank-new-end-poverty-tool-surveys-in-poorest-countries.

World Bank. 2016. *Poverty and Shared Prosperity: Taking on Inequality*. Washington, DC: World Bank.

World Bank. 2017. *Monitoring Global Poverty: Report of the Commission on Global Poverty*. Washington, DC: World Bank.

World Bank. 2018. *Poverty and Shared Prosperity 2018: Piecing Together the Poverty Puzzle*. Washington, DC: World Bank. https://www.worldbank.org/en/publication/poverty-and-shared-prosperity-2018.

World Bank. 2021. *World Development Report 2021: Data for Better Lives*. Washington, DC: World Bank. https://www.worldbank.org/en/publication/wdr2021.

World Bank. 2023. *World Development Report 2023: Migrants, Refugees, and Societies*. Washington, DC: World Bank.

World Bank. 2024a. "New World Bank Group Scorecard FY24-FY30: Driving Action, Measuring Results." World Bank, Washington, DC.

World Bank. 2024b. *Poverty and Inequality Platform Methodology Handbook*. Washington, DC: World Bank. https://datanalytics.worldbank.org/PIP-Methodology/.

World Bank. n.d. "Translating Our Vision." World Bank Group Scorecard online resource. https://scorecard.worldbank.org/en/scorecard/home.

World Food Programme. 2009. *Comprehensive Food Security & Vulnerability Analysis (CFSVA) Guidelines*. Rome: World Food Programme. https://www.fsnnetwork.org/sites/default/files/2020-07/Comprhensive%20Food%20Security%20%26%20Vulnerability%20Analysis%20Guidelines.pdf.

World Inequality Lab. 2024. "Distributional National Accounts Guidelines: Methods and Concepts Used in the World Inequality Database." WID.world. https://wid.world/document/distributional-national-accounts-guidelines-2020-concepts-and-methods-used-in-the-world-inequality-database/.

Yonzan, Nishant, Branko Milanovic, Salvatore Morelli, and Janet Gornick. 2022. "Drawing a Line: Comparing the Estimation of Top Incomes between Tax Data and Household Survey Data." *The Journal of Economic Inequality* 20 (1): 67–95. https://doi.org/10.1007/s10888-021-09515-5.